OXFORD POLITIC

Series Editors: David Miller

JUSTIFICATORY LIBERALISM

OXFORD POLITICAL THEORY

Oxford Political Theory presents the best new work in contemporary political theory. It is intended to be broad in scope, including original contributions to political philosophy, and also work in applied political theory. The series will contain works of outstanding quality with no restriction as to approach or subject matter.

OTHER TITLES IN THIS SERIES

Justice as Impartiality
Brian Barry

Multicultural Citizenship: A Liberal Theory of Minority Rights
Will Kymlicka

Real Freedom for All: What (if anything) Can Justify Capitalism?
Philippe Van Parijs

The Politics of Presence: Democracy and Group Representation
Anne Phillips

An Essay on Epistemology
and Political Theory

JUSTIFICATORY LIBERALISM

GERALD F. GAUS

New York Oxford
OXFORD UNIVERSITY PRESS
1996

OXFORD UNIVERSITY PRESS

Oxford   New York
Athens   Auckland   Bangkok   Bombay
Calcutta   Cape Town   Dar es Salaam   Delhi
Florence   Hong Kong   Istanbul   Karachi
Kuala Lumpur   Madras   Madrid   Melbourne
Mexico City   Nairobi   Paris   Singapore
Taipei   Tokyo   Toronto

and associated companies in
Berlin   Ibadan

Copyright © 1996 by Oxford University Press, Inc.

Published by Oxford University Press, Inc.,
198 Madison Avenue, New York, New York 10016

Oxford is a registered trademark of Oxford University Press

Library of Congress Cataloging-in-Publication Data
Gaus, Gerald F.
Justificatory liberalism : an essay on epistemology
and political theory / Gerald F. Gaus.
p.   cm. — (Oxford political theory)
Includes bibliographical references and index.
ISBN 0-19-509439-5 (cloth)
ISBN 0-19-509440-9 (paper)
1. Liberalism. 2. Social contract. 3. Justificaton (Theory of knowledge)
I. title. II. Series.
JC574.G38   1995
320.5'13—dc20   94-49138

1 3 5 7 9 8 6 4 2
Printed in the United States of America
on acid-free paper

For Kelly

PREFACE

This book completes, but in doing so extends, the project begun in *Value and Justification*. In that book I argued that nonpsychopathic people conceive of others and themselves as moral persons. We understand ourselves and others as capable of putting aside personal valuings, and of acting on norms that can be justified to all. To rid ourselves of this conception, I argued, would undermine our understandings of ourselves, others and social life, leaving us without rational grounding for most of what we hold dear. Given who we are, I argued, we are committed to the idea of a publicly justified morality.

In the last chapters of *Value and Justification* I sketched some of the main elements of publicly justified morality, focusing on a right to personal freedom and a morality advancing the common good. At the time I recognized that these were vague requirements; I assumed that further work would yield more specific political principles, a justification of certain political institutions, and, indeed, policy prescriptions of various sorts. This proved mistaken. As I try to show in this book, the public justification of a public morality has great difficulty advancing beyond abstract principles. Because of this, the further work that was required was not, as I originally envisaged, more detailed public justifications—the arguments for which were manifestly inconclusive—but an analysis of how political institutions cope with this inconclusiveness. The conception of political institutions as simply expressing or conforming to justified morality thus gave way to a more complex idea, that political institutions not only express what can be morally justified, but also respond to our pervasive inability to provide decisive justifications.

All this raises a fundamental puzzle: Each of us is committed to our political views, yet our arguments for them seem inconclusive. How can each of us be justified in embracing political views that, from a certain public perspective, are inadequately justified? To solve this puzzle we need a much more sophisticated account of justified belief than that employed in recent political theory. At least to me, one of the amazing features of contemporary political philosophy is the way in which it has taken a "justificatory turn," yet the work of epistemologists and cognitive psychologists has been all but ignored. I believe this is a serious mistake; epistemologists and cognitive psychologists have looked hard at these issues for many years, and they have much to teach us. To be sure, learning from them is not always easy; their arguments are rather more technical and formal than is typical in moral and political philosophy. But the effort, I think, pays off in a political philosophy that is clearer about what it means by justification, and so avoids many of the confusions that characterize so much contemporary writing on political justification. Part I of this book is thus a study in epistemology and cognitive psychology in which I develop an account of what it is for an individual to possess justified beliefs. I call this a theory of *personal* justification. Based on this theory, part II develops a theory of *public* justification—how moral claims can be justified to others. Finally part III analyzes *political* justification—the way political institutions cope with the inconclusiveness of public justifications.

As with everything I write, this book has been deeply influenced by my close association with Stanley Benn; if I had been able to argue with him about it, this would have been a much better piece of philosophy. My work on justification was spurred long ago by Fred D'Agostino; though we disagree about a good deal, I have learned a lot from him and his work, and I thank him for it. My philosophical conversations with Julian Lamont—in Melbourne, Brisbane, Wollongong and Atlanta—have been immensely beneficial. It is always enlightening, and always a joy, to talk philosophy with Julian. As should be clear to every reader, I have been greatly influenced by the excellent work of Bob Ewin; my thanks to him for writing such good philosophy. A very early version of my thesis was criticized by Loren Lomasky while we were shopping at the *Super One* supermarket in Duluth; I would like to thank him for pressing his case, and for the patience of the other shoppers who were a bit perplexed by the loud voices over the fish counter. I greatly benefited from comments on parts I and II by Julian Lamont, Fred D'Agostino, John Kleinig, Bob Ewin and Chris Morris. I also would like to thank Steve Macedo, Jeremy Shearmur, John Chapman, Eric Mack, David Gow, Carolyn Morillo, Jonathan Riley, Steve Buckle, Ian Shapiro, William Nelson, Philip Pettit, Stuart Warner, Daniel Shapiro and Jim Fetzer.

I learned a great deal from various presentations of parts of the book. One of the paradoxes of academic life is that one always wants one's presentations to "go well," but one almost always learns a lot more from those that "go badly," i.e., in which questions are asked for which one has no coherent answer. In a few cases it took years for me to formulate an answer. So my thanks to participants at seminars and sessions at the following, especially to those who embarrassed me: the North American Society for Social Philosophy, the International Economics and Philosophy Society, the American Political Science Association, the New Zealand Division of the Australasian Association of Philosophy, The Murphy Institute of Political Economy, the philosophy departments of the University of New England, LaTrobe University, the Australian National University, the University of Wollongong, and Bowling Green State University, and the politics and philosophy departments at Victoria University in Wellington, Monash University, and, of course, the University of Minnesota, Duluth.

A very early version of the argument of sections 13 and 14 appeared as "Public Justification and Democratic Adjudication" in *Constitutional Political Economy* (Fall 1991). A preliminary statement of the argument of sections 12 and 16 appeared as "Public Reason and the Rule of Law" in Ian Shapiro (ed.), *Nomos XXXVI: The Rule of Law* (New York University Press, 1994). Some material from section 9.1, on the idea of the reasonable, appears in "The Rational, the Reasonable, and Justification," *The Journal of Political Philosophy* (1995).

Initial work on this book was undertaken while I was a Visiting Fellow in Philosophy and Politics at the University of New England, in Armidale, New South Wales. I would like to express my appreciation to the University of New England for its financial support and hospitality during my visit. The first two parts of the book were written during my tenure as a Visiting Scholar at the Social Philosophy and Policy Center at Bowling Green State University. I am deeply appreciative of the support provided by the Center; I am particularly grateful to Fred Miller, Kory Swanson and Sterling Burnett. My thanks also to the University of Minnesota for its generosity in granting academic leaves and financial support. Lastly, I would like to express my appreciation to Alan Ryan and Oxford University Press for their early support of the project.

Duluth, Minn.   G. F. G.
March 1995

CONTENTS

ABBREVIATIONS   xv

1. INTRODUCTORY: EPISTEMOLOGY AND
   POLITICAL THEORY   3
   1.1. Justificatory Liberalism   3
   1.2. Moral Epistemology   5
   1.3. Public and Personal Justification   10
   1.4. Plan of the Book   12

PART I—PERSONAL JUSTIFICATION

2. BELIEVING FOR REASONS   17
   2.1. Giving, Having, and Believing for Reasons   17
   2.2. Reasons as Causes of Beliefs   19
   2.3. Sustaining Causes and Justified Belief   23
   2.4. Efficient Causation and Justification   25
   2.5. Are All Reasons for Beliefs Themselves Beliefs?   28

3. THE INTERNAL AND EXTERNAL
   PERSPECTIVES   30
   3.1. Open and Closed Justification   30
   3.2. Externalist Justifications   32
   3.3. Belief Commitments and Tacit Beliefs   35
   3.4. Relativism of Reasons   38
   3.5. Relativism and Belief Systems   42

4. TAMING RELATIVISM   45
   4.1. Why We Are Not Committed to Normative Cognitive Pluralism 45
   4.2. Natural Mental Logic   47
   4.3. Mutual Intelligibility and the Limits of Pluralism   48
   4.4. Stich's Objection to the Bridgehead   52
   4.5. Inferential Errors   54
   4.6. Are the Subjects Really Wrong?   59

5. INFERENTIAL JUSTIFICATION   63
   5.1. The Argument Thus Far   63
   5.2. Four Axioms of Inferential Justification   64

5.3. Defeating Reasons   66
5.4. Epistemic *Akrasia*   70

6. WHY ALL JUSTIFICATION CANNOT BE
   PURELY INFERENTIAL   74

6.1. The Regress Argument   74
6.2. Global Coherentism   76
6.3. Inferential Justification and Web Coherentism   81
6.4. Conclusion: Coherence and Inference   83

7. FOUNDATIONALISM AND INTUITIONISM   85

7.1. Coherence Theories and Self-Justified Beliefs   85
7.2. Weak Foundationalism   91
7.3. Moral Intuitionism   97
7.4. Reflective Equilibrium   101
7.5. Summary of Part I   108

PART II—PUBLIC JUSTIFICATION

8. PRIVATE, SOCIAL, AND PUBLIC REASONERS   113

8.1. Private Reasoners   113
8.2. Social Reasoners and Intersubjective Agreement   116
8.3. Why Reason Publicly?   120
8.4. Moral Demands and Moral Authority   123
8.5. Public Reason and Moral Demands   129

9. WHAT IS PUBLIC JUSTIFICATION?   130

9.1. Populist Theories of Public Justification   130
9.2. Openly Justifiable Demands   137
9.3. Defeated and Victorious Justifications   144
9.4. Undefeated Justifications   151

10. LIBERAL PRINCIPLES   159

10.1. Victorious Justification: Constraints and Resources   159
10.2. Toleration, Free Speech, and the Commitment to Public
      Justification   162
10.3. Immunities as Defeated Proposals   168
10.4. The Public and Private   171
10.5. Why the Reflexivity Requirement Is Misguided   175

11. INCONCLUSIVE PUBLIC REASONING   179

11.1. Two Unacceptable Responses to Inconclusiveness   179
11.2. Liberal Authority   184

PART III—POLITICAL JUSTIFICATION

12. THE RULE OF LAW   195

12.1. Three Aspects of the Rule of Law   196
12.2. The Internal Morality of Law   197
12.3. Rights   199
12.4. Constitutionalism   204
12.5. Liberal Constitutions and Constitutional Politics   213

13. TRACKING DESIDERATA FOR LAW-MAKING INSTITUTIONS   215

13.1. Law-Making Institutions   215
13.2. The Political Contract   217
13.3. Inconclusiveness, Indeterminacy, and Random Democracy   223
13.4. Widely Responsive Procedures   226
13.5. Deliberative Procedures   230
13.6. Non-Neutral Procedures   237

14. POLITICAL EQUALITY   246

14.1. The Limits of the Consequentialist Justification of Democracy   246
14.2. The Principle of Equality and Political Equality   248
14.3. On Political Inequality   253

15. CHALLENGES TO ADJUDICATIVE DEMOCRACY   258

15.1. The Challenge from Social Choice Theory   258
15.2. The Charge of Public Incompetence   260
15.3. Politics, Self-Interest, and Adjudication   263
15.4. Vote Trading   267
15.5. Adjudication versus Mediation   271

16. THE JUDICIARY AND THE LIMITS OF LEGISLATION   275

16.1. Judges as Umpires   275
16.2. Judicial Review   279
16.3. The Moral Obligation to Obey the Law and Its Limits   286
16.4. Revolution and Utopian Aspirations   288

Contents

17. CONCLUSION: JUSTIFICATORY LIBERALISM
    AND ITS RIVALS   292

APPENDIX: LIBERAL PRINCIPLES IN A
WORLD OF STATES   296

NOTES   303

BIBLIOGRAPHY   340

INDEX   363

ABBREVIATIONS

The following symbols are used in this book:

⊃	Implication ("if, then")
&	Conjunction ("and")
∨	Inclusive disjunction ("or, perhaps both")
⊻	Exclusive disjunction ("or, but not both")
→	One-way inferential justification
⇄	Two-way inferential justification
≡	Equivalence
≢	Not equivalent
∃	Existential quantifier ("for some")
∀	Universal quantifier ("for all")
~	Negation ("not")
∴	Therefore
α, β, Γ	Variables for sentences or beliefs
Φ, X, Ψ	Variables for actions
S	System of reasons and beliefs

JUSTIFICATORY LIBERALISM

CHAPTER 1

Introductory: Epistemology and Political Theory

1.1 Justificatory Liberalism

In the last decade a number of philosophers have advanced what might be called a justificatory conception of liberalism. On this view, to quote Stephen Macedo, "[t]he moral lodestar of liberalism is . . . the project of public justification."[1] Liberals, Jeremy Waldron tells us, "are committed to a conception of freedom and of respect for the capacities and the agency of individual men and woman," and, he continues, "these commitments generate a requirement that all aspects of the social world should either be acceptable or be capable of being made acceptable to every last individual."[2] In a similar vein, Charles Larmore holds that "[t]o respect another person as an end is to insist that coercive or political principles be just as justifiable to that person as they are to us. Equal respect involves treating all persons, to which such principles are to apply, in this way."[3]

Given the actual disagreement in our Western societies over liberal ideals, it is manifest that justificatory liberalism cannot explicate "publicly acceptable" principles as those to which each and every member of our actual societies, in their actual positions, actually assent. If that is the test of public justification, justificatory liberalism is most unlikely to vindicate substantive liberal principles. Justificatory liberals require a *normative theory of justification*—a theory that allows them to claim that some set of principles is publicly justified, even given the fact that they are contested by some. And this, in turn, appears to call for a moral epistemology, in the sense of an account of the conditions for justified moral belief, or at least justified adherence to social principles. Indeed, even leaving aside the fact of actual disagreement over liberal principles, one would expect that a conception that puts justification at the very core of political philosophy would proffer an explicit and rich theory of moral and political justification. Remarkably, the adherents of justificatory liberalism not only fail to offer such an epistemology, but insist that abstaining from presenting one is fundamental to their position. John Rawls, for instance, maintains that "reasonable justification" is a "practical" and not an "epistemological" problem.[4] For Rawls, "moral epistemologies" are "comprehensive" doctrines, which are open to rational dispute, and so are not in the requisite sense publicly justified.[5] Thus Rawls seeks to avoid any complex epistemological claims, relying instead on commonsense notions about reasonableness and disagreement. The problem, as Rawls and others see it, is to avoid contentious epistemological issues and focus on the practical political task of securing agreement.[6] Consequently, rather than "justificatory liberalism," Rawls, Larmore, and others describe their view as "political liberalism."

I believe this to be a fundamental error. If public justification is the core of liberalism (as I believe it is),[7] and because there is no such thing as an uncontentious theory of justification, an adequately articulated liberalism must clarify and defend its conception of justified belief—its epistemology.[8] I shall argue in part II that, in fact, political liberals do not really abjure epistemic commitments; instead, they rest their case on a vague, but nevertheless clearly erroneous, normative theory of justification.[9] Justificatory liberalism, I maintain, must articulate its moral epistemology, and show why it is to be preferred. Some philosophers believe that this is impossible, insisting that justification and public justification are "essentially contested concepts." According to F.B. D'Agostino, for example:

> To settle on a particular conception of public justification, it is therefore necessary to settle questions, at least to our own satisfaction, which are themselves properly political questions. The project of public justification therefore cannot be beyond or prior to politics itself. It is not a meta-political project, as some have wishfully thought; it is, rather, itself a part of properly political argumentation.[10]

D'Agostino maintains that theories of public justification inherently incline toward some political prescriptions rather than others. Rawls's "pragmatic notion of justification," he says, is inherently antipaternalistic, whereas more "rationalistic" accounts such as the impartial spectator theory incline toward paternalism. We need not pause here to consider his specific claims about the paternalist implications of different modes of justification. Let us agree with D'Agostino that a theory of public justification will not be "neutral with respect to the topics and outcomes of argumentation."[11] However, it does not follow from this that settling on a particular conception of public justification is to settle

questions that are *properly political*. If we have provided a sound case
for employing a particular conception of public justification, we are in
a position to insist that substantive political views that cannot be justified within this conception are properly ruled out. That, for instance,
the proper theory of public justification makes it easier to justify liberal
than statist views does not show that we are preempting "properly"
political questions; it shows, rather, that the proper domain of the political is circumscribed by the ideal of public justification. D'Agostino
disagrees because he is convinced that it is in principle impossible to
show that any one conception of public justification is superior to the
rest; consequently, the choice of a conception must, on his view, itself
be motivated by political preferences.[12] Appeals to what can be publicly justified thus appear as attempts to deify some political preferences
and thereby short-circuit political discussion.

Such skeptical challenges cannot be put to rest by avoiding moral
epistemology and relying instead on commonsense notions of justification. Indeed, the strategy of avoidance merely reinforces the skeptic.
For the skeptic's charge is that in the end all theories of justification
are manifestations of merely personal moral and political preferences.
Consequently, avoiding detailed defenses conjoined with the claim that
everyone agrees with one's rather vague understanding of justification
plays into the skeptic's hands; that, he says with a smile, is just what
one would claim when trying to pass off political preferences as reason.[13] And the skeptic is right about at least one thing. Political liberals
such as Rawls do rely on a theory of justification that is far from uncontroversial. As D'Agostino points out, the theory has a strong pragmatic bent, part of which is a heavy reliance on norms of commonsense
reasoning. But, as we shall see, there is overwhelming evidence that
such commonsense methods are normatively flawed. Thus, I shall argue, not only do political liberals rely on a normative theory of justified belief, but far from being uncontentious, it is one that must be rejected.

1.2 Moral Epistemology

1.2.1 Robustness

In this book I tread the path against which political liberals warn: I
develop a theory of the justification of our beliefs, including those
about morality and political justice. I shall thus approach some central
issues of moral and political philosophy through epistemological inves-

tigations. This approach has not, I think, been sufficiently exploited in contemporary moral and political theory. For most of this century, moral philosophers have focused on the meaning of moral language or the metaphysics of morals. Questions such as "What does 'good' or 'right' mean?" and "Are there any moral facts?" (or "Are there any moral truths?" "What is the nature of moral properties?") have been the staple of metaethics, as well as much normative ethics.[14] Here I wish to focus instead on "How do we justify our moral judgments, both to ourselves and others?"[15]

This approach, I think, has a crucial feature sought by political liberals, though not to the degree they seek it: robustness. Let us say that theory T_1 is robust vis-à-vis T_2 to the extent that changes in T_2—including the total rejection of T_2 in favor of some competing theory T_2'— do not weaken the justification of T_1. Robustness is to be contrasted with sensitivity; to the extent that the justification of T_1 is affected by changes in T_2, T_1 is sensitive to T_2. Now we can understand political liberalism as aiming to achieve maximum robustness in relation to various metaphysical and epistemological theories, views of the good life and of morality, and so on. That is, Rawls's aim is to articulate a set of political principles that are supported by an array of comprehensive doctrines, many of which are inconsistent with each other. Thus regardless of which doctrine is embraced or accepted as true—or indeed which one may someday be demonstrated true—political liberalism will be justified, and in this sense is robust.[16] I concur that robustness is a great merit in a political theory; if the justification of a political theory is highly sensitive to the justification of metaphysical, epistemological, and moral theories, and to substantive ideals of the good or the holy life, that theory is unlikely to provide a justified basis for a stable social order.[17] The question is how much robustness can be achieved, and at what cost. My central claim in this book is that justificatory liberalism cannot achieve significant robustness in relation to theories of justification; for good or ill, it can only be as strong as the account of justification on which it is based.

1.2.2 *Two Examples of the Robustness of Justificatory Liberalism: Realism and Emotivism*

This, however, is consistent with considerable robustness in other areas. For example, most of what I say in the following pages is robust in relation to the dispute between realist and nonrealist accounts of morality. Following David O. Brink, we can characterize moral realism thus:

MR: (1) There are moral facts or truths, and (2) these facts or truths are independent of the evidence for them.[18]

MR is not itself an account of how we justify our moral beliefs, but a doctrine about the relation of our justified beliefs to the world or to "facts." We can thus distinguish theories of justified belief from theories of truth. For a moral realist, a theory of justified belief would provide the standards for judging whether or not something is true; Brink, for example, embraces a moral epistemology that explicates justified belief in terms of coherence (see chap. 6). But his distinctive claim as a moral realist is not that justification is a matter of coherence, but that justified moral beliefs are about moral facts or truths, the existence of which is independent of the justified belief. Coherentist epistemology and realist metaphysics are detachable. One could embrace a coherentist moral epistemology but deny the existence of any moral facts independent of justified belief: the only moral "truth," one might say, is justified belief.[19] The distinction between epistemological and metaphysical commitments is perhaps even more obvious in a theory of empirical knowledge such as that developed by Laurence Bonjour, which explicitly combines a coherence account of justified belief with a correspondence theory of truth. We are, Bonjour maintains, justified in believing an empirical claim if it coheres in the right way with the rest of our beliefs, but what makes the claim true is that it corresponds to the way the world is.[20] In contrast, absolute idealists such as Bernard Bosanquet held both a coherence account of justified belief and a coherence theory of truth.[21]

The theory of justified belief—the epistemology—I defend in this book is consistent with realist and nonrealist metaphysics of morals; my concern is how moral beliefs are justified, and this is consistent with a range of views about the existence of moral facts. To this extent, at least, I agree with Rawls that questions of the truth or falsity of our moral judgments can be left to one side, and we can instead focus on whether they are reasonable and justified.[22] Many students of metaethics will resist this; the very statement of the problem—"How are moral *beliefs or judgments to be justified?*"—seems to presuppose what is often called a "cognitivist" metaethic. Because the notion of "cognitivism" is itself so vague, it is difficult to respond to this charge. In one of its many senses, cognitivism is much the same as moral realism—a metaphysical doctrine affirming the existence of moral facts or moral truths, or maintaining that moral judgments are about such facts.[23] My comments about robustness vis-à-vis realism apply, of course, to this notion of cognitivism. However, another version of cognitivism is more epistemological. In this version, whether or not it is appropriate to say that moral beliefs are about facts or can be true or false, moral judgments are cognitive insofar as they are genuine judgments that are at least sometimes supported by reasons.[24] My analysis does presuppose this sort of cognitivism. That is, although we can put aside disputes as to whether ethical judgments are true or refer to moral facts, I suppose that they can be justifiable, fitting, appropriate, mistaken, and so on.[25] Consequently, my account is not consistent with, say, forms of emotivism that deny that moral judgments are cognitive in this sense.

However, much of what I argue is robust even with respect to varieties of emotivism.[26] We can distinguish three broad types of emotivist theories.

1. *"Blind" emotive theories.* Richard B. Brandt called C.L. Stevenson's theory "blind" emotivism, meaning, roughly, that one's emotive reactions toward X can change independent of changes in one's "cognitive field."[27] Holding constant one's perceptions, beliefs, and expectations about the future, one's emotive attitudes toward X may nonetheless change. Brandt argued that on Stevenson's blind emotive theory, the relation of moral reactions to other beliefs is simply causal, not justificatory. One cannot say that a Stevensonian moral reaction is based on irrelevant beliefs or convictions, because the blind theory holds that the emotive judgments may change freely irrespective of the cognitive field. Thus arises the familiar criticism of Stevenson's theory that it does not allow for genuine moral judgments that can be reasonable or unreasonable.[28]

2. *Affective-cognitive moral judgments.* Because the most plausible accounts of emotions do not characterize them as purely blind, noncognitive, affective reactions, emotivist moral theories need not, and should not, be blindly emotivist. For example, suppose that the model of a moral judgment is something like: "Yuck! Those are despicable things." We might call this an affective-cognitive judgment; the moral judgment is composed of an affective or attitudinal response ("Yuck!") and a cognitive basis for it ("It is appropriate to feel this way toward things with those features. They are yucky things.") On this view, though an attitude is a necessary part of a moral response (and so is emotive in one sense), it also has a cognitive element that allows for justification and criticism of the response.[29] Such emotive judgments may be criticized as being ill-founded if they are based on unsound beliefs. Suppose, for instance, you are asked why you believe Hunan chicken is yucky, and you reply "Who wouldn't dislike chicken liver

covered with Hershey's chocolate syrup?!" In this case your grounding beliefs, and so your judgment, is unsound.[30]

3. *Affective-cognitive basic moral judgments.* The above theory characterizes every moral judgment as affective-cognitive. As a consequence, the space for inferential reasoning—of the sort that a moral belief β_1 implies another moral belief β_2—is restricted.[31] Insofar as (a) an affective response is held to be *necessary* for a moral belief and (b) whether or not a person experiences an affective response is not only a logical but a psychological issue too,[32] it will often be difficult to show, for example, that one moral belief follows from another. However, an emotive theory of ethics need not insist that an affective response is a necessary part of all moral judgments. The emotivist can distinguish basic or original moral judgments from derived or secondary ones, and hold that only original or basic judgments have a necessary affective element, while derived judgments can be inferred from the basic ones.[33]

The account offered here is clearly inconsistent with the first option, blind emotive theory. However, I think it will emerge that my account is consistent with the third, foundational, emotive theory. I will defend the idea of foundational judgments, though I shall not commit myself to an affective explanation of them. The relation between the moral epistemology defended in this book and the middle option, in which all moral judgments are affective-cognitive, is harder to divine. Though much of what I say ought to be relevant, my account gives a much larger role to inferential reasoning than is consistent with the pure affective-cognitive theory.

1.2.3 Robustness Distinguished from Uncontroversiality

I have tried to indicate that the analysis of moral beliefs and their justification may be surprisingly robust in relation to metaethical theories, and why such robustness is attractive to a justificatory liberal. Being robust is not the same as being uncontroversial. A theory may well be consistent with, say, a variety of metaphysical views, theories of meaning, personal ideals, and religious doctrines, but may nevertheless advance controversial theses. A philosophic justification is not to be confused with popular acceptance, rough consensus, or even probable acceptance by all reasonable parties. This, as we shall see in part II, is a major divide between my justificatory liberalism and contemporary political liberalism. My aim is to explore the nature of justification, and in so doing show why liberal democracy is justified; it is not to show that popular consensus on this justification can be obtained among all reasonable people.

This is not to belittle the goal of popular consensus. In the sociological sense of that complex word, the *legitimacy* of a liberal regime depends on widespread acceptance of its justification, or perhaps the justice of its institutions. And it would be as wonderful as it would be remarkable if the best justification of the regime were also the grounds on which most citizens support it. Nevertheless, a test for the justification of a political regime—the test as to whether it provides all citizens with good reasons to support it—is not whether that justification is widely accepted, or is uncontroversial.

Which is just as well, for in some respects the account of justification I present here is controversial. I shall challenge a fundamental orthodoxy in philosophy—cherished by Aristotelians, rational-choice theorists, and almost everyone else—of a sharp division between theoretical and practical reason, as well as the not-unrelated split between empirical and normative reasoning. Not that I claim all these are the same; reasons for belief can be distinguished from reasons to act, and normative beliefs are not the same as empirical beliefs. However, I shall contend that the general notion of a rational belief can be analyzed, and much of this analysis applies to moral as well as empirical beliefs. Thus most of part I is devoted to the general idea of a rational belief system; though topics familiar to moral philosophers such as reflective equilibrium (sec. 7.4) will be considered, the main focus will be on general epistemological issues.[34] The aim, then, is a general theory of rational belief and reasonable believers. This approach bears fruit in part II; armed with our general theory of rational belief, we shall avoid many of the perplexities and pitfalls that plague current discussions of public justification.

1.3 Public and Personal Justification

At the outset, the task of developing a theory of justification confronts a deep and sometimes highly charged controversy. Do we begin with an individual system of beliefs and how, within it, a person justifies her beliefs? Or do we commence by examining interpersonal justification—what beliefs can we justify to each other? Contemporary political philosophers incline toward the latter. The interpersonal conception of justification is most clearly articulated in Jürgen Habermas's discourse theory. For Habermas, moral justification is necessarily intersubjective, in the sense that it aims at reasoned agreement (under ideal conversational conditions) among participants in the discourse. His discourse ethics thus supposes that "the justification of norms and commands requires that a real discourse be carried out and thus cannot occur in a strictly monological form, i.e., in the form of a hypothetical process of argumentation occurring in the individual mind."[35] Given that justificatory liberalism is based on the primary commitment to public justification, it may well seem that nothing but the intersubjective or interpersonal focus could possibly serve as a starting point.[36]

Stanley Benn, however, cautions that "[t]oo much can be made . . . of this interpersonal concern." He continues:

Within the modern consciousness, practical reason is located in the first instance not in the mustering of knockdown arguments to persuade or justify oneself to others but in the process of individual choice and judgment. Each person's moral consciousness is something that he has to keep in reasonable shape. . . .[37]

Benn's analysis of the "modern consciousness" sets the stage for the problem of Rawlsian political liberalism, namely, that in a pluralistic society such as ours, people exercise their reason to arrive at competing, though often still reasonable, judgments concerning morality and the good life. Rawls and others call this the supposition of reasonable pluralism.[38] Now reasonable pluralism can occur only if people arrive at reasonable judgments that are not publicly justified; *ex hypothesi,* these are reasonable views, but they are many in number and are inconsistent with each other. The very idea of reasonable pluralism supposes that we have reasonable views that cannot be publicly justified.

Part I of this book analyzes how two individuals can arrive at justified beliefs that are incompatible with each other. This theory of *personal justification* shows how reasonable pluralism is possible. Possessing a justified set of beliefs does not require that the set be publicly justified: one can justifiably hold a belief β that cannot be publicly justified. Public justification, I shall argue, is a far more strenuous test than personal justification; many of our moral beliefs that are personally justified are not publicly justified. That is the crux of the problem of reasonable pluralism.

Talk of personal justification runs the risk of immediately alienating some readers, who may be tempted to reject the entire account as biased toward an individualistic, "monological" point of view, and therefore wrongheaded from the outset. And insofar as it does commence with personal justification, there is something to this, though understandably I do not think it is either biased or wrongheaded. However, many readers are, I think, apt to overestimate the individualistic nature of the analysis. Later (sec. 8.2) I shall try to show in what way all reasoning—including personal justification—is social; to say that all reasoning does not aim at public justification is not to say that it is thoroughly private and asocial. But these are complex issues, the discussion of which must wait until we have considered justified belief. For the time being, suffice it to note that the individualistic character of the analysis is moderated by three points.

1. As Benn quite rightly points out, a focus on personal justification is consistent with recognizing that an individual's cognitive and moral resources are in a significant sense a social inheritance. A person's principles and values are not, he reminds us, "the individual's inventions *ex nihilo*. They have been adopted, inculcated, absorbed from an enveloping social environment."[39] One can only engage in personal justification given such a social inheritance. However, in a pluralistic society this inheritance itself is diverse and conflicting, and so working out a justified view of the world is an individual achievement.

2. Second, we shall see that personal justification ultimately must be responsive to the challenges and responses of others. A fully adequate analysis of personal justification thus will lead us to interpersonal justification, so not even personal justification is strictly monological.

3. Finally, I shall argue that when making moral demands on others, personal justification is not sufficient; such demands must be publicly justified, and this is indeed a form of interpersonal justification. The gap between my account and Habermas's, then, is less than it might first appear, for his discussion of the intersubjective character of moral reasoning is primarily concerned with the justification of principles of justice, and here we agree that public justification is the ultimate standard.[40]

1.4 Plan of the Book

The argument of the book divides into three main parts. Part I advances a theory of personal justification, or, we might say, a model of justified systems of reasons and beliefs. This will allow us to explicate the idea of reasonable pluralism. Part II then turns to the ideal of public justification. I shall argue that the theories of public justification advanced by political liberals and other "intersubjectivists," while providing some insights, are incompatible with the best theory of justified belief. Based on the analysis of personal justification, I distinguish three main outcomes of public justification: victory, defeat, and inconclusiveness (undefeated, unvictorious beliefs). As I said earlier, I shall argue that, though some substantive fundamental moral principles can be victoriously publicly justified in our society, their number is modest. Victorious public justifications are fairly rare in a pluralistic society such as ours; in contrast, undefeated, unvictorious justifications—those that are reasonable but also contentious—abound. Part III then analyzes political life among citizens who typically confront each other with inconclusive public justifications. I argue here that the institutions of liberal constitutional democracy are publicly justified ways to adjudicate among the plethora of competing undefeated public justifications on substantive issues of justice and the common good. In this part I shall examine such topics as the justification of liberal democracy, constitutionalism, judicial review, and the rule of law.

PART I

PERSONAL JUSTIFICATION

CHAPTER 2

Believing for Reasons

2.1 Giving, Having, and Believing for Reasons

My ultimate concern in this book is with moral, and especially political, justification in which participants advance to others their reasons for beliefs, principles, and policies. But participation in political justificatory discourse presupposes that people enter with beliefs supported by reasons. When a person seeks to justify her belief to *others*, she ordinarily supposes that she has good reasons for it. As a participant in such interpersonal justificatory discourse, then, one typically endeavors to *show* others what one thinks already obtains, namely, that one has good reasons for what one believes. To be sure, as discussion proceeds one may revise this initial estimate; we shall see in part II that the effort to justify what one already believes often results in revision of one's beliefs. So I certainly do not wish to deny that interpersonal discussion is dynamic, and indeed ultimately necessary for personal justification. Yet none of this undermines the presumption that at any given time one enters any particular discussion with beliefs for which one already has reasons.[1] Indeed, interpersonal justification produces belief change just because participants are prepared to reply to queries about, and challenges to, their beliefs by pointing to specific reasons supporting them.[2] If others convince you that your supporting reasons are unsound, change of belief is apt to occur. Beliefs that are justified because they are supported by, or follow from, reasons I shall call *inferentially justified.*[3]

To possess an inferentially justified belief β, it is not sufficient that there is a good reason R from which there is a conclusive argument to β. At a minimum, one must accept R. Someone who justifies holding a belief by appealing to a reason he does not accept is not simply rationalizing rather than justifying the belief (see sec. 2.3), but is being hypocritical (sec. 9.2.2). Consider, for instance, Anna, a Freudian therapist who, after confronting research on the comparative effectiveness of various psychotherapies, concludes that Freudianism is bunk.

But she has a large practice and her patients expect Freudian explanations, so that is what she gives them. Say, then, she has a belief: "Little Hans has a case of hysterical phobia"—he is so afraid of horses he will not go out on the street. The Freudian reason supporting the diagnosis of neurosis or phobia is "one thing alone: the replacement of his father by a horse"—he has displaced his fear of being castrated by his father onto the horse.[4] Of course, Anna does not believe this; she believes that Little Hans certainly has a hysterical phobia, but she does not accept the Freudian account that she passes on to Little Hans's parents. She, in fact, has based her diagnosis on a New Age self-help book. Now assume that Freudianism actually provides the correct account and the New Age self-help book does not. Does Anna have a justified belief? We might say that her belief is *justifiable* in the sense that it could be justified, but given that Anna rejects the reason that would justify her diagnosis, we cannot say that *her belief* is justified. Being justified in believing β is not the same as being right; as we shall see, it is possible to be justified in holding a false belief. We see here that one can hold a correct belief but not be justified in doing so.

To be justified in believing β one must *have or accept* the reasons that justify it. But not even this is enough. As others have noted, to be justified in believing β one must not only *have or possess* a good reason that supports β, but must *believe β for good reasons.* Consider:

> Case 1: Alf Believes the Right Thing for the Wrong Reasons.[5]
> Alf and Betty are lovers, but Alf has many beliefs that indicate that Betty is unfaithful; he has seen receipts from little-out-of-the-way hotels in her pocketbook (and he hasn't visited such hotels with Betty since their affair before she divorced Charlie), she has been working late every night for two months now, she keeps calling him "Dearest Frank," and the like. Alf can be said to have perfectly good reasons for believing Betty is unfaithful. But suppose that, despite all the evidence that Betty has been unfaithful, and no counterevidence, Alf simply refuses to believe such a thing; he seeks to convince himself that it could not be true.[6] Assume now, though, that he enrolls in a night-school sociology course on "Relationships in the '90s" and discovers that there is a .25 chance that one's lover has been unfaithful in the last year. On the basis of this evidence, Alf infers that Betty has cheated in the last year. Alf now has a belief (that Betty has cheated) for which he has good reasons; is it a justified belief?

No, most obviously because, though the belief is justifiable given his belief system, Alf has not based his conclusion on the beliefs that could justify it. To infer in this way that something with a .25 probability has occurred is an inferential error (see sec. 4.5); if Alf had based his belief on his diagnostic evidence about Betty, it would be justified. In this case Alf has failed to make the right connections among his beliefs. He believes the right thing for the wrong reasons. To have a justified belief β, it is not enough, then, for Alf merely to have good (or even conclusive) reasons for believing β.[7]

The last few decades of analytic epistemology have been characterized by the abundance of somewhat eccentric counterexamples to almost every conceivable and reasonable proposal; we need to be cautious about following this path by placing too much weight on such examples.[8] It is, I think, unlikely that our understanding of justification (or anything else in philosophy) will be advanced if a plausible and theoretically well-grounded proposal can be dismissed with an argument of the sort, "But there is a rather bizarre example which helps to undermine this initial plausibility."[9] However, the above example is not just another odd case conjured up by analytic epistemologists. As Jon Elster observes in his analysis of the rationality of wishful thinking and ideology, "we have all met persons basking in self-satisfaction that seems both to be justified and not to be justified: justified because they have good reasons for being satisfied with themselves, and not justified because we sense that they would be just as satisfied were the reasons to disappear."[10] To take a more homely example: When teaching students, we often have occasion to distinguish when a student knows an answer from when, though he has all the relevant information at his disposal, he has just made a lucky guess. Having the information and getting the right answer are not enough; to have justified belief, one has to make the connection between the belief and the relevant considerations.

2.2 Reasons as Causes of Belief

If, then, a belief is justified because of its supporting reasons, it is not enough that such reasons are available to the believer; the belief in question must somehow be *based* on them. Stanley Benn believes this basing relation is causal. Following Bernard Williams, he holds that "rational beliefs are caused by the reasons which are their grounds."[11] This proposal is intuitively appealing; Alf's belief β is inferentially justified only if he has good reasons for β and these good reasons cause Alf to accept β. I believe this is basically right, though clarifying the nature of this causal link turns out to be a good deal more difficult than it appears.

Take a mundane causal claim: The broken window was caused by the high winds that blew the branch that smashed the glass. In this instance the wind was the impetus for the change. At first the branch was at rest and the window intact; the wind lifted the branch, which caused a change in the state of the window. Afterward the wind died down but the window remained broken. David Armstrong contrasts this sort of *efficient cause* to what he describes as a *sustaining cause*. In this second sense of cause we can say that pillars cause the roof to remain up; the roof will only remain up so long as the pillars remain.[12] In sections 2.2 and 2.3 I consider sustaining causal accounts of justified belief; I turn to efficient causation in section 2.4.

The crux of the sustaining analysis is that the justification of a belief turns crucially on why it is *now held*. This suggests a counterfactual test. Consider again the case of the pillar and roof. We might say that the pillars are the sustaining cause of the roof if eliminating the pillars would cause the roof to drop. So if the pillars were merely facades, eliminating them would not cause the roof to drop. Similarly, we might say (as a first approximation) that in Alf's belief system S, β is sustained by R only if dropping R from S would cause β to drop from S.

Unfortunately, this rather straightforward proposal will not suffice. Putting aside worries about the best way to explicate counterfactuals, we have at least to take account of the possibility of overdetermination.[13] To revert to our roof case, perhaps the builder was cautious and overengineered the structure. Not only do the pillars support the structure, but there is a backup system; cables hung from the outside would hold up the roof in case of pillar failure. In this case, as long as the pillars are in place, they alone support the structure, but as soon as the pillars give way, the cable system will engage and keep the roof from falling. This structure would not meet our counterfactual test: Even if the pillars were eliminated, the roof would not drop. Yet it certainly seems that right now the pillars are holding up the roof. In a similar way, when one set of sustaining beliefs is eliminated, another often engages.

Again, this is no mere philosopher's fancy. In an interesting series of experiments Lee Ross and his colleagues induced subjects to develop theories and opinions on the basis of information that was later shown to them to be false.[14] In one experiment subjects were given false feedback when sorting authentic suicide notes from fictitious ones. On the basis of their "successes" and "failures" in performing this task, subjects developed beliefs about their own competency and their future ability to make such discriminations. Afterward the subjects were extensively debriefed, and each subject acknowledged that his or her "performance" was strictly an artifact of the experimenters' manipulation. Nevertheless, even after the discrediting of the evidence upon which their beliefs were based, subjects showed marked belief perseverance. Similar results were achieved in an experiment in which subjects were induced to develop theories, on the basis of false evidence, about the relation between firefighters' professional performance and the firefighters' scores on a test for risk taking. Once again, despite being informed later that the scores were fictitious, subjects showed significant perseverance in their theories. One possible hypothesis in this case is that the subjects, having developed their beliefs, searched their memories for new support rather than abandon them.[15] Thus, just as the cables engaged to keep the roof from falling when the pillars were removed, subjects may have appealed to other reasons to sustain the beliefs about their skills once the supporting experimental feedback beliefs were discredited.

A more complicated counterfactual test is thus required. The sorts of cases I have been examining would seem to call for a modification along the following lines:

> In belief system S, β is sustained by R only if (1) dropping R as an element of S would cause β to be dropped as an element of S, or (2) dropping R as an element of S would cause some other reason R' to be invoked.

This seems to capture the sort of mechanism hypothesized in the belief-perseverance case in which subjects switched from one sustaining reason to another. We can imagine a series of sustaining relations; as each sustaining reason is dropped, a new one is invoked, and so on. Now this raises the worry that, in practice, the principle is immune from falsification. Say we seem to discover a case, such as the belief-perseverance study, in which the sustaining cause is eliminated and yet the belief remains. This would seem to be a counterexample to the belief-sustaining analysis. But now the defender of the sustaining analysis can always invoke some alternative reason R' that must be there to sustain the belief, apparently securing the analysis from any possible counterexample. But this doesn't follow: The sustaining analysis hypothesizes that there must be an alternative sustaining relation, but nothing follows about the impossibility of falsification. In any particular case the principle hypothesizes that "backup" sustainers will be evoked; if there is no evidence that this occurs, this hypothesis will be rejected.[16] On the other hand, we may find that people cite new evidence for their old beliefs—evidence that would not be invoked if the initial sustaining reasoning had not been discredited—thereby providing some support for the backup theory.[17]

Thus far I have been supposing that a clear order of priority can be determined, such that at any time we can distinguish the sustaining reason from the backup sustainers. But what of a case of overdetermination in which multiple sustainers operate at the same time? When a building is actually overengineered, the pillars and the external cables would be doing the job simultaneously. In the belief case, too, more than one reason may be holding up the belief. It will not do simply to say that all are to be included in the set of "sustainers" of β (or the roof) and leave it at that, as reasons can differ in their justificatory force. Surely a natural response to Ross's belief-perseverance experiment is that the first set of sustaining reasons were (initially) justificatory (see sec. 3.1) while the second set were not—they were not sound reasons.[18] To collapse these good and bad justificatory reasons into a single set of sustaining reasons would obscure the place of the basing relation in inferential justification. Still, we can begin in the way this proposal contemplates, by first identifying the set of all reasons that have a sustaining relation for β at time t. Let $\{R_1 \ldots R_n\}$ be the entire set of possible sustaining reasons for β in S at time t (it does not matter how widely we characterize this set). If this set were dropped, it would cause β to be dropped. Now consider all possible subsets of $\{R_1 \ldots R_n\}$. For each subset we can ask two questions: (1) If we drop the rest of $\{R_1 \ldots R_n\}$, is β sustained? (2) If "yes" to the first question, is it possible to drop any elements of the subset and still sustain β? If we answer "yes" to the first question and "no" to the second, we have identified a minimal sustaining subset of $\{R_1 \ldots R_n\}$; call it $R_{\{min\}}$. A set is $R_{\{min\}}$ if all other members of $\{R_1 \ldots R_n\}$ could be dropped except for $R_{\{min\}}$ and β still sustained, but no members could be dropped from $R_{\{min\}}$ without also dropping β. (Minimal sustaining subsets may overlap, e.g., reason R_2 may be member of more than one minimal sustaining subset.) Each subset $R_{\{min\}}$ might be called an elementary sustaining reason. Having identified each elementary sustaining reason, we then would be in a position to distinguish good sustaining elementary reasons for holding β from those that are unsound. In analyzing whether β is justified, we might then inquire whether any of the elementary sustaining reasons are good reasons for β; if any are, we may then conclude that β is justified (this is too rough; see sec. 5.3).

I shall not pursue this sustaining analysis further, though a great deal more could be said about sustaining reasons, as well as general issues about the analysis of counterfactuals. But further levels of complication and sophistication would not, I think, make the core idea either clearer or more (or for that matter less) compelling.

2.3 Sustaining Causes and Justified Belief

I believe something very much like the sustaining analysis is correct for justified belief, though I shall not even attempt to review all the possible objections to it.[19] However, one important objection is particularly germane to our concern with moral beliefs, and so needs to be considered.

Keith Lehrer is so deeply opposed to a causal analysis of the basing relation that he describes it as a "causal fallacy." He writes:

It is easy to imagine the case of someone who comes to believe something for the wrong reason and, consequently, cannot be said to be justified in the belief, but who, as a result of his belief, uncovers some evidence which completely justifies his belief. Suppose that a man, Mr. Raco, is racially prejudiced and, as a result, believes that the members of some race are susceptible to some disease to which members of his race are not susceptible. This belief, we may imagine, is an unshakable conviction. It is so strong a conviction that no evidence to the contrary would weaken his prejudiced conviction and no evidence in favor would strengthen it. Now imagine that Mr. Raco becomes a doctor and begins to study the disease in question. Imagine that he reads all that is known about the disease and discovers that the evidence, which is quite conclusive, confirms his conviction. The scientific evidence shows that only members of the race in question are susceptible to the disease. We may imagine as well that Mr. Raco has become a medical expert perfectly capable of understanding the canons of scientific evidence, though, unfortunately, he has become no less prejudiced as a result of this. Nevertheless, he understands and appreciates the evidence as well as any medical expert and, as a result, has reason for his belief that justifies it. He has discovered that his conviction is confirmed by scientific evidence. He knows that only members of the other race are susceptible to the disease in question. Yet, the reasons that justify him in this belief do not causally explain the belief. The belief is the result of prejudice, not reason, but it is confirmed by reason which provides the justification for the belief. Prejudice gives Mr. Raco conviction, but reason gives him justification.[20]

We need to take such a case seriously, as the basic model may well characterize many moral beliefs. A number of theories maintain that the grounds on which we initially accept moral principles are not the grounds that justify them. Jean Piaget and Lawrence Kohlberg, for instance, tell us that children adopt moral principles because they emanate from authority, and it is the stature of the authority and the desire to please the authority that initially sustain morality.[21] On their view, moral development is not so much a change in substantive judgments as a change in justifying those judgments, thus suggesting that as the child develops she may come to adopt very different justification for a belief that was caused by, for example, the desire to please parents.[22] However, these cases are not directly analogous to Lehrer's insofar as the original cause for the belief actually is dropped as the new, perhaps genuinely justificatory, supporting reasons are developed. Freud's analysis of the superego is much closer; it may well be that the original factors constraining the ego are still operative in adults, despite the more sophisticated reasons they can advance for their moral convictions.[23] In this Freudian picture, a normal moral agent may be much like the unsavory Mr. Raco; the cause of his moral belief is some unjustified and perhaps irrational consideration, though he may have other beliefs that show it to be justifiable.

Lehrer's case is a strong counterexample to an efficient causal theory (sec. 2.4) according to which a belief β is justified only if the reasons that originally caused β are good reasons for holding it. This requirement is much too strong. We originally come to hold our moral convictions for some notoriously fantastic reasons; if the justification of our current moral beliefs must be tied to those original causes, we would have few if any justified moral beliefs. These problems do not arise for a sustaining causal analysis; on this view, it is not important why we originally came to hold a belief, but why we now do so. But, it would seem, Mr. Raco and Dr. Freud still pose a problem for a sustaining analysis: Right now Mr. Raco holds his belief for bad reasons, and perhaps right now we hold moral convictions for obscure and confused reasons that we could not acknowledge. Whether Mr. Raco is justified in his medical beliefs depends on whether they are overdetermined. Suppose they are. Employing the method sketched in section 2.2, assume that if we deleted Mr. Raco's racist beliefs, the scientific evidence would sustain his beliefs about the disease. In this case we would have no difficulty agreeing that Mr. Raco's medical beliefs are actually justified, because there exists a justified sustaining relation. But what if we suspect that, were Mr. Raco to be brainwashed into becoming a more decent fellow, the scientific evidence would not sustain his beliefs about the disease? Mr. Raco's medical beliefs would then not be overdetermined; the scientific evidence would not be able to sustain them. Is the belief still justified? Lehrer thinks so; for him justification is a matter of what reasons one can give, or perhaps advance, not why one believes what one does.[24]

Lehrer's account, however, does not allow us to distinguish rational believers from those who manifest obvious defects of rationality.[25] Consider Alf, into whose head beliefs pop, and stay for a variety of odd reasons, such as outlandish racist theories, neurotic fantasies and fears, and so on. Alf goes through life holding such incredible beliefs without making any effort to adjust them to what is justified or sound. He surely is a radically defective believer, his mental processes exhibiting no link between good evidence and belief. Alf's beliefs are *free floating* and it is a mere happenstance if they latch onto a "justifying" basis.[26] Now suppose that a paternalistic epistemologist takes pity on Alf and wishes to raise him closer to the level of an adequate believer. But she does so in a way inspired by Lehrer. First she gives Alf a long true/false test on, for example, epidemiology, on which Alf scores 50 percent. She asks Alf the reasons for his answers, which prove to be as bizarre as his reasons always are. Subsequently, she gives Alf a list of all the correct answers and the reasons for them, which Alf memorizes. He then retakes the test. Because Alf's beliefs are causally uninfluenced by good evidence that he accepts—in this case, the good evidence is what the benevolent epistemologist says are the correct answers and the reasons for them—Alf again scores 50 percent, getting the same half of the questions correct. Our epistemologist claims to have vastly increased Alf's justified belief, because Alf can now cite, in addition to his own bizarre reasons, the correct reasons for the 50 percent of the questions he has always answered correctly. But surely Alf is no better a believer than he was before; some of his free-floating beliefs—free-floating, that is, in relation to evidence and good reasons—can be linked up with good reasons, but this is mere luck and has no effect on Alf's beliefs. Alf's ability to memorize and recite a list of reasons that has no impact on his beliefs does not, as far as I can see, increase the justification of those beliefs. Even epistemic justification is practical insofar as its outcome impacts on one's belief system. To divorce the analysis of justification from the account of why beliefs are held obscures this impacting relation.

2.4 Efficient Causation and Justification

It thus seems that for Alf to be justified in believing β on the grounds of R it is not only necessary that Alf believes R and that R justifies β but, additionally, that Alf believes β because of R in the sense that R sustains his belief. Is it also necessary that R be the efficient cause of β, in the sense that it originally caused Alf to believe it?

It is useful to pause briefly and consider why focusing on efficient as opposed to sustaining causes may be attractive. The most plausible path to this position is via a reliabilist theory of justified belief.[27] Consider, for example, a view according to which a belief is justified if and only if it was (efficiently) caused by a process that reliably produces true belief.[28] On this view, the historical pedigree of a belief is crucial: If β was produced by a process P, and if beliefs produced by P are reliably true beliefs, then β is a justified belief in virtue of its original (i.e., efficient) cause. Thus, for instance, one might say that our perceptual beliefs are justified because they are (efficiently) caused by a perceptual apparatus that reliably produces true beliefs.

It is widely supposed that such a theory of justified belief is either inapplicable to moral beliefs or else shows that moral beliefs cannot be justified.[29] Following in the path of Robert Nozick, though, we could maintain that just as justified empirical beliefs might be said to track truth because they are caused by a process that reliably causes true belief, normative beliefs could be said to track value or rightness because they are reliably caused by a process that yields correct evaluations.[30] Alexis Meinong, for instance, held that emotional responses provide a knowledge of values.[31] Thus it might be argued that just as the presentation of an object to our perceptual process under the correct conditions causes a true belief, the presentation of an object under the correct emotional conditions produces a correct valuation.[32] To be sure, the apparent diversity of moral beliefs leads many people to suspect that no such reliable mechanism is to be had. My point is that there is no theoretical bar to analyzing justified normative beliefs in this way, and indeed some seem inclined to do so.

The shortcoming of reliabilism as a theory of justified belief is that it supposes the notions of truth or correctness to be logically prior to justification. That is to say, on any reliabilist account we must first know what true or correct beliefs are before we can talk sensibly about what beliefs are justified. The concept of a justified belief logically presupposes that we can identify true (or correct) beliefs, and a reliable process that causes them. Now it seems that, in an important way, this is getting things backward. A theory of justified belief, we might expect, would help in determining when we hold true beliefs and when we go wrong; understanding the requirements of epistemic justification may serve as a route to truth. Epistemology is in a deep sense ultimately practical: It provides guidance about how to seek truth and how to know it when we come across it. But all this supposes that we can give an analysis of justified belief that does not presuppose access to truth.

Not only does reliabilism seem to invert the proper order of analysis between justification and truth, but it posits much too close a tie. Justified belief is usually a good path to the truth, but it seems perfectly intelligible that one can have a number of justified but false beliefs.[33] Although we should be wary of epistemologists' exotic tales in theorizing about justified beliefs, brains in vats and evil demons seem relevant here.[34] If we suppose that somehow all our perceptual inputs deceive us—we really are brains in vats, or an evil demon consistently and flawlessly leads us astray—we have no access to the truth.[35] But it still makes sense to talk of justification, of beliefs being supported by reasons. We can distinguish a brain in the vat that makes outrageous connections between beliefs from one whose beliefs are regulated by sound rules of inference, though neither has any access to the truth. To take a step back toward reality, it is manifest that attacks such as Richard Rorty's on the idea of truth as something "out there" in the world do not also constitute attacks on justification; indeed, in many ways Rorty wishes to replace the idea of truth with that of justification.[36] My aim is not to endorse Rorty's view, but to stress that his ability to articulate it intelligibly suggests that our understanding of justified belief is much more robust vis-à-vis the idea of truth than reliabilism would suggest. And that is, I venture, a good thing, for the general idea of truth is highly contested today, as the notion of ethical truth has long been. Analyses of justified belief that do not presuppose the concept of truth are much more apt to achieve the robustness that justificatory liberalism seeks (sec. 1.2).[37]

These comments relate to reliabilistic analyses of justification in particular, rather than the general claim that justified belief involves efficient causation. This latter claim need not imply the externalism that makes reliabilism objectionable.[38] However, the very idea—intrinsic to all efficient accounts of justified beliefs (including reliabilism)—that justification centers on the process of *belief formation* seems dubious. Why a belief was originally embraced is not crucial to whether it is now justified. This is, I think, particularly manifest with moral beliefs; as we saw, on a variety of accounts, moral development is better understood as an evolution of our reasons for our moral beliefs than of deep changes in the content of those beliefs (sec. 2.3). To show that the initial reason for embracing β is erroneous is only relevant if it shows that β is not now believed for an adequate reason; if we know that Alf now believes β for perfectly good reasons—they sustain his belief— then why he originally came to believe it is not relevant.

Still, efficient causation does seem relevant to evaluating a person's epistemic rationality. In our case of the free-floating beliefs (sec. 2.3), one of the things that made Alf such a defective believer was that good reasons to believe β were unable to produce β. Epistemic rationality requires a disposition to believe what one has good reason for believing. Given that I have already advocated a causal account of the basing relation, it seems most natural to explicate this dispositional feature of epistemic rationality as also causal, though in the efficient sense. It would, after all, be odd if reasons could causally sustain beliefs but were inefficacious in bringing them about.

All this suggests that, in analyzing the justification of a person's beliefs at any given time, we need only examine sustaining causation. To inquire whether Alf's belief β is justified, we need to know on what reasons it is based, and the sustaining analysis is required for that task. But when we take a dynamic view and consider rational belief change, we need to suppose efficient causation to account for why Alf changes his beliefs when confronted by good reasons.

2.5 Are All Reasons for Beliefs Themselves Beliefs?

If reasons are the direct cause of Betty's beliefs, they clearly cannot be understood as simply propositional. Propositions are not the sorts of things that can be causes.[39] Recognizing this, it may seem that we are committed to what epistemologists call the *doxastic presupposition*, namely, that all the reasons that can enter into (inferential) justification of Betty's beliefs must themselves be beliefs of hers.[40] It seems clear that one belief state can cause another belief state. Moreover, recall Benn's problem with which we began (sec. 1.3): the individual's concern with keeping her moral consciousness in reasonable shape. A person is concerned with evaluating her own beliefs in the light of the reasons she embraces. If Betty's concern is whether her acceptance of β is justified,[41] she must appeal to reasons that *she accepts* that support β. If Betty is asking herself whether she is justified in accepting β, it will be of no avail for her to cite reasons that she does not accept; they could not provide *her* with a reason to embrace β, and so they could not cause her to believe β.

None of this requires that we accept the doxastic presupposition; that only follows if a reason-state of Betty's is necessarily a belief-state of hers. But we should not embrace this constrained notion of reasons. Recall the emotivist analysis discussed in section 1.2.2. An emotivist theory might say that one of Betty's reasons for accepting a moral belief that Xs are bad is that she has a negative affect or feeling response toward Xs. This feeling state need not be a belief, nor need Betty believe that she is in this feeling state; the feeling state directed toward X just is a reason to ascribe to the belief that Xs are bad.[42]

William Lycan objects to calling such justification inferential: "Only when a belief is based on another belief do we speak of *inference*, but it seems always appropriate to describe any of the cognitive and perceptual states on which beliefs are based as being reasons in a usefully wider sense." [43] I confess that my linguistic intuitions are not as clear as his, but I don't think that anything significant hangs on the linguistic point. What is important is that (1) Betty can have good reasons for β that are not beliefs; (2) the justification of β can turn on these reasons; and (3) these reasons can cause her belief that β. Still, there is something in the worry that a belief can be justified simply by a nonbelief state such as a feeling. Suppose that Betty believes that Xs are bad, and cites as her only reason for believing this, "I feel boo toward Xs." It does indeed seem pretty odd to say that she infers the badness of Xs just from the boo feeling. Her "reason" seems simply a rather roundabout statement of "blind emotivism," which I suggested really has no place for the idea of a moral belief (sec. 1.2.2). But if, instead, Betty refers to certain features of X, describes how these features arouse negative affects in her, [44] and claims that objects with such features should be avoided, it seems that she really has given reasons for her evaluation, one of which is the arousal of a nonbelief state in her. Though it is hard to see any rule or principle that can be specified here, I venture that it does not seem implausible to cite nonbelief states as reasons that enter into an inferential justification of a belief, though the idea that a belief can be inferred simply from a nonbelief state does strike one (or, at least, me) as fairly implausible. In any event, I shall thus assume that nonbelief states such as feelings can enter into inferential justification, and remain skeptical that sense can be made of a belief that is inferred solely from, say, a feeling.

Adopting this broad view of inferential justification vastly increases the robustness of our account in relation to various emotivist theories. To restrict reasons in inferential justification to belief states would be to rule out, a priori, that feelings can be grounding reasons for beliefs. Nothing we have uncovered about the causal basing relation warrants such exclusion. Moreover, I think it is highly plausible to maintain that in some cases one's affective responses can provide reasons for evaluative statements. Thus, for instance, a positive feeling experience when eating ice cream can provide a reason for the belief that "Ice cream is delicious." [45] To insist on the need for an additional belief—"I believe I have a positive feeling when eating ice cream"—adds nothing to the justification of the evaluation, and seems otiose. [46] Of course, to say that such feelings are eligible as reasons—they are not conceptually unfit to serve as reasons—is not to endorse them as good reasons; just what reasons are good moral reasons is a substantive issue in ethics.

CHAPTER 3

The Internal and External Perspectives

3.1 Open and Closed Justification

Thus far I have focused on the causal dimension of the basing relation. But, of course, that one belief causes another does not show that it is a reason for it. As Pollock notes, our beliefs can be knit together causally in odd ways:

I might believe that I am going to be late to my class, and that might cause me to run on a slippery sidewalk, lose my footing, and fall down, whereupon I find myself flat on my back looking up at the birds in the tree above me. My belief that I was going to be late caused me to have the belief that there were birds in the tree, but I do not believe the latter on the basis of the former.[1]

To be sure, cases of this sort are more puzzling on an efficient causation account of the basing relation, as it seems manifest that one's belief that one will be late for class does not sustain one's belief that there are birds in the tree. Psychoanalysis is probably a richer source of examples of nonjustifying sustaining causes. That Little Hans fears horses because he is afraid that his father will castrate him does not justify his belief that horses are dangerous.[2] In short, reasons are justificatory. But how do we determine whether some consideration is a good reason—or any sort of reason at all—for Alf to believe β?

The idea of a "good reason" can be interpreted from the agent's internal perspective or from an external viewpoint.[3] For example, Alf may believe that Betty, his lover, is faithful; given the facts available to him, he has a number of beliefs upon which this conclusion is based. From an internal perspective, Alf has good reason to believe that Betty is faithful. However, it may be the case that she is having an affair with Frank unbeknownst to him; from an external perspective he has good reason to conclude that she is unfaithful. So, too, in the belief-preservation experiments (sec. 2.2). From the subjects' internal perspective, they had good reason to accept the feedback offered by the experimenters, testifying to the keenness of their ability to discriminate real from fictitious suicide notes; from a more comprehensive external perspective, in which we know the aims of the experiments, it seems that their beliefs were not really justified after all. Analyses of justification often go astray because they unaccountably and unconsciously switch back and forth between the internal and external perspectives. And this is understandable insofar as both are relevant to justificatory claims. After all, in a way Alf is justified in believing Betty to be faithful, and in another way he is not. We can avoid many pitfalls and confusions throughout the analysis by confronting this vexed question at the outset.

The situation of Ross's subjects before their debriefing session can be captured by distinguishing whether we view their system of beliefs as closed or open.[4] At time t, before the debriefing session but after the experiment, their beliefs in their skills are justified if we consider only their current beliefs and reasons—if we take their system of beliefs and reasons, S, as closed. At t, when the subjects are evaluating their capacities to distinguish, say, real from fictitious suicide notes, only those beliefs and reasons that are then a part of S can count for them. As is often said, one cannot escape from one's circle of beliefs.[5] Restricting themselves to the contents of their own S at time t, they made the justified inference: They were skillful on the task. However, the supposition of Ross and his colleagues was that, once additional information was brought to bear on the subjects' systems of reasons and beliefs, these beliefs would no longer be justified *in those systems*. For *open* justification, then, we treat S as open to new information and arguments and, from this external perspective, make judgments about what would then be justified in S. We ask (1) whether, given S, would the subjects have reason to accept some new reason for belief, R'; and (2) if they do have a good reason to accept R', would its inclusion in S require changes in S such that their belief in their discriminatory skills would no longer be justifiable on the basis of R?

The core idea of open justification is that, at any given time, a justified belief system is, ideally, stable in the face of acute and sustained criticism by others and of new information.[6] Full explication of the idea of open justification would thus require a counterfactual test, and once again we would meet all the difficulties that idea poses. But the intuitive point is, I think, clear enough. Open justification asks the question: Are there any considerations of which Alf could be made aware that are grounded in his systems of beliefs and, if integrated, would they undermine the justification of β given his revised system of beliefs?[7] Put somewhat more elegantly, if Alf's beliefs were subject to extensive criticism and additional information, does *his viewpoint commit him* to revise his beliefs? It is important to stress here that the question is whether Alf's viewpoint commits him to changing his beliefs, not whether he would actually do so. Perhaps, like Mr. Raco, Alf is so psychologically wedded to a certain belief that he just could not bring himself to drop it from his belief system no matter how unjustified it is. This would not show that the belief is openly justified, for, like Mr. Raco, we may be able to see that Alf's other beliefs and his inferential norms commit him to rejecting the belief, even if he refuses to do so. As we saw with Ross's belief-perseverance experiments, subjects often persevere in holding unjustified beliefs; their perseverance does not show that the beliefs are openly justified. Open justification, then, takes a person's current system of beliefs and asks, first, whether given this system that person is committed to accepting some new piece of information, and, second, whether that person is then committed to revising his or her system of beliefs in the light of that new information.

3.2 Externalist Justifications

Open justification might be described as weakly externalist. According to open justification, Alf's current belief, β, may not really be justified despite the fact that it is justified given Alf's current system of reasons and beliefs. So open justification takes an external perspective on what Alf is justified in believing. However, open justification takes Alf's current belief system[8] as the point of departure. Beginning with Alf's current system S, open justification asks: Given the beliefs currently constituting S, is Alf committed to accepting some new reason R' that would result in a new system S', in which R would no longer justify β (perhaps because R has been dropped from S')? Although the conclusion of an open justification can disagree with Alf's own (closedly) justified judgments based on his system of reasons and beliefs S, that system is always the point of departure for the external criticism.

Because it may seem that the external perspective is in some way privileged, a stronger form of externalism may appear called for. Whether Alf is justified in believing β, we might say, ultimately depends on whether there simply are good reasons for believing β. And whether there simply are good reasons for believing β does not depend on the nature of Alf's perspective, but is an objective, entirely external, matter. For example: Alf has good reason to believe that the earth is round just because it is true that the earth is round. If, somehow, Alf possessed a belief system that did not lead to this belief—even supposing open justification— that would not give Alf any less reason to hold it, though it would lead us to expect that he would not come to embrace it. So if β is true, Alf has reason to believe it even if it is not inferable from his other beliefs. As Joseph Raz puts it:

> Beliefs are sometimes reasons, but it would be wrong to regard all reasons as beliefs. It should be remembered that reasons are used to guide behaviour, and people are to be guided by what is the case, not by what they believe to be the case. To be sure, in order to be guided by what is the case a person must come to believe that it is the case. Nevertheless it is the fact and not the belief in it which should guide him and which is a reason. If p is the case, then the fact that I do not believe p does not establish that p is not a reason for me to perform some action.[9]

Raz's view clearly captures an important feature of discourse. If asked, for example, why he believes that the Minnesota Twins won the 1992 World Series, Alf could reply that he believes they did because they won and he saw them win. His *belief* that he saw them win, Raz might say, is not his reason for believing they won; the reason was *that* they won. A fact about the world is the reason for his belief. In general, then, on this view reasons are understood as facts about the world. To be sure, before some fact can cause a belief in the requisite way it must be internalized, but the crucial reason for the belief is the fact, not another belief.[10]

This account implies that reasons for true beliefs and reasons for false beliefs are, ontologically, deeply different. Of course, in one way they must be different, insofar as we suppose that reasons for true beliefs are typically good reasons, while reasons for false beliefs are usually bad reasons (but see below, sec. 3.4). But on Raz's account the difference is much deeper. The Minnesota Twins, after all, won the 1991, not the 1992, World Series, so the "fact" that they won in 1992 could not have been the reason for Alf's false belief that they won in 1992. Since even false beliefs can have reasons, we must suppose that the reason was some belief of Alf's, perhaps a result of faulty memory. What could not have been the reason for his belief was the fact that the Twins won in 1992, for there was no such fact. And neither could the reason for his belief that "The Twins won in 1992" be the fact that they won in 1991, though Twins' winning in 1991 is part of the causal explanation of why he arrived at his false belief.

Things can get even more complicated. Suppose Betty believes that the Apollo moon landings were faked; they were, she believes, televised from an Air Force base in California. Today we would conclude that the reasons for her belief could not have been that they were actually faked. But suppose that we discover in ten years that they really were faked; do we want to say then that this fact is, after all, the reason for her belief? But why change the account of her reasons and reasoning just because it turns out that she was correct? Our original accounting of her evidence, her perceptions, and her reasoning may be as sound after the discovery as it was before; the mere fact that she turns out to be correct does not in itself seem to require that we give a new account of her reasons for her belief that the moon landings were faked.

All this seems needlessly complicated. Moreover, it attenuates the link between our deliberations and our reasons. Betty's deliberations were the same before and after the "discovery" that the Apollo landings were faked, so it would seem that an account of her reasons should be the same, too. But we have seen that this is not so on a strongly externalist view; after the discovery we find that Betty has a crucial reason causing her belief of which we were not aware, namely, the fact that the moon landings were faked. Of course it can be said that she had such a reason all along but we never knew it. Then, of course, we can never know what a person's reasons are until the truth of the view is known. But that seems wrong; we can understand a person's reasons perfectly well without knowing whether they are correct or incorrect.

Our reasons for our beliefs are our perceptions, feelings, and our other beliefs, including beliefs about when perceptions and feelings are apt to lead us astray and when they are not. To be sure, our perceptions and feelings are caused by facts presented to us in certain ways, but these facts can only become reasons for us when translated into cognitive, affective, and perceptual states. Describing something as a fact is a way of talking about the world, whereas describing something as a reason is a way of talking about cognitive (i.e., belief and reason) systems, and in particular the connections that are appropriately made within a cognitive system. The weakly externalist view of open justification recognizes this. External reasons are perhaps best understood as reasons that the person does not now possess, but that her system of beliefs and epistemic norms commits her to accepting. This does not involve positing a unique sort of reason; it still understands reasons as cognitive states.

It follows from this view of reasons that if Alf's belief system is such that it is really impossible to show, even under open justification, that any element of it supports R's status as a ground for β, then R cannot be a reason for Alf. In my terms, then, suppose that even given open justification, under which we consider new information and arguments that might be addressed to Alf, R still could not enter S as a reason to believe β. While in such a case it makes perfect sense to say that R correctly describes some fact—say, that the Twins won the 1991 World Series—it would be wrong to say that this is a reason for Alf to believe that fact. If, *ex hypothesi*, we have to admit that nothing in Alf's system of beliefs could possibly show him that the Twins won in 1991 (which is implied by saying that even under open justification R is not a reason for β in S), it seems that we have yet to give him any reason to believe that they did.

An upshot of this view is that we must reject the idea of an inherently impersonal reason. On a strongly externalist conception of reasons there could be a fact F that was a reason to accept β, even if humans were incapable of recognizing F, conceiving of it, and so on; it would be a reason, but it could never enter into any human's cognitive system. And if humans were the only rational creatures, it would make sense to say that F was a reason but could never be part of any belief system. I do not doubt such facts exist. Our perceptual and cognitive capacities allow us to cognize and conceptualize the world in a variety of ways, but it seems intelligible (if disputed by some) that there exist states of affairs that humans simply can never cognize. This much, I think, is clear; but it is mysterious what could be meant by saying that they provide *reasons* to believe β. "Reasons for whom?" is the proper query. Facts become reasons when they enter into cognitive systems with inferential norms and are able to *justify* acceptance of a belief.

3.3 Belief Commitments and Tacit Beliefs

In explicating this conception of reasons, Stanley Benn and I described them as "commitments."[11] We employed this term not to suggest that accepting reasons somehow required an act of will (as one may voluntarily commit oneself to the Catholic Church), but rather to stress that one has a reason R in virtue of something else that one believes or accepts, and so one is *committed to R*. In this light, a mere fact about the world cannot be a reason for a person, even in an external sense, until it is a commitment—until, that is, one is committed to embracing a belief about it in virtue of other parts of one's system of beliefs and reasons. Closed justification, then, restricts itself to one's present commitments, whereas open justification concerns conjectures about what commitments would arise in the light of new information and arguments. But both understand reasons as epistemic commitments of a person arising out of her or his current belief system.

If reasons are commitments to believe one thing in light of one's acceptance of another, then systems of epistemic norms cannot be understood as simply permissive—as allowing, but not requiring, inferences.[12] On the face of it, this may seem implausible; it seems to commit us to an infinite number of beliefs—all those that follow from everything we now believe. In a sense, we do seem to have an infinite number of beliefs.[13] Yet, as Watson reports, Sherlock Holmes has a good argument against any such idea:

"You see," he explained, "I consider that a man's brain originally is like a little empty attic, and you have to stock it with such furniture as you choose. A fool takes in all the lumber of every sort that he comes across, so that the knowledge which might be useful to him gets crowded out, or is at best jumbled up with lots of other things, so that he has difficulty laying his hands upon it. Now the skillful workman is very careful as to what he puts in his brain-attic. He will have nothing in it but the tools which may help him in doing his work but of these he has a large assortment, and all in the most perfect order. It is a mistake to think that little room has elastic walls and can distend to any extent. Depend upon it that there comes a time when for every addition of knowledge you forget something that you knew before. It is of the highest importance, therefore, not to have useless facts elbowing out the useful ones."[14]

If we are to reconcile the idea that in some sense we have an infinite number of beliefs with Holmes's objection that we cannot store that much information, it seems we need some distinction between beliefs that we store and beliefs to which we are committed. I hesitate to add any detailed proposal to the complex debate about how memory works, and how this might relate to tacit beliefs,[15] but it certainly seems that we would want to distinguish the following types of beliefs Alf can be said to "have":

B1: Alf is sitting in a chair depressed, thinking "Betty is cheating on me."
B2: Alf falls asleep in the chair, but still believes "Betty is cheating on me."
B3: Alf believes that "No nuclear bombs have been dropped on Detroit this year."
B4: Alf believes that "The square root of the sum of 98,971 and 18,572,070 is 4321."
B5: Alf is a utilitarian. Although he has never read any philosophy,

he believes that "There can be conclusive moral reason to kill one innocent person to save nineteen others."[16]

B6: If Alf knew that the experimenters were misleading him, he would be committed to revising his estimation of his skills in distinguishing real from fictitious suicide notes.

B1 is an example of a *conscious belief;* it is in Alf's working memory.[17]

B2 is a case of an *explicit but not conscious belief.* The number of beliefs that can be brought into consciousness at the same time is obviously very small; we would certainly say that Alf has many more beliefs than he can think about at the same time. Explicit beliefs such as B2 probably should be understood in a dispositional sense: one who believes β is disposed to judge β, to affirm β, and so on.[18] Moreover, it seems likely that explicit beliefs are explicitly stored in passive or long-term memory; William Lycan hypothesizes that for any such belief there is some specific state of Alf that is referentially (representationally) related to it.[19] And there seems a sense in which the retrieval of an explicit belief into active memory yields no new information. Once Alf believes that Betty is cheating on him, repeated retrievals of that belief do not tell him anything new. Sherlock Holmes's brain-attic theory no doubt is applicable to explicit, nonconscious beliefs: There is a limit to the number of explicit beliefs that we can store, though Holmes probably underestimated his own storage capacity.

B3 is aptly described as an *obviously derivable belief.* Hartry Field understands tacit beliefs as obviously derivable from explicit beliefs.[20] In the case of B3, it seems doubtful that Alf stores this bit of information explicitly. However, it seems sensible to say that Alf believes that no atomic bombs have been dropped on Detroit this year; he would be disposed to judge so if the occasion arose in which such a judgment made sense.

The question is whether such tacit beliefs can be causes of other beliefs, in other words, whether they can serve as reasons for other beliefs. Two possibilities emerge. First, it might be held that somehow tacit beliefs are actual inner states of people, and as such can serve as causes. If this route is taken, the number of tacit beliefs, though quite large, cannot be infinite; it is hard to see how there could be an infinite number of actual inner states of a person. Alternatively, it may be held that tacit beliefs are essentially derived, that is, produced by the operation of inference rules on explicitly stored beliefs. In this case we could have an infinite number of tacit beliefs, but then tacit beliefs could not be actual inner states of people. They are, perhaps, possible inner states that can be quickly generated. But if they are not actual inner states, then they cannot serve as causes of other beliefs until they are actually generated.

B4 and B5 are examples of *beliefs to which we seem committed* by virtue of our other beliefs, though the derivation may be complex and ultimately surprising. If one takes the second option just discussed, they are simply a type of tacit belief; under the first option, they are not. Whatever sorts of beliefs they are, it seems clear that we can have an infinite number of them, though for the reason just explored it seems equally clear that they cannot causally sustain other beliefs. Perhaps rather than saying that Alf believes B4 we would want to say that he is committed to it by virtue of his other beliefs, making clear that no inner state now corresponds to it. Note that bringing B4 to consciousness does result in new information, in the sense that Alf has put together stored knowledge to yield a result that was not an object of explicit belief. B5 is much the same. Suppose that Alf is a straightforward act utilitarian; though he has never thought about the matter, and has never read Bernard Williams's story of Jim and Pedro, we might say that he was committed to the conclusion that one has a moral responsibility to kill one innocent person to save nineteen innocent others. In this case Alf's system of beliefs and reasons commits him to a certain moral judgment; if he continues to accept those beliefs and reasons, he must accept the conclusion. It is in this sense that systems of reasons for belief are not merely permissive, but constitute rational commitments.

B6 is *not a current belief* of Alf's in any way, not even the very extended way in which it might be proper to call B4 and B5 "tacit" beliefs of his. Open justification, which makes claims along the lines of B6, is an externalist perspective; it is not restricted to the justification of Alf's present beliefs, but focuses on what beliefs would be justified if *S* were subjected to criticism and new information.

3.4 Relativism of Reasons

If open justification is the strongest external standpoint, it seems that we are pointed toward a sort of relativism in relation to reasons. Given Alf's perspective, I have been arguing, it is possible that he has no reason to believe β, while given our system of beliefs, we do. This conforms to W. Newton-Smith's characterization of relativism, namely, that "*R* is a reason for holding that β is true for Alf while *R* is not a reason for holding that β is true for Betty." To Newton-

Smith this is to enlist in the cause of the devil: "Rationality requires
. . . having good reasons for one's beliefs. If relativism held with regard to reason . . . this would be a victory for the Kingdom of
Darkness." [21]

Newton-Smith maintains that relativism of *reasons* is incoherent because it implies relativism of *truth*. He writes:

> R is a reason for believing that β just in case there is an appropriate truth
> linking R and β. That my typewriter looks white to me is a reason for thinking
> that it is white just because things that look white in the sort of circumstances
> that obtain at the moment are or tend to be white. . . . Whether R is conclu-
> sive reason for β or merely a fallible indicator of β, whether R is semantically
> or contingently connected to β it remains true that R is a reason for β just in
> case there is a truth of the appropriate kind linking R and β. Thus, if relativism
> about truth is incoherent, relativism about reason is incoherent. [22]

Notice that Newton-Smith is supposing a strongly externalist view of
reasons according to which R is a reason if and only if the link between
R and β is a truth (a fact) about the world (and not merely about the
agent's belief system). Manifestly, he does not understand this link as
merely a necessary condition; a merely necessary link would be consistent with his characterization of relativism. Suppose that an R–β link
is a truth; then R could be a reason for Betty to believe β. But if it
were only necessary, R still may not be a reason for Alf to believe β.
This, though, is the possibility depicted in Newton-Smith's characterization of relativism, and is said to constitute a victory for the Kingdom
of Darkness. It thus follows that, for Newton-Smith, the truth of the
R–β link is a necessary and sufficient condition for R being a reason to
believe β.

But the problem is that one can have perfectly good reason to believe
what is false, and have no reason whatsoever to believe what is true.
This is so not only under closed justification (in which a person's system of beliefs and reasons is taken as given) but under open justification
as well (in which we subject a person's belief system to criticism and
new information). If a system is sufficiently unlike our own, it seems
possible in principle that even under open justification that system
might not admit R as a reason for β, even though it is a reason for us.
Reasons, I have argued, are not facts or simply mirrors of facts; they
concern the functioning of cognitive systems and the appropriate connections drawn between the elements of those systems. If we take this
view, then relativism with respect to reasons does not imply relativism
with respect to truth. In principle, a person can have impeccable reason
to believe what is false.

It might be thought that this cannot be right: If Alf believes β, and β is false, then there must be some flaw in Alf's system of beliefs such that, given open justification, his system would be revised so as to reject β. True beliefs, it may be thought, are a seamless web; one false belief anywhere in a system produces contradictions that give a person reason to reject the false belief. So one cannot have impeccable reason to believe what is false; under open justification, one must always have reason to reject all false beliefs. Perhaps, given the limits of time and cognitive resources, Betty may be unable to show how Alf's belief system, properly reconstructed, commits him to reject β, but this does not mean that he really has no reason to reject it. What we can show is justified, and what is justified, are quite different.[23] But, the objection continues, the important point is that if Betty believes that β is false, she must believe that Alf has reason to reject his belief that β.

The most plausible grounding for this line of thought is, I think, the conviction (already encountered in our discussion of reliabilism) that rational belief systems are ultimately to be characterized in terms of truth.[24] Brian Ellis calls this the "standard account," according to which "if a system of beliefs can be said to be rational, it is only because these beliefs could all be true."[25] Clearly, if we adopt this view, then a relativism of reasons is indeed going to be linked to a relativism about truth. Ellis, however, proposes an alternative analysis of rational belief systems:

> We can recognize a rational system of beliefs, or an irrational one, even where we cannot adequately specify truth conditions for the sentences in question. We do not even have to believe that the sentences involved are objectively true or false. Consequently it is at least plausible to maintain that knowledge of rationality precedes that of truth conditions.[26]

On this view, Alf's rational belief system S is modeled in terms of two main elements:[27] (1) the sentences Alf accepts *(A)*, the ones he rejects *(R)*, and the ones about which he is undecided *(X)*; (2) a set of logical operators (or, more generally, inferential rules) connecting the acceptance and rejection of one sentence with another. For example, in Ellis's system,[28] given a formal language L_0 and any two sentences α and β,[29] which may either be accepted or rejected, or about which a person is undecided, then S is a rational belief system if it conforms to the following conditions[30]:

C1: One and only one of $A\alpha$, $R\alpha$ and $X\alpha$ occurs in S.

C2: α and $\sim\alpha$ do not occur with the same A or R in S.

C3: (a) $A(\alpha \lor \beta)$ occurs in S only if $R\alpha$ and $R\beta$ do not both occur in S.

    (b) $R(\alpha \lor \beta)$ occurs in S only if neither $A\alpha$ nor $A\beta$ occurs in S.

C4: (a) $A(\alpha \ \& \ \beta)$ occurs in S only if neither $R\alpha$ nor $R\beta$ occurs in S.

    (b) $R(\alpha \ \& \ \beta)$ occurs in S only if $A\alpha$ and $A\beta$ do not both occur in S.

C5: (a) $A(\alpha \supset \beta)$ occurs in S only if $A\alpha$ and $R\beta$ do not both occur in S.

    (b) $R(\alpha \supset \beta)$ occurs in S only if neither $R\alpha$ nor $A\beta$ occurs in S.

C6: (a) $A(\alpha \equiv \beta)$ occurs in S only if α and β do not occur with opposite A or R evaluations in S.

    (b) $R(\alpha \equiv \beta)$ occurs in S only if α and β do not occur with same A or R evaluations in S.

C7: S is completable through every extension of L_0.[31]

My aim is not to defend Ellis's specific proposals. However, it may seem that the simple tripartite division among acceptance, rejection, and being undecided is just too simple. Ellis himself develops probabilistic models, as do Forrest and Gärdenfors.[32] Sometimes the issue is put in terms of degrees of belief. Hence:

> *Brute Strength Thesis:* One accepts some beliefs more strongly than others.[33]

Often the Brute Strength Thesis is explicated in strictly probabilistic terms, such that to each belief one accords a probability, the result being a measure of strength of belief. I think the idea of strength of belief is employed rather more often than it is understood; for example, it is not pellucid to say "I believe to degree .87 that my wife went to McDonald's today."[34] I think the useful idea in the Brute Strength Thesis can be explicated in terms of two rather more specific theses:

> *Degree of Implicatedness Thesis:* Some of one's beliefs are more deeply implicated in one's belief system, and so it would take a great deal of evidence to overturn them.

> *Likelihood of Error Thesis:* For many or all of one's beliefs, one not only accepts them, but has a view of how likely they are to turn out to be wrong or unjustified.

Both of the latter articulate the idea that beliefs have varying strengths, without asserting that holding beliefs itself is a matter of degree.

The Likelihood of Error Thesis is particularly relevant to inferential justification, for two reasons. First, it seems that the rational acceptance of a belief is necessarily related to the likelihood of error, but it is difficult to divine much in the way of hard and fast rules. Certainly it seems irrational to accept a belief that one thinks is more likely to be wrong (or unjustified) than right (or justified), but it does not follow from this that one should accept a belief that one believes is more likely to be right (or justified) than wrong (unjustified). After all, it can be rational to be undecided. Moreover, as the legal system suggests, different standards of proof will be suitable to different cases. In civil law, for example, all that is typically required is a preponderance of evidence in order to justify (the court's) accepting a claim; in criminal trials, the court remains undecided unless the likelihood of error is very low (i.e., no reasonable doubt remains).[35] I certainly do not wish to claim that justifications for different standards of proof for belief acceptance cannot be advanced, but it seems plausible that there will be considerable disparity among rational belief systems in just what standards they require in various cases for belief acceptance and rejection.[36] For example, in some sorts of cases a person might believe that she must decide either yea or nay, as, for instance, when one is in a burning house and must decide whether it is safer to jump out the window or try for the stairs. In cases of this sort we would be more than a little surprised by someone who refused to accept either belief until a higher standard of evidence was reached. On the other hand, in many matters we can wait: refusing either to accept or reject a belief may be appropriate. Often, I think, one's epistemic decision will be affected by one's broader values (sec. 5.4); differences in values may well lead to different openly justified standards of proof for different people.

Second, because we do accept beliefs with greater than a zero likelihood of error, inferential justification can be justification decreasing. If β_1 has a likelihood of error of $3/4$, and β_2 has a likelihood of error of $3/4$, then an inference from (β_1 & β_2) to β_3 may result in a conclusion with a likelihood of error of 50 percent.[37] Consequently, in such cases long inferential chains based on one basic belief are not apt to yield conclusions the acceptance of which is rational, even if the reasoning is impeccable.[38] This, as we shall see, points to the importance of systemic considerations in justification.

3.5 Relativism and Belief Systems

For the moment, I shall not pursue these matters. The important point at present is that a rational belief system is to be analyzed in terms of the relations among its members (reasons and beliefs) and not with reference to the idea of truth. By loosening the tie between rational belief and truth, my analysis is robust among conflicting theories of the nature of truth. This seems especially attractive if we wish to integrate moral belief into a general theory of rational belief. As I pointed out in section 1.2, throughout its history ethics has been divided between those who insist that its claims are truths, perhaps describing a certain sort of fact, and those who maintain that moral statements are neither true nor false. If we analyze rational belief systems in terms of admitting truths and only truths, it will be impossible for moral epistemology to be robust on this crucial issue of metaethics. And, insofar as justificatory liberalism supposes a theory of moral justification (sec. 1.2.1), this would tie it to intractable issues in metaethics. However, if we adopt a view along the lines proposed by Ellis, it not only coheres with the preferred internalist account of reasons, but allows us to proceed while putting aside these divisive metaphysical issues.

If we understand rational belief systems in this general way, two routes lead to a relativism of reasons. First, people start off with different sets of rejected and accepted beliefs. Even if different people impeccably employ the same logical operations on two such sets, there is no reason to believe that they will end up with the same belief sets.[39] Consequently, Alf's rational system may contain a belief β that Betty's rational system does not, even under open justification. Relativism of reasons would then obtain; let us call this *belief relativism*. Second, people may employ different logical or inferential connectives. Ellis, for instance, admits that his conditions C5(b) and C6(b) may seem counterintuitive, and he considers alternatives.[40] And, ultimately more important, different people may justifiably employ different standards of proof regulating belief acceptance and rejection. We need to be careful here; as we shall see shortly, allowing much in the way of *logical relativism* has considerable costs in mutual intelligibility. If Alf's rules of "inference" are totally foreign to Betty, it is unlikely that she will be able to recognize his system as a rational system at all. Nevertheless, it does seem that, at least to some degree, people can have systems of beliefs that contain different norms of inference and belief acceptance and still be able to recognize each other's systems as *rational*.[41] If so, then another source emerges for the relativism of reasons.

This second source of relativism is especially important to moral reasoning, as it is plausible that diverse logics connecting such operators as "ought" and their relation to notions such as "obligation" can be openly justified.[42] Consider, for example, what Bernard Williams calls the "agglomeration principle," according to which "I ought to do Φ" and "I ought to do X" imply "I ought to do Φ and X." Williams shows how combining this principle with the principle that *"ought* implies *can"* allows one to generate the following inconsistency:[43]

1. I ought to do Φ.
2. I ought to do X.
3. I cannot do both Φ and X.

From (1) and (2) by agglomeration:

    4. I ought to do Φ and X.

from (3) by "*ought* implies *can*":

    5. It is not the case that I ought to do Φ and X.

The result is a contradiction between (4) and (5). If, as seems reasonable to me, one accepts the principles of both agglomeration and "*ought* implies *can*," one seems committed to abandoning either (1) or (2); that is, it is not the case one ought to do Φ or it is not the case one ought to do X. Famously, however, many, including Williams and Susan Hurley, reject or modify the principle of agglomeration. Williams insists that we ought to do *each* act, Φ and X, but not *both*. And, as he points out,

[t]here are certainly many characterisations of actions in the general field of evaluation for which agglomeration does not hold, and for which what holds of each action taken separately does not hold for both taken together: thus it may be *desirable*, or *advisable*, or *sensible*, or *prudent*, to do Φ, and again desirable or advisable etc. to do X, but not desirable etc. to do both Φ and X.[44]

Either view strikes me as plausibly justified in a rational belief system.[45]

CHAPTER 4

Taming Relativism

4.1 Why We Are Not Committed to Normative Cognitive Pluralism

Thus far I have been arguing in favor of the possibility of a relativism of reasons. It may thus seem that we should endorse what Stephen Stich calls "normative cognitive pluralism":

> *Normative* cognitive pluralism is not a claim about the cognitive processes people do use; rather it is a claim about *good cognitive processes*—the cognitive processes that people *ought* to use. What it asserts is that there is no unique system of cognitive processes that people should use, because various systems of cognitive processes that are very different from each other *are equally good*.[1]

However, nothing I have said justifies such a strong claim. I have argued that reasons concern connections within belief systems, and because the initial set of beliefs may differ or because some of the logical operators may differ, Alf might have a reason to accept β while Betty has a reason to reject β, even though both their belief systems are openly justified.[2] Moreover, I have argued that Betty can recognize that Alf really has a reason to believe β though she does not have such a reason. This, I take it, is to endorse a sort of relativism of reasons. But it does not follow from this that Betty is committed to evaluating Alf's belief system[3] as just as good as her own. Indeed, given all her conceptual resources, it would seem that she is committed to seeing her own as superior. *Ex hypothesi*, given all she knows about what is to be believed, she seems committed to concluding that her own beliefs and inferential rules are superior (after all, that is why she uses them). From her perspective she must view Alf's system as inferior in the sense that it is not as well justified given everything she believes. If Alf's system is openly justified, Betty must acknowledge that Alf has no reasons to accept her view—it cannot be justified to him. But it does not follow that from all this she must conclude that his view is in some sense as good as her own.

The point might be put in terms of a contrast between impartiality and objectivity. Normative cognitive pluralism requires that one be impartial between one's own way of reasoning and those of others; the ways others reason are different from, but just as good as, your own. But it is hard to see how one can really believe this. If one's system is closedly justified, and one reflects on (what one considers to be) appropriate standards of evidence, the soundest inferential rules, and so on, one must conclude that it is one's own system. What resources could you possibly draw on that would allow you to evaluate others' systems of beliefs (including inference rules) as just as good, yet not give you any reason to alter your own? (Perhaps if, by some chance, your system was precisely tied with others, and no revision of yours would be superior, but that seems pretty far-fetched.) However, though one seems necessarily partial to one's own cognitive processes, one can still be objective in the sense of recognizing that what is a reason for you need not be a reason for others. This seems associated with what Jean Piaget has called "decentering": a process by which an individual comes to recognize that her own point of view differs from that of others, and therefore what are reasons for her are not necessarily reasons for others.[4] We can be objective in the sense that we can recognize that others, even under open justification, may not share our reasons without abandoning our partiality for our own belief system. Put simply, we can have good grounds for believing our own view is superior while nevertheless acknowledging that we may not be able to justify it to others, even supposing open justification.

To be sure, a temptation arises here to adopt a God's eye perspective: From the perspective of God, or of the universe, or a philosopher, aren't the various cognitive systems just as good as each other? Putting aside some very real worries about the intelligibility of appeal to such a transcendental judgment,[5] it is obscure just what the claim "as good as" amounts to. If it means only that the fact that R is a good reason for Alf to believe β does not imply that a perfectly rational Betty also has reason to believe β, then it is implied by what I have called objectivity. If it implies the strong claim that we should be neutral between their systems and ours, in the sense that we should be prepared to use them, it is incoherent. We could never have reason to employ what, from our perspective, does not give us reasons. Nor can the claim intelligibly imply, say, that we should be just as prepared to teach or recommend conflicting ways of reasoning; to recommend a system is to do so for a reason, but it is our own system that announces to us what are, and what are not, good reasons (but see sec. 9.2.2). All things considered, it seems best to leave aside the notion that other people's ways of reasoning are "as good as" our own. Stich's normative cognitive pluralism is too ecumenical.[6]

4.2 Natural Mental Logic

In sections 2.1 and 2.2 I endorsed the widely shared view that reasons are the causes of the beliefs they justify. Given this, if we adopt a view of rational belief systems along the lines proposed by Ellis, it seems natural to provide a causal interpretation of the sorts of inferential rules that, he says, characterize rational belief systems. Inferential rules specify rational connections between beliefs; if inferential reasoning (which is causal) is to be rational, it must conform to these inferential rules. But if these inferential rules are merely rules of art, informing us only about what are good and what are bad inferences in relation to some standard, it would be a little mysterious to discern how they affect the causal links between reasons and beliefs. One way to dissolve this mystery is to understand inferential norms not only as rules of art, specifying excellence in reasoning, but as causal laws of thought. As J.S. Mill put it, "Logic comprises the science of reasoning, as well as an art," and Ellis agrees.[7]

Though there is some dispute on this matter, psychologists investigating inferential reasoning have uncovered a good deal of evidence supporting the hypothesis that people employ a mental logic—a system of inference rules—in their actual reasoning. Indeed, most psychologists studying actual reasoning suppose some version of the mental logic theory.[8] And Lance J. Rips concludes that, in comparison with other approaches, theories that posit natural inference rules provide a better explanation of the data concerning how people actually reason.[9] However, it does seem that mental logic may depart from the standard propositional calculus. Psychologists studying English reasoners, for instance, have found that English speakers do not interpret connectives in a way consistent with standard logic. Particularly troubling are interpretations of "if, then" statements (as well as "or" connectives), which are not typically used in ways that correspond to standard analyses in logic.[10] In response to these findings, such psychologists as Rips and Martin D. Braine have developed sets of natural inferential rules that correspond to the way speakers of English employ connectives.[11] Rips has gone beyond this to develop rules modeling causal reasoning as well.[12]

Mental logic views incline strongly toward the hypothesis that these logics are in some way natural or innate, though precisely to what extent is open to investigation. There may well be a complicated interplay between language and logic, such that English speakers tend to employ some inferential rules not utilized by others. A plausible hypothesis is that the capacity to develop a mental logic is innate, though the precise developmental path taken depends on a variety of factors, including one's native language.[13] If so, this would certainly help tame a radical relativism of reasons. The set of possible mental logics—laws governing thought—is apt to be pretty severely constrained.

P.N. Johnson-Laird criticizes mental logic views on the grounds that they suppose people to be intrinsically rational: We are, as it were, wired to process thoughts in a rational way. Yet, he points out, a large body of evidence shows that people often depart from norms of rational inference. But how could they possibly do so if the laws of logic are the laws of thought?[14] Perhaps logic should be understood merely as an art, and whether one embraces logic depends on other factors. Some people may be "deductively driven," while others do not value such rationality.[15] I shall not attempt to enumerate, much less explain, all possible errors in reasoning, but at least three merit discussion: (1) simple inferential errors, in which people overlook the correct inferential rules; (2) inferential errors in which people rely on invalid inferential rules; and (3) *akrasia* of belief. I consider the first two in section 4.5, the third in section 5.4.

4.3 Mutual Intelligibility and the Limits of Pluralism

I have been arguing that evidence supports the view that people employ mental logic in their reasoning; that a plausible hypothesis is that the capacity to develop such logics is innate; and that the range of possible logics is constrained by our innate capacities. In short, we have reason to suppose that the variance in mental logics among people and peoples is limited. This conclusion is reinforced by the philosophy of anthropology and of language. When Alf confronts Betty and seeks to render her utterances intelligible, he must suppose that he and she share crucial inferential norms.[16] The problem becomes particularly clear in anthropological contexts, in which one is seeking to interpret those in an alien culture. Martin Hollis and Steven Lukes have argued that in such interpretive settings the anthropologist must build up an interpretation of the alien language by locating a "bridgehead." The assumption underlying the bridgehead strategy is that others generally perceive what we perceive and tend to say about it the sorts of things we would say.[17] Relying on these assumptions, the anthropologist begins by translating everyday, basic perceptual sentences such as "Yes, this is a brown cow" and "No, it is not raining right now." Hollis and Lukes insist that this bridgehead includes translations not only of beliefs, but of basic logical rules, since "what sentences mean depends on how the beliefs which they express are connected, and that to justify a claim to have identified a belief one must show the belief is connected to others." Consequently, in the main,

Native logic must either turn out to be a version of our own or remain untranslatable.

If this is right, '$\alpha \supset \alpha$', '$\sim(\alpha \& \sim \alpha)$' and '$(\alpha \& (\alpha \supset \beta)) \supset \beta$' express more than axioms in a particular system or rules in a particular game. They express, rather, requirements for something being a system of logical reasoning at all. To look at alternatives is like looking for a novel means of transport which is novel not only in that it has no engine but also in that it does not convey bodies from one place to another. Anything which satisfies the latter condition could not be a means of transport at all. If natives reason logically at all, then they reason as we do.[18]

The point is that the context that sets the stage for the possibility of relativism—that we confront others different from us but of whom we can make some sense—presupposes widespread shared norms of inference as well as beliefs.[19] Thus the very possibility of mutual intelligibility sets a limit on the extent to which we can understand others as employing cognitive processes different from our own. According to Donald Davidson's principle of charity, we proceed by

assigning truth conditions to alien sentences that make native speakers right when plausibly possible, according, of course, to our own view of what is right. What justifies the procedure is the facts of disagreement and agreement alike are intelligible only against a background of massive agreement. Applied to language, this principle reads: the more sentences we conspire to accept (whether or not through a medium of interpretation), the better we understand the rest, whether or not we agree about them.[20]

The degree of charity we can exhibit is apt to vary with the attitude we take to the bridgehead. Suppose we arrive at a translation for the bridgehead, and this provides us with a fixed point for the translation of less obvious utterances, for example, religious or theoretical ones. Hollis describes the bridgehead thus:

In upshot there has to be some set of interpretations whose correctness is more likely than that of any later interpretation which conflicts with it. The set consists of what a rational man cannot fail to believe in simple perceptual situations, organized by rules of coherent judgment, which a rational man also cannot fail to subscribe to. All interpretation rests on rationality assumptions, which must succeed at the bridgehead and which can be modified at later stages only by interpretations that do not sabotage the bridgehead.[21]

If, as Hollis argues, the bridgehead is a fixed point in our interpretations, this will constrain possible interpretations of some nonbridgehead (e.g., theoretical) sentence β. We cannot purchase the truth of β by modifying the bridgehead. At this point, a commitment to a natural mental logic account of reasoning supports a strong presumption in favor of maintaining the bridgehead. Natural mental logic gives us independent reason to suppose that the basic inferential norms regulating reasoning will not differ greatly from one society (or person) to the next. Natural mental logic, then, counsels that we should not practice charity by purchasing consistency for others by attributing to them different basic inferential norms. Consequently, the preferred interpretation may be that β is a mistaken or irrational belief.[22]

The best—most enlightening—interpretation of others, then, may attribute unjustified beliefs to them (in either the open or closed sense). If the only way to render those beliefs justified would be to undermine the bridgehead—that is, to suppose that their basic inferential norms differ from ours—such charity would inhibit intelligibility. Now the same insight applies to some nonbasic inferential norms.[23] We may do better to suppose that others share our basic inferential norms but also rely on nonbasic unsound ones, than to render them all sound by positing basic inferential norms that differ from our own. Consider, for instance, Mill's observation that people make causal attributions on the basis of the fallacious principle that causes tend to resemble their effects. Mill gives an example of "the celebrated medical theory called the 'Doctrine of Signatures.' " In the words of Dr. Paris, a nineteenth-century physician, the doctrine is "no less . . . than a belief that every natural substance which possesses any medicinal virtue indicates by an obvious and well-marked external character the disease for which it is a remedy, or the object for which it should be employed."[24]

The lungs of a fox must be a specific for asthma, because that animal is remarkable for its strong powers of respiration. Turmeric has a brilliant yellow colour, which indicates that it has the power of curing jaundice . . . and the Euphrasia (eye-bright) acquired fame, as an application in complaints of the eye, because it exhibits a black spot in its corolla resembling the pupil. The blood-stone, the Heliotropium of the ancients, from the occasional small specks or points of blood colour exhibited on its green surface, is even at this very day employed in many parts of England and Scotland to stop a bleeding from the nose.[25]

As Mill recognized, this inferential rule may be appealed to when interpreting the magical beliefs of other cultures.[26] In this case it would seem that we can maximize intelligibility by attributing to others an unsound inferential rule (effects look like causes, or by imitating an effect you can cause it), rather by insisting that, in some way, their beliefs and inferential rules must be rational.[27] Nisbett and Ross suggest that a similar procedure may be helpful in rendering psychoanalysis intelligible.[28]

Richard E. Grandy advances another reason why the aim of rendering others' behavior intelligible can be advanced by attributing error to them. Grandy maintains that "a causal theory of belief is embedded in our epistemological heritage,"[29] and, of course, I have advocated such a theory here. On this view, if Alf believes β, that belief is caused. Moreover, a mere fact cannot directly cause a belief (sec. 3.2), though of course acquaintance with a fact can. Grandy considers the case of Paul, who has just arrived at a cocktail party and remarks to the person next to him, "The man with the martini is a philosopher." Directly in front of Paul is a man (who is not a philosopher) at the bar drinking water out of martini glass, and there is no one else in sight drinking from a martini glass. However, unseen in the garden is a philosopher merrily drinking more than his share of martinis; indeed, he is the only one at the party drinking martinis. One strategy is to attribute to Paul a true belief, since the man at the party drinking a martini is a philosopher. But since there seems no way that this fact could have caused Paul's belief (he is not aware of the garden or the man in it), our theory of belief commits us to attributing an error to Paul. And by doing so we render his remark intelligible, whereas to translate it as true would, given our theory of belief, render it utterly mysterious.

These observations allow us to reject two radical principles of interpretation. According to what might be called the principle of *radical charity*, we can only achieve intelligibility through rendering other people's beliefs true, and so intelligibility is inversely related to the number of errors or false beliefs we attribute to others. Following Hollis, Lukes, and Grandy, I have argued that intelligibility can sometimes be better achieved by attributing errors, including inferential errors, to others.[30] On the other hand, we also must reject a *radical pluralism*, freely attributing to others all sorts of strange beliefs and odd inferential norms; to do that would render others unintelligible. Instead, if our aim is to achieve intelligibility—which, after all, is necessary for justificatory discourse—we must first secure a bridgehead of shared basic beliefs and inferential norms. Given this, we can render others' beliefs intelligible by sometimes attributing simple error to them, and sometimes attributing to them reasons for belief (and action) that are justified given their belief systems but not ours. For example, it seems at least plausible for a non-Catholic to interpret the religious belief of a devout Catholic that the Eucharist is the body and blood of Christ in this latter way.[31] Unlike the belief of, say, an Anglican, it would probably be wrong to provide a strictly symbolic interpretation of this belief; and it is not altogether clear that the devout Catholic's belief system is such that this belief can be shown to be openly unjustified.[32] In this case the Catholic could have an openly justified belief that is not, from some perspectives, justified. Hence the possibility of relativism, though of a rather tamed and limited type.[33]

4.4 Stich's Objection to the Bridgehead

Stephen Stich develops a particularly interesting objection to the bridgehead account of translation from Christopher Cherniak's discussion of feasibility orderings of inferences. Given the structure of human cognition, some inferences are easier than others. "Thus, other things equal, inferring $\alpha \supset \beta$ from $\sim\beta \supset \sim\alpha$ is typically easier (and hence more likely) than inferring $(\exists x)(\forall y)(Fx \supset Gy)$ from $(\forall x)Fx \supset (\forall x)Gx$, and the latter is much easier than one as difficult, say, as determining that the axiom of choice is independent of the other axioms of set theory."[34] Now, Cherniak asks us to consider a person who accepts the same inferences as we do, but whose feasibility ordering is vastly different. Stich continues the story:

For him, inferring "Socrates is male" from "Socrates is an uncle" and "If Socrates is an uncle, then Socrates is male" would not be possible, though inferences like determining the independence of the axiom of choice "would be an easy task, performed reliably and without prolonged investigation." . . . Cherniak claims, and I am inclined to agree, that despite the peculiarity in the inferential behavior of this imaginary subject, we would not find it totally beyond the bounds of intuitive plausibility to translate his sentence "If Socrates is an uncle, then Socrates is male" homophonically, and to view the belief state which underlies his sincere assertion of that sentence as the belief state that if Socrates is an uncle, then Socrates is a male. We would, in short, feel no overwhelming intuitive resistance to a scheme of intentional characterization for this subject which paralleled the one we use on less exotic folk. But, of course, the inferences our imagined subject finds impossibly difficult are just the ones Hollis would surely count among the bridgehead inferences, since they are the ones which are trivially obvious for more normal subjects.[35]

Although Stich's view may not be "totally beyond the bounds of intuitive plausibility" nor invoke "overwhelming intuitive resistance," there are good grounds to doubt that the belief states underlying the assertions would be the same in the subject as in ourselves. It seems far more plausible, I think, to suppose that the most obvious inferences are explicit beliefs (sec. 3.3); their retrieval is quick, and they do not yield new information. Such is, I venture, the case of 2 + 2 = 4 as well as the argument of *modus ponens*. In contrast, it seem highly doubtful that many of us explicitly believe that the square root of the sum of 98,971 and 18,572,070 is 4321, or that we hold as explicit beliefs extremely difficult inferences that follow from our system of inferential norms and beliefs. If they are all held as explicit beliefs, then Holmes's worries about the space in the brain-attic do indeed arise. Can it be that none of them are held as explicit beliefs—that only some sort of "atomistic" belief or rule can be held explicitly? I see no reason to suppose so; very few adults actually have to retrieve the rules of arithmetic to discover that 2 + 2 = 4.

If this is so, then although our set of explicit plus implicit beliefs may be the same as the inverse feasibility subject's conjunction of explicit and implicit beliefs, which beliefs are explicitly held, and which are implicitly held, will differ. Cherniak's subject will have explicit beliefs that are implicit for us (or, indeed, only belief commitments), and vice versa. And if that is so, then the belief states indicated by "If Socrates is an uncle, then Socrates is a male" will differ. Consequently, it would be inappropriate to include the inference in the bridgehead, at least insofar as we have reason to believe that the guiding assumption— that what is obvious to us must be obvious to them—fails.

This conclusion can be arrived at by a somewhat different route. It seems clear that Cherniak's subject's web of beliefs will look very different from ours; the reasons that support his belief that "If Socrates is an uncle, Socrates is a male" will differ markedly from ours. Now it seems that the content of a belief is affected by the inferential links relating it to other accepted sentences. We have already seen that these links are causal (secs. 2.2 to 2.3); so it would follow that the causal links among beliefs in our subject will differ markedly from those that obtain in us. If, as Davidson suggests, the cause of a belief is indispensable in determining the content of what we say, it follows that the content of "If Socrates is an uncle, then Socrates is a male" will be very different. Indeed, our beliefs may be so different that communication is impossible. "Communication begins where causes converge: your utterance means what mine does if belief in its truth is systematically caused by the same events and objects." [36]

The lesson from the inverted inference feasibility example is, I think, that the requirements for intelligibility are in some ways more exacting than the demands of inferential competency. We can acknowledge that in principle an inverted subject's inferences are impeccable, but it does not seem that this would be sufficient for us to engage in discourse with such a person, or sufficient to render his behavior intelligible. Beliefs and arguments that are central to our discourse and way of life would be almost inaccessible to him, and vice versa. Another way of putting this point is that a sentence in language L_1 cannot be translated into L_2 just because their truth conditions are identical. Thus, though the truth conditions for our "If Socrates is an uncle, then Socrates is a male" are identical to the inverted subject's "If Socrates is an uncle, then Socrates is a male," this does not mean they are translatable. As Davidson suggests, for translation we need to know why the sentences are held true in both languages, and that includes "the place of the sentence in the language as a whole, . . . the role of each significant part of the sentence, and . . . the logical connections between this sentence and others."[37]

4.5 Inferential Errors

Cherniak's idea of feasibility orderings of inferences maintains that some inferences are easier for us than others. One way of understanding this is that the retrieval of some inferential rules from memory is more difficult than others. Rips has uncovered the feasibility ordering shown in Table 4.1. The parameters indicate a measure of the availability of inference rules; they are ordered from most to least available. Thus if we accept Rips's theory of mental logic (or one along similar lines), not only can we explain the workings of a rational belief system, but we can predict when it is more and less likely to error, depending in part on the availability of the required inference rules.

John Stuart Mill seemed to believe that such retrieval errors were "casual mistakes" which, he said, stem "from a casual lapse, through hurry or inattention, in application of the true principles of induction."[39] In Mill's opinion such errors do not warrant philosophical analysis. Mill contrasted such casual errors to fallacies—the application of erroneous rules. It may well seem that the systematic application of erroneous rules poses a deeper challenge to the claims that the laws of logic are the laws of thought (sec. 4.4). If the laws of logic specify the causal relation among reasons, what are we to make of fallacious rules, which also specify causal relations among reasons? And what allows us to deem some causal relations as "rational" or "logical" and others as

Table 4.1 Inference Rules and Their Availability

Inference Rule		Parameter Estimate
Disjunctive *modus ponens:*	$(\alpha \lor \beta) \supset \Gamma$ α $\therefore \Gamma$	1.000
And introduction:	α β $\therefore \alpha \,\&\, \beta$	1.000
And elimination:	$\alpha \,\&\, \beta$ $\therefore \alpha$	.963
If introduction:	β can be deduced from α $\therefore \alpha \supset \beta$	.861
Or elimination:	$\alpha \lor \beta$ $\alpha \supset \Gamma$ $\beta \supset \Gamma$ $\therefore \Gamma$	.858
Modus ponens:	$\alpha \supset \beta$ α $\therefore \beta$	.723
DeMorgan's law:	$\sim(\alpha \,\&\, \beta)$ $\therefore \sim\alpha \lor \sim\beta$	.715
Disjunctive syllogism:	$\alpha \lor \beta$ $\sim\alpha$ $\therefore \beta$	.713
Not introduction:	$\alpha \supset \beta$ $\sim\beta$ $\therefore \sim\alpha$	.238
Or introduction:	α $\therefore \alpha \lor \beta$	.197

Adapted from Lance J. Rips, "Cognitive Processes in Propositional Reasoning," *Psychological Review* 90 (1983): 38–71, pp. 45, 62. Copyright American Psychological Association. Used with permission.[38]

fallacious? I want to suggest here that the analysis of fallacious rules is not in principle different from the analysis of casual errors; both turn on the fact that our cognitive resources are limited. The economic use of cognitive resources can result in an unjustified belief due to reliance on a fallacious rule, just as it can result in error because the correct rule is not retrieved from memory—or, to put it differently, the correct connections between beliefs are not made.

To see this, consider Mill's analysis of the fallacy that causes must resemble their effects, discussed in section 4.3. Mill calls this an "*a priori* fallacy, or natural prejudice," perhaps the "most deeply-rooted" of all.[40] This is an instance of the "representativeness heuristic" explored by Amos Tversky and Daniel Kahneman.[41] In seeking the cause of an event, we tend to look for factors that are representative of it, or resemble it. This same heuristic also explains more sophisticated errors. Consider the following three cases:

Case A: Nonexpert Errors in Probability Judgments. In a famous study of Tversky and Kahneman's, undergraduate subjects were given the following problem (the values in parenthesis are the numbers of subjects choosing each answer):

A certain town is served by two hospitals. In the larger hospital about 45 babies are born each day, and in the smaller hospital about 15 babies are born each day. As you know, about 50 percent of all babies are boys. However, the exact percentage varies from day to day. Sometimes it may be higher than 50 percent, sometimes lower.

For a period of 1 year, each hospital recorded the days on which more than 60 percent of the babies born were boys. Which hospital do you think recorded more such days?

The larger hospital (21)
The smaller hospital (21)
About the same (that is, within 5 percent of each other) (53).[42]

In this, and in many other instances documented by Tversky and Kahneman, most people make the faulty probabilistic inferences.

Case B: Expert Errors in Probability Judgments. Not only untrained people make such errors. Tversky and Kahneman show that members of the Mathematical Psychology Group and the American Psychology Association also make systematic erroneous probabilistic inferences. The following question was put to them:

Suppose one of your doctoral students has completed a difficult and time-consuming experiment on 40 animals. He has scored and analyzed a large number of variables. His results are generally inclusive, but one before-after comparison yields a highly significant $t = 2.70$, which is surprising and could have theoretical significance.

Considering the importance of the result, its surprisal value, and the number of analyses your student has performed, would you recommend that he replicates the study before publishing? If you recommend replication, how many animals would you urge him to run?[43]

Of seventy-five respondents, sixty-six recommended replication; the median recommendation was for a replication using twenty subjects. However, assuming that the mean and the variance are actually identical in the two samples, the chance of uncovering the significant result in the second sample is just above 50 percent. That is, the advice of the supervisors is to run a replication study in which there is almost a 50 percent chance that a significant finding would not be replicated. Tversky and Kahneman hypothesize that, in this and in other cases, respondents expect all samples to be representative of the population. "If we expect all samples to be very similar to one another, then almost all replications of a valid hypothesis should be statistically significant." [44]

Case C: Ignoring Base Rates. There is good evidence that, when confronted by specific diagnostic information, people rely on it almost exclusively, and thus ignore base rates. [45] Consider a simple problem posed by Richard Nisbett and Lee Ross:

The present authors have a friend who is a professor. He likes to write poetry, is rather shy, and small in stature. Which of the following is his field: (a) Chinese studies or (b) psychology? [46]

Tversky and Kahneman's research indicates that people will overwhelmingly select (a); the diagnostic information is "representative" of a professor of Chinese studies. Yet if we consider the relative size of the two populations—professors of psychology and Chinese studies— the probability is very much that the person is a psychology professor. To be sure, the diagnostic information would justify some small departure from the probabilities given by the base rates, but the evidence indicates that in such situations people tend to ignore base rate information, *even when it is supplied to them.* [47]

Tversky and Kahneman attribute these faulty cases of probabilistic reasoning to the representativeness heuristic. In Case C, the diagnostic information is representative of a professor of Chinese studies, so people ignore base-rate probabilities and are typically quite certain that the friend is a Chinese scholar. Case A also illustrates the representativeness heuristic. Small samples are regarded as representative of the general population; if the population as a whole manifests a 50/50 split, all samples should be representative of this, small as well as large. The same analysis applies to the specialist case, B. This leads Tversky and Kahneman to conclude that "people's intuitions about random sampling appear to satisfy the law of small numbers, which asserts that the law of large numbers applies to small numbers as well." [48]

That people are led to errors when relying on the representativeness heuristic does not mean that they are irrational to employ it. As Nisbett and Ross stress:

The representativeness heuristic is a legitimate, indeed essential, cognitive tool. Countless inferential tasks, especially those requiring induction or generalization, depend on deciding what class or category of event one is observing; such judgments inevitably hinge upon assessments of resemblance or representativeness. . . . Even in our examples, the use of the representativeness heuristic produced errors only because it was overapplied while other normatively important criteria were overlooked.[49]

But even overapplication of the heuristic may be, at least in one way, epistemically justified. A great deal of evidence indicates that people cope with limited cognitive resources by relying on "quick but dirty" inferential rules of thumb.[50] Relying on the representativeness heuristic is very likely an efficient way to make causal and probabilistic judgments. Given that we are faced with limited cognitive resources, it may well be efficient to adopt an inferential strategy that drastically reduces the demands on cognitive resources even though it leads to serious errors. This is not to say that these are not really errors. Say that one adopts the following strategy regulating one's beliefs about social justice: "Believe whatever John Rawls says." This may well be a pretty efficient rule, but, with all due respect to Professor Rawls, it will still lead to some mistakes. And they will be mistakes relative to one's own system of beliefs, and the norms it contains.

Moreover, it will not always make sense to improve upon the heuristic so that it does not produce error. That is, we might imagine a person reforming her cognitive processes such that she always applies the heuristic when it aids in making the correct inference, but not when it produces error. To be sure, all things being equal, this monitoring capacity will be a cognitive improvement, but of course all things are not equal; monitoring has costs. At this point it is tempting to proffer a technical formula, for example, monitoring should be adopted just to the point at which increased monitoring costs outweigh epistemic gains. And I suppose this is true, though I would not wish to have to explain how "costs" and "gains" can be explicated and compared here. The crucial point is that a reasonable person, coping with her inherently limited cognitive resources, will quite reasonably employ inferential strategies that will surely lead her into error. In such cases I wish to claim that (1) the person is not being unreasonable or irrational, for she has good reason to employ the strategy, yet (2) the belief that is produced is unjustified.

Representativeness is but one of the heuristics studied by cognitive psychologists; availability and vividness are also important.[51] Because much the same point applies to them, there is no need to catalog and explicate these various heuristics. However, a word about vividness might be useful, as it sheds light on deliberation and judgment. Evidence indicates that "information is weighted in proportion to its vividness."[52] Thus, for instance, concrete or emotionally salient information is more vivid, and hence is apt to play a dominant role in deliberation. At this point, it is impossible not to tell Nisbett's Volvo story:

> Let us suppose that you wish to buy a new car and have decided that on the grounds of economy and longevity you want to purchase one of those solid, stalwart, middle-class Swedish cars—either a Volvo or a Saab. As a prudent and sensible buyer, you go to *Consumer Reports*, which informs you that the consensus of their experts is that the Volvo is mechanically superior, and the consensus of the readership is that the Volvo has a better repair record. Armed with this information, you decide to go and strike a bargain with the Volvo dealer before the week is out. In the interim, however, you go to a cocktail party where you announce this intention to an acquaintance. He reacts with disbelief and alarm. "A Volvo! You've got to be kidding. My brother-in-law had a Volvo. First, that fancy fuel injection computer thing went out. 250 bucks. Next he started having trouble with the rear end. Had to replace it. Then the transmission and the clutch. Finally sold it in three years for junk.[53]

Nisbett acknowledges that this gives you a reason to make a very small adjustment in the repair rates given by *Consumer Reports:* Assuming that it was not in the original survey, you now have one additional observation. But is it likely to be weighed that lightly? More to the point, would one have the nerve to go out and buy a Volvo? On reflection, it would be silly for Nisbett to base a decision on a sample of one, when *Consumer Reports* provides a large sample. So the rational thing to do is to buy a Volvo. But this bit of information is so vivid that it is constantly apt to reassert itself; when it does, we'd expect Nisbett to waiver and, while knowing just how silly it is, decide that maybe a Saab would be a better way to go. (This helps explain *akrasia* of belief; see sec. 5.4).

4.6 Are the Subjects Really Wrong?

Stich asks us whether we can truly say—as my headings indicate—that the respondents are making errors, or are we simply imposing our own favored epistemic style on them? As he puts it, are we being epistemic chauvinists?[54] Some of the inferences are obviously mistakes; they are not even justified in the closed sense. In Case B, for example, the respondents all agree on the relevant norms of probability, and are committed to accepting that their recommendation of a retest using twenty subjects is too conservative, in the sense that it is too likely to cause the experimenter to reject significant findings. It is doubtful that the members of the Mathematical Psychology Group and the American Psychology Association embrace significantly different norms or beliefs (on these matters) than do Tversky and Kahneman. It is plausible to think that many of the other responses were not closedly justified.

But some cases are more perplexing. Suppose that (1) people are, as I have said, rational to adopt heuristics, and (2) even when their "errors" are pointed out to them, they remain unmoved. That is, even in the face of sustained criticism, their allegiance to the "wrong" inferences is unshaken. This seems to be the case with Ross's belief-perseverance experiments. However, the subjects' refusal to alter their beliefs is only definitive if one adopts not a relativistic, but a subjectivistic, account of justified belief. On a subjective theory of justification, Alf is justified in believing β if he actually believes β, or continues to believe β even after reflecting on new information.[55] If that was our theory of justification, then the subjects' failure to change their beliefs about their skills in distinguishing real from fictitious suicide notes would be decisive. But such subjectivism is implausible. Consider for a moment the rather unsettling findings of P.C. Wason and P.N. Johnson-Laird. In one experiment subjects were given three numbers and told that experimenters had in a mind a rule for the generation of a series of numbers, and that these three numbers fit the rule. The task of the subjects was to "test hypotheses" about what the rule might be by asking the experimenter questions of the form "Do numbers *n, m, o* fit the series?" in which the subjects themselves supplied various candidates. When the subjects felt sure they knew what the rule was, they were to announce it to the experimenters. Wason and Johnson-Laird found many subjects poor at such hypothesis testing, but of immediate interest are some of the responses of subjects once they discovered the error of their confident announcements about the rule regulating the series:

> *Experimenter:* If you were wrong, how could you find out?
>
> *Subject A:* I can't be wrong since my rule was correct for those numbers.
>
> *Subject B:* Rules are relative. If you were the subject, and I were the experimenter, then I would be right.[56]

In some cases subjects simply remained immune to the recognition that they had been wrong, often to the point of simply insisting that they *must* be right. As Wason and Johnson-Laird point out, the evidence that they were wrong was clearly before them and they obviously had good reason to accept it. After all, the rule they guessed was not the rule that was employed. Instead of acknowledging that their rule was not correct, some subjects employed devices to protect themselves from this conclusion. It may, of course, be held that they did not maximally reflect on their beliefs, so it remains possible that more criticism may have changed their minds. But the point is that the trick is to induce them to believe what, according to their own system of reasons and beliefs, was clearly justified. In closed, as well as open, justification, what people reflectively conclude is justified is not necessarily what is justified.

But perhaps in many of the cases people did the best they could with the knowledge they possessed, but did not possess the information necessary to arrive at the correct answer. Some evidence supports this.[57] The question still remains whether their answers would be the same given criticism and exposure to additional information. In the next phase of his work Nisbett investigated just this question. Nisbett and his colleagues have demonstrated that exposure to courses in statistics can markedly improve reasoning in conditional logic and statistical reasoning, both clearly relevant to Cases A–C.[58] Lehman and Nisbett thus conclude that "contrary to much contemporary theorizing about reasoning, highly general inferential rules can be taught and that the quality of people's everyday reasoning can be improved."[59] Stich might maintain that this just shows that indoctrination in the official epistemological ideology can be effective, but a more plausible explanation is that, in the face of criticism and new information, people tend to revise their system of beliefs because, given their current system, they see good reason to alter their beliefs. Nisbett's studies on the effects of education in eliminating errors indicate that in our cases the subjects' responses were not openly justified.

Of course, that people can be induced to change their minds is not definitive. As Stich and Nisbett point out, people can be "taught" to abandon correct views for incorrect ones. For instance, they induced people to wonder whether the gambler's fallacy may, after all, be correct.[60] "Our point, then," they write, "is that with suitable arguments subjects can be convinced of an invalid rule just as they can be convinced of a valid one. What is more, we know of no reason to think that valid rules are easier to teach than *plausible* invalid ones."[61] The qualification "plausible" is crucial here. Some fallacies—notoriously the gambler's fallacy—are plausible because they conform to "heuristics," or inferential shortcuts upon which we rely. Because these heuristics are part of people's belief systems, a deviant teacher can appeal to them to cast doubt on sound inferential rules that are inconsistent with them. Although the first response to the conflict between the heuristic and the sound rule may be to abandon the sound inferential rule, this pedagogical route will lead to increased contradictions. The student induced to give up the valid inferential rule for the unsound one backed by the heuristic will encounter more and more contradictions between his heuristic-based rule and other apparently sound inferences. Thus Stich and Nisbett's alternative pedagogy, while easy enough at the outset, should run into increased difficulties as the "education" proceeds, indicating that the wrong (i.e., anticonservative) belief revision was made at the outset (see sec. 7.1.1). In contrast, a pedagogical program based on limiting heuristic-endorsed inferences will become increasing stable as it proceeds. Stich and Nisbett's own suggestion that expert opinion converges on the normatively correct rules seems to support this hypothesis about the relative stability of the two pedagogies.[62]

In response to the worry underlying Stitch's position—"Who are we to say that the subjects are wrong?"—I think the reply is that the subjects themselves are committed to that evaluation.[63] However, recall that I am not claiming that relativism is ultimately impossible—indeed, I have argued that the possibility must be acknowledged. My point here is simply that the studies of human inference upon which Stich builds a good bit of his case provide meager support for it. Genuine cognitive relativism (in the sense of openly justified systems of beliefs and reasons that entertain inferential rules or beliefs that are inconsistent with each other) is, I suspect, rarer than Stich would have us believe; and when it occurs, it is less radical than Stich envisages.

CHAPTER 5

Inferential Justification

5.1 The Argument Thus Far

Before proceeding, it will be useful to sum up briefly what has been argued thus far, and to provide an idea of where we are heading. I began part I by considering just what is involved in justifying a belief by citing a reason. I argued that to justify a belief required more than merely having a good supporting reason in one's belief and reason system; it requires holding the belief because of that reason. A causal interpretation of "the basing relation" was thus defended; in particular I stressed that a sustaining causal relation is basic to justified belief, though efficient causation seems a part of epistemic rationality. Chapter 3 then turned to the notion of a "good" reason that was implicit in the account of the basing relation. I argued that good reasons are relative to a system of reasons and beliefs, and thus rejected strongly externalist views of reasons. However, the idea of open justification does endorse a modest form of externalism, allowing others to take up an external perspective and consider what reasons a person really has. But because the point of reference is always the person's system of beliefs and reasons, suitably modified to take account of new information and criticism, the possibility of a relativism of reasons emerged. However, chapter 4 tried to show that we have reason to believe the degree of actual relativism will be modest, and we certainly should not endorse anything so strong as normative cognitive pluralism.

At this point some readers may object that too much emphasis has been placed on general epistemic issues, and not enough on distinctly moral justification. Two defenses can be offered. First, one of my theses is that the gulf between general models of epistemic justification and moral justification is not nearly so great as many have believed. Though this may have been recognized by moral realists, I shall try to show that even moral subjectivism can be accommodated within a general account of epistemic justification. The crucial move here is to divorce the idea of a good reason from truth; once that is accomplished, a variety of moral theories can be brought under the same general epistemic theory. The second defense is that ultimately we shall indeed focus on distinctly moral justification, though we must still consider in more detail the general epistemic question of what is involved in justifying a belief by appeal to a reason.

5.2 Four Axioms of Inferential Justification

As I think has been clear all along, the core idea of pure inferential justification is that one believes β just because it is based on R—R sustains β and justifies it. Intuitively, the idea is that if β's justification is purely inferential, *all* of its justification comes from R; take away R and nothing is left. Pure inferential justification thus supposes:

> Axiom 1: If Alf's belief β is purely inferentially justified by R, and only R, and if Alf is not justified in accepting R, then β is not justified at all.

The analysis also supposes Axiom 2:

> Axiom 2: If Alf's belief β is purely inferentially justified by R, then $\beta \neq R$.

If $\beta \equiv R$, then β is self-justifying. We shall consider self-justification later (sec. 7.1), but it is clear that inferential justification is distinct from self-justification. The core idea of inferential justification is that a belief is justified by *other* beliefs or reasons. I also propose that:

> Axiom 3: Alf's belief β is irrational if it is unjustified.

This is more controversial; it insists that it is irrational to hold an unjustified belief. Some philosophers have seemed to accept that we could rationally entertain "unjustified justifiers": beliefs that are not themselves justified, but that justify others. Leaving aside the perplexities of this view, it would seem to run contrary to the *telos* of inferential justification. Inferential justification provides a warrant for holding a belief; we are thus unwarranted in holding a belief without good reason. Though philosophers disagree as to whether epistemic justification of β merely gives one epistemic permission to believe or commits one to believing it,[1] even the weaker permissive view implies that one does not have permission to hold unjustified beliefs. If this was not implied, the permissive view would be vacuous; it would imply that one is permitted to have justified beliefs, but one is also permitted to hold unjustified beliefs. Only against the background of a general epistemic principle that one is not permitted to hold beliefs that are not justified does the permissive view makes sense.

Charles Larmore seems to reject Axiom 3 for another reason:

It is usually assumed that each of our beliefs be justified. (Often the assumption takes the form of the requirement that beliefs serving to justify other beliefs must themselves be justified.) This assumption has become so routine and unthinking, that its original motives have come to be forgotten. Such a requirement has arisen, in fact, not so much from reason as from the metaphysical aspiration to view the world *sub specie aeternitatis,* an aspiration animating most of Enlightenment thought as well. The demand that each of our beliefs be justified is the demand that we undo the weight of historical circumstance and rethink our commitments on the basis of reason alone. . . . If we give up that metaphysical aspiration, and take as our rule that we must have positive reasons for thinking some belief of ours may be false if we are to put the belief in doubt *and so demand its justification,* the idea that our beliefs must be justified will fall away.[2]

The requirement that "our beliefs must be justified" is ambiguous between (1) "It must be the case that our beliefs are justified" and (2) "We must show that all of our beliefs are justified." Certainly (2) is mistaken. It is a waste of cognitive resources to show that beliefs are justified when we have no reason to doubt them. The Cartesian stance, doubting everything and demanding justification for everything, is epistemically profligate: Why embark on the *process of justifying* that which you do not doubt? And we have no standing reason to doubt everything. But to say that we have no reason to doubt β is just to say that we have no reason to doubt that it is justified—we suppose that β is justified until we have a reason to doubt it. But this is to suppose that (1) is the case: We suppose our beliefs are justified (see sec. 7.1). Axiom 3, then, is not to be interpreted as requiring that we offer justifications for all our beliefs; it requires only that any belief that is properly in our system must be one that is justified. It is perfectly consistent with Axiom 3 to suppose that a belief is justified until we have a reason to doubt it.

It might be thought that a weaker version of Axiom 3 would be superior:

Axiom 3*: Alf's belief β is irrational only if it is *unjustifiable.*

An unjustified belief, it will be remembered, is one that is not held for a good reason; such a belief may still be justifiable if the agent has within his belief system the resources to justify the belief (sec. 2.1). So, it might be argued, as long as a belief is justifiable, a person is rational to hold it. But recall here our story of the free-floating believer (sec.

2.3). Alf believed things for all sorts of fantastic reasons, and challenges to these beliefs never moved him. Even if we taught Alf the proper grounds for his beliefs, this would not make them rational, for Alf still did not connect the beliefs to their justifying reasons.

In that story I also argued that Alf manifested another defect of epistemic rationality: When presented with good reasons, he did not revise his belief system (sec. 2.4). This suggests the fourth axiom of inferential justification:

> Axiom 4: If (1) accepting (rejecting) β is openly justifiable in Alf's system of beliefs, and (2) he is aware of these justifying reasons, it is rational for Alf to accept (reject) β and irrational not to.[3]

The *telos* of inferential justification is to believe what we have the best reasons for believing and not to believe what we have reasons to reject, or have no reasons for accepting.[4] Axioms 3 and 4 sum up this idea.

5.3 Defeating Reasons

For Alf's belief β to be inferentially justified, it is not enough that it is based on a good reason in Alf's belief system. Although β may be based on some reason R_1, Alf might believe R_2, which defeats the inference from R_1 to β. To return to Alf's doubts about Betty's devotion, consider the following:

Case 2: Alf's Worries Are Rebutted. Alf and Betty are lovers, but Alf has many beliefs that indicate that Betty is unfaithful; he has seen receipts from little-out-of-the-way hotels in her pocketbook (and he hasn't visited such hotels with Betty since their affair before she divorced Charlie), she has been working late every night for two months now, she keeps calling him "Dearest Frank," and the like. Distraught over all this, Alf confides in Doris, who is Betty's confidant, but (unknown to Betty) Alf's close friend. Doris insists that Betty hasn't given the slightest hint about an affair, and in the past Betty has confided everything, important and trivial, to Doris. Despite all the evidence he has of Betty's unfaithfulness, Doris's testimony points to her faithfulness. Alf accepts Doris's testimony, and concludes that Betty is, after all, faithful.

In this case Doris's testimony defeats the circumstantial evidence. Following Pollock, let us say:

> If R_1 is a reason for Alf to believe β, R_2 is a *defeater* for this reason if and only if (1) R_2 is a reason of Alf's[5] (2) R_2 is logically consistent with R_1 and (3) (R_1 & R_2) is not a reason to believe β.[6]

If, then, Alf believes β on the basis of R_1, but he also believes R_2, which is a defeater of the inference from R_1 to β, the inference is defeated and β is not justified. Note that in the sort of nondemonstrative inference with which we are mainly concerned, Alf does not have to reject either R_1 or R_2; neither does he have to deny that the argument from R_1 to β is valid. Given Axiom 3, Alf must reject β (supposing it was, if justified at all, purely inferentially justified by R_1).[7]

As Pollock notes, defeaters come in two types. In our case of Alf's worries, the defeater rebuts his inference by justifying the opposite belief, namely, that Betty is faithful rather than unfaithful. More formally, then:

If R_1 is a reason for Alf to believe β, R_2 is a *rebutting defeater* for this reason if and only if R_2 is a defeater (for R_1 as a reason for Alf to believe β) and R_2 is a reason for Alf to believe $\sim\beta$.[8]

Thus, in our case, Doris's testimony rebuts the inference from the circumstantial evidence to the conclusion that Betty has been unfaithful, justifying instead the conclusion that Betty has been faithful.

It needs to be stressed that it is the acceptance of the conclusion to the argument that is rebutted, not the beliefs on which it is based or the reasoning connecting the grounding beliefs and conclusions. Thus Doris's testimony does not rebut any of the facts that Alf has uncovered, such as the hotel receipts or that Betty calls him "Dearest Frank" at especially inappropriate moments. Neither, importantly, does it refute the reasoning from these facts to a conclusion that Betty is unfaithful. What it rebuts is *acceptance* of the conclusion in light of the reasons pointing in the opposite direction.

This is important because, as it were, all the elements of the rebutted argument stay in Alf's belief system, and may be drawn upon again if additional evidence is uncovered supporting the original conclusion. This is most obvious in the way evidence is presented, rebutted, and then reevaluated in a criminal trial. The prosecution may introduce evidence that justifies the conclusion of guilt, which is then rebutted by the defense. But if new, additional evidence of guilt is then presented, the original rebutted argument, reinforced, rises again. This point is perhaps better brought out by contrasting a rebutting to an *undermining* argument.

Case 3: Alf Discovers the Truth. Alf hires a private detective. The detective's report explains away all of the evidence that pointed so strongly to Betty's unfaithfulness. It turns out that every night she stayed at work late to write a romantic novel. Since the romantic novel took place in many out-of-the-way hotels, she visited them (alone) as part of her research. And the central character—modeled, it turns out, after Alf—is named Frank. He discovers that Betty wanted to surprise Alf, giving him a copy of the manuscript on his birthday.

The detective's report undermines the reasons to believe Betty is unfaithful; it shows that they do not support that conclusion after all.[9] In this case the evidence no longer supports the original conclusion. Another way to undermine an argument is to show that it was based on a fallacious inference rule, so that, once again, the evidence no longer supports the original conclusion.

One may think, perhaps, that this only shows that Alf's original justification for his belief about Betty's unfaithfulness was mistaken; the absence of undermining reasons may be less of an additional requirement for justified belief than a reiteration that R_1 must really be a good reason for believing β. In a way I suppose this is right, but often the possibility of undermining a claim does not so much show that we have made a mistake as it allows us to come to a deeper understanding of our supporting reasons. Suppose, for instance, that Alf believes that speech should be entirely free, hence those producing pornography ought not to be interfered with. So Alf endorses the American Civil Liberties Union's case defending an admitted hard-core pornographic publishing company on the basis of his commitment to a belief that speech must be free. But then suppose an undermining argument is presented to Alf: Say it is claimed that hard-core pornography does not aim at communication, and so does not fall under the free speech principle.[10] If this undermines Alf's belief that pornography ought not to be interfered with (and his support of the ACLU's action in this case), it does show in a way that he was originally mistaken. But this, I think, is to miss the point that he has come to a deeper understanding of his free speech principle; in a sense he has arrived at a new interpretation of what follows from it. All this, of course, is very different from a case in which Alf's support of the ACLU's action is rebutted by, say, his principle that women should not be exploited. In this case he may conclude that while the free speech principle does indeed support the ACLU's action, he has other reasons, based on his feminist commitments, to oppose it.

Note that our discussion of undermining a belief has assumed Axioms 1, 3, and 4. When Alf discovers his belief that Betty has been unfaithful is undermined, it is (according to Axiom 1) not justified at all. And so the supposition has been that it is therefore required by rationality that he reject this belief and accept the alternative, that she is faithful (Axioms 3 and 4). So, too, when he concludes that his commitment to the free speech principle does not justify a belief that pornography should be unregulated, that belief is unjustified and so, I supposed, ought to be rejected.

A complication arises at this point. That R_2 defeats the inference from R_1 to β does not imply that, all things considered, a person is unjustified in believing β on the basis of R_1, for the defeater may itself be defeated.[11] Recall that the inference from R_1 to β is defeated by R_2 if $(R_1 \ \& \ R_2)$ is not a reason to believe β; in the case of a rebuttal it is a reason to believe $\sim\beta$. But there could be a reason R_3 such that $(R_1 \ \& \ R_2 \ \& \ R_3)$ rebuts $\sim\beta$, in other words, is a reason to believe β. In this case the defeating reason is itself defeated, thus reestablishing the original inference. Let us introduce the idea of an *ultimately undefeated inference;* an inference is ultimately undefeated either if it is simply undefeated or if, though defeated at one stage, all the reasons that defeat it are themselves defeated *once and for all.* That is, after a series of defeaters, themselves being defeated, and so on, the series ends with the argument's defeaters being defeated, and so the inference being vindicated.

We can now formulate a little more precisely the idea of pure inferential closed justification:

PICJ: Alf's belief that β meets the conditions of a (closed) purely inferentially justified belief only if:
  (1) Alf's belief that β is based on some good reason, R, that is part of his system of reasons and beliefs.
  (2) The inference from R to β is ultimately undefeated.

Mutatis mutandis, we can formulate such necessary conditions for an *openly* purely inferentially justified belief. Axioms 1 and 2 are assumed. An inferentially *justifiable* belief, of course, is less demanding; it requires only that a person have the reasons that would inferentially justify the belief, not that he actually hold the belief for those reasons.[12] Indeed, a belief can be inferentially justifiable even if one does not now hold it as an explicit or even tacit belief; one may, for instance, be committed to it by virtue of one's other beliefs (sec. 3.3).

Pure inference is a basic mode of justification. Surely *some* our beliefs, moral or otherwise, are purely inferentially justified. When we have occasion to justify our beliefs we cite the reasons on which they are based; undermine all those reasons and the belief is unjustified, so we abandon it, or at least should do so (Axioms 3 and 4). I propose, then, a modest requirement for any adequate account of justified belief: It must allow for *some cases* of pure inferential justification.

5.4 Epistemic *Akrasia*

My concern is inferential justification and, therefore, the conflict of reasons to believe, not directly with reasons to act. However, Susan Hurley has recently argued that conflicting reasons to act are fundamentally different from reasons to believe. I wish to digress here a bit to consider her argument.

The core of Hurley's argument is a distinction between *prima facie* and *pro tanto* reasons. In cases of conflicting reasons for belief, Hurley argues, the reasons are *prima facie*.[13] When a reason to believe β conflicts with a reason to believe ~β, she indicates, this conflict is only apparent in the sense that ultimately either β or ~β is true or correct; once it has been made clear which reason is the actual reason, the other has "no remaining residual force." She writes:

> The term *"prima facie"* seems appropriate for reasons that are like the reasons given by relational probabilities in that they can't come into ultimate conflict with one another. . . . *Prima facie* reasons are like rules of thumb, that give us reasons provisionally but may turn out not to apply when we learn more about the situation at hand, in which case they have no residual reason-giving force.[14]

In contrast, she insists, conflicting reasons for action do indeed have a residual reason-giving force, even when they are overridden:

> Conflicting reasons for action such as justice and kindness aren't *prima facie* in the sense that, like rules of thumb, they seem to give reasons to do acts that would be just or kind, but may turn out not to when we learn more about the situation. One could do the kind act because kindness requires it, even in the face of one's better judgment, namely, that all things considered one ought not to do the kind act but rather the just act. In doing so, one would be acting irrationally, in the way that the *akrates* acts irrationally. But one would still be acting for a reason, namely, because of the kindness of the act. The term *"pro tanto"* seems appropriate to describe such reasons, which might conceivably come into ultimate conflict with one another and thus can be the operative reasons in cases of *akrasia*.[15]

The claim that only *pro tanto* reasons can provide the basis for *akrasia*—weakness of will—is a central theme of Hurley's *Natural Reasons*. Because, as it were, even when a *pro tanto* reason is overridden in favor of another it still retains "residual force," it is always possible that a person will manifest *akrasia*—that she will ignore what she has better reasons to do, and manifest a weakness of the will by acting on this less important but still forceful reason. In contrast, Hurley is adamant that evidential *akrasia* is impossible because, once the "all things considered" judgment has been made, the overridden reason has lost whatever force it had, and is indeed shown not to be a reason at all. And since it is not a reason at all, it does not remain in a person's system to induce an *akratic* belief.[16]

Hurley's thesis would certainly be correct if defeated reasons were always eliminated from one's system of reasons and beliefs. If a defeated *prima facie* reason were in some way wiped out of one's system of beliefs, then clearly it could not resurface to produce an *akrasia* of belief. That is, suppose that the inference R_1 to β is defeated by R_2; if it followed that R_1 was deleted from the belief system as a result of its defeat, then clearly it would have no "residual force." But though this is a plausible analysis of the upshot of defeat by undermining, it does not make sense of a rebuttal. In the case of a rebutted inference, R_1 and the inference from R_1 to β both remain (though the acceptance of β is not justified). Indeed, as we saw, in one sense rebutted reasons do lay waiting to be revived should new evidence be gathered that increases their force, allowing them to be ultimately undefeated in justifying β. So, in a very real sense, the reasons remain in one's system of beliefs, and could resurface to produce an evidential *akrasia*.

If, then, rebutted reasons are to be understood as having no "residual force," it must be in a way that allows them to remain part of one's belief system, even after they have been rebutted. The emphasis must be on their lack of "force"; once defeated, they can have no power to produce belief without new evidence. After all, once Alf has concluded that Doris's testimonial evidence rebuts the circumstantial evidence, he has no reason to believe Betty to be unfaithful. As Hurley says at one point, pieces of evidence "yield automatically to better evidence."[17] But this does not really seem plausible in Alf's case. Nothing would be less surprising than Alf's believing periodically that Betty was unfaithful, despite his repeated assurance to himself that Doris's evidence confirmed her devotion. This is not simply a case of indecisiveness; Alf may be sure that Doris is extremely reliable, and yet give way to irrational doubts. In this case Alf may be entirely aware that he is not accepting the best evidence, but still he finds himself walking around the living room at 3:00 A.M., unable to sleep because he is sure (for a while) that Betty has been unfaithful.

It might be objected that this is because Alf has interests other than simple pursuit of the truth, such as his valuing of Betty's love. To be sure, but this is precisely the point. Though our beliefs about the world aim at truth, what truths we explicitly believe depend crucially on our practical interests.[18] Moreover, uncertainty allows a variety of values to affect our beliefs. This is so even in what for some of us is still the paradigm of a truth-centered practice, science. Because, as Hurley herself acknowledges, data underdetermines theories,[19] scientists draw on values in adjudicating among theories. As Thomas Kuhn writes:

> To a greater extent than other sorts of components of the disciplinary matrix, values may be shared by men who differ in their application. Judgments of accuracy are relatively, though not entirely, stable from one time to another and from one member to another in a particular group. But judgments of simplicity, consistency, plausibility, and so on often vary greatly from individual to individual. . . . Even more important, in those situations where values must be applied, different values, taken alone, would often dictate different choices. One theory may be more accurate but less consistent or plausible than another. . . .[20]

A scientist choosing among competing theories is thus not in such a very different situation from Hurley's person having to choose between justice and kindness. To use an example of Kuhn's, suppose a physicist early this century was faced with a choice between the old quantum theory and Einstein's. Perhaps on the basis of accuracy she selects Einstein's; Einstein's theory thus defeats the older theory. Yet plausibility remains a consideration, and at times it may have grounded a transient conviction that Einstein must be wrong—it is all so implausible! The value, as well as all the reasons that support the old quantum theory, remain, even though rebutted. Theoretical *akrasia* certainly seems possible.

A sharp division between conflicts of belief and conflicts of values seems misguided. As believers we are not passive processors of information, programmed so that rebutted evidence "automatically" lies still. Our deliberations as to what competing beliefs are rebutted by what others are impacted upon by a variety of practical and theoretical values, which allows for epistemic *akrasia*. Our reasons cause our beliefs, but some of these reasons are values. This is often epistemically appropriate: In theory choice, considerations of simplicity, plausibility, and consistency are well supported by epistemic norms. But as Hurley herself recognizes, values cannot always be quieted even after they have been duly considered and overridden, and so the same sort of weakness that characterizes her situation of moral choice can occur in a scientist's choice of theories or Alf's conclusions about Betty's faithfulness.

Still, it may be said that in one way Alf's situation differs radically from Hurley's agent deciding between acting on justice or on kindness. If all the information were in, ultimately one set of evidence or the other would dissipate. If we know everything, there is no conflict of evidence, whereas no matter how much we know there will always be a conflict of values. Perhaps this is ultimately Hurley's point. But not even this is uncontroversially true. Those whom Isaiah Berlin calls "monists" believe "that all positive values in which men have believed must, in the end, be compatible, and perhaps even entail one another."[21] Of course pluralists will reject this, but this shows that even this distinction between beliefs and values is not intrinsic to the very concepts, but is a consequence of a specific theory of values. In any event, nothing is to be gained by analyzing belief systems from the perspective of the omniscient. Real believers live their lives with conflicting reasons for belief, and even when one rebuts the other, that which is rebutted often allies with important values that, *akratically*, can induce its transient acceptance.[22]

CHAPTER 6

Why All Justification Cannot Be Purely Inferential

6.1 The Regress Argument

Surely some of our beliefs are purely inferentially justified. The idea that we are justified in believing one thing just because it is based upon other beliefs is attractive and familiar, and moreover seems applicable to many everyday instances of justification. It is tempting to suppose that purely inferential justification might be the only sort of justification. I now wish to argue that it cannot be. *If any of Alf's beliefs are purely inferentially justified, then all his beliefs cannot be purely inferentially justified.* That being so, the most an advocate of inferential justification can endorse is my minimal inferential requirement (sec. 5.3).

The argument in support of this claim is the famous, or perhaps infamous, regress argument advanced by epistemological foundationalists.[1] But foundationalists have sometimes claimed that this argument shows that foundationalism must be correct; it does not. Sometimes it has been claimed that the argument shows that coherence theories must be rejected; it does not do that either.[2] Nor does it show that circles cannot justify. What it does show is that all justification cannot be purely inferential.

Let us consider the regress argument in terms of Alf seeking to justify his belief β. Suppose that Alf justifies β by showing that he infers it from R_1; it is the reason upon which β is based. But Alf can appeal to R_1 as a support for β only if he is justified in holding R_1. If he is not justified in believing R_1, his justification for β is undermined. As Axiom 1 states, if a person's reasons for holding a purely inferentially justified belief are discredited, he is not justified in holding that belief. So for R_1 to be an inferential justifier for β, it must itself be justified. Hence, there must be an ultimately undefeated reason for Alf to believe R_1; call it R_2. But, of course, the same must apply to R_2; it can serve as a justifier for R_1 only if Alf is justified in holding it.

As long as justification is purely inferential, this process can only go three ways: (1) Inferential justification may come to rest on an unjustified belief. (2) The process may never terminate; having an infinitely large set of beliefs, Alf may simply keep on with inferential justification, always coming to new beliefs that themselves are inferentially justified by yet other new beliefs. (3) At some point the inferences form a circle: Alf justifies β by appeal to R_1, R_1 is inferred from R_2, R_2 is inferred from β, thus completing the circle.

I have already indicated that (1) is unacceptable for a purely inferential theory of justification. The *telos* of personal justification is that we should have only justified beliefs; that is why defeating the reasons for a belief shows that the belief should be jettisoned. If we dispose of that requirement, then showing that a belief has no supporting reasons does not show that we should not still believe it. This possibility thus is inconsistent with Axioms 3 and 4.

Laurence Bonjour suggests that the second possibility may have been entertained by Peirce.[3] Of course, if actually demonstrating an infinite regress of justifications is required for justifying a belief, Alf could never actually *justify* any of his beliefs, for it will be more than a little difficult to cite an infinite series of beliefs as his justification for β. More important, though, even if we restrict ourselves to what is required for his beliefs to be justified, this regress possibility would require that every justified belief be backed up by an infinite chain of supporting beliefs, for if any inferential chain comes to an end, the pure inferentialist is left with the first option. As Bonjour quite properly notes, this requires immense cognitive resources; only a belief system with infinite beliefs can have *any* justified beliefs![4] However, we have already seen (sec. 3.3) that the number of explicit beliefs we can entertain is surely limited by our cognitive capacity, so all the infinite beliefs could not be explicit. I also argued, though, that the only interpretation of the idea of tacit beliefs that allows them to be causes of other beliefs (and hence be justifying reasons) is that which rules out an infinite number of tacit beliefs (remember here that justifying beliefs are sustaining causes, not simply efficient ones). So, if justifying reasons are to be causal (which we have seen they must be, chap. 2), there cannot be an infinite number of them.[5]

This leaves us with the third option, circular justification. But this is not *inferential justification* at all; it manifestly violates Axiom 2, i.e., that the supporting reason, R, for β not be β. In the circle, β is inferred from R_1. According to Axiom 1, if R_1 is not justified, β has no justification at all. So only if R_1 is justified is β justified. The justification of R_1 is then said to turn on R_2; unless R_2 is justified, R_1 is not justified, and so neither is β. But R_2 is justified on the basis of β; only if β is justified is R_2, hence R_1, hence β justified. But because, according to Axiom 2, β cannot inferentially justify itself, the circle has not inferentially justified β.

One way to show that β is not simply justifying itself would be to contend that, as the inference passes through each stage, it picks up additional justificatory force. That is, an inference from β to R_2 to R_1 and back to β gives a stronger warrant for β than the simple argument from β to β. Suitably understood, I think this is correct (see below, secs. 7.2–3), but it is not a pure inferential justification.[6] The upshot of Axiom 1 is that a purely inferentially justified belief obtains all its justification from its grounding reasons. If, then, each element of the inferential series obtains all its justification from its grounding reasons, the series can only pass justification along. It cannot, as it were, amplify it as it passes through each stage.

It is important to stress that I am not claiming that circles cannot justify: the claim is that circles cannot purely inferentially justify. The upshot of the regress argument is that the modest requirement that there be some room for purely inferential justification requires that not all justification be purely inferential.

6.2 Global Coherentism

6.2.1 The Principle of Coherence Justification

I maintain that not all beliefs can be purely inferentially justified; another source of justification is necessary. This directly contradicts David O. Brink's assertion that, on his coherence theory, "no beliefs are noninferentially justified."[7] Since Brink is not an advocate of embracing unjustified beliefs (he, too, accepts something like Axiom 3), it follows that he believes that all justification is purely inferential according to his coherence theory. Not only do I disagree, but I wish to claim that, far from being thoroughly purely inferential, Brink's holistic coherence theory does not allow for *any* purely inferential justifications. The argument in support of this deep criticism of Brink's coherentism will occupy the rest of chapter 6 as well as section 7.1.

Brink sketches his coherence theory thus:

Coherentism . . . holds that no beliefs are noninferentially justified. One's belief p is justified, according to coherentism, insofar as p is part of a coherent system of beliefs and *p*'s coherence at least partially explains why one holds *p*. The degree of one's justification in holding *p* varies directly with the degree of coherence exhibited by the belief set of which *p* is a member. Moreover, coherence is not simply a matter of logical consistency. The degree of a belief system's coherence is a function of the comprehensiveness of the system and of the logical, probabilistic, and explanatory relations obtaining among members of the belief system.[8]

Brink distinguishes the explanation for one's believing *β* from the justification of *β*; the coherence of the belief set containing *β* at least *partially* explains why a person holds *β* but is the *full* justification of *β*.[9] Let us focus for the moment on the second, justificatory, claim.

For a coherentist such as Brink, justification is not a property of individual beliefs but of an overall system of beliefs.[10] Only systems of beliefs possess coherence; any particular proposition is justified only insofar as it is an element of a justified system of reasons and beliefs. This implies that, strictly, the coherence justification (CJ) of any particular proposition is always of the form:

CJ: *β* is justified to degree *x* because it is a member of system of reasons and beliefs *S*, which is coherent to degree *y*, where *x* is a positive function of *y*.

This takes account of Brink's (and other coherence theorists') principle that justification is always a matter of degree and varies directly with the degree of coherence exhibited by the belief set of which *p* is a member.

Given that the (coherence) justification of a belief is relative to the coherence of a belief set, it would seem that the justification of a belief would vary depending on which set we consider, from a simple two-belief set to one's entire system.[11] But employing as the relevant set any other but one's entire system can serve only as an approximation of justification. Suppose that *β* is considered in relation to two sets, {*α*,*β*} and one's entire belief set *S;* it coheres very well with the two-member set, but very badly with the overall system. In this case one cannot say that from one perspective *β* is justified but from another it is not. *S* encompasses {*α*,*β*}; if we know *β*'s coherence with *S* we know how well it is justified, and its distinct coherence with the two-member set becomes irrelevant to its justification. Coherence with proper subsets of one's system, then, is relevant only insofar as such less-than-global coherence is indicative of global coherence.

6.2.2 Two Types of Global Inference

Brink's claim, then, is that articulations of CJ render all justification purely inferential. Now we need to distinguish two apparently different ways in which coherence theories might be purely inferential: *globally* and *locally*. I consider global inference in this section (6.2); I turn to local inference in section 6.3.

Immediately we confront two very different versions of global inference itself. Consider first the absolutist coherence (AC) principle, a principle of both justified belief and justified belief change:

AC: (1) a belief is fully justified if and only if it is a member of the perfectly coherent system S^*;

(2) Alf is now justified in believing α, a member of his present system S_1, to the extent that S_1 approaches S^*;

(3) Alf would be justified in accepting a new belief β only if inclusion of β results in a new system S_2 which is closer to S^* than is S_1.

This absolutist coherence principle has strong affinities with the coherence theories of Absolute Idealism. Absolute Idealists held that to increase one's knowledge was somehow to come to a greater understanding of the Absolute, which alone was perfectly coherent. Only insofar as our finite systems came to grasp, in their own very meager way, the Absolute could we be said to have knowledge. An increase in knowledge necessarily brings our system of reasons and beliefs more in line with the Absolute.[12]

It is understandable that contemporary coherence theorists do not wish to follow Absolute Idealists along this path. God may be able to judge the relative coherence of all possible systems, but from our perspectives, our judgments must be based on what would best increase the coherence of our present system of reasons and beliefs. As a theory of justified inference, any plausible coherence theory must take our current belief set as the data to be operated upon. As Richard Foley observes:

One of the central doctrines of coherentism—perhaps the central doctrine—is expressed by the maxim "there is no exit from the circle of one's beliefs." In part, this maxim is meant to express a negative doctrine; it is meant in a suggestive way to express the idea that traditional foundationalist views about privileged access are indefensible—that there is no privileged and immediate access to the truth of propositions about our own psychological states or to the truth of any other propositions. However, the maxim has a more positive side; it is meant to express the idea that what is rational for a person to believe always is a function of what else he believes. So whether or not it is epistemically rational for a person to believe some proposition is not something that can be determined by looking at that belief, or that proposition, in isolation . . . one always needs to take account of the rest of his doxastic situation.[13]

If we are to employ it as a theory of justification, the coherence principle tells us whether we are justified in believing β *in the light of the other things we now believe.* As a theory of justified belief change, we must understand the principle of coherence akin to the Pareto principle: It can tell us what moves are justified *given a certain starting point.* If we are at some point and are deliberating whether to make an inference, it is (perhaps) intelligible to accept the dictum: "Make the inference that will best maximize the coherence of your current system of reasons and beliefs (and this includes expanding your present system)." Contrast the maxim: "Make the inference that would move your system of reasons and beliefs closer to most coherent system of beliefs, regardless of whether your current beliefs are members of this system." Given that we must reason from our own beliefs, it is more than a little difficult to see how this latter principle could ever be applied. But suppose it could; say the Master Epistemologist informed you that the most coherent system of belief was S_{912}, and unfortunately this had very little in common with your system. And, she adds, according to S_{912}, the proper inference is to belief β_{987}, which of course you cannot see as making any sense, but it really is coherence maximizing. I submit that this could not give you any reason at all to believe β_{987}.[14]

In place of the Absolutist understanding of global inference, it seems that a plausible theory must be a version of a situated coherence (SC) theory:

SC: (1) Alf's belief α is justified to degree x because it is a member of his current system of reasons and beliefs S_1, which is coherent to degree y, where x is a positive function of y, and this at least partially explains why α is believed by Alf.

(2) Alf is inferentially justified in accepting a new belief β only if doing so would bring about a new system S_2, which, judged from his present perspective, is more coherent than S_1.

Situated coherence theory takes one's present system of beliefs as the point of departure for all justification. A belief that is an element of one's current system is justified to the extent the system is coherent; to the extent a belief change increases the coherence of one's present system, it is justified. No appeal is made to the idea that knowledge is an approach to the single, perfectly coherent, system that characterizes the Absolute.

6.2.3 Global Inference and Justifying Oneself

Suppose that the only valid inference is global inference: that S inferentially justifies β. If this were the only way in which our beliefs could be justified, it would lead to a gulf between what can be justified and justificatory discourse. In justificatory discourse Alf always would have to make out one and only one justificatory claim: β follows from S. But surely it would be terribly odd if every time Alf was asked, "Why do you accept β?" he replied, "Because it follows from everything else I believe." Not only isn't this very helpful, but it is hard to accept that anyone actually holds any belief for such an abstract reason. Seldom—indeed, I suspect never—do we justify an inference by saying that it follows from everything we believe, or that the inference to β best enhances the coherence of S. To be sure, we might employ lack of coherence as a block to some inferences; perhaps there is always an implicit clause in all inferences such that "and as far as I can see, this inference is consistent with everything else I believe." But this hardly shows that the inference is made because one believes it enhances global coherence.

It is important to keep this in mind when we turn to public justification and justificatory discourse. Actual justificatory discourse involves challenging specific beliefs, and defending those beliefs by providing specific reasons. In this sense justificatory discourse is inherently local rather than global. Consequently, a theory such as global coherentism must distinguish the level of real justification, which is global, from the local level that is the focus of discourse. But, as we shall see, this leads to puzzles about the extent to which that which we take as justificatory—advancing certain claims, giving their reasons, and replying to challenges—is actually justificatory. None of this shows that global coherence theories are wrong. But it does seem that their split between the methods of justificatory discourse and the criterion of justified belief is an unwelcome cost of their picture of justification.

6.2.4 Global Inference and the Basing Relation

Let us put aside the way that pure global justification obscures the role of actual justificatory discourse. Problems remain. For one, it gives an inadequate account of the basing relation, undermining the idea that justified belief requires making the "right connections" between reasons and beliefs.[15] Because of this coherence theories are inadequate accounts of inferential justification.

In one way global inference accepts a basing relation. That β follows from S, says Brink, both justifies β and *partially* explains why one holds β. But this sort of basing relation cannot distinguish between Alf's having reasons in his system for believing β and Alf's believing β for those reasons (sec. 2.2). Recall Case 1 in our continuing saga of Alf and Betty, in which Alf had all sorts of good reasons to believe that Betty was unfaithful, but refused to accept this conclusion until he took the sociology course on "Relationships in the '90s" and wrongly inferred that if there was a .25 chance that one's lover has been unfaithful in the last year, Betty must have been unfaithful this year (sec. 2.1). In this situation, it seems that because Alf's total system of beliefs does indeed support the conclusion that Betty was unfaithful, the coherence theorist would have to say that it was a justified belief. But Alf failed to make the right connections between his beliefs, and so his belief that Betty is unfaithful does not, after all, seem justified.

Global coherence theories, then, cannot distinguish many justifi*able* beliefs from justi*fied* ones (sec. 2.1). One who has an inferentially justified belief not only accepts the requisite grounding reasons, but has made the correct connections between these reasons and the belief. It is important to stress this is not to insist that justified beliefs have the correct causal history.[16] Rather, the point is that a justified believer is not simply one who happens to have a set of reasons that provide justifications for a set of beliefs; she is one who makes the right connections between the two sets and who now holds the belief because she does so.

6.3 Inferential Justification and Web Coherentism

Coherence theorists are not unaware of the abstractness and oddness of global justification. Consequently, they typically distinguish systematic (or global) from contextual (or local) justification.[17] The basic idea is that on the systematic or global level—which is the epistemologically critical level—justification proceeds according to the coherence principle. But at the local or contextual level, justification *looks* linear, what I have called inferential. At the local or contextual level one takes certain beliefs as justified, and reasons from them; at this workaday level inferential justification appears (somewhat misleadingly, perhaps) as a linear movement from some specific beliefs to other specific beliefs.

On one interpretation of this view, local or linear inferences are merely evidentiary of global justification; the real justificatory work is done at the global level. A valid local inference from R to β is a sign of, but only a sign of, increased coherence. I consider this view briefly below (sec. 6.4). But on another, I think more interesting, interpretation, specific inferences from R to β take on a more constitutive role in coherence. Idealists, who were among the more ardent modern coherence theorists, explicated coherence in terms of the inferential relations among the members of the belief set. "Fully coherent knowledge," said Brand Blanshard, "would be knowledge in which every judgment entailed, and was entailed by, the rest of the system."[18] Bonjour weakens this to: "The coherence of a system of beliefs is increased by the number of inferential connections between its component beliefs and increased in proportion to the number and strength of such connections."[19] As the web of belief thickens, and new inferential relations between beliefs arise, this would seem ipso facto to increase coherence. Local or, as I shall say, specific inference thus seems always to be coherence increasing. Let us call this web coherentism: Overall coherence is characterized as a web of specific inferences. Is coherence theory purely inferential in this sense?

One problem with this proposal is that coherence is a multidimensional concept. Bonjour is rather more straightforward than most in stating its elements:[20]

(I) The coherence of S is a positive function of:
A. logical consistency of the elements of S;
B. probabilistic consistency of the elements of S;[21]
C. the number and strength of inferential connections.
(II) The coherence of S is a negative function of:
D. the extent to which S is divided into subsystems;
E. the presence of unexplained anomalies in S.

For my purposes, the specific dimensions do not much matter so long as: (1) coherence is multidimensional; (2) these dimensions are independent measures; and (3) specific inferential connections constitute one dimension.

Ideally, the coherence theorist would like to able to weight these various dimensions so as to arrive at all things considered judgments of overall coherence. That is, the coherence theorist would like to be able to compare one system, high in inferential connections but also high in anomalies, with one that is less rich in inferential connections, but also with fewer anomalies and perhaps some probabilistic inconsistency. The ideal would be a coherence function that would combine all weighted scores on each dimension to arrive at an overall coherence index for a system. A coherence theorist could then say that one is epistemically justified in moving from a system of reasons and beliefs S_1 to S_2 only if the coherence index of S_2 is higher than that of S_1.

As I write, Christmas is approaching, so let us grant the wish of the coherence theorist. Suppose we arrive at a scoring system in which all belief systems can be placed on a scale of 0–100 on each of the variables defined above. For simplicity's sake, say all the measures are assigned a weight of 1, though nothing turns on this. On these assumptions, we would have the following coherence index (CI) (using the letters in the above list as designating the five dimensions of coherence):

CI = Dimension A score + Dimension B score + Dimension C score - Dimension D score - Dimension E score.

It is manifest that the overall coherence of S_2 can be less than the overall coherence of S_1 even though the number of inferential connections in S_2 is higher than in S_1. Since local inferences are not the sole source of justification, but only an element of coherence, it follows that on the web view all justification cannot be accounted for in terms of local inferences. This conclusion cannot be avoided by a coherence index composed of only the inferential connections dimension. If all justification is specific inference, then we are back to the regress problem with which we began; in other words, no justification is purely inferential.

Thus, on web coherentism, all justification cannot take the form of specific, local, inferences. Indeed, we cannot be confident that an increase in inferential connections is always an increase in coherence. If we employ a standard, multidimensional conception of coherence such as Bonjour's, overall justification is not simply a function of specific linear inferences. If we abandon the multidimensional concept of coherence and take local inference as the only component of coherence, we are led back to the regress argument.

6.4 Conclusion: Coherence and Inference

This concludes our discussion of the positive claim that coherence theories are purely inferential. I began by distinguishing global from local inferences. Coherence theories based solely on global inferences, from the entire system to each belief, cannot provide a plausible account of the basing relation. Not only is it implausible to contend that the justifications of single beliefs are based on the entire system, but global inferential theories cannot make sense of the distinction between (1) what is believed and justified and (2) what is believed and justifiable but not justified. If, as I have argued, the basing relation is fundamental to inferential justification, global coherence justification is not inferential. I then turned to consider whether coherence theories can somehow be purely inferential in a way that relies on specific or local inferences rather than the single global inference. The idea that coherent systems are rich webs of inferential connections seemed to point to such a possibility. But I concluded that since coherence is a multidimensional concept, coherence justification cannot be explicated purely in terms of local or specific inferences.

Still, it might be said, valid local inferences are *evidence* of coherence. Perhaps; it is hard to say. One reason for the difficulty is that it is so hard to know, much less to measure, just what would constitute an overall increase or decrease in the coherence of an entire system of reasons and beliefs. At this juncture, the parallels between utilitarian ethical theory and coherence epistemological theory are striking. Both advance an ultimate master justificatory norm that places such extreme demands on our cognitive resources as to be, in practice, unusable. Consequently, in order to guide practice, both master norms must be translated into local, practically useful norms—individual rights and duties for the utilitarian,[22] local inferential justification for the coherence theorist. The challenge confronting the utilitarian and the coherence theorist is the argument that: (1) these local norms, not the abstract ultimate norm, are essential for guiding practice; (2) these local norms can be independently justified, or at least as easily justified as the master norm; and (3) it is not at all obvious that the master norm justifies strict allegiance to the local norms. The course of normative ethics over the last twenty years has, I think, shown that a good deal is to be said for all three anti-utilitarian claims; refuting them has proven most difficult. I see no reason why coherence theorists should be expected to have any easier time with their similar task.

CHAPTER 7

Foundationalism and Intuitionism

7.1 Coherence Theories and Self-Justified Beliefs

7.1.1 The Principle of Conservation of Beliefs

As Brink recognizes, if his theory is purely inferential it must follow that "no beliefs are noninferentially justified." Moreover, he explicitly recognizes that it follows from this that no beliefs can be self-justifying, for then some would not be inferentially justified.[1] In this section (7.1) I argue that plausible coherence theories are actually committed to some notion of a self-justified belief.

In section 6.2.2 I distinguished an absolutist conception from what might be called a situated understanding of coherence. Plausible coherence theories, I argued, are to be understood in the latter way; the coherence principle guides believers as to how they should modify their current belief system. The benchmark of coherence, then, is one's current belief system; the coherence principle instructs one how to go from S_1 to some new S_2. Plausible coherence theories require that all such moves conform to the principle of conservation of belief. As Quine and Ullian put it:

> The strategy . . . would seem in general to be a good one: divide and conquer. When a set of beliefs has accumulated to the point of contradiction, find the smallest selection of them that you can that still involves a contradiction. . . . For we can be sure that we are going to have to drop some of the beliefs in the subset, whatever else we do.[2]

When, in the interest of coherence, beliefs have to be dropped, the principle of conservation counsels dropping as few as possible. Other things equal, a conservative transformation of one's belief system is to be preferred to one that gains coherence (narrowly understood in terms of logical and probabilistic consistency) by a radical revision of one's beliefs. But why conserve as many beliefs as possible? The quick but nevertheless plausible answer is that we want as much truth, or at least justified belief, as possible. Now I think this must be roughly right; though we want coherence, we seek to purchase it as cheaply as possible, by giving up as few beliefs as possible. Doing that will assure us the largest stock of justified beliefs once the revision has occurred.

Although I think this makes sense, and in some version must ultimately be correct, it supposes that each belief is an epistemic asset. Though we are willing to spend some of them to purchase coherence (*qua* consistency), we seek to be smart consumers and minimize our costs. But just how do we, as it were, cash out the idea of "epistemic assets" and "epistemic costs"? Is (1) *every* belief an epistemic asset or (2) only every *justified* belief an epistemic asset? If (1) is a distinct option, it must be because it deems some unjustified beliefs to be epistemic assets. But this seems most odd. Clearly unjustified beliefs are, if anything, epistemic liabilities. As I argued earlier with respect to inferential justification (sec. 4.2), the *telos* of epistemic justification is to believe what is justified and reject what is unjustified (Axioms 3 and 4). As Quine and Ullian put it,"insofar as we are rational, we will drop a belief when we have in vain tried to find evidence for it."[3] So it is hard to see how possessing an unjustified belief can be an epistemic asset and therefore worthy of conserving. Justified beliefs are the assets that should be conserved.

We must, then, suppose that only justified beliefs are epistemic assets. Given this, if we accept the principle of conservation (which applies to all our current beliefs), we must accept that every belief that is presently a member of S_1 is to some degree justified. The principle of conservation, then, follows from a principle of credulity: Given one's current system S_1, every member is to some degree justified, just because it is member of one's current system.[4] This principle cannot be accounted for by the principle of coherence, according to which S_1 should be replaced by S_2 just because the latter is more coherent than the former; any members of S_1 that must jettisoned to bring about S_2 are necessarily inadequately justified, so jettisoning them cannot be an epistemic cost in terms of coherence. Indeed, on coherence grounds a principle of radicalism seems to make sense. According to the principle of radicalism, we should alter our beliefs as radically as necessary to achieve the highest possible levels of logical and probabilistic consistency. An advocate of the principle of radicalism could argue that all the beliefs that we must jettison are *ex hypothesi* inadequately justified, so that the radical transformation does not incur any unnecessary epistemic costs; it jettisons beliefs, but not *(ex hypothesi)* adequately justified beliefs. The principle of radicalism can only be rejected as epistemically wasteful if it is supposed that every belief one currently holds is to some degree justified, and so losing any belief incurs some epistemic costs.

It is likely that the coherence theorist will reply to this by insisting that it is based on a partial definition of coherence: It understands coherence in terms of consistency, but overlooks that comprehensiveness is itself an element of coherence. But comprehensiveness is not the same as the principle of conservation of beliefs, nor does it typically require it. Suppose we take consistency and comprehensiveness to constitute coherence; then the system that is most consistent and comprehensive is that which we have most reason to accept. But to accept this does not imply accepting the principle of conservation. If the Master Epistemologist informs you that the most coherent system of belief is S_{912}, and this has just about nothing to do with your system, you nevertheless would have reason to give up just about all you now believe and accept an entirely new set of beliefs. That you aim at the most comprehensive set of beliefs does not justify conserving your present set. Radical belief revision is entirely justified if, after the belief revision, one has a more comprehensive set than that with which one began. It is by no means obvious that the best way to maximize one's gains is to incur the smallest possible losses at each point; giving up a lot to get even more back is a reasonable strategy. Imagine, for example, an investment strategy that insisted that the very idea of maximizing one's fortune justifies the principle of conservative investment: Always prefer the investment that requires one to give up the smallest amount of one's present holdings. If the goal is to maximize our store of beliefs, why should we prefer a strategy that gives up as few as possible on each move? Surely we would have to weigh costs and expected gains, sometimes making big investments to secure even larger returns.

Still, it would appear that a commitment to comprehensiveness necessarily leads to a weak principle of conservation: one should not give up a current belief without some expectation of epistemic gain. To do otherwise would be to squander an epistemic asset—a belief that has epistemic value. This by no mean entails the stronger principle of conservation—that one should always opt for the belief change that minimizes the cost in terms of current beliefs—but it does imply that a rational believer will only jettison a current belief if she has some reason to expect epistemic gain. If this is the way in which the idea of comprehensiveness is to be understood, it becomes manifest that the commitment to comprehensiveness itself implies that, for the coherentist, every belief one now possesses is an epistemic asset. And if only beliefs that are to some degree justified are epistemic assets—it is hard to see unjustified beliefs as assets—we again are led to the conclusion that, on a coherence view, every belief one now possesses is to some degree justified.

7.1.2 Why Coherence Theories Admit No Purely Inferential Justifications

My aim above was not to defend the coherence theorist's version of the principle of conservation of belief; though I shall argue that some such principle is required to regulate revision of our belief systems (sec. 7.2), I shall recommend a considerably more modest version of the principle than that which is usually advanced. My aim was to show that situated coherence theories use the criterion of coherence to revise systems of beliefs about which it is assumed that *every member is to some degree justified*. Accounting for this leads us to the idea of a self-justified belief. As Nelson Goodman put it:

> We cannot suppose that statements derive their credibility from other statements without ever bringing this string of statements to earth. Credibility may be transmitted from one statement to another through deductive or probabilistic connections; but credibility does not spring from these connections by spontaneous generation. Somewhere along the line some statements, whether atomic sense reports or the entire system or something in between, must have initial credibility.[5]

Coherence theory follows the second route—the entire system must possess an initial credibility. And, I have argued, this ends up meaning that to the coherence theorist every belief we now possess, just because we now possess it, is to some degree justified; that is, simply because Alf now believes β, that itself to some degree justifies β. To be sure, this degree of justification is weak. That one may increase coherence by rejecting β will justify deleting β from one's system.[6] But that degree of self-justification is still sufficient to make each and every belief an epistemic asset, and so justify some principle of conservation. An implication of this is that, far from supposing that *all* justification is purely inferential, plausible coherence theories maintain that *none* of our present beliefs are purely inferentially justified. To some degree, every current belief is justified just because one holds it. Admittedly, the coherentist can allow that inferential connections can enhance a belief's justification; I certainly am not claiming that inferential justification plays no role in coherence theories. But I do claim that a situated coherence theory adopting some principle of conservation of beliefs must attribute some small degree of self-justification to every current belief, and so no belief is purely inferentially justified. If I am right about this, typical coherence theories fail to meet the modest requirement set out in section 4.3, namely, that in any plausible theory of personal justification at least some beliefs are purely inferentially justified.

7.1.3 Brink's Criticism of Self-Justification

Surprisingly, the problem with coherence theories is that they admit too many self-justified beliefs, in other words, all current beliefs. To some readers this may seem more perverse than surprising; Brink, after all, recommends his coherence theory over foundationalist epistemologies just because the latter require what is to him the unintelligible idea of a self-justified belief. We would do well to pause here and consider what Brink has to say about self-justified beliefs. He writes:

But can there be such [self-justified] beliefs? Justification is justification in believing true. In order to be justified in holding one's belief *p*, one must have a reason to hold *p* to be true. But *p* is a first-order belief that such and such is the case and, as such, cannot contain the reason for thinking *p* is true. Indeed, self-justification can be regarded as the limiting case of circular reasoning—that is, self-justification is the smallest justificatory circle imaginable. And everyone—even the coherentist—regards such small circles as nonexplanatory and, hence, as non-justifying. . . .

We can put the point in another way. To be justified in holding *p*, one must have a reason to hold *p*. If *p* is a first-order belief, this would seem to imply that one must base *p* on beliefs about *p*, in particular, on second-order beliefs about what kind of belief *p* is (e.g., under what conditions *p* was formed) and *p*-type beliefs are likely to be true. But this shows that one's belief *p* cannot be *self*-justifying.[7]

Brink's case depends on the claim that "in order to be justified in holding one's belief *p*, one must have a reason to hold *p* to be true." Let us interpret this for the moment as the claim that all justification is necessarily inferential, in the sense described in section 5.2. Interpreting it thus, it is clear that self-justification must indeed be the smallest circle possible, in the sense that β is the reason for believing β. But this violates the second axiom of inferential justification (sec. 5.2). The only way to avoid violating the axiom is to appeal to some other reason that we should believe β, but then, as Brink says, it clearly seems that β is not justifying itself.

To see our way toward an answer to Brink, let us consider a plausible description of purportedly self-justified belief. Some beliefs, as Lycan argues, arise spontaneously: "I find myself holding beliefs that are not (at least consciously) inferred from other beliefs. Typically these beliefs will be beliefs about my immediate environment, perhaps about some of my own mental states, or perhaps about something else."[8] Say, further, that when one comes to these spontaneous beliefs in an inferential chain, a person has no reason to doubt them. One finds them persuasive.[9] Two questions must be answered: (1) Are these beliefs justified in any way, or are they simply unjustified? (2) If they are in some way justified, are they inferentially justified?

(1) Such beliefs are, I think, justified in the sense that an account can be given of how we cannot get along without them. That is, according to the best theory of epistemic rationality, we must suppose that at least some beliefs have an initial credibility. It is highly plausible to suppose that reasoners who rely on such spontaneous beliefs, and embrace them until reason is found to doubt them, will do epistemically better than those who seek to find justification for beliefs that seem entirely persuasive and not open to any objection.[10] Let us call this a *cognitive efficiency justification* for embracing spontaneous beliefs. And it does indeed seem a justification in the sense that it distinguishes these spontaneous and persuasive beliefs from, say, a truly unjustified belief—one that we have no reason to continue accepting.

(2) It would seem that we have fallen into Brink's trap; by giving a reason for maintaining the belief, we have inferentially justified it. Recall, though, our characterization of inferential justification:

PICJ: Alf's belief that β meets the conditions of a (closed) purely inferentially justified belief only if:
    (1) Alf's belief that β is based on some good reason, R, that is part of his system of reasons and beliefs.
    (2) The inference from R to β is ultimately undefeated.

The justification of the spontaneous belief does not meet condition (1), for it is not based on (i.e., causally sustained by) the reason based on epistemic efficiency. I argued at some length in chapter 2 that a person with an inferentially justified belief holds that belief because of the justifying reason. It is not even enough that the person's belief system contains that reason; there must be the sustaining causal connection. But this is not true of the justification of spontaneous beliefs. Alf need not even possess the requisite theory of cognitive efficiency, much less accept the spontaneous belief on the basis of it, in order to be justified in having such a belief.

This, I think, is an important point, for it shows why traditional foundationalists were not, as Brink perhaps suggests, merely confused. To be sure, they identified reasons why certain beliefs are incorrigible, certain, or infallible.[11] But that is not to say that those reasons were the grounds for holding those beliefs. If that were true, then only if

Alf first accepted the requisite foundationalist claim of, say, the incorrigibility of perceptual experience could he be justified in his perceptual beliefs, for then the foundationalist claim could be the basis of his belief in incorrigibility of perceptual experience. But, clearly, philosophical foundationalism need not be embraced *before* one's perceptual beliefs become justified.

Two objections might be advanced to this view of self-justification. First, following Pollock, one might recall my earlier distinction between beliefs and reasons for beliefs.[12] I acknowledged that the reasons supporting an inferential justification need not themselves be beliefs, but perhaps other sorts of internal states. It may be argued that our perceptual beliefs, though perhaps not inferred from other beliefs, follow from other sorts of internal nonbelief states, such as internal sensations. If so, then the beliefs are inferred from these nonbelief states, and so the beliefs are, after all, inferential. But then the problem of self-justification is driven back to these nonbelief reasons: Are we justified in accepting these as reasons, or is that unjustified? I take it that though these nonbelief reasons are not themselves inferred from anything else, general epistemological theories such as Pollock's constitute a sort of general, noninferential justification for accepting these as reasons for belief. In that case, the account of self-justified belief simply transfers to nonbelief reasons.

A more fundamental objection is to question my interpretation of Brink's argument. Recall that I interpreted Brink's claim that "in order to be justified in holding one's belief *p*, one must have a reason to hold *p* to be true" as meaning that all justification is necessarily inferential. But perhaps the claim that β is self-justified is just the claim that no reason can be given for accepting β. If that is what self-justification involves, then it really will be impossible to distinguish it from the absence of justification. And if to justify β inferentially is merely to give any sort of reason why β should be accepted, then clearly the only alternative to inferential justification is silence, and no justification at all. In chapters 2–5 of this book, however, I endeavored to show that the idea of inferential justification is best understood as more specific than this, and once it is properly understood, conceptual space emerges for noninferential and, indeed, self-justification.

7.2 Weak Foundationalism

Even a coherence theorist has to admit some self-justified beliefs. But we need not follow the coherentist in attributing a degree of self-justification to all one's current beliefs. If we are to meet the plausible requirement that some of our beliefs are purely inferentially justified (sec. 4.3), we need to restrict the set of self-justified beliefs to a (proper) subset of our beliefs. In order to do this, we have to distinguish two categories of belief: The purely inferentially justified and the (at least partially) self-justified. Once we distinguish these two classes, we find ourselves driven toward a somewhat unfashionable doctrine— epistemic foundationalism. As I said above, foundationalism is typically identified with claims of incorrigibility, certainty, or indubitability, and so-called critiques of foundationalism are usually directed at these less plausible claims rather than the distinctively foundationalist thesis.[13] More careful analysis reveals two claims distinctive to foundationalism in general (FG):

FG: (1) Some beliefs and/or reasons are basic, i.e., at least partially self-justified.

(2) Any justified belief or reason is either basic or derives its justification, at least in part, from the fact that it is inferred from basic reasons and/or beliefs.[14]

One form of foundationalism in general might be called weak foundationalism (WF):[15]

WF: (1) Spontaneous reasons/beliefs possess weak initial credibility.

(2) Any justified belief/reason either is spontaneous and/or is partially derived from a spontaneous reason/belief.

This may seem implausible. Foley observes that "people can believe some very odd propositions" and it seems wrong to say that a person is justified in believing them just because they strike him as plausible.[16] Indeed, recall our radically flawed believer from section 2.3, who has beliefs popping into his head for all sorts of bizarre reasons. I insisted that such a person was epistemically flawed; haven't I now defended precisely this sort of groundless belief? Two points must be kept in mind. First, according to weak foundationalism these spontaneous self-justified beliefs have only a weak credibility; this is a marked contrast to Foley's subjective foundationalism, which accords basic beliefs an epistemically secure position.[17] Add to this the second point: One has a store of epistemic norms that will often lead one to jettison spontaneous beliefs. For example, say that Alf has a spontaneous belief that the moon is made of green cheese; the idea pops into his head, and he likes it. But he also is committed to a number of epistemic norms about evidence gathering and beliefs about astronomy, according to which this spontaneous belief is surely wrong. Indeed, Alf can see that it is worse than epistemically useless—it is defeated by the rest of his system of reasons and beliefs. So Alf has a spontaneous belief β, that the moon is made of green cheese, but the rest of his beliefs commit him to β, and these latter are highly implicated in his belief system, and so are in one sense stronger (sec. 3.4). He thus is committed to rejecting his wild spontaneous belief.

Thus we are led to a sort of negative analysis of spontaneous beliefs: One is justified in holding them until they are proven guilty by virtue of inconsistency with one's other epistemic commitments.[18] Foley apparently does not think this will do:

But why is this suggestion any more plausible than the suggestion that mere belief always provides a reason for what is believed? Again, it is worth remembering that people can have very odd beliefs, and sometimes these will be such that nothing else that is believed with comparable confidence can be used to argue against them. Indeed people can have momentary surges in the confidence with which they believe a proposition, coming to believe with tremendous confidence a proposition about which moments earlier they had significant doubts and about which only moments later they will again have significant doubts.[19]

From Alf's perspective, however, in what sense could β be odd and yet not run afoul of his other beliefs and epistemic norms? The very evaluation of it as odd implies that it somehow fails to live up to norms about justified belief. Moreover, because we have attributed to such beliefs only very weak credibility, it does not seem that odd spontaneous beliefs will be held so strongly that "nothing else that is believed with comparable confidence can be used to argue against them." Indeed, our epistemic norms are surely more deeply embedded in our system and thus provide stronger reasons than these spontaneous beliefs. Note that I have rejected brute interpretations of strength of belief (sec. 3.4). Consequently, that Alf feels quite certain is not to say that the belief is strongly held; on either the likelihood of error or the implicatedness criterion, the spontaneous belief will be weakly held.

It is worth stressing that I have not denied that coherence considerations enter into justification; I have simply argued that coherence cannot be explicated in terms of pure inferential justification.[20] Like the coherence theorist, the weak foundationalist will agree that spontaneous beliefs are to be embraced only until they are shown to be incompatible with other elements in the system of beliefs. These spontaneous beliefs are not epistemically privileged in the sense that they are certain, or even remarkably good, guides to what is true or justified; they do not possess a degree of justification that would lead us to retain them while rejecting numerous other beliefs with which they conflict. They are where our quest for justification begins. But to admit that is to accord them only a very modest foundational role: The structure of beliefs builds up from them, but once the structure arises, any spontaneous belief that ill fits the structure is to be rejected as unjustified. This, I take it, is the real insight of coherence theories.

Foley's own suggestion is that a person has a reason to accept β as self-justified only if, according to "his deepest epistemic standards," the argument "I believe β, thus β" is truth preserving: "However, the point is that this argument, unlike other arguments for β, can give [Alf] a reason to believe its conclusion even if he does not believe its premise. It is enough that the premise be true."[21] Still, requiring that the belief actually be supported by one's deep epistemic standards seems to come perilously close to saying that it is inferentially justified by those standards, and so the idea of self-justification becomes somewhat fuzzy.[22] In any event, it seems to me that a weaker test suffices: That the spontaneous belief must not conflict with one's deep epistemic standards or beliefs.

No doubt the idea that spontaneously arising moral beliefs are self-justifying will seem especially disturbing to some readers. It may seem to license prejudices or hatreds that apparently "arise naturally." Surely, it will be said, Alf's unreflective belief that, say, men are morally superior to woman is in no way justified just because he "spontaneously" believes it. But we have seen that for the coherence theorist every belief that Alf now possesses has an initial degree of credibility, so the coherence theorist agrees with the weak foundationalist that Alf must begin by viewing this unsavory belief as an epistemic asset. Of course the coherence theorist will quickly add that considerations of consistency, comprehensiveness, and so on, will show that Alf is better off without this belief. It is probably based on "empirical observations" that are ill founded and do not accord with standards of evidence implicit in his system, and it probably also is inconsistent with egalitarian commitments Alf possesses. And this seems precisely right.

The chief difference, then, between weak foundationalism and a plausible coherence theory adopting the principle of conservation of belief is that the former restricts the principle of self-justification to a smaller set of beliefs. It follows from this that the principle of conservation must also be restricted to a smaller set of beliefs. I argued above that, because the principle of conservation is applied to the entire belief system under plausible coherence theories, it must be the case that each belief is an asset, that it has an initial credibility. If weak foundationalism restricts the set of privileged beliefs to a subset of our total beliefs, it seems that the principle of conservation of belief must also be restricted to this smaller set. Moreover, this conclusion appears dictated by the first axiom of inferential justification (sec. 5.2): If β is justified just because it follows from R, then all its justification derives from R—it contributes nothing itself. It thus would seem that the principle of conservation should apply to R (assuming it is basic), but not β. So when applying the principle of conservation, we are to consider how many spontaneous (i.e., self-justified) beliefs are to be lost in a belief revision, but should not consider independently how many purely inferential beliefs would be lost. But this may seem objectionable. If, given two self-justified reasons for belief, abandoning R_1 would lead to rejecting a few purely inferential beliefs that rely on it, while rejecting R_2 would cause the loss of many such beliefs, a plausible principle of conservation of beliefs would apparently counsel dropping the former. On weak foundationalism, though, the question of whether to drop R_1 or R_2 appears evenly balanced, since whatever we do, one foundational belief will be lost.

This raises a dilemma. If we adopt what seems the most plausible interpretation of the principle of conservation of belief, in which we keep R_2 because of all the beliefs that are inferred from it, then it seems that we no longer view all those beliefs as purely inferentially justified. If they were purely inferentially justified, all their justification would stem from R_2; but if we adopt the principle of conservation and rescue R_2, some of its justification stems from the beliefs that rely on it (i.e., they would be lost if we reject R_2, so keeping R_2 is justified.) The only way to keep purely inferential justification is to restrict the principle of conservation of belief to spontaneous beliefs, but that seems to accord spontaneous beliefs an overly privileged place.

The solution to the dilemma is to recognize that we actually possess not two but three classes of beliefs:

1. Spontaneous beliefs/reasons, which justify other beliefs but are not justified by others.
2. Spontaneously justified beliefs, which are also justified by other beliefs/reasons.
3. Purely inferentially justified beliefs.

Thus far we have been considering (1) and (3); what of (2)?

Although foundationalist theories are usually seen as insisting that justification is one way and linear,[23] this applies only to (1) and (3). Recall that my use of the regress argument against coherence theories explicitly avoided claiming that circles cannot justify; the claim was that circles cannot purely inferentially justify. One of the principles of coherence theories is that, other things equal, assuming that α and β are both to some degree justified, their joint justification is greater if $\alpha \rightleftarrows \beta$.[24] This would not be a purely inferential justification, since neither is purely inferentially justified, but the inferential justification increases their justification (see, e.g., Bonjour's criterion of inferential richness). Call this *ampliative justification*.

Equipped with the idea of ampliative justification, consider the following. Suppose that α_1 and α_2 are to some degree self-justified. Assume further that $\alpha_1 \rightarrow \beta_1$ and $\alpha_2 \rightarrow \beta_2$,[25] where neither β_1 nor β_2 is to any degree self-justified, i.e., they are (thus far) purely inferentially justified. Assume, then, that although α_1 does not directly inferentially justify α_2, it is the case that $\alpha_1 \rightleftarrows \beta_1 \rightleftarrows \beta_2 \rightleftarrows \alpha_2$. In this case, although β_1 and β_2 are purely inferentially justified (by α_1 and α_2), they are necessary for the amplitive justification between α_1 and α_2. Consequently, in considering whether to jettison α_1 and α_2, the epistemic costs of abandoning the set $\{\alpha_1, \beta_1, \beta_2, \alpha_2\}$ will be greater than the epistemic costs of simply abandoning the set $\{\alpha_1, \alpha_2\}$. Thus, even though β_1 and β_2 are inferentially justified, the principle of conservation applies to them insofar as they are necessary elements of an amplitive justification. And it does seem that one of the real insights of coherence theory is that many justifications are ampliative in this way, and hence the principle of conservation of belief can apply to beliefs that are not themselves self-justified.[26]

It might be objected that the possibility of ampliative justification shows that circles can indeed be justificatory, and this rescues coherence theories from my argument that they must suppose beliefs to be self-justified (sec. 7.1). If $\alpha_1 \rightleftarrows \beta_1 \rightleftarrows \beta_2 \rightleftarrows \alpha_2$ is more justificatory than the combined force of $\alpha_1 \rightarrow \beta_1$ and $\alpha_2 \rightarrow \beta_2$, then it may seem that a network of inferences can create justification even though none of the elements individually has any degree of self-justification. That is, assume that the individual justifications of α_1 and α_2 are null; given ampliative justification, the combined justification might be greater than null, thus giving the coherence theorists what they need: justification for a set of beliefs none of which possess credibility alone. But the immortal words of a dean at the University of Oregon ring true here: "Twice nothing is nothing."[27] It is one thing to assert that initial credibility can be amplified through participation in an inferential network; we have reason to believe α_1, and the fact that it links up with other things we have independent reason to believe increases our conviction that both must be right. In some ways this is akin to having two apparently independent pieces of evidence for α_1 in which one has some, but not great, confidence, and then discovering that they each also provide evidence for the other; by increasing one's confidence in the two pieces of evidence, one has also increased one's confidence in α_1. But this is different from the case in which one has no reason at all to believe α_1 and no reason at all to believe α_2 and then discovering that $\alpha_1 \rightarrow \alpha_2$. Joining two beliefs that possess no initial credibility does not create credibility.

The only way around this, I suspect, is to see every *inference* as intrinsically epistemically valuable; though neither α nor β is an epistemic asset, the *inference* from one to other is. Thus it might be argued that in changing beliefs we should minimize the number of inferences that we must give up. But it is appropriate to ask why inferences are so valued. Surely what we care about are *beliefs*—our epistemic aim is to have well-justified beliefs. Inferences allow us to move between justified beliefs and to uncover new ones. A focus on preserving inferences can only make sense if it is ultimately a way to preserve justified beliefs. After all, if we have good grounds to believe that α is not justified, the inference from α to β is not an epistemic asset at all. It is not even an asset that is worth giving up for some reason (say, because α conflicts with some other beliefs); an inference from one unjustified belief to another is a simple waste of epistemic resources. If I know that my belief that I am incredibly good looking is totally unjustified, my reason to abandon this belief is not in any way lessened because it implies the further belief that women tend to dream about me. And this brings us back to our problem: Conserving inferences only makes sense if inferences not only can amplify justification but can, literally, create it out of nothing. And they cannot do that.

7.3 Moral Intuitionism

7.3.1 Weak Intuitionism Contrasted with Traditional Accounts

"The mere fact that intuitions have to be admitted in ethics cannot be made an objection against ethics," wrote A.C. Ewing, "since it has been shown that we also have to admit intuition with all knowledge outside ethics that involves inference."[28] I have not shown that we must admit distinctively ethical intuitions; thus far I have argued only that somewhere in one's belief system some foundations—intuitions— are required. If every "ought" can be derived from some "is," it would be possible for these foundations to be nonmoral, with all moral beliefs derived from more basic nonmoral beliefs. But, as Ewing suggests, once we recognize the need for something like intuitions (in the sense of self-justified reasons or beliefs) in any belief system, the standard objections to recognizing them in ethics evaporate. Moral intuitions, I maintain, are simply weak foundational moral beliefs. They are no more objectionable than nonmoral foundational beliefs. However, weak foundationalism is a very modest form of foundationalism, and consequently it provides the ground for only a modest form of moral intuitionism. In this section I compare and contrast, on several dimensions, this weak form of moral intuitionism with more traditional intuitionist doctrines.

Self-Evidence. It is generally agreed that central to moral intuitionism is a claim that intuitions are in some way self-evident.[29] As H.A. Prichard wrote, "The sense that we ought to do a certain thing arises in our unreflective consciousness, being an activity of moral thinking occasioned by the various situations in which we find ourselves."[30] Thus understood, moral intuitions are "spontaneous beliefs," and so are not inferentially justified.[31] To this extent, weak foundationalism is consistent with the traditional view of moral intuitions. However, the traditional intuitionist notion of self-evidence typically goes beyond this, to include certainty or, at a minimum, a degree of justification sufficient to constitute knowledge.[32] This, of course, parallels traditional foundationalist claims in epistemology (sec. 7.2). Some intuitionists, however, have jettisoned this stronger claim; Ewing insisted that moral intuitions are fallible, and recently Mark Platts has advocated a form of moral intuitionism in which "certainty plays no role."[33] In the interpretation I advocate here, far from possessing certainty, moral intuitions possess merely an initial credibility. They are thus much less of an epistemic asset than Rawls's "considered judgments," which themselves are sometimes depicted as a type of moral intuition (sec. 7.4).[34]

Strength and Level. As Ross pointed out, even the claim that moral intuitions are certain does not imply that they are absolute, in terms of being overriding. He wrote:

> Within Intuitionism, we can have at one extreme the view of Kant that duties of perfect obligation always outweigh those of imperfect obligation. At the other end we might have people who think the duty of promise-keeping to be *sui generis* but yet to be one which very rarely outweighs the duty of promoting the general good.[35]

Considered simply as possessing initial credibility, weak intuitionism warrants ascribing only a very modest strength to these moral beliefs; however, embedded in a system of reasons and beliefs, they may be strongly justified, though in these cases they would not be simply self-justified, but inferentially justified as well (secs. 7.2–3.) Sidgwick distinguishes several levels of intuitionism; the contents of basic intuitions, he said, can be specific judgments, rules, or first principles.[36] Any and all are consistent with weak foundationalism (see further, sec. 8.1).

Objectivity and Subjectivity. Though recent advocates such as Platts abandon claims of certainty, intuitionists often still insist that intuitions are "factually cognitive" in the sense that they constitute "claims about the world which can be assessed (like any other factual belief) as true or false, and whose truth and falsity are as much possible objects of human knowledge as any other factual claims about the world."[37] So central was this claim to the philosophical intuitionism of the 1930s and 1940s that the fact of diversity of intuitions and judgments was taken to be a basic problem for the theory.[38] If we intuit moral facts, it was questioned, why do our intuitions differ? Whether the argument from the fact of diversity is a strong challenge to objectivist accounts of morality is not my concern; the important point is that intuitionism was usually understood as upholding some variety of moral realism, and that is why intuitionists were apt to say that people with the wrong intuitions were "blind"— could not see the moral facts of the case. Yet subjectivist intuitionist theories are possible.[39] To the subjectivist, moral intuitions may have an affective basis, arising from a person's emotional reactions to situations and characters; the intuitions then derive from our essentially subjective responses to situations.[40] Obviously the subjectivist will not be worried by the argument from the fact of diversity; given the variability in people's affective natures, if intuitions are essentially emotional responses, we should expect great variability in intuitions. Again I propose to put aside this dispute about realism; both realist and subjective intuitions are compatible with weak foundationalism.

7.3.2 Coherence and Moral Intuitionism

A number of intuitionists, such as Sidgwick and Ewing, sought to combine intuitionism with coherence justification. According to Ewing, for example, "the criterion of the truth of a theory of Ethics is its ability to make into a coherent system as much as possible of our ethical intuitions (common sense ethics)."[41] David Brink has recently criticized Sidgwick's very similar proposal. Somewhat simplified, Brink's claim is that, according to an intuitionist, a moral belief β is self-justified, and

thus not inferentially justified. But, according to the coherence principle, if it is justified at all, β is inferentially justified because it coheres
with the rest of one's beliefs. Consequently, β cannot be both an intuition and justified through coherence. Sidgwick, however, held that in
rational benevolence "there is *at least a self-evident element,* immediately cognisable by abstract intuition."[42] But he also maintained that
utilitarianism, which articulates the requirements of rational benevolence, is justified because it makes common sense morality coherent.
Brink thus observes that "As a philosophical intuitionist, Sidgwick
must claim that belief in utilitarianism, when justified, is self-justified,
or non-inferentially justified. As such, its justification cannot consist in
the fact (if it is a fact) that utilitarianism sustains and explains various
precepts of common-sense morality."[43]

Sidgwick's position is complicated, and I do not wish to advance an
interpretation of his text on this point. However, the sentence quoted
above does point the way toward the resolution of this problem: Intuitions can be said to possess a "self-evident element."[44] According to
weak foundationalism, intuitions possess an initial credibility, which
warrants counting them as epistemic assets, and therefore applying the
principle of conservation of beliefs. But intuitions and their implications are apt to conflict with each other. Unless we have but one master
intuition, conflict is a constant possibility; when it occurs, some beliefs
have to be overridden or even rejected. As we saw in the analysis of
ampliative justification, an intuition that justifies a number of other
moral beliefs, and is in turn justified by them, will achieve a much
higher level of justification than an isolated intuition. Consequently,
when confronted with a choice between abandoning the integrated or
the isolated intuition, though both are self-justified, the former will be
a greater epistemic asset because of its inferential links with other moral
(and nonmoral) beliefs.

The coherence principle can be applied to intuitions if the self-
justification of intuitions is not so strong that they could not possibly
be rejected because they lack coherence with one's other beliefs, or
they could not achieve further justification through their inferential
links. Traditional intuitionism, which depicts intuitions as certain, may
well thus confront Brink's problem. (Sidgwick himself said that the
truth of intuitions must be manifest.)[45] In one sense at least, if we are
certain of β, it is as justified as it can be (though one might have additional reason to believe that β is certainly true). In any event, if self-
justification is highly defeasible, then the same belief may be both an
intuition and inferentially justified (though not, of course, *purely* inferentially justified).

7.4 Reflective Equilibrium

The much-discussed notion of reflective equilibrium points to a method for systematizing our many moral beliefs into an orderly structure. Moreover, though it is often advanced as a criticism, many have insisted that John Rawls's articulation of the method of reflective equilibrium in ethics is based on moral "intuitionism."[46] And some of those who charge Rawls with intuitionism also criticize him on the grounds that the apparently coherentist character of reflective equilibrium is an illusion; in reality, they maintain, it is really a sort of foundationalism.[47] I am in the somewhat embarrassing position of having embraced these positions that, to critics, if not quite *reductios*, certainly are intended to render reflective equilibrium less palatable. Nevertheless, I take some encouragement from the long-standing disputes about reflective equilibrium. I have argued that justification is foundational, yet also contains appeals to coherence considerations;[48] I have also endorsed "subjective intuitions" that are only weakly justificatory, and so can be dropped from belief systems when they clash with more strongly justified beliefs. All this at least points to the possibility that the complexities of reflective equilibrium may map nicely onto my own account of personal justification. I believe this is so: Weak foundationalism makes sense of the method of reflective equilibrium, at least on one—and I think the most plausible—interpretation of that method.

7.4.1 The Justification of Reflective Equilibrium

Rawls sometimes indicates that reflective equilibrium is simply a matter of coherence: "A conception of justice cannot be deduced from self-evident premises or conditions on principles; instead, its justification is a matter of the mutual support of many considerations, of everything fitting together into one coherent view."[49] This conforms to Goodman's account of reflective equilibrium as the method for justifying deductive and inductive rules:

> But how is the validity of rules to be determined? Here again we encounter philosophers who insist that these rules follow from some self-evident axiom, and others who try to show that the rules are grounded in the very nature of the human mind. I think the answer lies much nearer the surface. Principles of deductive inference are justified by their conformity with accepted deductive practice. Their validity depends upon their accordance with the particular deductive inferences we actually make and sanction. If a rule yields inaccaeptable [*sic*] inferences, we drop it as invalid. Justification of the general rules thus derives from judgments rejecting or accepting particular deductive inferences.

This looks flagrantly circular. I have said that deductive inferences are justified by their conformity to valid general rules, and that general rules are justified by their conformity to valid inferences. But the circle is a virtuous one. The point is that rules and particular inferences alike are justified by being brought into agreement with each other. *A rule is amended if it yields an inference we are unwilling to accept; an inference is rejected if it violates a rule we are unwilling to amend.* The process of justification is the delicate one of making mutual adjustments between rules and accepted inferences; and in the agreement achieved lies the only justification needed for either.[50]

I have already rejected the view that mutual fit is "the only justification." Without some initial credibility, I have argued, coherence seeking through the principle of conservation is not intelligible.[51] This is not, I should stress, a problem that is particular to taking considered judgments about morality as the initial data to be made coherent; it is a general point about coherence justifications.[52] If one begins with a body of belief without any initial credibility, making it all fit together could not introduce credibility. Suppose, then, that at the present Alf possesses a belief system comprised of initially credible beliefs and inferences made from and between them.[53] Hence he already possesses a *belief system.* How could pursuit of reflective equilibrium increase the overall justification of his system?

Given the idea of ampliative justification, Alf can increase the justification of his beliefs by increasing the inferential links between them. As Bonjour points out, one way to increase the inferential links within a system of belief is to develop principles that explain a number of one's beliefs—sometimes called explanatory coherence.[54] Understood in this way, reflective equilibrium aims at explaining our already (at least partially) justified beliefs, and in so explaining them increases their justification. Roughly following Ernest Sosa,[55] let us adopt the principle of abduction:

A: Alf is justified in accepting P by basing it on his justified belief of β and on his justified belief that P is the best of all accounts that one recognizes as possible explanations of β, and this abduction is not defeated.[56]

Typically, A is applied to perceptual beliefs or observation statements, and the abduction explains them in terms of reliable perceptual faculties. But moral intuitions can also be explained by reference, for instance, to moral principles that imply them. If a moral principle P is to be abductedly justified as an explanation of a set of moral beliefs (β_1 . . . β_n), it will not do for it to be merely an ad hoc rule, such as the "rule" β_1 & β_2 & β_3 & . . . β_n. Such a "rule" does not explain the set at all. Indeed, explanatory principles should account not only for (most of; see below) the initially credible moral beliefs, but the inferential relations between them as well. Let us call this the *explanatory coherence interpretation of reflective equilibrium*. I do not claim that this is Rawls's own interpretation (though he clearly understands reflective equilibrium to possess an explanatory dimension);[57] it is, rather, the view to which we are led once we understand plausible coherence justifications as necessarily building on weak foundations. Nevertheless, it retains the distinctive circular justification that Goodman described. The general principles are justified on the basis of the intuitions, and justification of the intuitions is enhanced by being explained by the principles. But the circular justification is ampliative rather than alchemical.[58]

7.4.2 Narrow Reflective Equilibrium

Suppose that Alf decides that something like Rawls's two principles of justice explains almost all of his justified beliefs about justice; he sees them as Rawls intends them—as regulative principles that not only organize his beliefs but also enlighten him as to his own views about justice. What is he to do about the few recalcitrant beliefs? According to narrow reflective equilibrium, Alf is to decide whether these beliefs are credible enough to modify the principles so as to include them, or whether their credibility is sufficiently doubtful that they should be dropped from the system. Several observations are in order here.

First, it is mistaken to think of the beliefs atomistically. They are already inferentially linked. To drop some moral beliefs from one's system may lead to a loss of a number of others, and the whole set may be highly justified because of the inferential relations among the individual members. This allows us to provide a better interpretation of the intuitive idea that some "considered judgments" are strongly held while others are not. To be sure, to some degree this may involve a mere brute difference in the credibility one attaches to the beliefs, but in many if not most cases it can be explained in terms of the way one moral belief is implicated in others (sec. 3.4). To reject a highly implicated belief would lead to the rejection of so many others that we cannot seriously contemplate "giving it up." In contrast, an intuition that really is atomistic, possessing no significant inferential links to other beliefs, would be a likely candidate for a rejectable belief.

Second, I hope it is obvious that moral intuitions can be reasonably rejected, even though they possess a degree of self-justification. They are, as I have said, epistemic assets insofar as they are at least weakly justified, but they may entail costs that outweigh their moral-epistemic benefits. Thus, upon engaging in reflective equilibrium, we may find that some intuition is inconsistent with our abductively justified principle, and so keeping it in one's belief system introduces a significant inconsistency. Still, because the initial moral beliefs possess some degree of justification, reliance on the principle of conservation of belief is appropriate. However, it does not seem that one must either explain (through a general principle) or reject all moral intuitions. Perhaps a perfectly rational believer would be able to explain all her moral beliefs through general principles, but real believers may often find themselves with powerful explanatory principles—which account for a large part of their moral intuitions—yet retain some moral intuitions (perhaps a rather small, isolated set) that cannot be adequately explained but whose rejection is not called for. If the principles are to be genuinely explanatory, they cannot be modified by ad hoc measures to explain the recalcitrant intuitions, but that they remain unexplained does not mean that the intuitions must be rejected. Thus, for example, someone accepting Rawls's principles of social justice may have a considered judgment that the basic structure of society is unjust unless children are educated to promote their Millian autonomy; such a person may not see how Rawls's argument can be modified to explain this intuition while still accounting for all her other judgments of justice, and yet she may not be prepared to abandon it. In such a case we might say that she is awaiting a better theory, as, no doubt, we all are, about everything.

After a person has engaged in reflective equilibrium she is almost certain to possess a new set of moral beliefs, different from that with which she started. These differences will be of two types: Some beliefs previously held will be rejected, while some new moral beliefs will enter into her system. These will be inferred from the justified principles; once our beliefs are organized and explained, we can see implications (belief commitments, sec. 3.3) of which we were not previously aware. The question arises whether the initial set of moral beliefs and the revised set must overlap. As DePaul shows, on at least some interpretations of reflective equilibrium, it is possible that the intersection of the prior and posterior belief sets could be empty.[59] A procedure aiming at systematizing one's moral judgments could lead one to abandon all of them (see sec. 7.1.1). However, this outcome is not possible on the explanatory coherence interpretation. According to the abduction principle, our explanatory principle is justified because it explains our initially credible beliefs. And while it need not explain all of these—they are only initially credible, not conclusively justified—it cannot justify rejecting all of them. That, indeed, would be a most odd way to account for them.[60] This, I think, accords with most people's understanding of the way narrow reflective equilibrium works—that it is not revolutionary[61]—suggesting that the explanatory coherence interpretation may underlie most views of reflective equilibrium.

7.4.3 Wide Reflective Equilibrium

In his important essay on reflective equilibrium, Norman Daniels distinguishes narrow and wide reflective equilibrium. Narrow reflective equilibrium—which we have thus far been examining—is a coherence or fit between "considered moral judgments" and "moral principles" (though it is important to note that these "considered judgments" need not be specific—as Rawls makes clear, these judgments can involve various levels of generality.)[62] Wide reflective equilibrium introduces "background" theories, and so "is an attempt to produce coherence in an ordered triple of sets of belief held by a particular person, namely (a) a set of considered moral judgments, (b) a set of moral principles and (c) a set of relevant background theories."[63] While narrow reflective equilibrium seems morally conservative, in the sense that we are trying to systematize and conserve our moral beliefs, this moral conservatism is greatly diminished by appeal to wide reflective equilibrium. It is possible—in principle, at any rate—that all one's moral intuitions may be rejected in wide reflective equilibrium. But this is not because wide reflective equilibrium is itself anticonservative or antifoundational.[64] Wide reflective equilibrium expands the set of beliefs to be made coherent, including not only moral beliefs and principles, but background considerations such as theories of the person. Thus, for example, if we accept Michael Sandel's critique of Rawls's theory of justice, we might conclude that although (1) Rawls's theory is in narrow reflective equilibrium with moral beliefs, (2) it supposes a highly objectionable view according to which the self is prior to the values it affirms, a view ultimately at odds with our beliefs about selfhood.[65] In this case one would reject Rawls's theory because it is not in wide reflective equilibrium. Daniels thus says that wide reflective equilibrium allows for "far more drastic *theory-based* revisions of moral judgments."[66] This is, perhaps, somewhat misleading. Because reflective equilibrium is not a method of belief revision special to morals, but applies to beliefs generally, we can see that theories of the person are themselves the product of narrow reflective equilibrium concerning beliefs about personal identity, notions about choice, values, and so on. Theories of the person thus can be understood as themselves abductedly justified from a number of justified beliefs. Wide reflective equilibrium is simply checking our various theories for consistency with each other; moral theories, theories of the person, aesthetic theories—in principle, all should be consistent with each other. Wide reflective equilibrium, then, has the power to revise our moral judgments radically because it brings the rest of our belief system to bear on morality. Yet for all this, the method is still conservative and, as I have interpreted it, relies on self-justified beliefs. The difference is that what is conserved, and the self-justified beliefs that are retained, need not in principle be moral, but can be metaphysical, epistemological, or religious.

But this alerts us to the complexities of wide reflective equilibrium. Let us call (β_m, MP, TP) the ordered triplet of moral beliefs, moral principles, and, let us say, the background considerations involving a theory of the person. To be in reflective equilibrium among these three would still not achieve full wide reflective equilibrium, since other theories besides that of the person constitute the relevant "background" theory, but let us put that complication aside. Wide reflective equilibrium, we are told, obtains when all these are in equilibrium. But, as I have argued, the background theory is itself the result of a narrow reflective equilibrium, involving specific beliefs about personal identity, our intuitions in various Parfit-like stories, and so on.[67] So TP was produced *via* a narrow equilibrium of our various beliefs about personal identity (β_p). In seeking wide reflective equilibrium, TP, as well as MP, could be altered. But altering TP in order to achieve reflective equilibrium with MP could upset the narrow equilibrium among beliefs about personal identity, which produced TP. That is, wide reflective equilibrium may yield a revised theory of the person, TP′—in equilibrium with MP—but TP′ may no longer be in narrow reflective equilibrium with one's beliefs about personal identity. A reflective equilibrator thus would be committed to going back to his beliefs about personal identity to check the adequacy of TP′. Ultimately, one is committed to an equilibrium among members of the quadruplet, $(\beta_m, MP, TP, \beta_p)$. And, of course, once we consider all the relevant background theories and the beliefs relevant to them, the number of beliefs and theories involved in wide reflective equilibrium becomes truly awesome.

This conclusion follows from two plausible suppositions: (1) "background theories" do not arise out of nothing, but are themselves products of narrow reflective equilibria, and (2) nonmoral theories are not necessarily privileged over moral theories. That is, a theory of the person might be rejected because it fails to match our moral theory, as well as vice versa. If so, then a nonmoral theory such as a theory of the person cannot be considered fixed when engaging in wide reflective equilibrium. Rawls, it should be noted, seems to maintain that the background theories, or what he calls the model conceptions of person and society, are extremely robust in relation to specific beliefs about personal identity, selfhood, and so on. He thus argues that they are widely shared: "They are as basic as the ideas of judgment and inference, and the principles of practical reason."[68] On his view, although background theories do not arise *ex nihilo* they are deep elements of our conception of practical reason, and so are not, it would seem, the upshots of their own narrow reflective equilibria.

7.4.4 Two Doubts about the Prospects for Success in Achieving Wide Reflective Equilibrium

If Betty's epistemological norms commit her to consistency among her beliefs, she will have reason to pursue the method of narrow reflective equilibrium. Moreover, cognitive efficiency considerations also suggest pursuing it: To the extent that many beliefs can be explained by general principles, deliberation is greatly simplified. Rather than searching a vast number of beliefs, a person who has developed general explanatory (but also, in their turn, justificatory) principles will be able to use her cognitive resources efficiently. Nevertheless, though the method is certainly valuable, two considerations suggest that a person's success in actually achieving reflective equilibrium, especially of the wide or expansive sort, will be limited.

First, as Cherniak argues, because our belief system is so vast, considerations of cognitive efficiency require that we divide it up into a number of subsystems:

In terms of the rationality conditions on a cognitive system, the major cost of structuring the contents of long-term memory in this way is that inconsistencies and useful inferences that involve beliefs in different subsets are likely to be unrecognized. . . . Logical relations between beliefs in different "compartments" are less likely to be recognized than relations among beliefs within one compartment, because in the former case the relevant beliefs are less likely to be contemporaneously activated, and . . . it is only when they are activated together that such relations can be determined. The result is, as Herbert Simon had noted much earlier in another connection, actual human behavior "exhibits a mosaic character," a patterned lack of integration; "behavior reveals 'segments' of rationality . . . behavior shows rational organization within each segment, but the segments themselves have no very strong interconnections."[69]

Given this, we are greatly limited in our ability to bring into coherence beliefs about personal identity, theories of the person, moral theories, and moral beliefs, as well as relevant psychological theories and beliefs, sociological theories and beliefs, and so on. Thorough searching of the various subsystems for inconsistencies with our moral theories would be terribly costly; if we attempt it at all, it will be a rather haphazard and partial affair. Thus pursuit of various narrow equilibria seems generally a more fruitful path.

Second, I have argued that principles are to be justified in terms of their explanatory power vis-à-vis our other justified beliefs. Thus reflective equilibrium is based on an abductive hypothesis about the best possible explanation of our beliefs. The problem is that a great deal of evidence indicates that people make serious systematic errors in such matters. As we saw in section 4.5, people focus on the most easily available and most vivid information, so their explanations are almost certainly based on a biased sample of their beliefs.[70] Moreover, once people do develop theories, these remain remarkably robust in the face of contradictory evidence.[71] Once a person has accepted a theory, it is very likely to survive even if it conflicts with a great many beliefs.

Neither of these considerations indicates that reflective equilibrium does not increase the overall justification of one's belief system by enhancing consistency and increasing inferential connections. But they do caution us that, as a method for keeping one's moral consciousness in reasonable order, reflective equilibrium, especially wide reflective equilibrium, is of limited value.[72] More important, perhaps, we should expect that most people, employing their cognitive resources in a reasonably efficient way, will neither aspire to, nor obtain, such equilibrium. This, we shall see, is matter of considerable consequence for public justification.

7.5 Summary of Part I

The theory of justified belief presented in this part of the book can be summed up as possessing five attributes.

1. *It stresses local inference rather than global coherence.* Justification, I have argued, focuses on specific inferences and their grounding reasons. Coherence considerations are certainly justificatory, but they are not, as it were, the meat and potatoes of justification. This, I think, is just as well, for global coherence is almost impossible to measure (sec. 7.4), and so we have very little idea of whether we possess it or not. But we do have a good grasp of having reasons for our beliefs, upon which the justification of those beliefs depends.

2. *It is weakly foundational and intuitionist.* I have embraced what

are often presented as the two bogeymen of current epistemology and ethics. But I have tried to show that, paradoxically, the theory is less intuitionist and foundational than plausible coherence theories. The attempt to do without any foundations, I have argued, leads to attributing a degree of self-justification to all beliefs. I have tried to limit the set of such self-justified beliefs.

3. *It is somewhat epistemologically relativistic but does not embrace cognitive normative pluralism or epistemological subjectivism.* We have good reason to suppose a core of universally shared inferential norms; both the theory of interpretation as well as evidence about mental logic support this supposition. But there is also good reason to suppose that Alf can possess an openly justified inferential norm that Betty's openly justified belief system does not include. Inferences concerning operators such as "ought" are, I think, a clear example.

4. *It is weakly externalist.* I have argued that reasons are not external facts, but relate to the appropriate connections within a belief system. Thus the status of something as a reason depends on the other beliefs that person holds as well as the epistemic norms that are justified in that system. This does not mean that it is impossible to say that a person "has" a reason to which she is not presently committed; it can be argued, for instance, that additional evidence would so interact with that person's beliefs as to commit her to a reason she does not now recognize.

5. *It is causal, but accounts for errors in reasoning.* I have maintained throughout that reasons are not simply justificatory, but causal as well. Moreover, I argued that inferential rules are the laws of thought. But, if so, how do people make errors? If the inferential rules are the laws according to which people link the reasons that cause their beliefs, how can they ever make mistakes? They can do so because they can succomb to epistemic *akrasia*, because the rules are not always properly retrieved from memory, and, more important, because cognitively efficient people also employ quick but dirty inferential rules—everyday deviant logics that help a good deal, but lead us astray as well.

PART II
PUBLIC JUSTIFICATION

CHAPTER 8

Private, Social, and Public Reasoners

8.1 Private Reasoners

As I warned at the outset, the analysis of personal justification in part I may have struck some readers as overly individualistic and "monological." Justification was analyzed as essentially internal to a person's system of reasons and beliefs, and I allowed for considerable justifiable variation from one person's set of beliefs to another's. Some individualistic version of relativism seemed to emerge (chaps. 3–4). This is an incomplete, indeed, on its own, a distorting view of human reasoning. Thus far we have treated people as essentially private reasoners. Each has his own system of reasons and beliefs, and the moral beliefs he is justified in accepting and rejecting are determined by that system.

Many insist that such private reasoners are an illusion. The most familiar critique arises out of certain interpretations of Wittgenstein's private language argument. Following a rule—for instance, an inferential norm—requires that one be able to distinguish successful following of the rule from making a mistake. Or, as Susan Hurley puts it, one must be able to distinguish eligible from ineligible interpretations of the rule. And, she argues, no thoroughly individualistic account can adequately articulate this difference. Quoting Wittgenstein, she maintains that

the difference between making a mistake in following a rule . . . and following a different rule, or none at all, is not to be found among the intrinsic, non-relational, individualistically identified properties, movements, or states of an individual: [as Wittgenstein says] "What, in a complicated surrounding, we call 'following a rule' we should certainly not call that if it stood in isolation"—or in a different surrounding.[1]

In evaluating this argument, we need to distinguish two perspectives from which it can be made: that of the interpreter and that of the rule follower. The interpreter—the perspective on which Hurley focuses—

must rely on the principle of charity in determining whether another's activity can be understood as following a rule (sec. 4.2). If Betty is interpreting Alf's acceptance of β as an instance of his application of a rule in certain circumstances, it would appear that she must (1) be able to make some sense of the rule, and (2) understand the acceptance of β as an eligible or sensible interpretation of the rule in those circumstances, which requires that she be able to distinguish eligible from ineligible applications. But, so the objection runs, this cannot be done simply by resorting to facts about Alf and his system of reasons and beliefs. This, I think, is entirely correct, and that is why relativism is necessarily tamed (chap. 4). Our interpretation of another as following a norm must be intelligible by our own lights (that is what it means to say that it is *our interpretation*), and that significantly restricts our freedom to attribute to others norms and beliefs that we do not share and do not believe are justified. Moreover, as I argued above with respect to the inverse-feasibility subject (sec. 4.4), neo-Wittgensteinians such as Hurley are quite right that Betty's interpretation of Alf will not rest simply on a manual equating the truth of his utterances with hers, but on the ways in which beliefs are connected—a form of life.[2] But we have seen that, far from precluding the attribution of different beliefs and norms to others, interpretation and its search for mutual intelligibility almost certainly requires it (sec. 4.2), while at the same time limiting it.

In many ways the perspective of the agent can be reduced to the perspective of the interpreter: When the agent is seeking to follow a rule he can be understood as replicating the deliberations of an interpreter, who tries to understand which interpretations are eligible. What Betty can do for Alf—interpret his actions in relation to a rule and its sensible application—he can do for himself. Alf, we can say, is a self-interpreter.[3] *Prima facie*, this contradicts the Wittgensteinian analysis of a person following a rule. If, as Hurley believes, "Wittgenstein argues . . . that no course of action can be determined by a rule, because every course of action can be made out to accord with the rule, and also to conflict with it,"[4] Alf's efforts at self-interpretation would seem senseless. If Alf's norms, as they are embedded in his current system of beliefs, are really so radically indeterminate, then clearly he needs to go outside of himself—to a social practice—to get any handle on how to apply them. But surely this is too simple a picture. At any given time, Alf has a series of precedents to which he can appeal—past decisions about what the rule calls for[5]—as well as other beliefs about the point of the rule and its justification. And he can draw on these to limit indeterminacy. In Ronald Dworkin's terms, a person so reflecting on his system of reasons and beliefs engages in constructive rather than conversational interpretation—interpreting the rule in the light of one's beliefs about its purposes and (one's) past interpretations of it.[6] Such constructive interpretation of one's own system is part and parcel of the method of reflective equilibrium (sec. 7.4). Because the principles and theories justified through reflective equilibrium explain one's intuitions and other beliefs (which include rules), those principles and theories provide constructive interpretations of one's belief system, including the point, aim, or rationale of one's norms. Though reflective equilibrium—and thus constructive interpretation of one's system of beliefs—will always be incomplete and approximate, it provides significant constraints on eligible interpretations of any single rule or norm.

Some Wittgensteinians insist that this solves nothing, because the indeterminacy that plagues the original rule merely replicates itself at other levels. How to interpret our past decisions, general principles, the *telos* of a rule—all these, it might be argued, are as indeterminate as the original problem of how to apply the rule. If no single rule interprets itself, neither can a system of rules. This is implausible. Even though, taken one at a time and in isolation, the applications of rules may be highly indeterminate, in the context of a system of rules, in which the interpretation of one has consequences for others, the range of eligible interpretations can be greatly reduced. This, I think, is one of the important lessons of Dworkin's analysis of hard cases in law (sec. 16.1).[7] Consider, for example, the statute according to which "it is a federal crime for someone knowingly to transport in interstate commerce 'any person who shall have been unlawfully seized, confined, inveigled, decoyed, kidnapped, abducted, or carried away by any means whatsoever. . . . '"[8] According to this rule, is it a federal crime for a man to persuade a "young girl that it was her religious duty to run away with him, in violation of a court order, to consummate what he called a celestial marriage"?[9] Taken in isolation, it may seem that either an affirmative or a negative is equally eligible, thus confirming the neo-Wittgensteinian's claim that the rule itself does not tell us how to go on. But in the context of other rules and justificatory principles with interlocking interpretations, Dworkin shows, the indeterminacy is greatly reduced, if not eliminated.[10]

It cannot, I think, seriously be maintained that belief systems are radically indeterminate in the sense that, at any given time, a reasoner does not have within her belief system the resources to constrain eligible interpretations of her beliefs and norms. Advocacy of such a radical indeterminacy, I think, presupposes a singularly odd picture of humans as cognizers of their environment. Imagine a species that developed beliefs, including beliefs about the world, but at any particular time, it was always an entirely open question what these beliefs involve, and only by appeal to the understandings of others could they give one any guidance about *what to do next.* Such creatures, let us say, would be *purely social reasoners* because their private deliberations about their beliefs would be hopelessly indeterminate, and only through some sort of intersubjective agreement could they lock on to determinate interpretations of their beliefs. Intersubjective agreement would serve as a convention that identifies one out of an innumerable set of eligible interpretations as the coordination point (see sec. 9.4.3). A person excluded from the social deliberation would be paralyzed, not possessing the resources on her own to decide what to do, or what to believe, next.

The notion of a purely social reasoner is, of course, a caricature. So far as I know, no philosopher has seriously proposed such a view. But, I think, it resonates in much contemporary writing about rationality and deliberation, which simultaneously often makes too little of the determinacy of individual deliberation and too much of social conventions. People are private reasoners in a modest, obvious, but nonetheless crucial sense: At any given time, they can deliberate on their beliefs and norms and decide, without engaging in conversation, what to do or what to believe. Moreover, because (1) we have rejected a strong externalist account of reasons (sec. 3.2) and (2) one can be intelligible to others even when one accepts norms they do not believe are justified (sec. 4.3), we are private reasoners in a less obvious but crucial sense: The justification of any specific belief or norm does not depend on intersubjective agreement.

8.2 Social Reasoners and Intersubjective Agreement

I do not intend to deny that in important respects individual deliberation is inherently social. I stressed that at a particular time a person has a system of beliefs and reasons that provides the basis for interpreting her specific beliefs and norms, and crucial to this system is a series of precedents about how a norm was applied in past cases. But a person develops her system of reasons and beliefs through interaction with others; indeed, it is only because a person can successfully interpret most of what others do that she can understand herself as inhabiting a social world with intelligible others. Shared understandings—indeed, a more or less common "lifeworld"—are the background for any particular individual deliberation.[11]

Furthermore, though one can deliberate privately about how to apply rules, Wittgenstein was certainly right that one's own judgments of success and failure cannot be definitive. Even under closed justification, which takes the person's current system as the alpha and omega of what she has reason to accept and reject, it must be sensible to say that the person has made a mistake (secs. 4.4–4.5). And this suggests that, in order to be a deliberator, one must be a member of a community in which one's beliefs and rules are intelligible to others.[12] Imagine a person who was not a member of any such community; because her beliefs and norms were not intelligible to others, others could never make any intelligible judgments as to when her beliefs were (even closedly) justified and when they were not. If this really were the person's standard condition, the distinction between what was justified for her to believe and what she thought was justified would be of little consequence—who would remain to tell the difference? This would begin to seem indistinguishable from justificatory subjectivism (sec. 4.5). However, to avoid such subjectivism it is not necessary that everyone share all of one's norms—indeed, it does not require that anyone does.[13] What is essential is that there are others to whom one's norms and beliefs are intelligible, so they can understand what one is trying to do when applying the norm, and have the basis for saying that one has got it wrong.

Consequently, we must resist any tight connection between the notion of justified belief and rational consensus. For example, it seems wrong to insist that "ultimately, there is only one criterion by which beliefs can be judged valid, and that is that they are based on agreement reached by argumentation."[14] A person can be inferentially justified in believing β even though he knows that β cannot be openly justified to others—they can be given no reason to accept it. Indeed, a person might even accept β as true even though he is convinced that it cannot be openly justified to others and sees no prospect that he can so justify it in the future.[15] We need to be careful here, though. That one can possess a justified belief that one rightly believes could not be the object of rational consensus does mean that *all* one's beliefs and norms could be individualistic in this way. Philosophers such as Richard Rorty are surely right that in some ways justification is a social phenomenon.[16] And one of these ways is that we could not make sense of a person who uniformly reports justifications that we could not accept. But, as I have been arguing, we cannot move from the truth that a great deal of consensus is necessary for intelligibility to the claim that irreconcilable disagreement is always a source of unintelligibility. Moreover, because some of my beliefs cannot be openly justified to another, and because both of us may know this and yet remain intelligible to each other, it follows that discourse does not necessarily aim at rational consensus. As such, we must dissent from Habermas's insistence on an intimate connection between mutual understanding *(Verständingung)* and agreement *(Einverständnis)*.[17] Habermas rightly observes that communication involves making oneself intelligible to others—it requires that we understand the reasons of others—but I dissent from the view that one can only understand a reason of another insofar as it is taken seriously and evaluated as a good reason.[18] Because the radical principle of charity—according to which intelligibility is gained only through attributing sound reasons to others—is to be rejected (sec. 4.2), successful interpretation as well as successful discourse can proceed on the basis of intelligible error.

For much the same reason, it follows that objectivity cannot in general be characterized in terms of intersubjective agreement, whether actual, prospective, or counterfactual.[19] Rorty, for instance, argues that the problematic notion of "objectivity"—which he associates with a confused attempt to transcend our perspectives to get at the world "as it really is"— is best replaced by the idea of unforced intersubjective agreement.[20] However, once we have rejected the general doctrine that justified belief must be the object of intersubjective agreement of some sort, it becomes difficult to see why objectivity should be tied to agreement. Indeed, one is tempted to turn Rorty's thesis back on itself and speculate that this identification is the final effort at transcending our own perspectives, reaching outside of ourselves (to what is socially accepted) to see things as they really are. Rorty, of course, is adamant that such transcendence is a fantasy, as we cannot escape from our own circle of beliefs.[21] In a way, though, seeking objectivity in interpersonal agreement is an effort to get outside our own system of reasons and beliefs, looking for the objective in what is outside of ourselves. But surely our commitment to, and understanding of, objectivity is itself a cluster of beliefs and epistemic norms. It is no more outside our system of beliefs than are our inferential norms or other beliefs.

Recall the contrast between impartiality and objectivity briefly introduced in section 4.1.[22] Following Piaget—and on this point Habermas as well[23]—I maintained that developing an objective view of others involves "decentering," coming to see that one's own point of view is not necessarily shared by others, and that they can possess reasons that you do not and vice versa. It is all too easy to imagine that decentering involves transcending one's perspective, thus obtaining a God's-eye view.[24] Or, in ways sometimes suggested by Thomas Nagel, it is tempting to depict objectivity as a *thinning* of the self, achieving "a rather austere universal objective self."[25] But the metaphors of both transcending and thinning point in the wrong direction: The decentering agent renders her perspective more objective by developing a more complex theory about the relations of her belief system to those of others. The decentered individual *expands* and complicates her perspective.[26] The individual comes to believe that what counts for her as a reason does not necessarily count for others as a reason. And that belief is as much a part of her system of beliefs as any other. Consequently, beliefs about objectivity—what it is and how it is to be achieved—are justified in precisely the same way as any other beliefs, namely, in relation to one's system of reasons and beliefs. The justification of beliefs about objectivity is thus no more closely tied to intersubjective agreement than the justification of more mundane empirical beliefs.

Yet, for all this, Rorty is right that the desire for objectivity is related to agreement.[27] As Nagel observes, "because a centerless view of the world is one on which different people can converge, there is a close connection between objectivity and intersubjectivity."[28] To see both the truth and the limits to this claim, let us distinguish *metaphysical* from *epistemological* objectivity. A belief, let us say, is metaphysically objective if it accurately represents the way the world is (Rorty, of course, gives no quarter to such beliefs). If there are such metaphysically objective beliefs (and I am not supposing here that there are), they are only contingently a matter of intersubjective agreement. Some people may have openly justified systems that do not give them any reason to accept such beliefs; they can be fully justified in rejecting the truth (sec. 3.4). Only if we suppose that, somehow, everyone converges on true beliefs does metaphysical objectivity imply intersubjective agreement, but this turns out to be an extremely dubious supposition.[29]

More interesting is epistemological objectivity. This is what I had in mind in my account of decentering: I stressed that Alf's being inferentially justified in believing β does not imply that others are openly justified in believing β. Or, more simply, his having reason to believe something does not imply that all rational others have reason as well. The possibility emerges that, given epistemic objectivity, since Alf acknowledges that Betty does not have a reason to accept his personally justified belief β, he will not criticize her as in any way epistemically defective for not believing β. To insist in such cases that she accept his merely personally justified belief would really be a sort of "epistemic chauvinism" (sec. 4.5). If everyone is epistemically objective in this way, this will lead to an epistemic tolerance insofar as people will refrain from making certain sorts of epistemic criticism of others. But, though we shall see that is important, this in itself does not produce intersubjective agreement. Alf may continue holding β and Betty $\sim\beta$, despite their both being committed to epistemic objectivity.

Epistemic objectivity does, however, have one important link to intersubjective agreement. One's theory of objectivity can serve as a filter, distinguishing considerations that are reasons for oneself, or *personal* reasons, from *public* reasons, those that are not only justified within your system of reasons and beliefs, but can be at least openly justified to others as well. A person who has developed a theory of objectivity, then, is in the position to offer arguments that *can be* the object of rational consensus. Being able to distinguish personal reasons from public ones, an epistemically objective person can fashion arguments to which rational others would assent, because such arguments provide them with considerations that are reasons given their systems. This, as we are about to see, is indeed significant. But the order of explanation here is not from consensus (under some idealized conditions) to objectivity, but rather from an epistemic theory of justified belief, to a theory of what reasons we do and do not share (a theory of epistemic objectivity), to arguments based on shared reasons (arguments on which rational people can converge). Hence the foundational role of epistemology in the analysis of public reason.

8.3 Why Reason Publicly?

Kant identifies three maxims of "common human understanding . . . (1) to think for oneself; (2) to think from the standpoint of everyone else; (3) to think always consistently." [30] Thus far we have been exploring aspects of the first and third maxims; our capacity for objectivity leads us to the second, what Kant called the public use of reason. [31] Because we can distinguish personal from public reasons, we can address arguments to others in the sense that we can provide reasons *to them*—considerations that are reasons given their own systems of beliefs. The question arises, however, why we should be interested in, or committed to, such public reasoning; granted that we have the capacity to develop a decentered theory of our belief system's relation to that of others, why should we bother to "think from the standpoint of others?" [32]

One appealing reply must be dismissed, namely, that we are justified in holding only beliefs that can be publicly justified. In the narratives of Alasdair MacIntyre and Richard Rorty, a fundamental aspiration of the Enlightenment was "to provide for debate in the public realm standards and methods of rational public justification by which alternative courses of action in every sphere of life could be adjudged just or unjust, rational or irrational, enlightened or unenlightened. . . . Rational justification was to appeal to principles undeniable by any rational person. . . ."[33] Our account of personal justification abandons this aspiration. One can have a fully justified belief β that others have no reason to accept, and so it cannot be justified through the use of public reason. Thinking from their perspectives, I can see that my belief is not openly justified in their systems (chaps. 3–4). But that does not imply that my belief is not justified; given my system of reasons and beliefs, it may well be an epistemologically impeccable belief. In short, a belief can be personally but not publicly justified, and that is quite enough to justify a person's holding it.[34] Once we allow that justified belief need not be publicly justified—justified from the standpoint of everyone—our general epistemic commitment to have justified beliefs (sec. 5.2) cannot account for a commitment to public reasoning. We are back to our initial question: Why bother with public reason?

A partial answer derives from the requirements of mutual intelligibility. Interpreting the utterances and beliefs of others requires a great many common beliefs (sec. 4.3); without a solid core of publicly justified beliefs, we would be pushed into a solipsistic world, inhabited by creatures of whom we could make no sense.[35] Everyday discourse appeals to reasons that are justified from everyone's perspective. As Kant put it, in such cases we are "addressing the real public (i.e. the world at large)."[36] But, as I have been insisting, our general commitment to publicly justified beliefs is not all-pervasive. Assuming the publicly justified core, further intelligibility can be achieved without public justification. Again, a belief can be justified though not publicly justified. Are there any beliefs that are inherently and necessarily publicly justified if they are to be justified at all?

Although I have been critical of Habermas's general intersubjective account of reason and justification, his analysis of claims of justice points to a valuable insight. Habermas distinguishes "*evaluative* questions, which fall into the general category of the good life and are accessible to rational discussion only *within* the horizon of a concrete historical form of life or an individual life style," from truly "*moral questions*, which can in principle be decided rationally in terms of criteria of *justice*."[37] The latter issues, Habermas argues, are to be determined from the moral point of view, which is intersubjective—the justified norms must be acceptable to all.[38] What, though, is special about justice that requires beliefs about justice to be publicly justified?

Moral commitments, especially beliefs about justice, presuppose public reason because they combine two features: demandingness and culpability. Consider first the way in which morality constitutes a system of demands. In ways remarkably similar to Habermas, Joel Kupperman distinguishes ethics in the wide sense—which includes value judgments— and morality as that part of ethics constituting "a system of strong demands."[39] Some ethical evaluations of others—as meeting or falling short of standards, or as exhibiting excellences—are not moralistic because we do not typically demand that people share and live up to these standards or experience resentment and indignation when they do not.[40] "This was Nietzsche's view; and it is one of the reasons why, although he felt free to make value judgments of various sorts, he was opposed to morality."[41] The crucial concept here is the notion of a duty, which always constitutes a *requirement*, the performance of which can be demanded.[42] Requiredness in general should be distinguished from specific claims on others that follow from someone's possessing rights. As Mill argued, a person may have a duty—a requirement—that she practice charity, but this does "not give birth to any right. . . . No one has a moral right to our generosity or beneficence, because we are not morally bound to practice those virtues against any given individual."[43] So one may be subject to a requirement that is not correlative with a claim of another person. When a specific person is warranted in claiming an action as her due— when she can insist that others do what is required of them because it is owed to *her*—the requiredness of morality is expressed in claims made by some on others, i.e., rights.

The understanding of morality as a system of demands or requirements is often confused with the idea that morality is coercive. On Mill's view, for example, "we do not call anything wrong, unless we mean to imply that a person ought to be punished in some way for doing it."[44] And it certainly seems plausible that applications of coercion stand in need of public justification, perhaps even an especially compelling one.[45] But coercion is a way to enforce requirements or to motivate compliance. Alf can believe that Φ is required of Betty without in any way threatening her, or thinking that punishment is appropriate if she fails to accede to the demand. Demands may justify coercion, but they are not themselves coercive.

Morality, of course, is not unique in issuing demands: muggers, toddlers, and dictators all specialize in issuing demands. However, when Alf makes a moral demand on Betty, he not only seeks to impose on her but, in the event of her ignoring his demand, he appropriately can blame her, resent her, feel indignation, and so on. Blaming another or feeling resentment that your moral demand has been ignored are only appropriate when someone has ignored demands when, as we say, she should have known better. These reactions are thus not appropriate toward babies or those who could not possibly have known about the relevant norm, rule, or principle. The culpability of others for ignoring moral demands, then, supposes that they had a reason for accepting the norm and acting on it, but failed to pay heed to this reason.[46] If one admits that others had no reason to accept the norm, then it is inappropriate to resent them or blame them for failing to act on it; it would be certainly odd to expect them to feel guilty for not acting on it. If there really was no good reason for Betty to accept the norm, she cannot have the reason to do what Alf demands. Thus it is not the case that she should have known better. In issuing a moral demand, Alf must be able to claim that there was a reason for Betty to embrace the demand. And given that we have rejected strong externalism (sec. 3.2), he cannot claim that there just *is such a reason, whether or not Betty has access to it.* Given that open justification is the only sort of externalism we have admitted, Alf must suppose that he can openly justify the moral demand to Betty—he can show that she has reason to accept the relevant norm.

8.4 Moral Demands and Moral Authority

Let us look more closely at the idea of a moral demand. An intriguing, though I think ultimately unacceptable, analysis is provided by what might be called a first-person expressivist analysis of demandingness. Alan Gibbard, who develops such a view of norms, considers what we might say to an "ideally coherent anorexic" who embraces norms according to which it is better to starve herself than to remain alive at the cost of being "plump." Gibbard writes:

I, along with many other others, think that course of action irrational. Now suppose I tell her so. Why should she give heed? All analyses aside, I seem to be claiming that she must. I seem to be claiming that, in some important sense, I am right and she is wrong. Perhaps I am indeed expressing my acceptance of norms that forbid her starving, and perhaps I do accept higher order norms that tell everyone else to do so. I seem, though, to be doing something more as well. *I am demanding, with purported right, that she change her view of the situation.*[47]

As Gibbard points out, such a demand seems to presuppose that the norms I accept are authoritative—to demand acceptance of a norm is to claim a type of authority.

Analyzing demandingness in terms of normative authority allows us to distinguish a normative demand from mere browbeating. As Gibbard notes, if the anorexic should ask why she ought to accept my norms, I might simply browbeat her: "I might issue demands for which I myself think I have no basis."[48] In this case, let us say, one is *merely* demanding; one simply asserts that the other must accede to one's view, but this assertion is devoid of what Gibbard calls normative authority. Her ignoring it would thus not ground the supposition of culpability. Gibbard's emotivism is sophisticated just because he refuses to reduce moral demandingness to browbeating: A moral claim is not, as it were, just a very firm insistence that you must believe what I believe, or act as I would have you act.⁴⁹ To understand moral demandingness—a demand backed up by appeal to normative authority— we must understand how a moral belief can claim authority over others. Gibbard explores several types of moral influence.

The first he deems "contextual," as it draws on a supposition of shared norms. Suppose that Betty claims that the current policies of the Federal Reserve Bank are unjust to the unemployed; when might Alf take Betty's judgment as authoritative for him? As Gibbard points out, Alf might believe that, in a sense, Betty's reasoning can be substituted for his. That is, Alf may believe that he shares Betty's general views about justice, and also that if he came to understand economics, he would embrace her sort of view. In this case, Alf treats Betty as *an authority* on these matters, and embraces her judgment (sec. 11.2.2).⁵⁰ Just as Alf can accept Betty's authority because he believes that she reasons well on the basis of beliefs that he accepts, or would accept if he knew more, Betty can herself claim authority on this basis. That is, she can claim that Alf is committed to her judgments about the Fed in the sense that they can be openly justified to him. Given his current system of reasons and beliefs, in the light of new information and criticism, Alf is committed to these conclusions. For Betty to demand that Alf accept her conclusions about the Fed is to say that she attributes authority to them *in the sense that they can be openly justified to Alf*. "Authority is contextual, then, if it stems from a presupposition that the speaker is guided by norms the audience shares, so that the audience can use the speaker's reasoning as a proxy for its own."⁵¹

Contextual authority explains the distinction between a mere demand or browbeating and normative authority. And contextual authority presupposes public reason: The essence of contextual authority is the claim by the speaker that the demand is justified from the perspectives of those on whom it is being made. The speaker, that is, claims to be able to think from their standpoint, and it is on that basis that she rationally demands that they embrace her judgment. Much the same is involved in what Gibbard calls "Socratic influence." Sometimes, he writes,

hearers come to accept what a speaker says even without according him authority. The speaker may prod hearers to think along certain lines and come to their own conclusions. . . . It is the kind of influence that Socrates exercises on the slave boy in the *Meno*. One way to exert Socratic influence is just to say the thing that one wants the hearers to conclude. Hearers may accept what a speaker says not because the speaker accepts it, but on the basis of things they were prone to accept anyway if they thought along certain lines. Lectures in mathematics can proceed in this way. Socratic influence, then, can work by assertion, so long as the assertions produce conviction solely by prodding listeners to work things out for themselves, on the basis of what they already accept.[52]

Socratic influence is both more and less demanding than contextual authority. It is less demanding in that the wielder of such influence does not claim authority to override the judgment of the other. As we shall see presently, to claim to reason better than others, so that your judgment should replace theirs, is a difficult claim to justify adequately. Those exercising Socratic influence do not make this overridingness claim; they seek the assent of those whom they seek to influence. Yet in some ways Socratic influence is even more demanding than contextual authority. Contextual authority contents itself with showing that a belief is *justifiable*, that the person over whom authority is exercised is rationally committed to such a belief (secs. 2.1, 9.2.1). Those who would exercise Socratic influence, however, seek to make others see the "right connections" between their beliefs. As in the *Meno*, where Socrates sets out with the conviction that the slave boy already has all the appropriate beliefs but fails to draw the "right connections" among them, the Socratic influencer seeks to *produce justified belief*—she seeks to induce the person to "see the truth," to believe what is justified for the right reasons. This distinction, we shall presently see (sec. 9.1.2), is fundamental to an analysis of public justification. For now, however, the relevant point is that, these differences notwithstanding, both contextual authority and Socratic influence suppose that the person exercising influence is reasoning from the perspective of the other, and so both are based on a commitment to public reasoning.

Gibbard, however, believes that normative demands can be based on a "kind of fundamental authority" different from either contextual authority or Socratic influence. Gibbard's worry, it will be remembered, is the ideally coherent anorexic; the coherence of her belief system precludes your claiming contextual authority or Socratic influence. (This, I think, is not quite right; as we saw, a person can possess a coherent belief system, yet still not draw the proper connections between her beliefs; sec. 6.2.4.) However, Gibbard denies (though he does not put it thus) that all justification is inferential. "A person," he says, "may find a norm credible, fully or to some degree, indepen-

dently of the other norms that support it."[53] This, of course, is fundamental to weak foundationalism (sec. 7.2). Gibbard proposes, then,
that because (in my terms) norms are often at least partially self-
justifying, one can press a norm on a person even though it is not
inferentially justified by that person's system of reasons and beliefs.
And this is precisely what he proposes in the case of the ideally coherent anorexic:

> I claim rather to be "seeing" something that she doesn't: that the fundamental
> norms she accepts just don't make sense [i.e., are not rational]. I am claiming
> a kind of fundamental authority, an authority that does not stem from any
> common acceptance of more fundamental norms. I am claiming that her norms
> are crazy, so that my own are, in a fundamental way, more to be trusted
> than hers.[54]

Gibbard thus indicates that the sort of foundational view I defended in
part I provides the basis for "fundamental authority." Moreover, he
believes that this sort of "influence," in which people press on others
partially (or fully) self-justified norms, is an inevitable part of social
life, and occurs continuously in the development of a person's moral
system. Gibbard summarizes his argument in favor of the legitimacy of
such influence thus:

> 1. I must accord legitimacy to past influences from others. My present norma-
> tive views stem pervasively from their influence. The norms I accept must not
> tell me, on that account, to throw out all my present judgments—for if they
> do, I am left a bleak skeptic. To some past influences, then, I must accord le-
> gitimacy.
> 2. That means I must accord legitimacy as well to future influences—not to all
> of them, but to the ones that meet certain standards. I have no plausible story
> of why past influences were all right but future ones will not be. There is
> nothing special about now as now.
> 3. In a discriminate way, then, I must accord others some fundamental au-
> thority.[55]

The argument, I believe, fails. In the first step Gibbard points out
that, as a matter of fact, many of our beliefs and norms have arisen
from the influence of others. So deep is this influence that it cannot be
corrected. Moreover, someone who denied its legitimacy—sought to
purge from her system all such beliefs and norms—would be led to a
sort of "bleak skepticism." So we must accord these past influences
"legitimacy." But here we must distinguish two very different ways of
according legitimacy to a past influence. We may, indeed must, acknowledge that many of our current beliefs were produced by a variety
of mechanisms—traditions, schooling, parental attitudes, and so on.

Gibbard is certainly correct that the ways these beliefs were produced do not disqualify them, in the sense of rendering them illegitimate or unjustified. And that is because the justification of our beliefs does not depend on their causal history, but on why they are now held; the sustaining rather than efficient view of the basing relation is correct (sec. 2.3). However, to acknowledge that these influences are "legitimate" qua not rendering past beliefs illegitimate is not to say that they are legitimate qua justificatory or possessing normative authority. A variety of factors may have given rise to beliefs—not just the influence of others, but, perhaps, rivalry with other philosophers to develop distinctive views—and these are all "legitimate" in the sense that a believer can acknowledge them without abandoning those beliefs. But in no way do they justify those beliefs.

What, then, of future influences? The parallel that Gibbard would have us accept is by no means obvious. If past influences have been legitimate, Gibbard argues, future ones must be, too; to deny this would be to insist in some way that at this moment one is at the height of one's powers, and further influences should be resisted, though in the past they were a good thing. However, we are indeed a good deal more suspicious of future influences than of past ones. Part of our understanding of a rational believer is that one adopts new beliefs because of their grounding reasons (secs. 2.3 to 2.4). Consequently, a rational believer contemplating the future will be most hesitant about putting herself in situations in which her beliefs will be caused by a variety of extrarational influences, though in contemplating the past she may easily acknowledge that many of her current beliefs were produced by exactly those influences, and that does not render them illegitimate. The difference in one's perspectives on past and future influences does not stem from the idea that now as now is special. Rather, it derives from the difference between evaluating whether one's current beliefs are justified (which does not involve a commitment to how they were produced) and a rational believer's commitment to adopt new beliefs for good reasons (which does involve issues of efficient causation).

Leaving aside Gibbard's formal argument, his central intuitive claim merits attention: If another person finds a norm independently credible, then I must "favor the norm in my own eyes."[56] As I have stressed, this is particularly relevant to the view I advanced in part I. Like Gibbard, weak foundationalism (as opposed to coherentism) insists that a "person may find a norm credible . . . [at least to] some degree, independently of other norms that support it."[57] For Gibbard, the fact that another competent agent finds a norm independently credible gives us a reason to embrace it. And this is the intuitive root of his idea of fundamental authority. That others believe that it makes no sense to starve oneself to death to avoid being plump should, says Gibbard, count with the anorexic. More than that, others can insist that she is irrational not to embrace the norm, and demand that she do so. This attitude towards one's norms, Gibbard believes, is part and parcel of treating them as objective.

Gibbard's observations do, I think, show that the following epistemic norm is openly justified for all of us: *When lots of others arrive at beliefs conflicting with one's own, consider their views closely to see if you have made an error.* And if some such norm is indeed justified, the fact that many others hold conflicting intuitions gives the anorexic reason to reflect that, perhaps, she should abandon her intuition about the nastiness of plumpness because, say, it conflicts with her other beliefs. Or perhaps she, too, has the intuition that her behavior doesn't make sense. Such reflection seems eminently reasonable, but Gibbard has something much stronger in mind. Gibbard's anorexic, remember, is perfectly coherent, so we must presume that no matter how much she reflects, she will not have any reason to reject her "better dead than plump" norm and instead embrace our "better plump than dead" norm. That is to say, if she canvasses everything that could count for her as a reason, she simply has no reason to revise her system of beliefs and accept our norm. Presumably her system does not contain, or overrides, the foundational "better plump than dead" norm. Even so, Gibbard believes that just because others arrive at the "better plump than dead" norm, that in itself provides grounds for her to accept it. And that is because he believes that (assuming certain disqualifying conditions do not hold) many others' believing β justifies a belief that β. But that seems a strikingly strong and conformist norm that his formal argument does not establish.

Gibbard indicates that the anorexic who not only persists in her deviant belief but refuses to accept the contrary beliefs of others as a reason to alter her views must see herself as very special. "Is there anything special about me as judge—or at least is there anything that should be special about me to myself?"[58] It is hard, I think, to avoid the conclusion that a deliberator deliberating about her own beliefs does have a special status—simply that she is deliberating about *her* beliefs. Our understanding of a deliberator cannot be divorced from the fact that deliberators operate on their own understanding of the world. To each, the deliberator's status vis-à-vis her own beliefs is indeed unique and special. To be sure, any deliberator can be wrong about her own beliefs and their implications, but that does not undermine the idea that deliberators, as such, are determiners of what they believe. Though they can and should consider the deliberations of others, a self that considered its own deliberations as just one opinion among others as to what it should believe would be radically and deeply alienated. Indeed, it would be doubtful that such a self could avoid dissolution.[59]

To conclude: Gibbard's notion of a demand on others resting on fundamental authority supposes that rational believers are committed to a metanorm, *If under good conditions many others find a norm independently credible, I must look favorably on the norm.* I have tried to show that, given the account of personal justification offered in part I, Gibbard's formal argument for this metanorm fails. Consequently, I conclude that the individual who seeks to exercise fundamental authority over the fully coherent anorexic does indeed engage in a form of browbeating. You are insisting that she accept your norm, though you acknowledge that she has no epistemic resources that would lead her, even under ideal conditions, to accede to your demand.[60] That is, even if she exhausts all her epistemic resources and admits all the new information that her system acknowledges as relevant, she still would have no reason to believe what you would have her believe, or to embrace the norm you would have her embrace.

8.5 Public Reason and Moral Demands

The failure of first-person expressivist accounts of demandingness—of which Gibbard's is a remarkably sophisticated version—means that genuine moral authority depends on public reason. To make genuine moral demands on others, and not browbeat them or simply insist that they do or believe what you want, you must show that, somehow, their system yields reasons to embrace your demand. Morality, then, requires that we reason publicly, from the standpoint of others. Of course, if the rational standpoints of everyone were identical—if fully rational people always had identical systems of reasons and beliefs—the requirement to reason publicly would be easily met. To reason from one's own justified perspective and to reason publicly would be the same. But we have seen that justified belief systems may diverge significantly, and from this arises the distinction between what is personally and what is publicly justified.

If our relations with others are to be morally informed, we must reason publicly. I shall not try to show here why our relations should be moral, though I have tried to do so elsewhere.[61] For now, the important point is that the requirement to reason publicly is not an epistemic requirement, nor is it a requirement entailed by being a member of a linguistic community or a rule follower; it is a requirement of moral life.

CHAPTER 9

What Is Public Justification?

9.1 Populist Theories of Public Justification

9.1.1 The Actual Assent Thesis

Understanding the nature of justified belief and our commitment to reason publicly allows us to approach in a new light political liberalism's most vexing issue: *Just what does it mean to reason publicly?* The wrong answer to this question distorts and confuses all that comes after, including the analysis of the liberal state and politics. And it is on this issue, more than any other, that political liberals have erred (chap. 1).

Suppose that Alf, a moral agent, demands that Betty accept norm *N*. Because he is a moral agent he thus acknowledges a commitment to publicly justify his demand on Betty—he refuses simply to browbeat her into embracing *N*. As Rawls says, to have a sense of justice is to "expresses a willingness . . . to act in relation to others on terms that they also can publicly endorse."[1] It is tempting to interpret this as meaning that Alf refuses to override Betty's own judgment by imposing *N* on her.[2] To impose a demand on Betty would be to insist that she conform to it whether or not she wants to or agrees to it.[3] And that, in turn, seems to imply that to avoid imposing his view on her, Alf must obtain Betty's assent to *N*.

The attraction of this proposal—let us call it the *actual assent thesis*— is considerable. Alf, let us say, believes that *N* is publicly justified, while Betty disagrees. For Alf to go ahead and impose *N* on her is for him to override her judgment and insist that she follows his. Alf thus appears to be asserting that his perspective is somehow privileged; after all, Betty believes that *N* is not publicly justified, so we appear to have a simple confrontation of perspectives. Who is Alf to say that he is correct? The commitment to public justification derives precisely from the recognition that one's own perspective is not necessarily definitive.

The actual assent thesis is an instance of what I shall call Justificatory

Populism; it supposes that Alf's and Betty's judgments are on par in the sense of being epistemological equals. Since all judgments are epistemologically equivalent, for one person to override the judgment of another can only be a brute assertion of his own view that is inconsistent with the commitment to public reason.[4] Consequently, only if agreement can be obtained is the commitment to objectivity honored.[5] Despite its initial attractiveness, this radical form of Justificatory Populism is implausible. People can withhold their assent because of obstinacy, selfishness, laziness, perversity, or confusion. That an obstinate Betty simply refuses to assent to any of Alf's moral demands cannot demonstrate that Alf has failed to publicly justify them, for what Betty says she is committed to is not necessarily correct (sec. 4.6). Surely actual assent cannot be necessary.[6]

9.1.2 The Reasonable People Thesis

A plausible Justificatory Populism must be a little less populist and a little more elitist; some idealizing conditions must be accepted, so as to allow Alf sometimes to conclude that N is publicly justified even though Betty actually dissents. At a minimum, for instance, it must be allowed that only if Betty is deliberating in good faith and doing her best to reason things out is her agreement required.[7] More generally, it may be allowed that only the agreement of reasonable people is necessary; call this the *reasonable people thesis*. Such a view is advanced by John Rawls. According to Rawls, "to say that a political conviction is objective is to say that there are reasons, specified by a reasonable and mutually recognizable political conception . . . sufficient to convince all reasonable persons that it is reasonable."[8] Rawls's conception of the reasonable is multifaceted; at least five elements stand out:

1. A reasonable person is ready to propose and abide by principles that can be publicly justified. This is to say that reasonable people are moral persons.[9]
2. A reasonable person recognizes the "burdens of judgment." Reasonable people will often disagree because (a) it is difficult to assess the bearing of evidence on disputed questions; (b) they disagree about the relative weight of different factors; (c) their concepts are vague; (d) their social position affects the way they weigh evidence and weight values; (e) it is difficult to balance normative considerations that may weigh on different sides of an issue; and (f) values conflict, and there may be no correct answer as to how they should be traded off against each other.[10]

3. Reasonable people believe that it is unreasonable to employ political power to repress reasonable doctrines.[11]
4. Reasonable people are free from the standard defects of reasoning.[12]
5. In their public justifications, reasonable people rely only on methods of reasoning accessible to others, in particular commonsense reasoning and the non-controversial conclusions of science.[13] Call this *the accessibility condition.*

As Rawls emphasizes, this is by no means a purely epistemological conception of a reasonable person, though it certainly contains epistemological elements.[14] The first and third conditions are, in a fairly straightforward sense, moral traits. I have been assuming the first, that we are moral persons and so are willing to propose and abide by public justifications. The third condition, that we are not willing to employ force to repress reasonable doctrines we do not share, is closely related to the commitment to justify our moral demands on others to them—we refuse to browbeat others into embracing our norms.[15] The second condition, the "burdens of judgment," will occupy us presently. For now I wish to focus on the fifth, the accessibility condition.

The accessibility condition is widely embraced, and indeed seems a defining characteristic of political liberalism.[16] Stephen Macedo, for instance, holds that the liberal conception of public justification "honestly acknowledges the substantive characteristics of *public* moral justification: it does not aim to identify what are simply the best reasons, where best is a function of only the quality of the reasons as reasons leaving aside the constraints of wide accessibility."[17] It is because Rawls and Macedo embrace the accessibility condition that they are justificatory populists. Though they partially idealize the subjects of justification, so that only the assent of reasonable people is required for a successful public justification, the principles of reasoning appealed to must be those accessible to all and sanctioned by common sense.

Rawls and Macedo, I think, understand the accessibility condition as a minimalist theory of reason, specifying "plain truths."[18] That is, they seem to believe that, although the accessibility condition may exclude some sound but complex inferences, it only sanctions sound inferences. More precisely, to constitute a minimal theory of reason, any inference that meets the accessibility condition must be valid. If this is not the case, the accessibility condition constitutes a deviant rather than a minimalist theory of reason. Suppose, for instance, that Betty wishes to demand that Alf accept the moral belief β, and she employs genuine commonsense reasoning in her justification to show that Alf's belief α

commits him to β. Assume further that Alf's belief system S contains an openly justified inferential norm N according to which the inference α → β is not valid: N undermines the inference from α to β. In this case, from Alf's perspective, commonsense reasoning is not a minimalist but a deviant theory of reasoning. If so, Betty has not provided Alf with a reason to accept β. Remember that the commitment to objectivity and public reasoning requires that Betty provide Alf with reasons for him to accede to her demand that he embrace β; here, appealing to the commonsense argument that sanctions α → β does not provide *him* with such a reason.

Does it matter that Alf is unable to publicly justify his norm N to Betty? I have been assuming that Alf's openly justified system of beliefs can contain an inferential norm that is not a part of Betty's system (sec. 3.5). To Betty, N is not a reason to reject the inference from α to β. But this in itself is not a problem for Alf. Betty is making a claim that Alf has reason to accede to a certain moral demand: Her public justification aims to show that Alf has a reason to accept β. But if in Alf's openly justified system of reasons and beliefs this is a bad inference, then Betty has failed to show that Alf has reason to embrace it. Because Alf is not demanding that others accept his inferential norm, he does not have to publicly justify it—we have already rejected the Enlightenment's principle that all justified beliefs are publicly justified (sec. 8.3). Hence Alf can possess a personally justified inferential norm N that is not publicly justified, which determines what he has reason to believe; Betty's justifications addressed to Alf must conform to it.

If commonsense inferential norms are to be part of a minimalist conception of public reason rather than (from the openly justified perspectives of some) a deviant theory of reasoning, it must be the case that commonsense inferential norms are endorsed by at least all openly justified systems of reasons and beliefs. Now if we mean by commonsense reasoning something like "methods of reasoning and inferences readily sanctioned by a large majority, even after significant reflection," then it seems pretty clear that commonsense reasoning is deviant from the justified perspectives of many. There is considerable evidence, for instance, that people tend to accept as valid the gambler's fallacy[19] as well as heuristics that lead them to ignore base rates and make grave errors in probablistic judgments (sec. 4.5) and in causal judgments (sec. 4.3); that they are subject to epistemic *akrasia* (sec. 4.6); and that many inferences based on "if, then" reasoning as well as inferences based on negation seem puzzling to a great many people.[20] It may be replied that people can be induced to abandon these faulty ways of reasoning, so a "refined common sense" would not sanction deviant norms. And this is right; as I pointed out in section 4.5, people can be taught the correct inferential norms. But that people can be taught normatively correct reasoning does not mean that whatever reasonable people can be induced to accept is normatively appropriate. As we also saw, people can be induced to abandon valid norms in favor of the gambler's fallacy (sec. 4.5). And in any event, some people simply refuse to admit that they make mistakes (sec. 4.5). If, though, the claim is that valid inferential norms are those that reasonable people would accept *if they appreciated their errors,* we have abandoned the reasonable people thesis for a stronger normative theory of justification.

My claim, then, is that commonsense epistemic norms and practices lead to normatively inappropriate results, and this causes problems for Rawls's theory. There is, for instance, a very strong case that commonsense epistemic norms are inconsistent with what Rawls himself describes as reasonable. Consider his crucial claim that reasonable people recognize the "burdens of judgment," that we often disagree because matters are complex, multiple criteria must be traded off against each other, and so on. Good evidence indicates that this is not a commonsense attitude toward disagreement, if by "commonsense" we mean what most reasoners reflectively believe is appropriate. In their study of ordinary reasoners from their teens to their sixties, Deanna Kuhn and her colleagues found that at least half the subjects were "absolutists." In Kuhn's study, ordinary reasoners were asked to formulate theories explaining crime, unemployment, and children failing in school. Her absolutists were confident that experts knew with certainty the answers to these complex issues, and were likewise apt to be equally certain of their own opinions. Consider the following replies:

How sure are you about what causes prisoners to return to crime?
  "Sure, because it's my opinion."
Could someone prove that you were wrong?
  "No, because I think I'm right."
  "Well, if I truly believe in what I'm saying, I don't think anyone could prove me wrong.
  "If I believe in what I say, I don't think anybody can make me wrong."
How sure are you of your own view, compared to an expert?
  "More sure. I feel strongly about my opinion. I think it is the right one."[21]

More than half of Kuhn's subjects endorse epistemic norms according to which their holding a belief entails that it is almost surely correct, and it is thus almost impossible to prove that they are wrong. Kuhn describes her absolutists as advocating an epistemic theory of sorts, and on this (the most popular view among Americans of all ages) the idea of the "burdens of judgment" is rejected. Either Rawls allows this commonsense epistemic theory, in which case most people will be justified in rejecting his crucial doctrine of the "burdens of judgment," or he insists that, however appealing the widely accepted epistemic norm of "belief implies certainty," it is normatively inappropriate. Clearly only the second option is eligible, but to endorse it we must apply normative standards not sanctioned by most people's common sense. To be sure, a Rawlsian can always reply that by "common sense" Rawls means nothing so crude as what common people believe (!), but rather a philosopher's interpretation of common sense. This certainly leads to a less populist theory of justification, but, as should emerge in what follows, it is doubtful that this understanding of common sense is an adequate basis for Rawls's pragmatic aims.

As I stressed in part I (sec. 4.5), this is not to say that these unjustified norms are closedly justified for the many that would assent to them (nor does it show that the justified norms are not closedly justified for those that have difficulty seeing them). But it does show that what is even reflectively accepted by commonsense logic—if this means actual everyday reasoners and their practices—constitutes a deviant and not a minimalist theory of reasoning. If, though, we leave aside the idea of commonsense reasoning, we can identify a minimalist theory of reasoning that meets an accessibility condition. In sections 4.3 and 4.4, I defended Hollis's and Lukes's notion of the bridgehead, in which are included basic inferential norms that we necessarily ascribe to all. We necessarily suppose these norms not only to be widely shared, but basic to everyone's system of beliefs.[22] Methods of reasoning that are part of the bridgehead, then, are in the relevant sense accessible to all, and provide a shared minimum standard of reasoning.

It may seem that ultimately this is merely to quibble about words: Rawls and Macedo appeal to widely shared commonsense notions of reasoning that everyone acknowledges, while I have located the minimalist accessible core in bridgehead beliefs and inferences. This may appear a distinction without a difference. However, it is crucial to keep in mind that many people may resist conclusions to which their own system of beliefs and reasons commit them, as seems to occur frequently with, say, "if, then" reasoning and inferences based on negation. If so, then the minimalist accessible standards of reasoning I have defended may still be puzzling to many people, and in one sense controversial.[23] Even more important, there is considerable evidence that many ordinary reasoners find it difficult to grasp counterarguments to their positions or respond appropriately to good evidence that appears to undermine their positions.[24] All this means that conclusions based on normatively minimalist and accessible reasoning may be not be appreciated as such by a great many people. It seems that political liberals such as Rawls and Macedo cannot accept this. Rawls is very clear that his aim is to articulate an understanding of public justification that induces stability, because citizens actually appreciate the inferences.[25] Unless the principles and ways of reasoning are actually available and acknowledged by citizens, the justified principles will not be "widely seen to be reasonable"[26] and citizens will not "*regard* [them] as justified."[27] Given Rawls's and Macedo's pragmatic concerns, they must interpret the accessibility condition as only allowing inferences that are widely *regarded* as valid and convincing, but that means that they sanction a deviant and not a minimalist theory of public reasoning. And that, in turn, implies that the "justificatory arguments" may not be normatively justificatory at all.

Let me sum up this somewhat complicated argument. I have argued that Rawls and Macedo advance a populist theory of public reasoning: Genuine public reasoning is characterized as what is sanctioned by commonsense reasoning. This, I have argued, is not an accidental feature of political liberalism, but arises directly out of the aim to articulate a stable conception of justice, the justification of which citizens will be able to appreciate and by which they will be convinced. But overwhelming evidence indicates fundamental divergences between commonsense-sanctioned inferences and normatively appropriate inferences. Consequently, Rawls's and Macedo's populist theory of public reason can generate arguments that are widely accepted but are not justificatory, while arguments that are based on shared bridgehead norms may be resisted by many. Thus, while I have accepted a version of the accessibility condition, it follows that normal people may dissent from accessible conclusions.

This points to a more general problem with identifying what is publicly justified with what reasonable people will accept.[28] We saw in section 4.5 that it is reasonable to rely on heuristics and other quick-but-dirty inferential methods. But those who employ these methods may (1) arrive at beliefs that are not justified by their own systems, and (2) fail to be persuaded by normatively valid (from their own perspective) reasoning that conflicts with the heuristic. Consequently, nothing is quite so common as reasonable people believing what is not well justified, or failing to believe what is well justified. Public justification, then, cannot be identified with that to which all reasonable people will assent, even after reflection.

9.2 Openly Justifiable Demands

9.2.1 Justified and Justifiable Beliefs

Let us return to Betty's problem: Accepting that moral demands are to be publicly justified, she acknowledges that her demand that Alf accept β must be justified to him—that she must provide him with reasons for accepting β. But we have yet to decide what this involves. Having rejected populist theories of public justification that focus on what Alf assents to, or readily sees as justified, let us take a more normative tack and consider the ways that Betty may justify β to Alf.

A demanding requirement is that Betty must lead Alf to embrace a justified belief β. This is essentially what Gibbard called "Socratic influence" (sec. 8.4): Her argument for β must be such that at the end Alf actually has embraced it as an explicit justified belief (sec. 3.3). Although this seems terribly demanding, it is very much in the spirit of political liberalism and, indeed, the social contract tradition. If our aim is to secure the assent of the other to our claim, justification of the demand should bring about the belief in the other, for then (assuming sincerity on the part of our justificatory partner) assent can be secured. Moreover, this proposal is not subject to some of the worries associated with the actual assent or consent proposals. If simple assent is sufficient, a justification would count as genuine even if Betty hoodwinked Alf into assenting through bogus arguments. But if the aim is to produce assent through Socratic influence—bringing about *justified belief* in the other—assent to unjustified proposals would not be justificatory.

But *requiring* Socratic justification—actually inducing the justified belief—seems far too demanding. A person, as we have seen (sec. 2.1), can be presented with impeccable reasons for embracing β, and yet fail to draw the right connections between these reasons and β. In these cases the person has available all the necessary reasons to bring about the justified belief, but nevertheless fails to accept it. Here β has not been Socratically justified; the argument has not resulted in a justified belief. To take an example, suppose that Betty seeks to justify the norm that "Women philosophers should have equal opportunity for tenure." And suppose that Betty gives Alf all sorts of excellent and compelling reasons why this is a well-grounded belief, reasons that are openly justifiable in Alf's own system of reasons and beliefs. But suppose that Alf nevertheless refuses to accept the norm; he insists, for example, that women cannot do philosophy, and so any arguments she advances must be flawed in some way. Does it follow that Betty cannot make a moral demand on Alf based on the norm? Importantly, if she does and

Alf fails to take notice, would it be appropriate for Betty to hold Alf blameworthy (sec. 8.3)? Well, Betty can certainly say that Alf should have known better. He is just as blameworthy as a chauvinistic American who speeds in Australia because he refuses to believe that the speed limits in Australia are not posted in miles per hour. Despite its being pointed out to him, he insists that this must be nonsense: This is the American century, he drives an American car, and speed limits must be in miles per hour. The fact that he had a false belief that prevented him from accepting the norm does not mean that he isn't blameworthy, for he had available all the reasons necessary to act appropriately.

In cases of this sort, Betty can claim contextual authority: She can claim to show that the acceptance of the norm was *justifiable* given Alf's system of beliefs. Here she does not seek to elicit Alf's assent by actually bringing about the justified belief, but makes a normative demand based on her conclusion that the norm is justifiable in Alf's system. To say this is to allow that, because of inferential errors (sec. 4.5), Alf may fail actually to accept the norm, though he has the reasons that justify doing so. Betty claims normative authority over Alf. It is not mere browbeating; she claims that the norm is a justifiable part of Alf's own system, and so he does have good reason to embrace it. If she shows that, then she has justified the norm to Alf, even if she has not brought about a *justified acceptance* of it.

9.2.2 Closed versus Open Justification

To justify her norm to Alf, is Betty required to show that it is justifiable given Alf's current system of beliefs and reasons? This would require that she establish that the norm is already an explicit or tacit belief of Alf's (sec. 3.3).[29] From a normative perspective a serious objection tells against this requirement. Alf may currently hold beliefs that could not withstand critical scrutiny and new information, and Betty may know this. Moreover, it could well be that were Alf to reject these unjustified beliefs, his epistemic norms would commit him to a major revision of belief system. If, because they are important members of Alf's current system of reason and beliefs, she was required to appeal to these beliefs in her justification, Betty would be committed to appealing to what she considers to be bad reasons. For Betty to appeal in her justifications to what she thinks are, *from Alf's perspective*, flawed beliefs seems cynical. For her to try to "justify" Alf's accepting β by showing that it follows from a belief of his that he would be committed to rejecting if given new information strikes one as more of an attempt at manipulation than justification. Suppose, for example, your three-year-old child asks why she has to go to bed at seven-thirty and you reply, "Santa Claus says seven-thirty is the bedtime for three-year-olds, and if you don't go to bed Santa won't bring you any presents." This may do its pragmatic job, but it hardly counts as a justification. Persuasion, yes, but certainly not a sincere attempt at justification. Justification gives way to mere rhetoric (and perhaps cynicism) when one "justifies" a belief to another by citing reasons that one thinks are inadequate even from the perspective of the person to whom they are presented.[30] Justifying your beliefs or principles to others does not involve simply *giving others reasons that they will accept*, but in some way advancing reasons that you think are good reasons for them to accept. This suggests what might be called a *principle of sincerity*.

A radical sincerity requirement would hold that unless R is a good reason to accept β in her own belief system, Betty cannot appeal to R in justifying β to Alf. But this seems too demanding. Suppose that Betty proposes a norm, "Child health care should be funded by the state." Betty is a feminist atheist, while Alf is a Roman Catholic who strongly supports right-to-life groups. And let us also suppose—what many might deny—that Betty accepts that Alf's views are openly justified in his own system of reasons and beliefs. It would seem entirely appropriate for Betty to put forward the following sort of argument: "Someone with your religious beliefs about the sanctity of a child's life should support child health care." Given that Betty thinks Alf is justified in holding his beliefs, there is nothing cynical here about her appeal to them. She runs the danger of lapsing into cynicism when she bases her case on appeals to reasons of Alf's that she thinks *he* has good reason to abandon.

We should reject, then, the very strong principle of sincerity according to which, if Betty justifies β to Alf by appealing to his reason R_A, it must be the case in her own system that R_A is openly justified. But what if β itself is not justified in her system? For example, drawing on his religious sentiments, Betty justifies to Alf a norm that redistribution to the poor is justified, and so she demands some of his holdings. But when he presses her to contribute her share to the relief of the poor, she insists that she is a Scroogian: Redistributive norms cannot be justified to her, so she has no commitment to contribute. This really does seem a failure of public reasoning. Betty is not reasoning with others; she is reasoning from their perspectives to justify conclusions with which she disagrees, but that may in some way benefit her. This certainly is manipulative. If Betty's justification of norm N is to be

sincere, it must at least be the case that she has a justified acceptance of
N. *The norm—though not necessarily the grounding reasons—must be
openly justified in her own system of belief.*

Bringing these considerations together, let us adopt the following
principle of sincerity (PS):

> PS: Betty's argument justifying N to Alf is sincere if and only if (1)
> she is justified in accepting N; (2) she has a justified belief that
> N is justifiable in Alf's system of reasons and beliefs.

It should be noted that, according to PS, a person could unintention-
ally offer an insincere argument, such as if Betty advances a justification
for N mistakenly supposing that she is justified in holding N. So in this
respect, "sincerity" is somewhat misleading. Nevertheless, the important point is that for Betty to offer an acceptable public justification
of N, she must be justified in accepting N, and she must have a well-
grounded belief that the other person is committed to it.

Betty's justifications should be open justifications. Given his current
system of reasons and beliefs, Betty's aim should be to show that, all
things considered, Alf is presently committed to β. Open justification,
we saw, is weakly externalist; it allows for Alf to have reasons for
beliefs that are not presently a part of his system, but his commitment
to the new reasons must be based on his current system as revised by
new information (sec. 3.2). Unlike stronger forms of externalism, open
justification genuinely addresses Alf, and genuinely shows that *Alf has
reason* to embrace β. On the other hand, open justification does not
hold Betty hostage to Alf's current errors, *as long as they are errors
from the perspective of Alf's system of beliefs.* If, however, Betty is
quite firmly convinced that Alf is in error, yet she cannot show that,
given his current system of reasons and beliefs, he is mistaken, then
she cannot, in her public justification, suppose that these beliefs are not
properly a part of Alf's system. As a result, her public justification is
sincere only if she is justified in believing that the reasons to which she
appeals are openly justifiable in Alf's system of reasons and beliefs.

Our rejection of strong externalism is important here (sec. 3.2). Suppose that we had embraced a strong externalist theory, according to
which R is an impersonal reason to accept β; it is simply a fact that
provides *anyone* with conclusive reason to accept β. Then Betty could
reasonably insist that she justifies β to Alf by citing R even if nothing
in Alf's current system of reasons and beliefs commits him to accepting
R as a good reason for β. Thus, if Betty was an atheist feminist, she
could justify abortion on demand to fundamentalist Alf by showing it
to be central to feminism, the true doctrine. William Galston appar-

ently endorses justifications of this type. Commenting on Charles Larmore's insistence that the imposition of political principles on another requires that they be "just as justifiable to that person as they are to us" (sec. 1.1), Galston writes:

> Larmore . . . may well be right that the norm of equal respect for persons is close to the core of contemporary liberalism. But while the (general) concept of equal respect may be relatively uncontroversial, the (specific) conception surely is not. To treat an individual as a person rather than an object is to offer him an explanation. Fine, but *what kind* of explanation? Larmore seems to suggest that a properly respectful explanation must appeal to beliefs already held by one's interlocutors; whence the need for neutral dialogue. This seems arbitrary and implausible. I would suggest, rather that we show others respect when we offer them, as an explanation, what *we take to be our true and best reasons for acting as we do.*[31]

Galston's switch from Larmore's concern with making principles "justifiable" to providing "explanations" of our action could perhaps indicate that he simply is not concerned with justification at all. We can *explain* our actions perfectly well by pointing out our own reasons, without thinking this *justifies* the actions. Of course, explaining our actions doesn't show respect; murderers often explain their reasons, but we hardly take this as showing respect for others. But suppose that Galston really is interested in justifying impositions on others. The idea that we best justify our impositions by citing "what we take to be our true and best reasons for acting the way we do" only makes sense if we suppose an externalist account of reasons, according to which, if something is a good reason for us, it is because it simply is a good reason, but that means it must also be a good reason for everyone. If we accept such an account, citing our good reasons does justify to others. However, having rejected the strong externalist conception of reasons, this collapsing of personal and public justification is not available.

9.2.3 Two Examples

As should be clear, Betty's commitment to sincere open justification of her moral demands *on* Alf *to* Alf requires that she refrain from appealing in her justificatory arguments to considerations that, while openly justified in her system, are not openly justified in Alf's. I argued in section 3.5 that such relativism of reasons is possible, but thus far we have only considered the problem abstractly. Let us briefly consider two elements of moral and political life characterized by such relativism: personal values and religious convictions.

The liberal account of values, ends, and projects insists on a distinction between the personal importance of these values and projects to an agent and their public standing. As Loren Lomasky puts it:

An individual's projects provide him with a *personal*—an intimately personal— standard of value to choose his actions by. His central and enduring ends provide reasons for action that are recognized as his own in the sense that no one who is uncommitted to those specific ends will share the reasons for action that he possesses. Practical reason is *essentially differentiated* among project pursuers. . . .[32]

Hence, observes Gilbert Harman, "we only fool ourselves if we think our values give *reasons* to others who do not accept those values."[33] It is, then, because liberalism conjoins a commitment to public justification and a theory of values as primarily of personal importance that, as Thomas Nagel rightly points out, "it distinguishes between the values a person can appeal to in conducting his own life and those he can appeal to in justifying the exercise of political power."[34]

Liberals often apply this same doctrine to religious convictions, treating them as merely personal projects or values.[35] Understandably, those with such convictions typically resist this description: They insist that their religious beliefs are not at all like personal projects or values that a person may or may not choose to pursue, but are fundamental truths about the universe and the point of human existence. And, I think, this is right; basic metaphysical beliefs are not to be equated with values or personal projects. But we can now see that liberalism is not a doctrine that focuses on the personal nature of values, but rather on the requirements for sound public justifications. Because one's values do not necessarily provide reasons for others to act, they are ineligible as grounds for public justifications. And so, too, are most religious convictions, not because they are values but because they cannot be openly justified to others.[36] A liberal citizen with deep religious convictions thus refrains from appealing to these convictions in public justifications not because they are mere personal choices, not because he doubts that they are fundamental truths, but simply because they do not provide other (i.e., secular) liberal citizens with reasons to accede to his demands.

In his discussion of the place of religious convictions in politics, Kent Greenawalt maintains that such compartmentalization of belief is as unattractive as it is impossible:

To demand that many devout Catholics, Protestants, and Jews pluck out their religious convictions is to ask them how they would think about a critical moral problem if they had to start from scratch, disregarding what they presently take as basic premises of moral thought. Asking that people perform this exercise is not only unrealistic in the sense of the impossible; the implicit demand that people try to compartmentalize beliefs that constitute some kind of unity in their approach to life is positively objectionable.[37]

Greenawalt concludes "that the threads of publicly accessible reasons cannot be disentangled from religious convictions and personal bases of judgment, and that strenuous efforts to make the separation would carry psychological costs and impair people's sense of individual unity."[38]

Two issues must be distinguished. Suppose, as Greenawalt argues, Alf cannot "disentangle" religious beliefs that are merely personally justified from those norms that can be publicly justified. In itself, this does not mean that those norms are not justified for Alf; that he accepts the norm for religious reasons does not undermine its status as an openly justified belief of his. Where Alf will have problems is in addressing justifications to others. If he cannot distinguish what are reasons for him from what are reasons for others, it is unlikely that he will be able to publicly justify his norm. He will be unable to disentangle reasons that others share from those that are openly justified to him and not others. Consequently, he will not be able to engage in public reasoning on this matter. Moreover, if he believes that the religious reasons are necessary to justify the norm, but that they are not openly justifiable given the belief systems of others, then any attempt to justify the norm would run afoul of the principle of sincerity.

For Alf to engage in sincere public justification he must be able to advance arguments that abstract from his merely personally justified beliefs and provide others with reasons (from their perspectives) to accept the norm. I see no reason to doubt that people can do this; as I have argued, the ability to decenter and reason from the perspective of others is a normal cognitive achievement (sec. 8.2). Moreover, because global coherence accounts of justification are to be rejected, so, too, must we reject Greenawalt's picture of belief systems as akin to seamless webs. Although beliefs implicate each other, much justification is locally inferential, and system-wide coherence is difficult to achieve. Our belief systems, as Cherniak argues, are compartmentalized (sec. 7.4.4). Furthermore, a person's beliefs may be overdetermined (sec. 2.2). More than one set of reasons may sustain a belief. This, pretty obviously, allows for both secular and divine justifications of the same belief. Because the justification of each belief does not implicate all others, a devout person can possess a fully secular justification for N that can be advanced to fellow citizens. Public justification becomes possible when the devout become participants in a shared discourse with those who do not embrace their religious convictions, and that assumes, given the circumstances of modern life, at least a nondenominational and most likely a secular discourse (see sec. 10.4).[39]

9.3 Defeated and Victorious Justifications

9.3.1 Challenges to Proposed Justifications

Public justification supposes that normal adults develop a conception of impartiality or objectivity, allowing them to distinguish personal or idiosyncratic reasons from public reasons. The latter are to provide the basis of public justifications of demands on others. Suppose that on the basis of her understanding of impartiality, Betty offers a public justification of the form $R_1 \to \beta$, with β being the conclusion that Alf must redistribute some of his holdings to Charlie. For Betty to offer a sincere open justification, then, it must be the case that (1) she is justified in accepting β, (2) reason R_1 is openly justifiable given Alf's system of reasons and beliefs, and (3) the inference from R_1 to β is likewise openly justifiable.

It is fairly likely that Alf will challenge Betty's argument. How might he do it? Putting aside for a moment the charge of insincerity, for Alf to show that Betty's argument does not justify β to him, he needs to establish that the inference from R_1 to β is defeated in his system of reasons and beliefs. To do that, he must advance a defeater reason. Recall that, following Pollock (sec. 5.3.1), we characterized defeater reasons in the following way:

> If R_1 is a reason for Alf to believe β, R_2 is a defeater for this reason if and only if (1) R_2 is a reason of Alf's and (2) R_2 is logically consistent with R_1 and (3) $(R_1 \& R_2)$ is not a reason to believe β.

Recall also that we distinguished rebutting and undermining defeaters. Alf may try to undermine Betty's justification by advancing a defeater reason showing that β cannot be inferred from R_1. For example, Betty may appeal to Alf's acceptance of the Lockean proviso that for justified holdings, enough and as good *must* be left for others; because, she claims, Alf's acquisitions have not left as much and as good for Charlie, his holdings are unjustified. But Alf replies that the Lockean proviso implies no such thing; he claims that it specifies a sufficient, but not a necessary, condition for justified appropriation.[40] So even if his appropriations did violate the proviso, it wouldn't follow that they are unjust. In this case Alf seeks to undermine Betty's justification, showing that the inference does not hold.

Alternatively, Alf may advance a rebutter. Again, recall from section 5.3.1 that:

> If R_1 is a reason for Alf to believe β, R_2 is a rebutting defeater for this reason if and only if R_2 is a defeater (for R_1 as a reason for Alf to believe β) and R_2 is a reason for Alf to believe $\sim\beta$.

Alf may admit that Betty's argument is a perfectly sound inference based on reasons he accepts; R_1 does imply β. Alf, for instance, may acknowledge that Betty has advanced a genuine reason for him to support redistribution, but he may advance a counterreason that he insists rebuts her argument for redistribution. Suppose Alf admits that (1) yes, in Lockean theory the proviso is a necessary condition for justified appropriation, and (2) his appropriations did violate it vis-à-vis Charlie. But he adds (3) utilitarian considerations are also relevant, and the importance of not undermining the sense of security of present owners overrides any Lockean redistributive argument.[41]

Finally, Alf may claim that Betty is not being sincere, that she is not justified in accepting β. Here the focus is not on what Alf believes, but on what Betty believes: Alf can seek to show that *in Betty's system of reasons and beliefs β is not justified*. This may seem an odd response; why should the fact (assuming it is one) that Betty is not justified in accepting β show that Alf can reject β? After all, regardless of whether β can be inferentially justified in Betty's system, if the inference is ultimately undefeated in Alf's system, then he does indeed have reason to believe β. The principle of sincerity begins to look questionable.

Two types of justificatory encounters must be distinguished: (1) one in which Betty is seeking to enlighten Alf about his own beliefs and commitments, and (2) one in which she is maintaining that a belief or norm is endorsed by public reason, and so is demanding that everyone embrace it.[42] Both types of justificatory discourse require Betty to base her case on what Alf is committed to, but the latter argument is stronger. In the latter Betty is not merely alerting Alf that he is committed to the belief, given his other beliefs and reasons; she is demanding that he embrace it. But for her to demand that he embrace β while refusing to accept it herself (or not having good reason to do so) is for her to demand that Alf embrace a belief that is not verified by public reason (as it is not verified from her own perspective), and indeed that she cannot see as justified. And this seems inconsistent with the status of her demands as moral. Although it is not advisable to rely on stipulative definitions of terms such as "moral," the notions of morality, impartiality, and universalizability are quite clearly intimately linked.[43] Arguments that are self-serving, in the sense of inducing others to accept claims that you do not accept, seem manifestly lacking the requisite impartiality. Certainly Kant stresses that the aim of public reason is to attain a universal point of view;[44] public reasoning thus articulates the requirement that moral judgments must be impartial and universalizable.[45] In any event, I shall suppose that insincere arguments do not qualify as bona fide public justifications, though little turns on this in what follows.

9.3.2 Defeat

One outcome of this justificatory exchange may be that Betty's proposal is *defeated* by Alf. Remember, Betty's claim is that the inference $R_1 \to \beta$ is ultimately undefeated (sec. 5.3.1) in *Alf's* system of beliefs (considered as an open system). This is of the utmost importance; her claim is not just that $R_1 \to \beta$ is justified in her own system, but that it is justifiable in Alf's system. On some views this may be a distinction without a difference. If one adopts a strong externalist view of reasons (sec. 3.2), whatever Betty has a reason to believe, Alf does too (and *vice versa*). But weak foundationalism allows for a relativism of reasons, so even if Betty is perfectly justified in believing β on the grounds of R_1, she cannot extrapolate from this that Alf must be, too. Consequently, if the inference from R_1 to β is defeated in Alf's system, a public justification that relies on it is defeated. Note that it would be too sweeping to say that if the inference from R_1 to β is defeated in Alf's system, Betty's public justification is defeated. Betty's justification of β may suppose that different people have different reasons for endorsing it; she may justify β to Charlie by arguing from R_1 to β, while justifying it to Alf by appealing to his belief R_2 (see sec. 15.5). So even if the inference R_1 to β is defeated in Alf's system, Betty's public justification is only defeated if she relies on that argument when showing that Alf is committed to β. We can think, then, of a public justification as a set of arguments for a proposal; sometimes the set may contain only one argument, at other times it may involve several (though the Principle of Sincerity limits the number of different arguments one may have advanced). For simplicity's sake, however, in what follows I shall focus on the case in which one offers a single argument to publicly justify a policy.

From Betty's perspective, then, for her to conclude that Alf has defeated her justification, she must judge that, given Alf's system of beliefs, the inference is defeated. Her task is to replicate Alf's openly justified reasoning. This means that she must take seriously beliefs and norms that are openly justified in Alf's system, but that are not so justified in her own. Consider again our redistributive example. Suppose that in Alf's system a strong utilitarian principle is openly justified, and this principle rebuts Betty's redistributive proposal. It will rebut it even if no utilitarian principle is openly justified in Betty's system. And this seems right; if Betty's aim is to show Alf what he is committed to, she cannot ignore openly justified beliefs of his that she does not share.

It is worth stressing again that for Betty to reason from Alf's perspective is not to say that she must gain his assent or that her conclusions (about what Alf's perspective commits him to) must agree with his own conclusions. I stressed in the first part of this book that a person can be wrong about his own epistemic commitments; consequently, what is openly justified for Alf to believe and what he thinks is openly justified are not necessarily the same thing. As a moral person committed to advancing public justifications, Betty ultimately has no choice but to evaluate the cogency of Alf's challenges. Even if she seeks to rely on the judgment of a third party whom she believes has superior wisdom, this still could be justified only if Betty has grounds for believing that the third party is better able to evaluate the cogency of Alf's challenges; that means that Betty's response to Alf's challenge would ultimately be based on her conclusion about its merits. In the end, Betty cannot help but rely on her own cognitive resources in deciding what constitutes a genuine public justification.

9.3.3 Victory

One judgment Betty might make, then, is that Alf has indeed *defeated* her proposed justification. In this case she would be committed to withdrawing her demand that β be accepted on the basis of R_1. Alternatively, she may conclude that Alf has failed to defeat her justificatory arguments—she may reject each of his challenges as inadequate. However, this seems insufficient reason for her to claim that her public justification is *victorious*.[46] In order to claim victory—to conclude that her justification $R_1 \to \beta$ is a bona fide public justification—at least two other conditions must be met.

1. The Publicity Condition. Betty cannot have reasonable confidence that her proposed public justification is victorious unless and until challengers have had ample opportunity to try to defeat it. Remember,

Betty is claiming her justification is ultimately victorious—no counterarguments defeat it—so she cannot have reasonable confidence that all challenges are defeasible until all available ones have been confronted. As Deanna Kuhn and her colleagues show, most people have difficulty constructing objections to their own proposals. Recall that in Kuhn's study, ordinary reasoners were asked to formulate theories explaining crime, unemployment, and children failing in school. Kuhn found that slightly fewer than half of her subjects were able to generate a counterargument to their own theory.[47] This suggests that the proposer of a purported justification is not likely to be an efficient canvasser of possible counterarguments to it. Cognitive efficiency considerations point to the same conclusion. It is a Herculean task, quite beyond our cognitive capacity, to scan even our own system of beliefs for all inconsistencies or defeaters; even Hercules would flinch at the task of scanning the systems of everyone else as well. The only accessible way to have reasonable confidence that a proposal is publicly justified is to put it forward and invite specific challenges from others. To rely on one's own conjectures about possible defeaters seems inadequate.

Thus the affinities between Habermas's theory and that advanced here may be greater than I suggested in section 8.2. Habermas insists that normative justification depends on actual discourse being carried out between the parties, and so cannot occur in the mind of a single person.[48] In one way I have disputed this, insofar as I have insisted, first, on the importance of personal justification, and second, on the necessity of each person's making up his own mind whether he has defeated challenges, and therefore the ineligibility of seeking to avoid this decision by appealing to consensus, even the possible consensus of reasonable people.[49] However, Habermas is surely correct on the crucial point that "monological" reasoning is insufficient to ground claims that a norm is publicly justified. This point is reinforced by another of Kuhn's findings. Although almost half of her subjects were at least able to generate possible counterarguments to their proposals, only a relative few were able to reply adequately to counterarguments.[50] Again, the evidence strongly suggests that the generation of challenges and replies is a scarce social resource, and only by taking advantage of the social division of argumentative labor—by actually putting forward proposals in the public forum, and so inviting challenges and replies—can one have reasonable confidence that one's proposal is publicly justified.[51] Public justification, then, is public not only in the sense that it must show that each has sufficient reason to accept the justification but, additionally, in the sense that it must meet the *publicity condition.*[52]

2. *Epistemic Authority and the Standard of Proof.* Suppose that the publicity condition has been met, and Betty concludes that all challenges have been defeated. Alf disagrees: As he sees it, some of his challenges have not been answered. As I have been stressing, this is not itself a bar to Betty's declaring that her justification is victorious. Yet it is also true that for Betty to declare victory in the face of Alf's dissent means that she believes that she knows better than does Alf what beliefs Alf's system commits him to. This is a strong claim. As I indicated in section 8.4, it would seem basic to our understanding of a person that, *normally*, a person is presumed to be the epistemic authority about what he has best reason to believe. I stress that this is a presumption, and certainly can be defeated. But any counterexamples one may devise are only compelling against a background according to which, in the normal state of things, Alf's conclusions about what Alf is to believe have a very special status. Consider again just how odd it would be to deny this. Suppose that Alf considers his own deliberations about what he has reason to believe as having no special status as determiners about what he should believe: Betty's conclusions and Charlie's deliberations about what Alf has reason to believe, he thinks, are just as relevant as his own when it comes to what he, Alf, is to believe. It should be clear that this view would go far beyond Alf's recognition that, for example, Betty is much more knowledgeable than he is about some area. In the latter case, although Alf does take Betty's deliberations as a substitute for his own, that acceptance is based on his deliberative conclusion that Betty is the person to turn to in this area. (It is worth noting here that Alf assents to Betty's conclusions, a matter we will return to presently.) The case I am considering here is informed by a radical dissociation of Alf-as-deliberator and Alf-as-believer. As he sees it, the first is not properly privileged as determiner of the second; Betty-as-deliberator has just as much epistemic authority to decide what Alf-as-believer should believe as does Alf-as-deliberator.

I suspect that renouncing this fundamental authority over one's own beliefs would evidence a sort of psychosis.[53] This is why those who, because of indoctrination, have been displaced as the determiners of their own beliefs persist in conceiving of themselves as self-determined believers. As John Wilson observes:

The indoctrinated beliefs are those which a person may think that he has accepted freely, for good reasons, but which in fact he has accepted when his will or reason have been put to sleep or by-passed by some other person, who has a sort of moral (as we significantly say) hold over him, by virtue of authority or some other power-bestowing psychological factor. The indoctrinated person, as Sartre would say, is in a state of self-deception: he is sleep-walking, or (in extreme cases) double-thinking.[54]

The supposition that individuals possess such an epistemic authority over their own belief systems is hardly unique to liberalism. The horror of Orwell's *1984* is the possibility of beings who really have ceded epistemic authority over their own beliefs, and are for that very reason no longer recognizable as persons. But I shall not insist on this. As my concern here is within liberal theory—individuals seeking to justify their moral demands to each other—it will do no harm to suppose that according this epistemic authority to the self-as-deliberator over the self-as-believer is a distinctly liberal position.

The important point is that Betty's claim that, despite Alf's dissent, she has publicly justified β to him seeks to override this epistemic authority of Alf over his own beliefs. It bears stressing that Betty can indeed sometimes be warranted in overriding this authority. In cases of what Gibbard calls "contextual authority," Betty can be warranted in claiming that she knows better than Alf what Alf should believe (sec. 8.4). Yet it seems that Betty must have a particularly strong case to warrant such overriding. Recall that in section 3.4 we saw that beliefs can be held with various degrees of confidence. Moreover, I argued that different people in different situations will justifiably employ different standards of proof; in one sort of case a person may employ, perhaps, a "preponderance of evidence" standard, while in other instances the "beyond reasonable doubt" standard is appropriate. Now Jeffrey Reiman argues that in claiming moral authority over another— claiming to override a person's own judgments and substitute your own—something like the reasonable doubt standard is required. According to Reiman, to make a moral demand is to seek to override the judgment of another, but such attempts at overriding are always suspect. They may be no more than mere attempts at *subjugation*—with this term understood very broadly to characterize any case in which the judgment of one person prevails over the contrary judgment of another simply because it can and thus without adequate justification for believing that it should."[55] Justification, Reiman thus maintains, seeks to "refute the suspicion of subjugation." And to do that, it must attain a very high standard of proof. "We must," Reiman says, "be able to show that the other person is mistaken. . . . For that, we must be able to show that the principle invoked is somehow true or valid beyond a reasonable doubt."[56]

In cases of reasonable doubt, Alf's epistemic authority over his own beliefs is decisive. After all, if there is reasonable doubt whether β or $\sim\beta$ is justified, and Betty believes β while Alf believes $\sim\beta$, why should Betty be accorded the authority to decide what Alf is to believe? This, I submit, explains why so many liberal analyses of justification seek to elicit the assent of citizens. Although I have argued against actual assent views of public justification (sec. 9.1), their attraction is that they do not involve overriding an individual's epistemic authority. If assent can be obtained, a lower standard of proof suffices. Thus assent is so attractive in justificatory arguments not because a person's agreement to a proposition renders it justified (how could it do *that?*), but because assent invokes rather than overrides a person's epistemic authority over his own beliefs, and thus can justify a proposition with a lower standard of proof.

Still, I have insisted, assent is not necessary to justification (neither is it sufficient). If Betty has shown that β is justified beyond a reasonable doubt, she has a genuine claim to contextual authority. Writes Reiman:

If some moral principle could be proven beyond reasonable doubt, then anyone who disagreed with that principle would be mistaken. If the winner appealed to that principle, then the winner prevails because she is right, not simply because she can. Otherwise the two confront each other as two people with incompatible judgments, and one prevails because he or she is able to.[57]

9.4 Undefeated Justifications

9.4.1 Inconclusiveness Distinguished from Indeterminacy

Carl Wellman describes justificatory encounters as trials by combat that are usually "terminated by an admission of defeat or a proclamation of victory or both."[58] Indeed, epistemologists who adopt this general approach to justification typically maintain that defeat or victory are the only options. If one does not meet (i.e., defeat) every challenge, it is often said, one must abandon one's claim.[59] It should be clear, however, that defeat and victory do not exhaust the possibilities; proposals can be *undefeated but not victorious.* In section 9.3.3 I argued that victorious justifications are not simply undefeated; in addition, they must satisfy the publicity condition and attain a high standard of proof.[60] The possibility thus emerges that Betty's justification may remain undefeated—none of Alf's challenges defeat it, so she continues to believe justifiably that she is correct—but because either the publicity condition has not been met or she has not attained the requisite standard of proof, she cannot claim victory. She is justified in believing that Alf is committed to $R_1 \to \beta$, yet she must acknowledge that she has not shown this beyond a reasonable doubt. That is, though she has (given her own epistemic norms and standards of proof) satisfied *herself* that Alf's system commits him to β, she has not been able to attain the requisite standard of proof to *show* Alf that he is committed to β. And because of Alf's epistemic authority over his own beliefs, satisfying herself that the inference is justified is not sufficient to override Alf's contrary judgment. As Bernard Williams argues, showing your own beliefs to be reasonable is not equivalent to showing competing beliefs to be unreasonable.[61]

Undefeated (but not victorious) public justifications arise chiefly because the considerations justifying β are typically *inconclusive*. The arguments are complex, and though Betty's judgment may achieve a standard of proof sufficient to justify her acceptance of β, it is insufficient to override Alf's epistemic authority and demand that he accept β. Because our belief systems are so complex, and so many considerations are relevant to disputes about what is publicly justified, it is often impossible to achieve victory. To be sure, it is not always impossible; we must be careful not to press the point too far. I shall suggest presently that we have good reason to think that liberal theory has had some important victories; principles of free speech and other civil rights are, I think, elements of a publicly justified conception of justice. Yet even these important victories point to the limits of public reason; as John Gray emphasizes, as soon as we move beyond these abstract principles to their application in specific cases, "indeterminacy" arises.[62] However, talk of "indeterminacy" can easily lead us astray. Indeterminacy and inconclusiveness are distinct; a great deal of trouble is avoided if we see this clearly.

The inconclusiveness of the justification $R_1 \to \beta$, I have been arguing, concerns the degree of proof offered for $R_1 \to \beta$ compared to a standard of proof: If the justification meets a higher standard, it is a conclusive justification, while justifications that fall short of the standard are inconclusive. I have been focusing on the interpersonal case, in which a person believes that $R_1 \to \beta$ but is unable to attain the high standard of proof required by public justification. Inconclusiveness, of course, can also exist within a single person's system of belief. Indeed, nothing is more commonplace. We all believe many things, with good reason, but not conclusively. In order to make this idea intelligible, we need only to distinguish (1) the minimum standard of proof required to accept or reject a sentence, and (2) the standard of proof need for firm belief, knowledge, or certainty. Justifications that meet (1) but not

(2) are inconclusive—as the dictionary tells us, the arguments are not "fully convincing" or "decisive." Because, as cognizers, we live in a complex world and operate with limited cognitive resources, we often must do with inconclusive beliefs. We usually cannot wait for decisive proof.

Inconclusiveness is to be distinguished from indeterminacy. Let us say that:

> System S is closedly/openly indeterminate with respect to β if and only if neither the acceptance nor rejection of β is closedly/openly justifiable.

Note two points. First, because we take either an internal or an external perspective on justification, we can take also take either an internal or an external perspective on whether some issue is indeterminate in a system of beliefs. Given Alf's current system of reasons and beliefs, he may not be justified either in accepting or rejecting β; of course, this indeterminacy may or may not be resolved once we move to an external perspective.

Second, I have characterized indeterminate beliefs[63] as those neither the acceptance nor rejection of which is justified. Recall that Ellis characterized belief systems in terms of sentences accepted, rejected, or about which one is undecided (sec. 3.4). Let us characterize S as indeterminate with respect to β if neither $A\beta$ nor $R\beta$ can now be justified in S.[64] It is thus manifest that, on this analysis, indeterminacy arises when the minimum standard of proof required for acceptance or rejection is not met. We can, then, distinguish inconclusiveness from indeterminacy: The justification for accepting (or rejecting) a belief is inconclusive if the justification meets the minimum standard of proof for acceptance (rejection) but falls short of some high standard of proof for conclusiveness, certainty, knowledge, and so on. A justification for accepting (or rejecting) a belief is indeterminate if it falls short of the minimum degree of proof required for either justified acceptance or rejection.

This, I think, is an intuitively attractive understanding of indeterminacy—the system of beliefs does not determine a response to β because neither its acceptance nor rejection can be justified. Consequently, if Alf's system of beliefs is really indeterminate with respect to β, he cannot either accept or reject it. Although this may seem a trifle too obvious to stress, keeping it in mind allows us to avoid understanding indeterminacy as equivalent to "anything goes" or "you can't go wrong." T.K. Seung and Daniel Bonevac, in their analysis of "Plural Values and Indeterminate Rankings" maintain that "The ranking of A and B is indeterminate just in case it is reasonable to conclude that A is better than B, that A is worse than B, and that A and B are of equal value."[65] Thus, "the essence of indeterminate ranking" is that there is "more than one right solution for your choice."[66] For the moment, let us take this as meaning that the following sentences all are justifiably accepted within the same system of belief: (1) *A* is better than *B*; (2) *B* is better than *A*; (3) *A* and *B* are of equal value. If we suppose that *A* is better than *B* implies that ~(*B* is better than *A*), then (1) and (2) are inconsistent and thus believing both violates a basic rationality condition (sec. 3.4). In something of an understatement, Seung and Bonevac admit that this "sounds paradoxical." Seung and Bonevac insist that this indeterminacy is "ontic" and not "epistemological": Epistemological indeterminacy derives from uncertainty (e.g., due to lack of information), while their "ontic" indeterminacy concerns the relations among rankings.[67] I cannot pause to pursue such matters here, but insofar as believers are to integrate sentences containing ontic truths into their belief systems, this conception of indeterminacy—be it ontic or epistemological—commits them to strictly inconsistent beliefs.[68] This seems a consequence worth avoiding.

9.4.2 Public Discourse and Inconclusiveness

Justifications are often inconclusive—they are open to doubt, not fully convincing, or not decisive because of the complexity of our belief systems and our limited ability to process all the information at our disposal. We have good grounds for forming (or rejecting) beliefs, but because so much information is available that cannot be adequately canvassed, we can seldom be confident that defeaters for our beliefs are not lurking, ready to overturn our conclusion (sec. 5.4). Victory is rare. Public debate is, I think, typically inconclusive in this way: The relevant information is so great that we are rational to form beliefs on the basis of what we have access to, but other people pick up on other information, coming to different conclusions. Because matters are so complex, neither side can typically claim victory. This is important, for it is inconsistent with the popular view that public debate is indeterminate, that neither acceptance nor rejection of the competing public justifications (qua public justifications) is rational. This is Kent Greenawalt's view. As he sees it, public reason often "runs out," and so must be supplemented by private reasons.[69]

Pace Greenawalt, it is precisely because our moral disputes are *not* typically indeterminate that it makes sense to form opinions and keep arguing about them. If the totality of reasons is really insufficient to form a conclusion, forming *any* opinion is unreasonable. Now some insist that reasonable disagreement arises out of indeterminacy; reasonable people, it is said, come to differing conclusions on questions for which there is no determinate answer.[70] If so, then no conclusion is publicly justified. And if some form opinions by relying on essentially personal reasons, to demand that others accept those opinions is to abandon the liberal commitment to public justification. Moral debate among liberal citizens makes sense because we can and do form opinions on the basis of public reasons; it is so inconclusive because so many considerations are relevant, either directly or because problems about which of two reasons is "weightier" can only be discussed by appealing to yet other, background, considerations, thus reintroducing problems of complexity.

Consider, for instance, disputes about the protection of animals. Greenawalt would have us believe that publicly accessible reasons simply are not enough to tell us what to do;[71] one who restricted herself to public reasons would be unable to form any justified belief about this matter. Greenawalt leads us to this conclusion by examining the differing, but very definite and not at all uncertain, views of such philosophers as Peter Singer and Tom Regan.[72] Assuming that neither Singer nor Regan has achieved victory on this issue, there are three possibilities: (1) neither has any epistemic warrant for forming any views, since the relevant reasons do not pass the threshold for justified belief; (2) since the public reasons are not sufficient to ground a conclusion, Singer and Regan are only warranted in forming opinions by relying on essentially personal considerations that do not provide others with reasons to accept their views; or (3) their reasoning is genuinely public insofar at they do present reasons for us to embrace their proposals, but because questions of agency, consciousness, and moral rights are so complex, they defend different positions, neither of which defeats the other.

The last is the most plausible. Belief systems are vast and complex; *our standard epistemological situation is an overabundance, not a paucity, of reasons.* This is, I think, a fundamental point: Given our inability to scan our belief systems for all possible inconsistencies and all justified inferences, it is entirely unsurprising that people arrive at opposing conclusions. Today, especially in ethics, it is fashionable to explain moral disagreement by appeal to incommensurability of values, or a basic plurality of equally valid valuational or moral perspectives. I do not wish to deny that such plurality is defensible, or that it can ground conflict; it will be recalled that I have defended a version of epistemological relativism. Still, given the complexity of our belief systems, it is, other things equal, always plausible to conjecture that any given disagreement is an instance of inconclusive reasoning, resulting from the complexity of the issues and our inability to declare victory for our view.

In response to this, one may wonder why such persistent dispute plagues ethical issues and not empirical ones, or why ethical issues are not subject to the orderly methods of investigation and conflict resolution indicative of empirical investigations. But surely, as soon as we put the question thus, the illusory nature of the implied contrast is apparent. Some moral issues, such as the injustice of slavery, are not subject to real dispute, while vast areas of social science are. As the complexity of the issue and the number of relevant variables increase, so does disagreement; hence the moderate disagreement about tomorrow's weather forecast, and the deep disagreement about patterns of climatic change. Again, I am not claiming that this demonstrates that basic indeterminacy never characterizes moral or political disputes—my point is that the observation of seemingly intractable disputes among experts does not, as Greenawalt suggests, provide evidence that the experts are relying on personal beliefs not subject to public justification.

9.4.3 Indeterminacy and Public Justification

My criticism of Greenawalt depends on my claim that when indeterminacy arises, public justification is impossible. If, under open justification, Alf's system of beliefs is indeterminate between the acceptance or rejection of β, then it is quite hopeless for Betty to seek to justify his accepting or rejecting it. Her aim in public justification is to show what Alf is committed to; if *ex hypothesi* he is not committed to anything on this issue, her task is hopeless. Public justification thus cannot occur on truly indeterminate issues. Since Alf cannot justifiably believe anything about the matter, Betty's claim that he is committed to some belief must be unsound. For Betty to make moral demands on Alf when she knows they cannot be justified to him is to browbeat him.

There is one exception to this. In cases of what might be called *nested indeterminacy*, Alf's system gives him no reason to choose, say, A, B, or C. Betty, I have been arguing, thus cannot publicly justify choosing one. But it may, and often is, the case that Alf does have good reason to accept $\{A \lor B \lor C\}$. In this case Betty could justify the set of possibilities to Alf, and given that only one (but no one in particular) is justified, she may be able to justify to Alf some procedure for selecting one of the set. This idea is formalized in analyses of multiple equilibria pure coordination problems in game theory, as in Figure 9.1. Neither Alf nor Betty has reason to select one equilibrium point

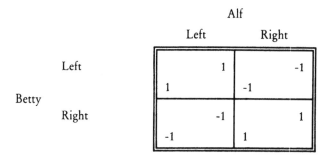

Figure 9.1 A Pure Coordination Problem

rather than the other, but both have a reason to select (the same) one. Thus, for example, we might say that Betty could not justify to Alf either a rule of driving on the left or a rule driving on the right, because his system of beliefs is strictly indeterminate between the two. But she could justify {Everyone drives on the left or Everyone drives on the right}; having justified the disjunctive belief, a procedure may be justified for selecting one of the disjuncts. (Just how procedures can be justified will occupy us in pt. III.)

Cases of nested indeterminacy need not be so trivial. Jon Elster believes that in child custody cases, the principle that the interest of the child should be the "sole, main or paramount" consideration is typically indeterminate between paternal or maternal custody.[73] Let us assume that he is correct, though it may well be that the principle is usually inconclusive. In any event, as Elster points out, even if the principle is indeterminate between the typical mother and the typical father, it does justify denying custody to manifestly unfit parents, those whose guardianship would very likely be harmful to the child because they have "been shown to have neglected the needs of the child, to have physically or sexually abused the child, to be financially unable to provide for the child, or to have character traits that render them emotionally inadequate."[74]

Just as there can be nested indeterminacy, a person's belief system can, and almost always does, contain *nested inconclusiveness*. Alf, for example, can have an inconclusively justified belief β; though he reasonably believes that β, the justification of β has not attained the requisite high standard of proof for firm belief. He still entertains the possibility that, rather than β, there is a substantial case for α, and he acknowledges that a justified α would defeat β. Yet he may have conclusively justified $\alpha \lor \beta$, which entails that Γ, a third competing sentence, is conclusively defeated. In this case, then, we can say that Alf's system of beliefs inconclusively justifies β and conclusively justifies

$\alpha \veebar \beta$. Of course, it is not simply any conjunction of inconclusively justified positions that constitutes what I have called nested inconclusiveness. The members of the set must be plausibly understood as competing interpretations of a more general, victoriously justified, notion. The concept/conception distinction employed by H.L.A Hart, John Rawls, and Ronald Dworkin is helpful here. It will be recalled that Rawls, borrowing from Hart, distinguishes various competing conceptions of justice, all of which are explications of the concept of justice.[75] The concept of X, according to Dworkin, involves "ideas that are un-controversially employed in all interpretations," while the conceptions employ and interpret these ideas differently, in ways that typically compete with one another.[76] The idea here, then, is that the concept is a highly abstract notion on which there may be agreement (or, in my terms, it may be victoriously justified). But numerous interpretations (conceptions) are advanced, each articulating the core abstract idea in a different way, none of which is victorious over the rest. This would be a paradigm case of nested inconclusiveness. We shall have occasion to return to it below.

CHAPTER 10

Liberal Principles

10.1 Victorious Justification: Constraints and Resources

As I have said, the requirements for victorious justification are exacting. It may help to review some of my main claims in order to appreciate just how exacting they are:

1. Because we have rejected strong externalism, Betty cannot make a good argument that, because she is justified in accepting β on the basis of R_1, everyone, including Alf, necessarily has a similar reason to embrace β.

2. Because we have rejected global coherentism, the following argument is not available to Betty: (a) Since all coherent systems converge, (b) that she is justified in believing β on the basis of R_1 is strong evidence that others with equally coherent systems would also believe β, and so (c) anyone who does not believe β has either (i) a less justified set of beliefs than does Betty or (ii) a better justified set. In either case, they should all converge on the same beliefs.

3. Because we have accepted weak foundationalism, Betty must accept that Alf can openly justify moral intuitions or religious beliefs that are not openly justifiable in her system, and yet defeat her public justification.

4. More generally, because we have accepted a form of epistemic relativism, it follows that what is justified for Betty may not be justified in Alf's belief system.

5. Betty cannot claim "fundamental authority" to influence Alf's beliefs.

6. And because it has been argued that Alf has epistemic authority over his own beliefs, a high standard of proof is required for Betty to override his judgments about what he is justified in believing.

Some conclusions *supporting* the possibility of successful public justification have also emerged:

7. Interpretive necessity requires that we attribute to others shared basic inferential norms and beliefs, ensuring a common basis for public reasoning.

8. By rejecting global coherence theories of justification in favor of weak foundationalism, which gives greater weight to local inferences, we have helped to localize the problem of justification. That is, the justifiability of any specific inference can, at least to a considerable extent, be isolated from a person's total set of beliefs.

9. We have rejected populist theories of justification, and thus need not suppose that sound justifications will be widely embraced.

10. We have concluded that public justification requires open, not closed, justification, thus embracing a weak form of externalism.

11. Public justification need not produce justified belief in others; it need only show that the norm or principle is openly justifiable.

Given these constraints and resources, the question arises whether any moral principle or claim can be victoriously justified to each and every member of a large community.[1]

"Liberalism," says Thomas Nagel, "takes various forms, but they all include a system of individual rights against interference of certain kinds, together with limited positive requirements of mutual aid, all institutionalized and enforced under the rule of law in a democratic regime."[2] Although the precise contours of the basic rights endorsed by liberals differ, we cannot go far astray by taking John Stuart Mill's analysis of liberty as canonical: Any liberal theory must provide a strong defense of freedom of speech (as Mill does in chap. 2 of *On Liberty*) and a protected private sphere in which one has great freedom to live one's life as one chooses (as Mill endorses in chaps. 3 and 4). Additionally, basic to the liberal tradition in politics has been a special commitment to religious toleration.[3] The first challenge confronting justificatory liberalism is, then, to show that these basic liberties are indeed victoriously justified; if this cannot be shown, it is unclear whether what I have called "justificatory liberalism" is, in a substantive sense, really liberal at all. As I pointed out in chapter 1, political liberals insist that public justification is the "moral lodestar" of liberalism and, manifestly, justificatory liberalism shares this view. Yet it is not entirely clear what is distinctively *liberal* about this commitment; it certainly seems plausible to conjecture that most political theories in the history of Western thought have claimed to be supported by good reasons that all rational citizens should be able to appreciate.[4] If public justification is an inherently liberal idea, we need to see how it is necessarily related to basic substantive liberal principles such as noninterference, toleration, freedom of speech, and freedom of religion.

In an important sense, nothing I could say here could add much of significance to the weight of the case that liberals have built up over the last few centuries. The entire history of liberal political theory has aimed to demonstrate that all citizens have conclusive reason to embrace a regime of equal liberty. Very little would be accomplished by presenting a synopsis of these crucial yet familiar arguments here.[5] Moreover, the intuitive appeal of these liberties is remarkable; it is quite possible that the attraction of these liberties is greater than any justificatory "foundational" argument seeking to show us why they are attractive.[6] They are, I believe, basic moral intuitions, and as such are at least partially self-justified (sec. 7.3). Nevertheless, it seems hopelessly contentious simply to assert that these basic liberties are obviously victoriously justified, and leave it at that. I shall try to demonstrate how, given a commitment to public justification, fundamental liberal principles follow. This, I think, will enlighten us not only about the justification of basic liberties, but about their relation to the idea of public justification.

On one matter, however, I shall remain silent. Liberals divide sharply of the question of whether the system of victoriously justified norms includes the right to private property. Although it is something of an oversimplification, probably the fundamental divide between the "new liberalism" and classical liberalism is whether private property and the market are victoriously publicly justified.[7] I think it is worth stressing that the mere fact that there is dispute on this matter—that "egalitarian" liberals such as Rawls dispute the classical liberal claim that a regime of private property is conclusively publicly justified and so part of the constitutional essentials[8]— does not itself show that the classical liberal claim is mistaken. A conclusive justification that private property is publicly justified need not be uncontentious. Once again, political liberalism and justificatory liberalism disagree. After telling us that the right to private property is not required by the fundamental principles of justice, Rawls says:

Moreover, even if by some convincing philosophical argument—at least convincing to us and a few like-minded others — we could trace the right of private or social ownership back to first principles or to basic rights, there is good reason for working out a conception of justice that does not do this. For . . . the aim of justice as fairness as a political conception is to resolve the impasse in the democratic tradition as to the way in which social institutions are to be arranged if they are to conform to the freedom and equality of citizens as moral persons. *Philosophical argument alone is most unlikely to con-*

vince either side that the other is correct on a question like that of private or social property in the means of production.[9]

Much depends on what Rawls means by "convincing." If by a philosophical argument "convincing to us, and a few like-minded others" he means that it relies on assumptions that cannot be openly justified to all members of the public, then I concur. But his aim of "resolving the impasse" in the democratic tradition, and his general claim that philosophical argument alone is unlikely to *convince*, is more plausibly interpreted, I think, as implying that his aim is to achieve widespread assent.[10] The aim of justificatory liberalism is not so practical: The fundamental goal is to live up to our commitment to justify our demands on others, and this can be accomplished by a philosophical argument that fails to convince many, yet is openly justified to all.

In what follows I shall not attempt to resolve this fundamental dispute between the classical and new liberalism. Both, I shall argue, can embrace the main elements of justificatory liberalism, though they disagree about what has been victoriously justified and what remains inconclusive.[11] In this respect, justificatory liberalism is not a competitor to these two traditions, but aims to put both in a wider justificatory perspective.

10.2 Toleration, Free Speech, and the Commitment to Public Justification

10.2.1 The Fundamental Liberal Principle

Our concern is whether the attempt to publicly justify principles comes to naught. We are thus supposing that people are committed to public justification—they do not seek simply to browbeat others into accepting their norms or into doing what they would like them to do.[12] I leave aside, then, the skeptical alternative of simply rejecting morality and public justification and instead embracing browbeating, coercing, or ignoring others. Now the reverse side of our commitment to justify imposing our norms on others is a commitment to refrain from imposing norms that cannot be justified. Those committed to public justification seek only to advance what they believe to be justified demands; consequently, they refrain from issuing unjustified demands. This commitment leads directly to liberal toleration; a principle of great practical significance.

Consider, for example, a religious sect with strongly held views about how others should live. Suppose, for instance, they believe that homosexuals are an affront to God and are to be punished. The lives of the members revolve around the sect; its teaching structures their outlook on the world. It is manifest that the sect could not publicly justify a law discriminating against homosexuals. No matter how strongly they hold their views, they will be unable to justify the imposition of discriminatory norms on homosexuals. Unless they ignore their commitment to public justification, they cannot justify their demands on others by citing their religious beliefs. Hence, they must refrain from imposing norms or rules on homosexuals that can only be justified by appeal to their religious beliefs.

That much, I think, is obvious. However, it may seem that the homosexuals are no better off, for they seem equally unable to justify a nondiscriminatory rule to the members of the sect. Within the belief systems of members of the sect, such a nondiscriminatory principle seems assured of defeat. And one can easily see how similar objections might defeat a variety of principles of equal liberty. But I think it is erroneous in this case to depict the homosexuals as demanding that the sectarians accept a norm of nondiscrimination against homosexuals (though, of course, in some cases such a norm may be proposed). Insofar as they are demanding tolerance, the homosexuals merely insist that the sectarian's discriminatory norms cannot be justified to them, and so may not be legitimately imposed on them. That is, they insist that the sectarians live up to their commitment to publicly justify themselves; if they cannot justify their demands, they must refrain from issuing them.

On the basis of this sort of reasoning, many philosophers have endorsed a right of each person to be treated equally, or, as Hadley Arkes says, an "equal right of each to be treated only with justification."[13] S.I. Benn and R.S. Peters, for example, defend the principle that *"none shall be held to have a claim to better treatment than another, in advance of good grounds being produced."*[14] They continue:

Understood in this way, the principle of equality does not prescribe positively that all humans be treated alike; it is a presumption against treating them differently, in any respect, until grounds for distinction have been shewn [sic]. It does not assume, therefore, a quality which all men have to the same degree, which is the ground of the presumption, for to say that there is a presumption means that no grounds need be shewn. The onus of justification rests on whoever would make distinctions.

. . . Presume equality until there is a reason to presume otherwise.[15]

This is an immensely popular argument; Richard Flathman, Isaiah Berlin, and William Frankena—to name just a few—endorse it.[16] Such philosophers uphold the principle of equality (E):

E: Any discriminatory act, any action that provides differential advantages or burdens, stands in need of justification.

However, nothing so strong follows from the practice of public justification and the accompanying notion of liberal toleration. Consider again our religious sect. The principle of equality would seem to require that the sectarians refrain from disadvantaging homosexuals because, *ex hypothesi*, they cannot justify such disadvantages to the homosexuals. But surely this is unreasonable. Suppose that members of the congregation are about to sit down to their Sunday afternoon brunch, and a slightly hungry homosexual appears at their door. Does liberal toleration require that the sectarians justify not inviting him— that they must come up with a sound justification (one that the homosexual has good reason to accept), or else invite him to brunch? At one point Benn thought so; he insisted that "discrimination in treatment between persons requires *moral* justification: it is not enough simply to *prefer* one to another since that involves regarding another person solely from the point of view of one's own satisfactions; respect for a person involves a right to be considered from his *own* standpoint."[17] So it would seem that the sectarians have to justify to the homosexual, from his standpoint, why he is not being asked to brunch. But surely this is implausible: The sectarians are not being intolerant or disrespectful when they choose to eat together rather than invite itinerant homosexuals.[18] Nor does it seem that they are in any way required to justify their actions to him. To put it baldly, with whom they decide to have brunch is none of his business. To be sure, in some societies a special nondiscrimination norm may be justified, according to which one does have to justify discriminatory behavior if, for example, one is offering services to the public.[19] But in the absence of such an explicit norm, it does not seem that one must justify every action that disadvantages others.

To tolerate others does not require that we have much to do with them, much less invite them to brunch. After all, we tolerate that to which we object, or of which we disapprove, and so it is not surprising that we will seek to distance ourselves from it.[20] Toleration is a minimal but fundamental requirement that we not impose upon others without justification. Tolerance requires, as Bruce Ackerman says, that we allow "others to go their own way"[21]—that we respect the freedom of others by refraining from imposing our personal norms, principles, and values on them. So liberal toleration does indeed prohibit unjustified impositions on homosexuals by the sectarians, such as demands that homosexuals conform to discriminatory norms or interferences. Rather than the principle of equality, underlying liberal public justification and tolerance is what might be called the liberal principle (L):

L: Imposition on others requires justification; unjustified impositions are unjust.

Certainly this is fundamental to liberal political and legal theory.[22] As Joel Feinberg says,

most writers . . . have endorsed a kind of "presumption in favor of liberty" requiring that whenever a legislator is faced with a choice between imposing a legal duty on citizens or leaving them at liberty, other things being equal, he should leave individuals free to make their own choices. Liberty should be the norm; coercion always requires some special justification.[23]

The basic idea, then, is that freedom to live one's own life as one chooses is the benchmark or presumption; departures from that condition—where you demand that another live her life according to your judgments—require additional justification. And if these demands cannot be justified, then we are committed to tolerating these other ways of living.

To be sure, this is a vague principle. My formulation refers to the general idea of "imposition," while Feinberg has in mind "coercion"; alternative formulations focus on the notion of "interference."[24] None of these is identical, and considerable interpretive work needs to be done before the principle ushers in specific prohibitions. This is precisely my point about justified principles. Recall John Gray's objection (sec. 9.4.1) that even if accepted, such principles are so vague as to be of little or no worth. As soon as we attempt to specify precisely what freedom requires, the principle, suggests Gray, becomes hopelessly indeterminate. As Alexander Bickel remarked about "majestic concepts" such as freedom of speech, "men may in full and equal reason and good faith hold differing views about . . . [their] proper meaning and specific application."[25]

If no relatively precise interpretation of the concepts can be justifiably selected over others, Gray's charge of indeterminacy or vagueness would be damning. What possible good could it do to justify principles so vague as to be inapplicable? This is a fundamental challenge to justificatory liberalism on which I shall focus in chapter 11. But note for now that the very vagueness or abstractness of principles greatly *enhances* their justifiability. The claim that some specific interpretation of the liberal principle can be victoriously justified over all others seems pretty dubious: There is lively debate on the nature of freedom, coercion, and interference, and it is hard to see how any interpretation specific enough to guide legislative decisions can be victoriously justified for all members of the public. In essence, it seems that victoriously justified liberal principles are cases of nested inconclusiveness (sec. 9.4.3). What is victoriously justified is a range of conceptions of, say, the fundamental liberal principle; within that range, as we shall see, it may be impossible to victoriously justify a particular interpretation. But that is quite consistent with claiming that a principle has been publicly justified, namely that {Conception$_1$ $\underline{V}$ Conception$_2$ $\underline{V}$ . . . Conception$_n$} is justified, and hence Conception$_{n+1}$ is defeated. This provides a nonpopulist interpretation of Rawls's "method of avoidance":

> The work of abstraction, then, is not gratuitous: not abstraction for abstraction's sake. Rather, it is a way of continuing public discussion when shared understandings of lesser generality have broken down. We should be prepared to find that the deeper the conflict, the higher the level of abstraction we must ascend to get a clear and uncluttered view of its roots.[26]

The idea is not that the actual assent of everyone, or even the actual assent or support of all reasonable citizens, can be achieved in this way.[27] Nor does it follow—though of course it is a hope—that once abstract principles haven been (victoriously) justified, discussion may proceed to victoriously justify more specific interpretations. The point is that the abstract principles serve to exclude defeated proposals and delimit the range in which justifiable controversy can occur. This, as we shall see, is by no means insignificant.

10.2.2 Free Speech and Public Justification

In his work on constitutional interpretation, David A.J. Richards has shown that the basic notion of liberal toleration, and its accompanying ideas of respect for the right of conscience and the liberty of others, can be understood as the organizing principle of American constitutionalism.[28] The right to free speech has an especially intimate relation to the idea of public justification. I have already argued that, given our epistemic situation, we can claim victory for our justifications only if they meet the publicity condition (sec. 9.3.3). Dissenters, I argued, must have ample opportunity to challenge and try to defeat our proposed justifications before we can declare victory. This idea is the core of Mill's case for free speech; he insists that only if people are allowed to challenge a belief can we have confidence in it:

> There is the greatest difference between presuming an opinion to be true, because, with every opportunity for contesting it, it has not been refuted, and assuming its truth for the purpose of not permitting its refutation. Complete

liberty of contradicting and disproving our opinion, is the very condition which justifies us in assuming its truth for purposes of action; and on no other terms can a being with human faculties have any rational assurance of being right.[29]

The core liberal commitment to freedom of speech, then, flows directly from the requirements of public reason.[30] "The public use of one's reason must always be free, and it alone can bring about enlightenment among men."[31]

That *public* reason should be free merits emphasis. As Locke stressed, moral reasoning is the proper concern of everyone, and so free moral inquiry is not to be restricted to an elite.[32] Suppose for a moment that a moral elite does exist, in the sense that some reasoners are apt to reach more reliable conclusions than are others about what is publicly justified (see sec. 11.2.2). Because of Betty's epistemological authority over her own beliefs (secs. 8.4, 9.3.3), she has a privileged (though not unassailable) position regarding what she is justified in believing. Since the conclusions of the elite about what she is justified in believing are likely to be less than conclusive, unless her assent is obtained (hence invoking, rather than overriding, her epistemic authority), the elite will not be in a position to demand that she embrace their conclusions. Furthermore, since she does have privileged access to her own beliefs, unless Betty is able to contribute to the discussion by proposing defeaters to the elite's justifications, the elite will not be able to claim that the publicity condition has been met, so they will not be able to achieve the requisite standard of proof to claim victory.

The principle of free speech is thus foundational to liberalism; it is understandable that liberals such as Mill have insisted that "human beings should be free to form opinions, and to express their opinions without reserve."[33] Of course, even Mill acknowledges that speech loses its protection when it becomes an incitement to "mischievous acts." However, even if we consider speech simply as speech, it seems possible that our liberty to speak could rightfully be limited in the interests of public justification itself. As Stephen Holmes has shown, public discussion may be protected and enhanced by "gag rules."[34] Suppose, for example, a society is deeply divided on religious matters; each side presses its own inconclusive justifications on the other. So intensely do people feel about these matters that public debate is dominated by religious disputes, yet so inconclusive are these views that there is little hope of achieving any sort of closure to the debate, either in an epistemological or a practical sense (see chap. 11). This religious standoff may distract from a number of other important issues on which justifications may actually be forthcoming. In such a society, a gag rule that prohibits public debate on the religious matters—for example, in the legislature— may well advance the interests of public justification. Freed from this intractable and distracting controversy, public debate and justification may be improved.

I note this only as a possibility, to underline the extent to which even a principle as fundamental as free speech is subject to limitation. Despite the insistence of Justice Hugo L. Black—who famously announced that the First Amendment's proclamation that Congress shall make "no law respecting an establishment of religion" meant just what it said: "no law"—it seems impossible to insist that no restrictions to speech can be justified.[35] However, I do not wish to endorse Stephen Holmes's interpretation of the First Amendment as a gag rule for, as I shall now argue, another—or, rather, a complementary—interpretation suggests itself.

10.3 Immunities as Defeated Proposals

Normally we think of liberalism as upholding a number of basic rights, such as the right to free speech and the right to worship as one wishes. But the First Amendment to the U.S. Constitution does not assert *rights* to religion, free speech, or freedom of the press.[36] Rather, it announces that "Congress shall make no law respecting an establishment of religion, or prohibiting the free exercise thereof; or abridging the freedom of speech, or of the press. . . ." In Wesley Hohfeld's terms, the First Amendment gives citizens an *immunity* corresponding to a disability on the part of Congress to pass such laws; that is, the crux of the "right to freedom of religion" as specified by the First Amendment is an inability or lack of authority on the part of Congress to pass laws establishing a religion.[37] If we conjoin the fundamental liberal principle with an understanding of the First Amendment as announcing Congress's lack of authority to impose laws establishing a religion or interfering with the free exercise of religion, we are led to interpret the First Amendment as affirming that no such laws can be justified. That is, the First Amendment is to be understood as a conclusion drawn from several hundred years of religious debates: No religious sect can justify the imposition on others of its religious doctrines. All purported attempts to do so—and, as we know, the sixteenth and seventeenth centuries were characterized by many such attempts—had been defeated. Although each sect claimed to have the truth, each was notoriously unable even to begin to show that others were committed to it. As Locke observed:

For whatsoever any church believes it believes to be true; and the contrary unto those things it pronounces to be error. So that controversy between churches about the truth of their doctrines and the purity of their worship *is on both sides equal;* nor is there any judge . . . upon earth, by whose sentence it can be determined.[38]

Consequently, religion was determined to be a matter of private judgment—individuals have diverse beliefs on religious matters, none of which can be publicly justified.

An objection can be raised: Arguments, not conclusions, can be defeated. That is, at most the several centuries of religious dispute could be taken as showing that none of the arguments raised thus far were successful, but this does not show that the claim "Religion X ought to be established" cannot be publicly justified. And strictly speaking, this is so; inferences, not beliefs, are subject to defeat. Nevertheless, several centuries of argument did provide a considerable presumption that a successful argument establishing a religion was not on the horizon. As Locke pointed out, conflicting arguments based on religious premises are unable to establish their claims publicly, while Rousseauean insistence that a public religion was necessary for civil peace or harmony was belied by the ensuing civil disruption engendered by religious conflicts.[39] The conclusion to be drawn from the religious politics of the sixteenth and seventeenth centuries was that all known arguments endorsing establishment were notoriously weak, and that establishment was for this reason to be taken off the political agenda.

The removal, of course, was not for this reason alone. Stephen Holmes is surely right that the establishment clause was also intended to free politics from this hopelessly divisive issue. And I am not rejecting the more traditional narrative, according to which religious strife led to a sort of exhaustion, and was removed from the political agenda for the most practical of reasons. But these practical accounts have their limits. Holmes's analysis of gag rules, for instance, applies not only to the First Amendment, but to the gag rule of 1836, in which the U.S. House of Representatives resolved that "all petitions, memorials, resolutions, propositions, or papers, relating in any way, or to any extent whatsoever, to the subject of slavery, or the abolition of slavery, shall, without being either printed or referred, be laid on the table, and that no further action whatever shall be had thereon."[40] Although this, too, may have served the practical aim of allowing normal politics to proceed, it clearly is a different sort of accommodation from the First Amendment, for a public justification on this issue was indeed available. In contrast to the 1836 gag rule, underlying the First Amendment is an epistemological tale: Confidence that religious arguments provided the requisite sort of public reason faded and eventually was extinguished.

The claim, then, is that liberal political theory removes certain proposals from the political agenda, not simply on the practical ground that they are too divisive, but because they have been defeated in public discussion. This liberal conviction—that impositions of religion were defeated—evolved into a more general conviction that justifications for imposing ways of living were also defeated. To be sure, this is an idea even more vague than that of establishment; indeed, it seems consistent with a commitment to a public, though abstract, idea of "human flourishing."[41] It does, though, seem to rule out claims that any relatively specific ways of living—in terms not only of God to be worshipped, but of occupations to be followed, personal ideals to embraced, and so on—can be justifiably imposed on us. Many suppose that this shows that liberals are committed to a "pluralism" of basic values, but as Charles Larmore has stressed, this does not follow:

> [Pluralism] . . . asserts that the forms of moral concern, as well as the forms of self-realization, are in the end not one, but many. It stands, therefore, in opposition to religious and metaphysical conceptions of a single source of value. Liberalism, however, does not arise from an acceptance of pluralism. Instead, it seeks to found the principles of political association upon a core morality that reasonable people can accept, despite their natural tendency to disagree about comprehensive visions of the nature of value, and so in particular about the merits of monism and pluralism. The expectation of reasonable disagreement lies at a different, more reflective, level than pluralism. It responds to the religious and metaphysical disenchantment of the world, not by affirming it, as pluralism seems to do, but rather by recognizing that like other deep conceptions of value this disenchantment is an idea about which reasonable people are likely to disagree, as indeed they do.[42]

Leaving aside the reliance on political liberalism's reasonable people thesis (sec. 9.1.2), Larmore seems right that liberalism insists that all arguments endorsing the imposition of some specific vision of the good are defeated, and so no state has the authority to "establish" a theory of value. However, the plausibility of pluralist arguments is not quite so irrelevant to this as Larmore's analysis suggests. Suppose a liberal is committed (as many are) to some form of pluralism. Given this, a monist who seeks to impose his way of living on others must justify to the pluralist that the monistic imposition is justified. Now suppose that among pluralists, pluralism is personally justified; all efforts to show the pluralist that she is committed to a monistic theory have been defeated. The liberal pluralist's main claim—that the imposition of specific ways of living cannot be justified—is thus upheld. And this would be true even if the pluralist could not show that everyone must adopt pluralism.

This merits emphasis. A doctrine such as pluralism can be a *defeater doctrine* even if it cannot be conclusively publicly justified. If pluralism is openly justified for some citizens, then proposals to "establish" some view of the good life will be defeated. This is entirely consistent with some citizens' being openly justified in rejecting pluralism. We can now appreciate the fundamental role of a number of doctrines associated with liberalism—such as pluralism, value subjectivism, or the fundamental value of individual autonomy—which, though not themselves conclusively publicly justified, nevertheless are defeaters of illiberal "establishment" proposals. Doctrines that are not themselves publicly justified can play a crucial role in public justification.

10.4 The Public and Private

10.4.1 Private Matters

Freedom of religion, and more generally freedom of conscience, constitutes a recognition that certain issues are off the public agenda. As I have put it, liberals have concluded that proposals to impose public religions or specific ideals of life have been defeated, and so cannot overcome the barrier posed by L, the liberal principle. This idea of taking certain areas off the political agenda can be extended to the general idea of a private sphere. As Stanley Benn writes:

The conception of privacy is closely bound to the liberal ideal. The totalitarian claims that everything a person is and does has significance for society at large. He sees the state as the self-conscious organization of civil society, existing for society's well-being. The public or political universe is all-inclusive: *all* roles are public, and every function, whether political, economic, scholarly, or artistic, can be interpreted as creating a public responsibility for and in its performance.[43]

In *Liberty* Mill famously argues for a criterion distinguishing those acts for which one may be responsible to the public—either in the form of the government or to other individuals—and that part of one's life in which one is not subject to the authority of others. Mill insists that "the only part of the conduct of any one, for which he is amenable to society, is that which concerns others. In the part which merely concerns himself, his independence is, of right, absolute. Over himself, over his own body and mind, the individual is sovereign."[44]

It is often maintained that Mill's distinction between actions that concern others and those that merely affect oneself is "a completely untenable doctrine" because it is "quite impossible to distinguish that part of a person's behavior which affects himself and that part which concerns others."[45] However, as C.L. Ten has argued, rather than interpreting Mill as distinguishing two distinct spheres of action—the self-regarding and the other-regarding— we ought to understand him as distinguishing two types of reasons for interfering with a person's actions. As Ten points out, "there are various reasons why people may wish to interfere with the conduct of others. Mill's point is that the case for intervention must rest on reasons other than, for example, the mere dislike or disapproval of the conduct."[46]

On Ten's interpretation, Mill's harm principle disallows some reasons for interference—mere dislike, conviction that another's action is sinful, ungodly, or unnatural—while admitting that harm done to another is always a reason for intervention (though not always conclusive).[47] The harm principle is thus a further articulation of the idea that we are immune to justified interferences on the grounds of religion or ideas of the good life. Impositions on others justified in terms of dislike, disapproval, sinfulness, and so on, are disallowed—they are not good reasons for intervention. And to say that is to declare that they are defeated—those who do not share the disliking or understanding of sinfulness have no reason to accept such justifications. And, since Mill accepts the liberal principle that "in practical matters, the burthen [sic] of proof is supposed to be with those who are against liberty; who contend for any restriction or prohibition,"[48] it follows that one is immune from interventions based on such reasons. These immunities— held against not only government, but individuals generally—mark out the private sphere.

10.4.2 Public Concerns

Mill's harm principle is not simply about what cannot be justified; harm to others is a reason that can overcome the presumption against interference. Basic to liberalism is the claim that government is justified in interfering with a person's life to protect what Locke called the "civil interests" of others—"life, liberty, health and indolence of body; and the possessions of outward things, such as money, lands, houses, furniture, and the like."[49] Unless these basic interests are protected against invasion by others, peaceful social life cannot be attained. Consequently, liberal social contract theories have been insistent that the benefits of civil peace—and the costs of conflict—are so great that all rational individuals have conclusive reason to embrace norms that protect these interests. Although social contract theorists have often relied on some form of actual consent to justify public enforcement of these norms,[50] it should be manifest that, according to justificatory liberalism, hypothetical contractual arguments are genuinely justificatory. When the hypothetical contractualist argues that all rational individuals would consent to norms protecting these interests, it is being claimed that we all have conclusive reasons to adopt these norms: if (1) people are rational, (2) they have conclusive reason to embrace norms that are necessary for peace, then (3) they would do so. Thus, hypothetical contractual arguments are justificatory because the claim that some set of norms "would be (universally) consented to" indicates that they are publicly justified. It cannot be overemphasized that for hypothetical contractual arguments to justify, they must provide conclusive reasons for their preferred principles. Because they do not rely on actual consent, hypothetical contractual arguments claim to override the epistemic authority (sec. 9.3.3) of actual individuals who withhold consent. In contrast, actual consent contracts can make do with far less compelling arguments, as they employ, rather than override, the epistemic authority of the consenting individuals.

Liberalism, then, does not turn on the claim that we all consent to the conditions of peace, but rather that all individuals have conclusive reason to embrace norms protecting basic interests. Lockean "civil interests" are sufficiently general that, regardless of an individual's values, each prefers a regime of (1) universal protection of the basic interests to (2) universal nonprotection. This, certainly, is the upshot of Hobbes's account of the state of nature. The real challenge to this contractualist claim is not, I think, that everyone has reason to prefer (1) to (2), but that many have good reason to be free riders, and so prefer to universal protection (3) a regime in which others comply, but they do not. Again, though, we must remember that our concern is not simply people's preferences, but what norms can be publicly justified. Keeping this clearly in mind, the public justification of norms embodying (3) is not possible: Free riders will not be able to justify their free riding to the compilers.

Confronted by the choice between a normative system protecting everyone's basic interest or no normative system at all, the Hobbesian conclusion is unassailable. As Kurt Baier concludes, "Hobbes' argument is sound. Moralities are systems of principles whose acceptance by everyone as overruling the dictates of self-interest is in the interest of everyone alike."[51] David Gauthier's theory is also an example of this approach:

If social institutions and practices can benefit all, then some set of social arrangements should be acceptable to all as a co-operative venture. Each person's concern to fulfil her own interests should ensure her willingness to join her fellows in a venture assuring her an expectation of increased fulfillment. She may of course reject some proposed venture as insufficiently advantageous to her when she considers both the distribution of benefits that it affords, and the availability of alternatives. Affording mutual advantage is a necessary condition for the acceptability of a set of social arrangements as a co-operative venture, not a sufficient condition. But we may suppose that some set affording mutual advantage will also be mutually acceptable; a contractarian theory must set out conditions for sufficiency.[52]

Gauthier, then, argues that an institution is justified only if it advances the good of (i.e., benefits) all. It is unlikely that any arrangement will maximize the promotion of value from every perspective; individuals may have to compromise on arrangements that promote the values of all to a reasonable extent, but do not maximally promote anyone's values. But the important point is that if (1) we are committed to making moral demands on others (sec. 8.4) and (2) so are committed to public justification, then (3) we all have good reason to embrace moral principles that promote the values of all to a reasonable extent, for such principles can be justified to everyone. We are thus led to the idea of a system of moral demands that promotes the good of each or, we might say, the common good.[53]

It hardly needs to be pointed out just how abstract is the notion of such a system of moral demands. Although, in the abstract, a system of moral demands is clearly justified, for everyone has excellent reason to embrace it, the specific requirements of the justifiable system are a matter of reasonable dispute. And even those elements that we can be confident are conclusively justified—for example, norms prohibiting harm to the civil interests of others, specifying some system of holdings, allowing a person to control information about her personal relations,[54] protecting basic interests in health—are themselves subject to legitimate interpretive controversy. Indeed, the very idea of a harm to another turns out to be exceedingly complicated and contentious.[55] Once again we confront a nested inconclusiveness: The notion of a harm to another can be articulated through a number of competing conceptions. But it does not follow from this that the concept of a harm to another is altogether empty, or that no explications of it are defeated.

10.4.3 Liberal Principles

My aim is the foregoing was nothing so grand as identifying the complete set of victoriously justified liberal principles. First and foremost, I have tried to show that public victorious justifications are possible; second, I have attempted to identify some of the basic components of a publicly justified liberal morality. Freedom of speech, religious toleration extended to wide toleration of competing conceptions of the good life, antiestablishmentarianism (aimed at both religion and substantive views of human perfection), and a sphere of privacy are fundamental liberal commitments. Liberal public concerns focus on honoring these commitments but also on protecting fundamental civil interests, such as bodily integrity. Civil interests also include the maintenance of some sort of justified system of property rights. Most abstractly, liberal moralities accept that a system of restraints that advances the interests of everyone can be publicly justified; hence appeal to the common benefit is both legitimate and important in liberal moral discourse.

10.5 Why The Reflexivity Requirement Is Misguided

Paradoxically, the most powerful challenge to the possibility of publicly justified moral principles emanates from some proponents of public justification. For some proponents have been persuaded to accept the *reflexivity requirement,* namely, that a theory of public justification itself must be publicly justified.[56] To embrace the reflexivity requirement is to transform the ideal of public justification from the basis of an ethic of respect to the point of departure for skepticism. Happily, to embrace the requirement is also misguided. Much of the effort of such philosophers as Fred D'Agostino has gone into showing that public justification is an essentially contested concept, and so cannot itself be publicly justified. I shall simply grant the latter claim. It is not unduly modest to admit that the argument for weak foundationalism in part I, and the analysis of public justification in this part, are not conclusive. They have not, even I must admit, resolved the problems of epistemology beyond reasonable doubt. Consequently, the epistemic theory on which the public justification of liberal principles rests is not itself publicly (conclusively) justified.

A reflexivity requirement certainly appears to be warranted. Liberals claim that we cannot browbeat others into accepting our norms—they must be conclusively justified. But since what constitutes a conclusive justification is itself reasonably disputed, it would appear that liberals for

just that reason have failed to justify their basic moral principles conclusively. Aren't liberals just browbeating nonliberals when they insist that
their basic principles are conclusively justified? Someone with a religious
epistemology will argue that liberal principles are not conclusively justified, perhaps because they do not have divine sanction. Liberalism thus
appears as just another sect trying to impose its views on others.[57]

Throughout I have been stressing that the commitment to justify oneself to others arises out of one's own belief system: It is because Betty is
committed to making moral demands on others that are not mere brow-
beatings that she is committed to justifying herself to them. Let us, then,
remain firmly fixed on Betty's perspective, and see how things look to
her. She is, as I said, committed to the use of public reason because she is
committed to the practice of moral demands; confronting Alf, she acknowledges that her demand that he embrace norm *N—if it is to be a
moral demand rather than browbeating*—must be openly justified to Alf.
Surely at this point, her understanding of what it means "to openly justify herself to Alf" is just that, *her understanding*. Given her moral and
epistemic norms, she is committed to employing her public reason in
making demands, and she concludes that these must be openly justified
to Alf. Suppose that, accepting weak foundationalism, she does this.
Given her acceptance of WF, when making up her own mind whether
her demand is justified, she must examine Alf's beliefs and his epistemic
norms. That is, given her own epistemic commitments, to answer the
question "Is *N* openly justifiable to Alf?" she must consult Alf's beliefs
and norms. Suppose that she has done all this, and concludes that *N* is
victoriously justified.

Alf, however, disagrees. Alf, let us say, embraces a religious epistemology of some sort, according to which *N* is not justifiable in his system
of beliefs. In considering this, Betty has to decide whether the fact that,
according to his favored epistemology, Alf does not have reason to embrace *N* implies that he does not have a conclusive reason to embrace *N*.
A sound argument for the reflexivity requirement would be based on the
following claim:

(1) If (a) Alf is justified in accepting an epistemological theory T_A;
and (b) according to T_A his acceptance of norm *N* is not justified;
then (c) it must be that his acceptance of *N* is not *conclusively*
justified.

Underlying this seems another claim:

(2) If (a) Alf is justified in accepting T_A and (b) if T_A rejects *N*, then
(c) it must be reasonable for him to reject *N;* but if (d) it is

reasonable for him to reject *N*, it cannot be the case that he has a conclusive reason to accept it.

Claim (2) is mistaken. Alf can be openly justified in accepting an epistemology that says *N* is not justified when in fact he really has conclusive reason to accept it. And that is because:

(3) One can be justified in accepting an epistemological theory that yields bizarre judgments in some cases.

Even good theories can lead to some very odd results. Alf's acceptance of T_A may pass the threshold for a credible belief, yet, like so many theories in epistemology, it may sometimes yield some pretty strange results. Indeed, the last twenty years of analytic epistemology show that every plausible theory can generate some bizarre judgments.

Betty, then, can have both of the following as justified beliefs: (1) Alf is justified in accepting an epistemological theory according to which *N* is not conclusively justified; (2) *N* is conclusively openly justifiable in Alf's system of reasons and beliefs. The important point here is that Betty's commitment to public justification and Alf's epistemic authority require that she only demand that he accept a norm when he has conclusive reason to do so. This requirement can be met even if Alf dissents on the basis of his justified acceptance of a competing epistemology.

So Betty is not committed to concluding that, just because Alf's epistemological theory deems her proposal to be unjustified, she must be mistaken to believe it is conclusively justified. But this may not appease proponents of reflexivity. What they want to know is why Betty can base her conclusions about what is publicly justified on *her* view of conclusive reasons, when she cannot publicly justify that view. How can she employ it as the basis of her claim that *N* is victoriously publicly justified? If Alf has epistemic authority to decide whether or not to accept *N*, which can only be overridden by a conclusive justification, then doesn't Alf also have epistemic authority over what epistemological theory he embraces as showing what is a conclusive argument?

Alf surely has epistemic authority over what epistemic theory he accepts to explain his beliefs. But it does not follow that Betty's justification of a moral norm must be endorsed by Alf's theory. And that is because:

(A) Betty justifiably believes that *N* has been conclusively justified to Alf.

is distinct from, and does not in any way imply:

(B) Betty has conclusively justified to Alf that she has conclusively justified N to him.

As a moral agent committed to public justification, Betty is committed to having justified beliefs of type (A) before she demands that Alf accept a norm. That is, she must have a justified belief that the demand she is imposing is one that Alf has conclusive reason to accept. It is a philosophic confusion—perhaps the result of a quest to ground our justified beliefs in something outside of our own belief systems—to conclude that she can only be justified in holding (A) if she is justified in holding (B). According to (B), Betty must not only conclusively justify N to Alf; she must conclusively justify that she has conclusively justified it by showing Alf that the standards of conclusive justification she employs are conclusively justified. If it is not enough that (A)— that Betty has a justified belief that she has conclusively justified to Alf that he is committed to N—why is it enough that she justifiably believes (B)—that she has conclusively justified to Alf that he has been conclusively shown that N is the thing to believe? What if Alf disputes (B)? It would seem that the logic of the reflexivity argument would drive Betty toward having to *show* Alf that he has *been shown* that he has *been shown* that N is the thing to believe. And why stop here?

The requirement that one must publicly justify one's understanding of public justification has, I think, affinities to the "Know, Know" thesis in epistemology—that to know β, one must know that one knows it. For D'Agostino and others, to publicly justify N one must publicly justify that one has publicly justified it. Just as in the case of the "Know, Know" thesis, this leads to skepticism. And because many proponents of public justification embrace the reflexivity requirement and succumb to its attendant skepticism, they are driven toward a consensual and populist notion of public reason. As with the "Know, Know" thesis, I conclude that we ought to reject the requirement that we must publicly justify our concept of public justification.

In developing an account of liberalism, our first aim is to show that fundamental liberal principles are victoriously justified—that the case for them is conclusive. To accomplish this, we formulate a theory of liberalism. Our theory of liberalism can accomplish its task of showing that liberal principles are conclusively justified without showing itself to be conclusively justified. Our concern is the conclusive justification of substantive liberal political principles, not the conclusive justification of any specific philosophical theory of liberalism.

CHAPTER 11

Inconclusive Public Reasoning

11.1 Two Unacceptable Responses to Inconclusiveness

11.1.1 The Inconclusiveness of the Particular

I argued in the previous chapter that liberal public justification is possible. As John Gray stresses, however, the great difficulty confronting liberal public justification is the generality and abstractness of the victoriously justified principles. The principles that can be victoriously justified, I have suggested, are really instances of nested inconclusiveness.[1] Although the requirements of victorious public justification can be met, they are demanding; it is to not be expected that relatively specific interpretations of these principles can also be victoriously justified.[2] We should expect that even though a set of proposals can be victoriously justified, within the set no conclusive arguments will be forthcoming. Although we can justify embracing the concept (e.g., a right to free speech), no specific conception can be justified. But, as Rawls tells us, a conception supplies the principles and rules required to apply the concept in actual cases.[3] Consequently, if the justifications of specific conceptions are inconclusive, liberals have no way to apply their justified principles. Although I have insisted that the abstract principles have exclusionary force—they exclude some possible norms as permissible—it must be acknowledged that they often provide little in the way of positive guidance.

Philosophers can keep arguing (and publishing) about these unresolved issues—indeed, *these* are just the issues that philosophers typically *do* argue and write about. However, as citizens we are in a different position. Whether the right to life allows or prohibits abortion, whether it includes some animals, whether income is to redistributed, whether property rights are to be limited or altered to protect the environment—all these are pressing matters of practice, not just material for philosophical reflection. If, as seems likely, most of our specific moral disputes result in epistemological standoffs, what are liberal citizens committed to public justification to do right here and now? If Betty has an undefeated justification for redistributing Alf's wealth to Charlie, but she acknowledges that it is not victorious, what should she do? Let us consider two obvious, though ultimately flawed, options: waiting for victory or making moral demands based on her inconclusively justified belief.

11.1.2 Waiting for Victory (or Defeat): Moral Anarchism

On the face of it, there is much to be said for waiting until her proposal is victorious (or has been defeated). Betty is, after all, committed to public justification, and in a fairly obvious sense she has yet to justify her demand to Alf; she has not yet *shown* that he has reason to adopt her view and abandon his competing position. So imposition of her view on him would seem unjustified. This response seems to respect both Alf's epistemic authority (sec. 9.3.3) and the liberal principle (sec. 10.2.1). If interference with another requires justification, then the burden of proof would seem to fall squarely on Betty, for she is making a demand that would limit Alf's liberty. Until her public justification of restraints is shown to be victorious, she seems committed to noninterference. Supposing that outright victory is rare, the upshot would be a regime of minimal restraints, or perhaps even some version of anarchism in which we simply "agree to differ."[4]

To evaluate this option we must distinguish two sorts of inconclusive public justifications: what I have already called nested inconclusive justifications and what might be deemed *merely inconclusive* justifications. As I have stressed, a nested inconclusive justification appeals to a victoriously justified principle for which no victoriously justified specific interpretation is to be had.[5] In contrast, a merely inconclusive proposal is one that is not put forward as an articulation of a victoriously justified principle, but stands, as it were, on its own. The distinction between these two sorts of inconclusive proposals is not hard and fast or clear for all to see, and some may seek to present the latter in the guise of the former. Nevertheless, providing an interpretation of a justified principle can be distinguished, if not always clearly, from offering a distinct principle. Compare, for example, the following two sorts of claims:

(A) Alf claims that "Victoriously justified principle P requires Φ," where what is inconclusive is the claim that P requires Φ, not that P is a victoriously justified principle.

(B) Betty claims "Principle P requires Φ," where it is inconclusive whether P is a publicly justified principle.

In case (B), the wait-for-victory option really does seem appropriate; it has not been adequately justified. Here Betty is seeking to override other people's epistemic authority but has not been able to show that they are committed to *P*. It seems quite right that the liberal principle is a barrier to such proposals; it insists that others should be free to go about their business unless interference is justified *to them*, and this is precisely what Betty has not been able to do. Alf's demand (A) is more complicated. Here, we suppose, a principle *P* has been victoriously justified, so others such as Betty have conclusive reason to embrace it and to act in accordance with it (other things equal). The problem, however, is that it remains an open question just what action *P* requires: Alf has an undefeated, unvictorious case that *P* requires Φ, but Betty offers a competing inconclusive opinion. This seems a genuine instance of nested inconclusiveness—he is offering an undefeated yet unvictorious interpretation of a victoriously justified principle. In this case, Alf's ultimate appeal is to a principle that Betty has been shown she has reason to accept. For Alf and Betty to do nothing at all in this case would be, for practical purposes at any rate, to embrace the *defeated* option that *P* is not justified or is irrelevant to practice. If Alf waits until his specific proposal is victorious, and Betty waits until her specific proposal is victorious, then no specific course of action will be justified—*P* will be of no consequence.

It is tempting to think that the distinction between nested and merely inconclusive proposals is empty: Any proposal, it might be said, can be framed in terms of an appeal to some vague principle. But this is to miss the point. Recall C.L. Ten's interpretation of the harm principle as constraining public discourse by disallowing some sorts of reasons (e.g., paternalist and perfectionist) and requiring that cases be made out in terms of harm to others (sec. 10.3.1). In a similar way, the requirement that proposals to impose demands on others be anchored in victoriously justified principles regulates public discourse, insisting that reasonable cases for regulation must be plausibly construed as following from victoriously justified principles.

The distinction between merely inconclusive and nested inconclusive proposals, I believe, allows us to unite two aspects of public reason. Rawls understands public reason as reasoning based on justified principles: "Only a political conception of justice that all citizens might reasonably be expected to endorse can serve as *a basis* of public reason and justification."[6] On the face of it, this is puzzling; one would think that the justified political conception is the *outcome* of public reason, not the *basis* of it. Both descriptions are accurate. First, the public conception of justice is indeed the outcome of public reasoning insofar as it is victoriously justified. But once articulated, the public conception becomes the basis of further public reasoning. Although victorious justifications are no longer forthcoming, inconclusive proposals based on the public conception are exercises in public reason. In contrast, inconclusive demands on others that cannot be expressed in terms of the public conception—merely inconclusive demands—must be dismissed.

11.1.3 Imposition of One's Judgment: Moral Dogmatism

Always waiting for victorious justification would commit us to a life in which victoriously justified principles find no expression. The alternative would seem to rely on one's best judgment about what is publicly justified, and take that as determining what moral demands one can make on others. For Kant, relying on one's individual judgment characterizes the state of nature:

Although experience teaches us that men live in violence and are prone to fight one another before the advent of external compulsive legislation, it is not experience that makes public lawful coercion necessary. The necessity of public lawful coercion does not rest on a fact, but on an a priori Idea of reason, for, even if men to be ever so good natured and righteous before a public lawful state of society is established, individual men, nations and states can never be certain they are secure against violence from one another because each will have the right to do what *seems just and good to him*, entirely independently of the opinion of others.[7]

Kant goes on to insist that justice is absent in the state of nature because each relies on his own judgment, and thus "when there is a controversy concerning rights *(jus controversum)*, no competent judge can be found to render a decision having the force of law."[8] Indeed, Hobbes, Locke, and Kant all maintain that the chief inconveniences of the state of nature arise from individuals relying on their individual, controversial, judgments about natural rights and natural law.[9] The basic problems are two, one moral and one practical.

The moral flaw of the state of nature ruled by individual judgment is that we act without justification. As I have already argued, to impose an undefeated but unvictorious public justification on another fails to meet the demands of public justification. To have satisfied yourself that your demands are justified is far short of showing others that your demands are justified. If public justification is the moral lodestar of liberalism, and reflects a commitment to respect for persons,[10] relying on one's individual judgment in this way manifests disrespect and is unjust. Recall that Jeffrey Reiman argues that imposing inadequately

justified principles on another is an act of *subjugation:* One is sup-
planting the other's own judgment about what the other should do,
and replacing it with one's (merely personal) judgment about what the
other should do (sec. 9.3.3).

Leaving aside its moral shortcomings, a state of nature (i.e., a situation in which people all relied on their undefeated but unvictorious
judgments) would be characterized by uncertainty and conflict, undermining the basis for cooperation. Inconsistent interpretations of
each other's rights and responsibilities would lead to conflict and
thwart the development of settled expectations. This, of course, is a
familiar theme in liberal, and especially contractualist, political philosophy; Hobbes's, Locke's, and Kant's accounts of the state of nature all
aim to establish variations of it. Although on some matters we can
agree to differ, disputes engendered by competing judgments block
common action and, as R. E. Ewin points out, this includes "common
recognition of the limitations on individual or private action."[11]

It may well seem that I have ignored a third possible response to
the conflict of our inconclusive moral judgments: what Macedo calls
principled compromise. If Alf and Betty offer competing inconclusive
interpretations of a justified liberal principle, perhaps they should compromise on some "middle ground" that "gives something to each
side."[12] Now no doubt people who disagree about the demands of justice would do well to see if there is some third principle that they both
believe is justified; in this case conflict is replaced by consensus. Moral
relations among those who know each other well—friends, neighbors,
colleagues and family members—are often characterized by this sort of
agreement. But two considerations indicate that this is not at all likely
to be an effective solution to the clash of private judgments in a diverse
society. First, and most obviously, it is manifestly implausible to suppose that actual consensus on any principled compromise will emerge
in a diverse society, in which we often confront each other as strangers.
And, as we have seen, even if, say, actual consensus among all reasonable people is obtainable, it would not be necessarily justificatory (sec.
9.1.2). Because actual consensus—even consensus among all reasonable
people—is a chimera, a realistic commitment to a principled compromise would involve each person pressing his own conception of what
would be a fair compromise among competing positions. However,
people's ideas about what constitutes a fair compromise are as controversial as their ideas about other matters of justice. If so, Alf is apt to
propose P_3 as a fair compromise (between P_1 and P_2) while Betty
would advocate P_4. And even if they could agree on the best "middle
ground," specific interpretations of *that* compromise will engender dis-

agreement. Again, Alf is confronted with the options of either waiting until he can victoriously justify his interpretation, or going ahead and imposing it. Second, as I shall argue later (sec. 15.5), compromise seems an inappropriate response to epistemological disagreement. If Alf believes that P_1 is publicly justified, and Betty believes P_2 is publicly justified, that both can live with P_3 does not show they both believe it is publicly justified. We must remember that Alf and Betty are not in a dispute because Alf thinks that one interpretation works to his advantage and Betty believes a different one is in her interests—in these sorts of conflicts compromise is often appropriate. But when a disagreement is epistemological, when we disagree about what is the case, or what is indeed justified to all, a compromise that "gives something to each" may well lead us away from the right answer.

11.2 Liberal Authority

11.2.1 Umpires as the Voice of Public Reason

Relying on our undefeated but unvictorious judgments thus would lead to injustice and conflict. For Kant, if one "does not wish to renounce all concepts of justice," one must "quit the state of nature, in which everyone follows his own judgment" and subject oneself to "public lawful external coercion."[13] Hobbes, Locke, and Kant concur that an umpire or judge is required to make public determinations of our rights and duties. Says Hobbes:

And because, though men be never [sic] so willing to observe these laws [of nature], there may nevertheless arise questions concerning a man's actions; first, whether it were done, or not done; secondly, if done, whether against the law or not against the law; the former whereof, is called a question *of fact;* the latter a question of *right,* therefore unless the parties to the question, covenant mutually to stand to the sentence of another, they are as far from peace as ever. This other to whose sentence they submit is called an ARBITRATOR. And therefore it is of the law of nature, *that they that are at controversy, submit their right to the judgment of an arbitrator.*[14]

The social contract theories of Hobbes, Locke, and Kant are, first and foremost, justifications of an "arbitrator," "umpire," or "judge" whose task is to provide public, definitive resolutions of conflicting judgments. The "judge," as Hobbes said, provides "public reason" to which private reason "must submit."[15]

11.2.2 Contextual Authority

In order to grasp the nature of the umpire's authority, let us begin by considering a sort of authority with which umpiring is often confused, namely, the "contextual authority" explored in section 8.4. Suppose that Alf and Betty are locked in an inconclusive argument—such as whether justice demands redistributing some of Alf's property to Charlie—and so consult a sage, one who has superior access to what is publicly justified, and whose practical judgments more closely track the publicly justified morality than do their own. We could say that such a person is a contextual authority on morals.[16] The sage, priest, elder, or moral philosopher is, on this view, taken to have superior epistemological insight. And surely we sometimes do seek the counsel of those with such wisdom. But for this option to be a genuine solution to Alf and Betty's difficulty, three requirements must be met:

1. There must exist some people who possess superior moral insight.
2. They must be publicly identifiable. It will not do for Alf to grant authority to his libertarian friend while Betty grants it to her priest. This only transfers their dispute to different people. It must be the case that one or the other can show that it is unreasonable to reject his or her nominated sage.
3. Those who are publicly recognized as moral authorities must exhibit more convergence in their opinions than does the public at large.

We can grant (1); the problems arise with (2) and (3). It would seem that the dispute about who are the proper moral authorities would be just as inconclusive as the initial disagreement about what is to be done. Alf, opposing the redistribution of his holdings to Charlie, suggests we let his libertarian friend decide; Betty believes that her priest would provide sounder advice. If, *ex hypothesi*, neither is able to defeat the other's substantive views, it is doubtful that it is going to be any easier to defeat the other's preferred moral authority. But perhaps this is too quick; given that we have ruled out appeal to religious beliefs in public justification, maybe we can justify appealing to secular moral authorities. Let us grant this and turn only to professional moral philosophers. But then (3) is surely a daunting problem. Deep disagreement is characteristic of moral philosophy, not only on fundamental theory but on practice, too. If our sages disagree about so much—if, indeed, they often exhibit contempt for each other in their venomous denunciations of each other's views[17]—appeal to these sages is not apt to solve our disputes.

11.2.3 Coordinating Authority

Jan Narveson is quite right: The liberal recognizes "no high priests of morals." [18] But Alf and Betty may conclude that this is no real loss. After all, what is really necessary is that they resolve their practical dispute about what to *do;* they need not settle once and for all their epistemological controversy. As in scientific discourse, they can leave that matter open, hoping that in time a conclusive public justification will be forthcoming. In terms of Richard Friedman's analysis, Alf and Betty may well conclude that they are in no need of *an* authority on morals; they require only that someone be *in* authority to end the practical dispute. According to Friedman, to be *an* authority is to have superior knowledge such that others are warranted in accepting your judgments:

The basic purpose of this sort of authority is to substitute the knowledge of one person for the ignorance or lesser knowledge of another person, although what the person who defers thereby comes to possess as a surrogate for his ignorance is not knowledge, but "true belief" in the sense of belief that is indeed justified, though the believer knows not why. [19]

Friedman contrasts this conception of authority with a second, which he calls being "in authority." The key to being *in* authority is that others recognize your judgments as a reason for them to *act,* even if they do not accept them as a reason to *believe.* As Friedman puts it, instead of acting on one's "private judgment," one who follows such authority acts on the will of another. In this case one follows the will of another even if it conflicts with one's own private judgement: On this matter the person *in* authority will decide what is to be *done.* Her decision replaces yours about *what you are to do.* Particularly important in this regard is that one's obedience to the directives of the authority is not dependent upon agreeing with their wisdom. Indeed, the whole point of recognizing another as being *in* authority is that the authority of the directives is not dependent upon their soundness. As Friedman says:

The idea being conveyed by such notions as the surrender of private judgment or individual judgment is that in obeying, say, a command simply because it comes from someone accorded the right to rule, the subject does not make his obedience conditional on his own personal examination of the thing he is being asked to do. Rather, he accepts as a sufficient reason for following a prescription the fact that it is prescribed by someone acknowledged by him as entitled to rule. The man who accepts authority is thus said to surrender his private or individual judgment because he does not insist that reasons be given that he can grasp and that satisfy him, as a condition of his obedience. [20]

Consider, then, a practical authority entirely divorced from any claim to being an epistemological authority. The authority would instruct Alf and Betty to Φ, without making any claim that, on its understanding of the liberal public morality, Φ is the morally required act or policy. Certainly this type of authority is possible; it is the authority of a pure coordinator. If Alf and Betty are in a coordination game, it matters little to them what they do so long as they both do the same thing.[21] Recall again our earlier example of rules of the road: Alf and Betty desire to drive on the same side, but they have no justifiable beliefs that one coordination point is better than the other. Hence, the authority can solve the practical dispute simply by issuing a directive, without purporting that it is based on an examination of the relative merits of driving on the right or the left. The authority makes no claim to resolve the underlying epistemological dispute because there really is no such dispute: Alf and Betty's problem is a purely practical one.

This is all Betty and Alf require for cases of nested indeterminacy (sec. 9.4.3). In these cases, it will be recalled, there is a public justification that, say, our behavior be coordinated in some way, but it is simply indeterminate which of many possible coordination points should be chosen. No justifiable beliefs can be offered on this matter. In these situations Alf and Betty need a coordinator, someone or some procedure that will select from the justified set, and allow them to proceed.

A coordinator is not sufficient for cases of nested inconclusiveness, in which Alf and Betty each have undefeated beliefs, for example, about the proper regime of private property: Alf and Betty's practical controversy is based on an epistemological dispute. And because this is so, it seems doubtful that they would be satisfied with a dispute resolution procedure that makes no attempt to track the underlying epistemological issue. After all, they conceive of themselves as disagreeing about what *to do* because they disagree about *what is right;* to resolve the latter entirely independently of the former treats their moral dispute as if it were no more than a conflict of preferences.[22] Because (1) Alf and Betty are both committed to the public justification of demands on others and (2) they both believe that the disputed question has a right answer (and so it is not merely indeterminate), they thus have reason to support a procedure that is *justification tracking.* Justification-tracking methods of dispute resolutions seek to come as close as possible to the most justified answer(s), and thus rely as much as possible on the competing justifications (sec. 13.4). In contrast, purely coordinative procedures make no effort to draw on the competing justifications, for none are to be had: No even minimally justifiable beliefs exist as to what would be the best thing to so. My claim, then, is that, as participants in an inconclusive public debate, Alf and Betty have reason to resist a way of resolving their dispute that ignores its epistemological foundations, treating it as no more than a coordination problem. They would, then, seek a justification-tracking way to resolve the dispute; they would seek adjudication. As Leslie Green observes:

> When a judge decides a case at law, she settles the dispute in a way that is binding even if it wrong. But the justification for this can not be that it doesn't matter who wins, or even that who wins matters less than having some final settlement of the dispute. It is that such a procedure is thought to promote, however imperfectly, a correct resolution of the dispute. Thus, although indifferent choice may sometimes play a role in explaining the validity of . . . [authority], it cannot do so in general.[23]

11.2.4 The Umpire Model of Authority

Alf and Betty appear trapped in a dilemma. They rejected the purely practical account of authority because it makes no attempt to relate the resolution of the practical controversy to the proper solution of the epistemological disagreement. But they rejected contextual political authority because they are unable to identify an authority that could resolve their epistemological controversy.

The social contract tradition's notion of an umpire provides a way out. Consider more carefully the idea of an umpire in a game.[24] Players require an umpire because they have practical disputes based on their different views on how the rules of the game apply to particular situations. Often the dispute is simply about matters of fact, such as, "Did Betty hit the ball in foul territory?" But not all the time: When a player is penalized for unsportsmanlike conduct, the dispute is not simply about what was done, but whether it constituted prohibited conduct. Neither in law nor in sporting matches do rules apply themselves; they need to be interpreted, and the application requires practical judgment. The umpire, then, makes her practical determinations on the basis of her epistemological judgments concerning the rules of the game. This makes the umpire appear to be something of a sage. But players typically do not see the umpire as a sage, and nothing about accepting an umpire requires that they must. Players certainly may, but usually do not, take the umpire's decisions as a reason to believe; quite often they do not acknowledge her to be a contextual authority, and so refuse to defer to her judgments about what to believe. Players typically continue to believe what they did before the umpire decided—they accept her judgment as a resolution of the practical dispute, though not the epistemological dispute. Yet the participants expect the umpire to deliberate about what to do on the basis of the rules and the facts. Although the problem is essentially a practical one, the umpire's resolution is to be based on her determinations concerning the facts and the rules of the game, both epistemological matters.

Umpireship, then, constitutes a complicated mix of epistemological and practical concerns. The umpire's aim is to produce practical determinations that best track what the rules require. Yet players need only conceive of her as a practical authority (they see her as being *in* authority, not *an* authority). Indeed, it follows that players are committed to accepting the umpire's practical authority even when they believe her decision is wrong. Unless players are prepared to do so, they could not proceed with the game. Situations will arise in which one player reasonably believes that the rules render Φ appropriate, whereas another reasonably believes Ψ is appropriate. Unless they are prepared to follow the umpire's decisions in these cases, the umpire could not fulfill her role. To be sure, there are limits. At some point we say things like, "These just are not even reasonable calls; this ump is either blind or has been paid off." Even when we disagree with an umpire we can usually grasp how someone seeking to apply the rules of the game would make that decision. But if an umpire consistently acts in ways that, as far as we can tell, have nothing to do with the rules of the game, then we will conclude sooner or later that she isn't really being an umpire or that she is unqualified to perform the job. We can say, then, that the players only accept the practical authority of the umpire for decisions within some range of justifiable decisions. This range is specified by the set of nested inconclusive judgments, disputes about which the umpire is seeking to resolve.

This analysis of umpiring does not depend on the supposition that in a game such as baseball the umpire is applying a specific set of rules. Indeed, the umpire's chief role in baseball—calling strikes and balls—is anything but the application of a clear set of rules. Calling strikes and balls is much closer to the application of a vague concept—the idea of a strike zone—than the application of a set of rules. More generally, my analysis supposes that umpiring is appropriate when (1) there are some principles, rules, and so on, that are victoriously justified; (2) the application or specific interpretation of the rules is often a matter of reasonable dispute; (3) these disputes have an epistemological dimension—they are not simply about what people want, but what they believe is justified by appeal to the general principles; (4) it is necessary to resolve the practical dispute arising out of these different interpretations even if the underlying epistemological controversy remains.

11.2.5 A Summary

The argument of this section has been somewhat complex; it will be helpful to summarize it. I have argued that (1) when offering interpretations of victoriously justified principles, inconclusive reasoning is still genuinely public reason; (2) when interpreting justified principles, liberal citizens can neither wait until specific interpretations are victorious nor simply go ahead and impose their inadequately justified interpretations. Consequently (3) they must somehow resolve their dispute about the interpretation of these principles. But (4) they cannot, *ex hypothesi*, resolve the epistemic issue about what is best justified, not even by resorting to the opinions of others. Yet (5) they can at least resolve the practical issue about what is to be done. Now (6) insofar as their disputes are really indeterminate, as, for example, in pure coordination problems, I have argued that a *coordinator* is all that is required—some way to resolve the practical problem by instructing them what to *do*. However (7) I have maintained that disputes based on inconclusive public reasoning are not mere coordination problems; such disputes are ultimately epistemological (in the sense that citizens disagree about what is publicly justified), and the disputants have reason therefore to embrace justification–tracking dispute resolution procedures over those that simply instruct them what to *do* without taking account of the competing justifications. Thus (8), as Hobbes, Locke, and Kant argued, to resolve disputes based on inconclusive public reasoning, liberal citizens require an umpire, judge, or arbitrator. The umpire model of political authority yields two requirements for any decision procedure for resolving moral disputes:

1. It generally must be practically decisive.
2. It must yield decisions that are typically within the range of competing undefeated unvictorious justifications.

The first criterion follows from the practical necessity to resolve disputes: We turn to an umpire to resolve the practical dispute about what is to be done. But the umpire model of political authority also requires that the umpire's decisions be within the range of reasonable (i.e., inconclusive) opinions about what is publicly justified.

11.2.6 Exclusionary Reasons

An umpire thus seems to provide what Joseph Raz has called "exclusionary reasons."[25] Suppose that the umpire decides that redistributing Alf's holdings is not publicly justified. Because Betty does not treat the umpire as a sage, the fact that she accepts the umpire's verdict does not mean that it defeats her own conclusion that a norm allowing redistribution is publicly justified. Her position remains undefeated. But when she accepts the umpire, she accepts that the umpire's decisions provide exclusionary reasons for action. In our case, the umpire's decision gives Betty a reason to refrain from issuing demands based on her own evaluation of what is justified and, therefore, to leave Alf's holdings alone. Though Raz sometimes suggests that Betty is thus convinced it is not up to her to reason about the merits of the case,[26] this seems too strong. Betty can reason all she wants about the merits of the case; what she is excluded from is making a moral demand based on her evaluation of the merits.

In this case, then, Betty's own deliberation about what is publicly justified provides one set of reasons for action, and the umpire's decision provides another, conflicting, set. To say that Betty recognizes the authority of the umpire is to say that the reasons provided by the umpire exclude her from issuing demands of her own. Now Raz acknowledges that an exclusionary reason possesses a certain "scope": It can exclude Betty from acting on some of her reasons and not others.[27] However, it is often maintained that though the scope of authoritative directives can be limited, they are nevertheless *content independent*. Consider, for example, Leslie Green's analysis of authority:

A has authority over B if and only if the fact that A requires B to Φ (1) gives B a content-independent reason to Φ and (2) excludes some of B's reasons for not-Φ-ing.[28]

The second clause is an acknowledgment of the possibility of limitations of scope; the first insists that if A has authority to exclude B from acting on her reasons $R_1 \ldots R_n$, then A's authoritative direction to Φ excludes B from acting on those reasons regardless of the content of A's directives. We have seen, though, that the authority of the umpire is not content independent in this strong sense. An umpire's directive is only authoritative if it is within the range of justifiable decisions.[29] We might say, then, that instead of being content independent, the exclusionary force of the umpire's decision is content robust.[30] That the directives are content robust and not content independent, we shall see, is an absolutely fundamental characteristic of liberal authority.

PART III

POLITICAL JUSTIFICATION

CHAPTER 12

The Rule of Law

As I observed in chapter 11, the social contract tradition as exemplified by Hobbes, Locke, and Kant has sought to justify an arbitrator, umpire, or judge whose task is to provide public, definitive resolutions of conflicting judgments. Although we typically conceive of social contract theory as justifying "government," Locke's phrase is far more accurate and revealing: To escape the state of nature, in which each relies on her own moral judgments, we require rule by an "Umpire, by settled standing Rules, indifferent, and the same to all Parties"[1]—that is, umpiring through law. For all three philosophers law as articulated by the umpire, is the definitive voice of public reason. "CIVIL LAW," said Hobbes, "*is to every subject, those rules, which the commonwealth hath commanded him, by word, writing, or other sufficient sign of the will, to make use of, for the distinction of right, and wrong. . . .*"[2] In part III I aim to show that such an umpire can be victoriously justified. This requires two tasks. First, I must show that an umpire who rules through law can be victoriously justified. Unless that can be done, disputes about the publicly justified umpiring procedure will simply replace disputes about justice. As Nozick observes: "When sincere and good persons differ, we are prone to think they must accept some procedure to decide their differences, some procedure they both agree to be reliable or fair. [But] . . . this disagreement may extend all the way up the ladder of procedures."[3] Showing that the disagreement does not extend all the way up the ladder of political procedures is the main concern of social contract theory; I turn to it in chapters 13 and 14. Second, it needs to be shown why umpiring *through law* is required to solve the problems raised by a clash of private judgments. That is, leaving aside which umpiring procedure we should employ (i.e., what form of government is justified), why does the analysis of conflicting private judgments indicate that the set of justifiable umpiring procedures must be restricted to those that rule through law? It is to this question that I now turn.

12.1 Three Aspects of the Rule of Law

The ideal of the rule of law is multifaceted; three aspects are of particular relevance for our present purposes.

1. The rule of *law* is often contrasted with the rule of *men*, rule by mere will or caprice of political authorities. "In this sense," said A.V. Dicey, "the rule of law is contrasted with every system of government based on the exercise by persons in authority of wide, arbitrary, or discretionary powers of constraint."[4] Clearly, then, a dictator who rules through fiat based on passing whims does not rule through law. However, on many interpretations this ideal of the rule of law demands more than a Hartian union of primary and secondary rules. If Rex enacts vague statutes giving his secret police sweeping discretionary powers to decide what is a crime, or if he singles out political opponents by name and enacts regulations directed to them alone, his claim to rule through *law* is dubious.[5] This understanding of the rule of law leads to something very much like Lon Fuller's "internal morality of the law," that is, the defining characteristics of distinctly *legal rule* such as generality, publicity, exclusion of retroactive legislation, clarity, stability, exclusion of legislation requiring the impossible and the congruence of official action and declared rule.[6]

2. As Dicey pointed out, the ideal of rule of law has a less formal and more substantive dimension: the protection of personal freedom.[7] Ronald Dworkin stresses this substantive aspect of the rule of law (though expanding it beyond protection of personal freedom), which he calls the "rights conception" of the rule of law:

> It assumes that citizens have moral rights and duties with respect to one another, and political rights against the state as a whole. It insists that these moral and political rights be recognized in positive law, so that they may be enforced *upon the demand of individual citizens* through courts or other judicial institutions of the familiar type, so far as this is practicable. The rule of law on this conception is the ideal of rule by an accurate public conception of individual rights.[8]

3. Dworkin makes clear that the ideal of the rule of law requires not only that government rule *through* laws, but also that it be ruled *by* laws; courts are to enforce rights "against the state as a whole." This is one way in which the rule of law requires an independent judiciary: If citizens are to enforce their legal rights against government, the judiciary cannot be a mere instrument of the executive or the legislature.[9] This aspect of the rule of law also points to a tie between constitutionalism and the rule of law, insofar as a constitution is viewed as articulating a "fundamental law" that limits the authority of the legislature itself.[10]

My aims in this chapter are three. First, I wish to show that these features of the rule of law—formal requirements, individual rights, and the legal regulation of political authority—are part of a coherent ideal, rather than a hodgepodge of unrelated legal aspirations.[11] Second, as the rule of law is a central component of the liberal conception of justice,[12] I want to demonstrate how the theory that unites these three legal aspirations follows closely from basic liberal commitments. Last and, given the aims of this book, most important, I shall argue that the umpire account of political authority provides the basis of the liberal theory uniting these legal aspirations. In this chapter, then, I begin to develop a liberal theory of the rule of law based on the umpire account of political authority, though it will remain incomplete until the justifications of judicial review and the moral obligation to obey the law are presented in chapter 16.

12.2 The Internal Morality of Law

As I stressed in the analysis of liberal authority, the conflicts engendered by the inconclusiveness of our public justifications possess both a moral-epistemological and a practical dimension. Moral agents have an epistemological disagreement about what can be publicly justified, but this disagreement manifests itself in a wide array of practical disputes. People have practical disagreements about such matters as who owns a bit of property or whether obscene speech should be stopped. To grasp the distinctively practical problems brought about by the clash of inconclusive individual judgments, it may help to imagine individuals who are concerned only with the moral-epistemological problem. That is, suppose everyone has only one aim: to get the best possible answer to each moral dispute. Such relentlessly philosophical agents would *not* desire that laws be settled, *if* the cost of being settled is that the umpire continues to uphold older, marginally worse judgments, rather than adopt newer, marginally better, public judgments. Call LM the ideal liberal morality, that which sanctions all, and only, those impositions that are truly publicly justified. Although we cannot identify LM in detail, it is a regulative ideal for agents committed to public justification. Now call lm_i any particular set of judgments that seeks to approach LM.[13] Purely epistemologically motivated individuals absolutely prefer lm_2 to lm_1 if lm_2 more closely approximates LM than does lm_1.[14] If each change from lm_i to lm_{i+1} moved the law closer to the most justified liberal morality (as far as this could be discerned), our purely philosophical agents would not agree that a "law that changes everyday is worse than no law at all."[15] To be sure, if stability was itself a desideratum of LM, then at some point the change from lm_i to

lm_{i+1} would lead away from LM. But still, since purely epistemologically motivated agents have an absolute priority of enlightenment over
stability (insofar as the latter is not included in the former), they would
commend any change in the law that moved them closer to the ideal
liberal morality. Neither would such agents have objections to retroactive laws that corrected previous mistakes if this moved them closer to
LM. Better that than to let moral errors go uncorrected.[16] More generally, we can imagine such agents rejecting umpiring through the enactment of general laws that are simple and clear enough for all to follow.
As I have stressed, moral disputes are complex; perhaps only a wise
judge ruling on a case-by-case basis could possibly come close to what
is best justified. Of course, if agents were really purely concerned with
the epistemological dispute, they would not seek an umpire at all, but
the opinions of sages.[17]

Shifting, particularistic judgments are not obviously inappropriate
for purely epistemologically motivated agents. But we are not like that.
Our interest in public justification is ultimately practical; we have lives
to lead, and aspire to reason publicly to formulate principles regulating
our dealings with each other. It is because each seeks morality as a
framework for living a life that the components of Fuller's inner morality of law—stability, generality, publicity, simplicity, nonretroactivity,
noncontradiction—are critical virtues. An umpire that gave shifting,
particularistic, secret, overwhelmingly complex, and retroactive rulings
simply would not solve the practical problem of Hobbes's, Locke's, or
Kant's state of nature, no matter how wise it might be. Thus, in contrast to our purely epistemologically motivated agents, liberal citizens
have reason to prefer laws that are further from the ideal liberal code,
but provide better satisfaction of the demands of practice. In this sense,
Fuller's theory of law coheres well with liberalism; for justificatory liberalism the ideal of the rule of law has a *telos*—resolving conflicts fairly
and providing a framework for cooperation through decisions by an
umpire—and so contains within it the criteria of its own perfection.[18]

That the *telos* is a *fair* resolution of disputes merits emphasis. A
cardinal virtue of umpires is fairness or impartiality. One can be practically certain that in some cases the umpire will make decisions that, on
one's own evaluation of the merits of the case, appear quite wrong. So it
is a practical certainty that sometimes one will be instructed to Φ on the
basis of what one sees as flawed reasoning; moreover, in such cases, one's
Φ-ing may benefit others at a cost to one's own interests (e.g., Alf may
be instructed to redistribute some of his holdings to Charlie). For adjudication to achieve its practical aim in such cases, it must be manifest that
the umpire is impartial. Thus Hobbes's eighteenth law of nature:

No man in any case ought to be received for arbitrator, to whom greater profit, or honour, or pleasure apparently ariseth out of the victory of one party, than the other: for he hath taken, though an unavoidable bribe, yet a bribe; and no man can be obliged to trust him. And thus also the controversy, and the condition of war remaineth, contrary to the law of nature.[19]

Hence the demand that laws be impartially applied to all citizens and be stated in general terms.

Here the principle of equality is indeed justified. Earlier (sec. 10.2.1) I argued that public justification presupposes the liberal principle and not the principle of equality, according to which any discriminatory act, any action that provides differential advantages or burdens, stands in need of justification. The principle of equality, though not a basic principle of liberal morality, is a basic demand of the rule of law, requiring that every determination of the umpire be justified. In this respect public officials differ crucially from private citizens. Whereas private citizens are free to act as they see fit until, as it were, they run up against the rights of others, or seek to impose on others, this presumption does not hold for public officials. Public officials must be able to provide publicly accessible reasons justifying what they do in their official capacity; if they cannot do so, they lose their status of impersonal umpires who adjudicate conflicting demands in the light of public principles.[20] The principle of equality thus manifests a commitment to public reason. It places the onus of justification on public officials: Citizens are to be treated equally unless relevant grounds can be demonstrated for unequal treatment.[21] This requires that the state advance public reasons for its treatment of citizens. Governments become arbitrary when their actions are based on the private or idiosyncratic concerns of officials; a government that makes no distinction between the private concerns of its officials and public reasons is the paradigm of rule by will (or men), not by law. The principle of formal equality before the law thus articulates the liberal state's commitment to rule through public reasons only.[22]

12.3 Rights

12.3.1 Rights as Spheres of Authority

On the account I have been offering—which I have claimed is at the heart of the great contractarian theories—law strives, first and foremost, to provide definitive public resolutions of disputes between citizens. As Hobbes stressed, the inconveniences of the state of nature stem from the clash of people's private reasoning about what is best or just.[23] One way to understand the root of the problem is that in the state of nature each person divides social life into two areas of jurisdiction—those over which he is (to use Mill's phrase) "sovereign" and those areas in which others have authority. Problems arise because people dispute the boundaries of these two areas. To fix ideas, consider a simple case. Suppose Alf and Betty live in the forests of northern Minnesota, and both lust after a huge pine tree, the biggest they have ever seen. Alf wants to cut it down to build a sailing ship, while Betty wants to make it a tourist attraction. Alf starts toward it with his saw in hand, Betty seeks to block his path. They both claim jurisdiction over the tree.[24]

One way to solve their problem would be to resort to an umpire to determine what should be done with the tree. But constant appeals to the umpire would be inefficient and costly, so it is manifest that all will benefit from having known and predictable rules that would allow them to anticipate the umpire's judgment. That reasoning, we have seen, leads to something like Fuller's idea of the inner morality of the law. But settled rules that dictate the proper resolution of all future disputes, taking into account all the relevant details of every case that may arise, seem beyond the ability of even a legal Hercules. For example, suppose that Betty's justification for blocking Alf's way isn't that she wants a tourist attraction, but to save this environmental treasure for future generations. Or perhaps Alf's justification for cutting the tree is that it is blocking the sun on his beach. Or maybe Betty aims to thwart Alf's activity out of spite. How many details should the rules take into account?

The difficulty in formulating determinate rules to cover unknown future cases is familiar and important in both law and ethics (see sec. 16.1). Although this problem can only be mitigated, never completely solved, the development of a system of individual rights is critical in coping with it. Often—especially in political theory—rights are understood as ways to protect an individual against interference by the government or other citizens, and they certainly have this function (recall our discussion of immunities in sec. 10.3). But more basic to the idea of individual rights is that they serve to distribute discretionary authority in a community. For example, if in our simple case Betty owns the tree, then, within wide though certainly limited bounds, she has authority to decide what is to be done with it. Whether she wants to protect the tree to make a fortune from tourists, preserve our natural heritage for future generations, or spite Alf is not relevant—she has the authority to decide. Over a certain area of social life, Betty's decision settles the matter. As R.E. Ewin emphasizes:

rights take precedence over private judgments of right and wrong; the person who has the right makes the decision. There can be no question here of the right's being overruled on the grounds of kindness or the common good; what is at issue is who makes the decision, not the grounds on which it is made.[25]

Rights distribute authority over various areas of social life to different agents. Consequently, rights can be analyzed as types of authority relations. Just as the umpire's authority yields directives that exclude moral demands based on (at least some) first-order reasons (sec. 11.2.6), one who holds rights also issues exclusionary directives. If Betty has a right to the tree, her decision that it is not to be cut provides Alf with content-robust reasons to refrain from cutting it, reasons that exclude his acting on (at least some of) his own evaluations about what is the best thing to do. Alf may be entirely convinced that it would be best to cut the tree, and that Betty is objecting only out of spite. Nevertheless, that she has a right to the tree, and objects to its cutting, provides Alf with a reason to abstain from logging, even though he believes in the goodness, value, and justice of his project. A system of justified rights thus allows people to live together in peace and coordinate their activities while honoring their commitment to publicly justify themselves, despite the fact that they regularly, if not typically, disagree on the merits or justice of particular actions. It is, then, fundamental to the notion of a right that Alf can consistently acknowledge (1) that Betty has a right to Φ, and thus (2) she is justified in Φ-ing,[26] even though (3) Alf is justified in believing that Φ-ing is a bad or even an evil act.[27]

A liberal regime, in which individuals live together honoring their commitment to public justification in the face of pervasive moral disagreement, must be a regime of rights. A regime of justified rights copes with the fact of moral disagreement by decentralizing and dispersing moral authority. The argument for rights, then, is simply a special case of the general argument for an umpire. When liberal citizens confront each other with incompatible demands, none of which can be victoriously justified, if one of the parties has justified authority to decide the matter under dispute—in other words, has the right to decide—they can avoid both the dogmatism of simply imposing one's justified beliefs on others and the anarchism of refraining from ever imposing less-than-conclusively justified demands (sec. 11.1).

12.3.2 Rights and Recognition

If rights are to fulfill their moral and practical functions, they must be widely recognized and accepted. Ewin stresses this point:

A mere claim to have a right settles nothing if it is not, in the end, accepted by the relevant community, even if some members of the community finally accept it only as a result of appeal to a public procedure used to resolve disputes about who has what rights. . . .

Rights make a peaceful social life possible with people who are willing to live a peaceful life, people inclined to resolve disputes without recourse to fighting. . . . But a right that cannot be agreed on by people willing to settle disputes cannot serve the function of a right, so it is ineffective and no right at all unless it is made definitive by, for example, reference to a public procedure.[28]

It is this feature of rights that is uppermost in the minds of those who insist that, to use T.H. Green's phrase, "rights are made by recognition."[29] For rights to resolve disagreement by apportioning discretionary authority, they must be specified and distributed in a publicly definitive manner. Thus, as Ewin indicates, it is not enough that a right be a valid claim or be justified; it must be recognized.[30] The requirement that rights be authoritatively recognized stems from their practical, but also their moral, functions.

Consider first the practical function of rights. If rights are to resolve conflict by apportioning authority, they must be widely recognized and agreed upon. But differences of opinion about the scope and nature of rights will always arise (as I said, the problem of conflicting judgments can only be mitigated, not done away with). As Nozick recognizes, it is from this that the "inconveniences" of the Lockean state of nature arise:

Private and personal enforcement of one's rights . . . leads to feuds, to an endless series of retaliation and exactions of compensation. And there is no firm way to *settle* such a dispute, to *end* it and have both parties know it is ended. Even if one party *says* he'll stop his acts of retaliation, the other can rest secure only if he knows the first still does not feel entitled to gain recompense or exact retribution, and therefore to try when a promising occasion presents itself.[31]

An effective system of rights must allow for adjudicating disputes about both factual matters (who did what) and about the scope of rights, and the proper way to resolve apparent conflicts of rights. Rex Martin thus properly insists that the scope of rights must be authoritatively set (to preserve their content) and that without such setting and adjustment of scope, rights will conflict—conflict internally and with one another and with other (nonrights) considerations. Since such conflict can only be resolved or prevented by the action of agencies that can formulate and harmonize rights (through scope adjustment, competitive weightings, and so on), rights that lacked such agencies would necessarily conflict and the set of them could not be coherent.[32]

The upshot, then, is that for liberal rights to perform their task of allocating authority to individuals, they must be embedded in, and regulated by, an authoritative system of law.[33]

Authoritative recognition, then, is necessary for an *effective* system of rights. But it is also necessary for a system of rights to allow us to avoid moral dogmatism. That Alf has a well-grounded belief that he has a valid claim to the pine tree is insufficient; so long as his justification for the right is inconclusive, imposing the right on Betty would be inconsistent with his commitment to public justification. In this sense it is entirely correct to say that although rights have a moral basis, (almost) all rights are necessarily political, and so genuine rights must typically be embodied in a system of law. For almost all rights will be inconclusively justified, and it is only through a system of law that one of the competing inconclusive claims can be publicly identified a right.

In an important and fundamental sense, then, rights are indeed made by recognition. However, none of the following claims, often associated with the "rights are made by recognition" thesis, are justified:

C1: Every right authorized by a legal system is a justified claim, power, immunity, and so on.[34]

C2: No individual can have a right to Φ unless that right is recognized by a legal system.

C3: No one can have a right to Φ if the legal system asserts there is no right to Φ.

Hobbes's account of rights in civil society seems to embrace all three claims: Because individuals employing their private judgment disagree about what is just or best and therefore find themselves in intractable disputes, they submit to an umpire who *establishes what is just.* As Ewin shows in his excellent account of Hobbes' moral theory, "as an artificial right-reason or second-order decision-procedure between contending views of justice, the sovereign *determines what is just for us to do and, therefore, can do no wrong.*"[35] What the sovereign proclaims to be a right is a right (C1) and there are no rights apart from what the sovereign pronounces (C2).[36] In contrast, on the Lockean view, C1 must be rejected. The umpire, as I have argued, is to adjudicate competing undefeated but unvictorious proposals; it is *here* that we need an authority to render public determinations of our rights. However, if the umpire systematically ignores publicly justified rights—those that *have been* victoriously justified—its rulings depart from the *telos* of law. Such an umpire seeks to "resolve" issues that have already been decided.[37] Thus, for example, an umpire that denies the right to speak freely, or one that sought to abolish the citizen's immunity from regulation of her religious or private life would be rightly accused of tyranny—the attempt to overturn our natural (in the sense of prepolitical) rights.[38] The rulings of such an umpire simply could not establish that there was, say, no right to freedom of speech or religious toleration.

Our reason for rejecting C1 (that every right authorized by a legal system is a justified claim, power, immunity, and so on) also leads us to reject C2 and C3, the claims that individuals cannot have a right unless it is recognized by a legal system and certainly cannot have a right explicitly denied by the legal system. Some rights, I have argued, are victoriously publicly justified: They are bona fide rights, and the umpire commits an injustice when it violates them. As Dworkin puts it, on this view the rule of law "is the ideal of rule by an accurate public conception of individual rights."[39] Note that Dworkin identifies the rule of law as rule by an *accurate* public conception of individual rights; rule by deeply flawed conceptions does not constitute rule by law. Locke thus properly stresses that the tyrant, ignoring the rights of citizens, does not act through law; regardless of the procedures employed, an umpire who tramples the publicly justified rights of citizens cannot be said to rule though law.[40]

12.4 Constitutionalism

12.4.1 Fundamental Law, the Social Contract, and Constitutionalism

Both the internal and the external morality of law constrain what counts as law (in the sense of achieving the *telé* of legal rule). The liberal theory of the rule of law, implying as it does rule by an *accurate* conception of individual rights, thus endorses the idea of substantive moral principles that bind the umpire. Given that the umpire is only empowered to make determinations about what is justified—particularly about our justified rights—within a restricted set of moral disputes, it undoubtedly follows that the umpire's authority to make law is limited. The umpire itself is constrained by a law that is morally prior to its authority and its rulings. This suggests an interpretation of the social contract as a statement of fundamental law, specifying the power of the umpire and its limits. Fundamental law is the law that both empowers and constrains the umpire. The social contract can thus be understood as identifying that part of public morality that is conclusively justified, and by doing so identifies the bounds of a legitimate umpire. As Rogers M. Smith observes in his study of the relation of Lockean liberalism and constitutionalism:

Liberal regimes promise to decide a wide range of controversies fairly through decisions based on established, known, impartially applied rules and procedures—to provide, in short, the rule of law. The very notion of government as originating in a "contract" already gives liberal political theory a legalistic cast. When the original contract is understood to set standards for what governments may do, and when it requires officials to apply those standards in nonarbitrary, regular, and equitable ways, even the governors can be said to be governed by the laws. When the purposes and provisions of the original contract are held to embody principles of natural justice . . . then the laws men consent to in forming that contract can claim to be binding in every sense.[41]

This in turn leads to one aspect of the idea of liberal constitutionalism: Constitutions are understood to embody the social contract's identification of fundamental law. Early American jurisprudence acknowledged this connection among fundamental law, the social contract, and (state) constitutionalism. Constitutions were understood as articulating the social contract, which was fundamental law.[42] In *Federalist 78* Hamilton was clear that he viewed the Federal Constitution similarly: "A constitution is, in fact, and must be regarded by judges as, a fundamental law."[43] Constitutionalism, in the sense of a fundamental law that applies to the umpire, is inherent in the liberal theory of law. Stephen Macedo is quite right: "The Constitution, in order to be authoritative, must be capable of being read as a reasonable approximation to principles that pass the test of public justification."[44]

The idea that liberal constitutions imply substantive moral constraints on governments is, of course, not at all novel.[45] It is one element of Madisonian constitutionalism, and is the basic idea underlying the Bill of Rights.[46] Surprisingly, however, analyses of substantive constitutional provisions as articulations of fundamental law often fail to distinguish two very different ways these provisions function: the limiting and the empowering.[47]

If one's model of substantive constitutionalism is the Bill of Rights, the former understanding suggests itself: A constitution articulates fundamental moral principles that government may not violate. As one scholar puts it, "the objective of bills of rights is to give special protection for rights which are felt to be of fundamental importance."[48] A government is unjust if it enacts legislation that oversteps these bounds by, for example, seeking to establish a religion or severely curtailing freedom of speech. However, in the eyes of some, as long as a government respects these constraints, its legislation is just.[49] This view is advanced by Robert Bork:

The United States was founded as a Madisonian system, which means that it contains two opposing principles that must be continually reconciled. The first principle is self-government, which means that in wide areas of life majorities are entitled to rule, if they wish, simply because they are majorities. The second is that there are nonetheless some things majorities must not do to minorities, some areas of life in which the individual must be free of majority rule.[50]

Bork articulates inadequately the liberal ideal of limited government. His underlying claim is that a majority may properly legislate its preferences except when it runs afoul of constitutional restraints.[51] This is limited government of a sort—the majority is not allowed to do some things. But the limits are just the type that apply to individuals. As a private individual, one can do as one wishes up to the point at which one violates the rights of others. Bork's gloss on Madisonian democracy appears to depict the majority as an individual writ large—it can do as it wishes as long as it does not violate the minority's rights. But, given the fundamental liberal principle, almost every legislative act by the majority, because it constitutes an imposition on the minority, stands in need of justification (sec. 10.2.1).[52] Hence the importance of the principle of equality to the rule of law (sec. 12.2).

Many democratic theorists, of course, would reply that the majority can justify itself by appealing to the basic democratic principle that the *demos* can legitimately determine the matters on which it will speak. According to Robert Dahl, for example, "the demos must have the exclusive opportunity to decide how matters are to placed on the agenda of matters that are to be decided by means of the democratic process."[53] But this is not a principle of Madisonian democracy or of the liberal understanding of limited government.[54] "Justice," said Madison, "is the end of government,"[55] and justificatory liberalism concurs. The basic problem that requires the existence of political society, according to traditional social contract theory and justificatory liberalism, is that our opinions about the demands of justice are inconclusive. Because of this, and because of our commitment to justify our demands to others, we are led to embrace an umpire, judge, or arbitrator. The authority of the umpire is based on its claim to adjudicate disputes about what can be publicly justified. The umpire is empowered to speak only on these matters.

12.4.2 The Liberal Rechtstaat and the Limits of Policy

Fundamental liberal principles determine the proper scope of the umpire in two ways. First, by specifying those proposals that have been defeated (such as establishing a religion) and those principles that have been victoriously justified (such as free speech), liberal constitutionalism announces that the government may not overturn these outcomes of public justification. This is the limiting role of constitutional principles. Second, however, liberalism insists that government is empowered to secure limited ends or to perform limited tasks. Even if a legislation does not run afoul of basic rights and liberties, if a government is not empowered to act in that area the law is unjustified. Now it may seem that justificatory liberalism can provide a simple, if abstract, account of this end which government is empowered to pursue: To adjudicate disputes among citizens that arise from inconclusive judgments as to what is publicly justified. But that is too simple. Recall the distinction (sec. 9.4) between merely and nested inconclusive judgments. A nested inconclusive judgment is based on a victorious principle or judgment as, for example, the claim that "Victoriously justified principle P requires Φ," where what is inconclusive is the claim that "P requires Φ," not that "P is a victoriously justified principle." In contrast, a merely inconclusive judgment is an undefeated unvictorious claim that is freestanding; it does not present itself as an interpretation of a more abstract victoriously justified statement. I argued that an individual committed to public justification is committed to the "wait and see" strategy when advancing an inconclusive public justification (sec. 11.1.2). Since the person proposing the justification has not been able to show that others are committed to accepting the demand, the fundamental liberal principle requires that she refrain from imposing her view on others. Consequently, because citizens are not committed to adjudicating these disputes, they remain outside of the competency of the liberal umpire. Citizens are only committed to adjudicating disputes that can be plausibly represented as cases of nested inconclusiveness: Only in these sorts of disputes are liberal umpires competent to rule.

This ideal of the state, devoted to adjudicating disputes through the rule of law, can be rightly described as a liberal *Rechtstaat*—a legal state whose interventions are based solely on law. This ideal leads, as its critic Carl Schmitt correctly observed, to a "general 'juridification' of the entire life of the state."[56] However, the analysis of authority I have offered is doubly juridical. Not only must government interventions in the lives of citizens conform to the internal and external morality of law, but the essential task of the state is juridical: *to adjudicate disputes among citizens about the proper interpretation of justified principles.* This juridical conception of government is deeply rooted in the classical liberal tradition.[57] As Macedo observes of Oakeshott's theory, it

extends the full blooded ethic and persona of the conscientious adjudicator from judges to legislators and citizens: utterly impartial adjudication becomes the defining moment of politics as a whole. The liberal citizen as much as the legislator and judge occupy not positions providing opportunities to advance narrow interests, but public offices in a scheme of politics concerned to articulate and enforce the best reasons of public morality. By extending a strict conception of moral purpose from law to politics as a whole, all political roles and all proper participation in politics come to entail the renunciation of narrow interests. Reasons of public morality provide the ends for, and not simply side-constraints upon, political action.[58]

The scope for what is typically called "public policy" is restricted in liberal juridical regimes. In *Taking Rights Seriously,* Ronald Dworkin distinguished rights-based arguments from policy arguments, the latter of which "justify a political decision by showing that the decision advances or protects some collective goal of the community as a whole."[59] Famously, Dworkin insisted that individual rights "trump" collective policy goals, but this itself supposes that it is legitimate for a government to pursue collective goals so long as it does so in a way consistent with individual rights.[60] Thus, for example, Dworkin allows that the government "may devote special resources to the training of exceptionally talented artists or musicians . . . because a community with a lively cultural tradition provides an environment within which citizens may live more imaginatively and in which they may take pride."[61] Given the generalization of the argument against establishment (sec. 10.3), it is not easy to imagine a plausible argument, justifying taxation supporting the arts, addressed to all citizens—bowlers and fans of country and western music as well as middle class supporters of the arts—on the grounds that such taxation promotes community pride and imaginative existences. And absent such a justification, a liberal regime devoted to the rule of law provides no room for collective pursuits of such values, no matter how attractive to some, even a majority, of citizens.[62]

It may well be objected that this is far too narrow a conception of the ends of government. According to Rogers Smith, not even Locke seemed to restrict government to the umpiring function.[63] Recall that, on Locke's view, government is directed to "no other end, but the *Peace, Safety,* and the *publick good* of the People."[64] Madison, too, allows that the general welfare is an end of government.[65] But justificatory liberalism is not so very different. We have seen that liberal principles endorse policies protecting the civil interests of everyone, or more generally those that benefit everyone (sec. 10.3.2). We might say, then, that a fundamental liberal principle is that government can justifiably act to advance the public interest or common good. One, perhaps the greatest, object of public dispute concerns precisely the sort of policies that advance the good of everyone. Consequently, to restrict the umpire to adjudicating disputes about basic liberal principles in no way precludes government from taking action to promote policies that benefit everyone.

On first glance, accepting policies premised on furthering the common good may seem to undermine the liberal case for limited government, driving us back toward Bork's thesis that the majority may basically do as it wishes so long as it does not violate relatively specific rights of the minority. To say that the government has the authority to advance the common good may seem tantamount to saying that it can do whatever it likes. But clearly this is not so. Although, like all political principles, this one may be distorted and subverted in practice, by no means does it constitute a license for far-reaching majoritarianism. If taken seriously, the requirement that a justified policy must advance the interests of everyone is extremely demanding. Typically, I think, this requirement only appears empty if one adopts a collectivistic or majoritarian analysis of the public, or the common good, such that a policy can benefit "the public" without advantaging everyone.[66] But collectivism is inconsistent with the basic individualistic assumption of justificatory liberalism: To publicly justify a principle is to show that each and every member of the public has conclusive reason to embrace it.[67] For the same reason, we must reject the all-too-easy equation of the common good with the majority's interests.[68]

But this now would seem a hopelessly demanding requirement: What policies could possibly be justified as serving *everyone's* interests or good? Public goods, it may be insisted, just don't come that pure. Suppose for a moment that this is so; assume that policy G can be justified only if it secures a public good, but in fact *there is no inconclusive (i.e. not defeated) argument* that G advances the good of each and every person. If so—if every argument justifying G as benefitting everyone is decisively defeated—then it really does seem quite clear that collective, mandatory, pursuit of G is unjust. *Ex hypothesi,* some citizens are being co-opted into the pursuit of others' interests *without justification.* Surely it would be a damning criticism of "public policy" if all policies were like G—policy would always be premised on some browbeating others into serving their interests. I suspect that those who support more extensive state policy making but who also insist that no goods benefit everyone still believe that, somehow, policies are openly justifiable to everyone. Perhaps they believe that justice demands the provision of basic services (in which case it is not a matter of the common good at all); or perhaps they believe that the citizens who do not benefit from the policy can be given some other good reason to endorse it. If so, then, of course, these proponents of policy believe that the test of public justification can be met in the end, although not simply through common good arguments.

In any event, I suspect that the supposition underlying the objection—that no policies can meet a strict test of universal benefit—should not be so easily granted. For, first, there may be a plausible argument that a policy advances the interest of every member of some section of the public, such as motorists.[69] If a policy is universally beneficial among some section of the public, then mandatory taxation restricted to that section may well be justified. (We need to remember that the universal benefit test does not suppose that there will be universal consent to the policy—some may seek to free-ride or simply be wrong about what promotes their interests. See section 13.6.3). Moreover—and this is a point to which we shall return (sec. 15.4)—policies might in principle be bundled in various ways such that a reasonable case can be made that the universal benefit test is met. Perhaps it can be argued that a set of policies over a number of years meets the test.

Some might object that, despite my earlier protestations, this last suggestion shows that, after all, the common good requirement really is vacuous: If the requirement is not applied to individual policies or individual acts of legislation, it becomes simply hand-waving. The "requirement," one may object, can always be met if we are vague enough about what set of policies it is supposed to apply to. Again, I think this is too pessimistic, but it is not an issue that can be resolved here. Precisely what sorts of justifications are victorious is a properly political issue. In a liberal political order, for instance, more libertarian-minded citizens are apt to object to a variety of governmental policies on the grounds that they manifest illicit transfers from one group to another while others will maintain that, considered as part of a package of policies, they promote the good of all. Political theorists have often tried to resolve such disputes by providing detailed blueprints for justified policies. But this aspiration is misguided. We have seen that reasoning on these matters is almost surely inconclusive; consequently, the claim that a specific position is part of fundamental law, and so can be removed from the political agenda, cannot be justified. The proper aim of political theory is not to advance a preferred set of policies, claiming that they are conclusively justified and so beyond politics, but to articulate the sorts of reasons that are justificatory, and the general *ethos* of law making. And a system of laws that took seriously the demand that policies benefit everyone, and so was not prepared to mask majoritarian imposition as "public" benefit, would very likely differ from that which obtains today.

12.4.3 Procedural Provisions

Liberal constitutionalism empowers the umpire to adjudicate only those disputes that arise from inconclusive judgments about the proper interpretation and application of publicly justified liberal principles, including what policies advance the good of everyone. And, of course, the umpire is only empowered to adjudicate these disputes in ways that do not conflict with other justified principles as, for example, specified by a bill of rights. But constitutionalism is not exclusively concerned with such substantive constraints. Indeed, the great contribution of constitutional political economists has been to emphasize the way in which procedural provisions are at least as important, even perhaps more fundamental, to the Madisonian vision of limited government.[70] Constitutional procedures play two very different roles in a juridical state: identification of the umpire and ensuring that the umpire perform its juridical task properly.

The first function is often taken for granted. In his classic work on the concept of law, H.L.A. Hart stressed that in a legal system some of the rules "are *constitutive* of the sovereign."[71] What Hart called "secondary rules" do not aim to adjudicate disputes among citizens, but to identify what constitutes a genuine law—a determination of the umpire. It is worth stressing that secondary rules are so important in a legal system because the validity of a law cannot be determined from its content. This is not a conceptual truth about legal systems, but the consequence of a particular theory of law. Consider, for example, a more Platonic theory of law and government according to which rulers are genuine and acknowledged political experts—they are *an* authority on politics (see sec. 11.2.3). If the authoritativeness of the law were entirely dependent on its content—its wisdom—and if citizens could generally recognize expertise when they saw it, determining the validity of a proposed law would not require appeal to secondary rules that determine what acts of whom constitute legal regulation. However, because the authority of the umpire does not depend on the wisdom of its directives—its authority claims to be largely independent of its content—legal validity turns largely on whether the purported legal rule emanates from the authorized procedure. Secondary legal rules, as Hart stressed, identify who (under what conditions) has authority to issue valid primary rules.

The importance of secondary rules in identifying valid primary laws is, then, an essential part of political and legal theories that accord the state authority that is to a great degree independent of the content of its directives. Interestingly, on the Madisonian interpretation, the other important function of constitutional procedures points to the way in which the authority of laws does derive from their content. Given our acceptance of the idea of fundamental law, it is clear that on justificatory liberalism the content independence of political authority is restricted to inconclusive disputes about the proper interpretation of justified principles (sec. 11.2.6). Madisonian constitutional procedures aim to keep the government within its proper sphere of activity. Thus, in defense of the federalist principle Madison wrote:

Justice is the end of government. It is the end of civil society. It has ever been and ever will be pursued until it be obtained, or until liberty be lost in the pursuit. . . . In the extended republic of the United States, and among the varieties of interests, parties, and sects which it embraces, a coalition of the majority of the whole society could seldom take place on any other principles than those of justice and the general good; whilst there being much less danger to a minor from the will of the major party, there must be less pretext, also, to provide the security of the former, by introducing into government a will not dependent on the latter, or in other words, a will independent of society itself.[72]

My concern is not the details of Madison's argument for an extended federal republic, but that Madisonian constitutionalism employs procedures to keep the government within the bounds of justice; the reason of the public, he insisted, ought to control the government.[73] Madison's problem is much the same as justificatory liberalism's: While insisting that the government ought to be kept within the bounds of justice and guided by public reason, Madison was quite aware that on questions of justice, even "when men exercise their reason coolly and freely . . . they inevitably fall into different opinions on some of them."[74] We require government because our opinions differ on political issues, but government becomes tyrannical when it sets itself up as "will independent of society itself" and attacks the civil rights on which public reason concurs. The main problem of Madisonian constitutional design, then, is to minimize the likelihood that government will operate outside its proper bounds.

12.5 Liberal Constitutions and Constitutional Politics

Political theorists run the risk of two, opposite, errors. On the one hand, in theorizing about what a justified political order would look like, they are apt to preempt actual politics and substitute their own judgment as to what political decisions should be reached. Faced with this danger—which seems to smack of theoretical hubris—some political theorists respond by insisting that everything must be "left to politics." But whatever its appeal to, say, conservatives or Marxists, this response to theoretical hubris is not open to liberal political theorists, for liberals adamantly deny that all decisions must be left open to politics. Some things are beyond politics.[75] First, the commitment to substantive liberal principles is beyond politics insofar as the *legitimacy* of the principles is not properly on the political agenda. Freedom of speech, religious toleration, toleration of widely different views of what makes life worth living, antiestablishmentarianism, and the sphere of privacy that these tolerations lead to—such matters are off the political agenda. So, too, are the basic commitments of the rule of law. Justified adjudicative procedures, I have argued, are restricted to those that umpire through and by law. Hence, for instance, the rights associated with due process are fundamental to liberal authority, because they are central to the umpire's claim to decide issues fairly, and consistent with the principle of equality.[76]

Liberal theory, then, claims the right to dictate practice on matters of abstract fundamentals.[77] But even on fundamentals liberalism must allow for a certain sort of politics, for two reasons. First, we disagree about what has been conclusively justified, and second, in writing constitutions, we disagree about the best way to codify what has been conclusively justified. In an important sense, any specific liberal citizen knows precisely what substantive clauses should appear in a constitution: If and only if Alf is justified in believing that a clause has been conclusively justified does he have good reason to accept it as a constitutional constraint or requirement. Recall that our ultimate commitment to liberal authority derives from both moral *and* practical reasons: We wish to justify our demands on others, but such demands are part of living a life. Consequently, although citizen Alf may have a very clear idea of the ideal constitution, he may have solid practical reasons for accepting less. To serve its purposes, a constitutional order must not only be justified, but must be widely perceived as such. Traditionally, moral theory has looked askance at the idea of trading off moral commitments for mere practical benefits; but morality is itself a practical activity. As a moral agent Alf must decide what arrangements are most conducive to honoring his commitment to justify himself; confronted with a choice between an ideal constitution that is widely rejected and a less than ideal constitution that is widely embraced, Alf may rightly concur that the latter actually is more conducive to moralized social relations. To insist on what he believes to be right may lead to conflict, the breakdown of political order, and a return to the state of anarchy in which moralized relations are not generally available. Of course, at some point the less than ideal may be too much less, forcing a citizen to reject the constitution as a hindrance to a moral life. I shall have more to say about that problem in section 17.4. But for now, I merely wish to stress that a constitution that is less than perfect from the standpoint of admitting all that is, and nothing that is not, publicly justified may nevertheless be the best constitution from the perspective of actually leading a life informed by moralized relations.

There is, then, great merit in the idea of a distinctively constitutional politics—a search for justified principles on which there is wide consensus.[78] However, in contrast to political liberalism, we need to be very clear that these are distinct requirements—what is publicly justified and what is the object of wide consensus. To be sure, we would expect genuinely justified principles to be agreed to widely, but I have stressed that consensus is neither necessary nor sufficient for public justification. In contrast, widespread consensus is fundamental to the *efficacy* of a constitutional arrangement. As Henry Knox pointed out with regard to calls for a constitutional convention in the United States in 1787, a convention that did not appeal to the people of every state would be "inadequate" and "inefficacious."[79]

Liberal constitutional theory, then, does not replace constitutional politics and its search for consensus on fundamental substantive principles, nor does it dictate the justified procedures for legislation and the application of general rules to specific cases. Again, though, liberal political theory does not give full sway to "the voice of the people." As we are about to see, justificatory liberalism also insists on institutions of a certain sort.

CHAPTER 13

Tracking Desiderata for Law-Making Institutions

13.1 Law-Making Institutions

Let us suppose that liberal citizens have partially completed their constitutional task: *They have achieved widespread, though of course not complete, consensus* on what substantive principles are publicly justified. We have seen that liberal citizens committed to public justification would restrict the set of feasible procedures to those that umpire through law. A justified umpiring procedure must conform to the internal morality of the law, including the principle of equality; it must specify and respect the rights of citizens; and it must respect fundamental law. The critical justificatory task now confronts our liberal citizens: To justify an umpiring procedure to resolve their disputes about the proper interpretation of the demands of fundamental law. The complete umpiring procedure will be complex; it requires both (1) a legislative procedure that adjudicates citizens' competing inconclusive judgments about the requirements of liberal principles by formulating laws, which are the definitive voice of public reason, and (2) a judicial system to adjudicate competing judgments about the application of laws to specific cases. In addition, a complete account of the juridical state would have to consider the justification of the executive, which enforces the definitive public judgments articulated by law.[1] In what follows, however, I shall focus on the main adjudicative functions of government.[2] In chapters 13–15 I examine legislative adjudicative procedures; I turn to the judiciary in chapter 16.

It will help to clarify at the outset the idea of a law-making institution, and to distinguish it from outwardly similar ideas employed in social choice theory. Our interest is in systems that translate individual judgments into laws. Let us call L_i a law-making institution that yields a law on issue i, given the set of individuals each of whom have judgments on the issue. The set of judgments is that of all the public—the people to whom a law must be justified if it is to be publicly justified.[3] The idea is that we have a set of individuals (Alf, Betty, Charlie, etc.), each of whom has a judgment on an issue. A law-making institution, then, takes the set of individual judgments and generates a law on issue i.

A law-making institution can be, but typically will not be, what A.K. Sen describes as a "collective choice rule," which transforms individual preference orderings over a set of options into a social decision.[4] Most important, most law-making institutions employ representative assemblies of various sorts. Law-making representative systems involve four main steps: (1) voters form judgments on candidates; (2) some electoral rule translates their judgments into a representative assembly; (3) individual legislators form judgments about various proposals; and (4) some legislative voting rule translates their judgments into laws. While steps (2) and (4) can be modeled in terms of collective choice rules, the entire institution involving (1) to (4)—citizen judgments to legislative outcomes—cannot be usefully understood as a formalized collective choice rule.

Because of this, the findings of axiomatic social choice theory are of limited usefulness in deliberating about what law-making institutions are justified. This limitation is nicely brought home by considering the formal criterion of monotonicity. If our focus is only on collective choice rules, there is an overwhelming case for imposing the condition that, roughly, as individual voters come to favor an option, the collective choice rule responds positively by making it more socially preferred, or at least not less socially preferred. Assume, given some profile of individual judgments, a collective choice rule determines that x is better than y. Now suppose that only Betty changes her opinion; she previously thought y was better than x, but now she believes that x is better than y. It seems manifest that the collective choice rule should still select x over y; if it originally deemed that x was preferred to y, and now even more people agree, the social choice should remain that x is better than y. As William Riker says, "it would be perverse in the extreme if increased votes for an alternative contributed to its defeat."[5] Yet collective choice rules that involve elimination procedures, such as the single transferable vote employed in elections to the Australian House of Representatives, can respond negatively to increased support.[6] But in the Australian electoral system the single transferable vote is not itself the law-making institution, but is part of steps (1) and (2), translating individual judgments about candidates into legislative seats. If we take a wider perspective and consider entire electoral systems, the results are very different. David Austen-Smith and Jeffrey Banks show that when considering full electoral systems, depending on the assumptions one makes about the ways voters decide to cast their ballots, either all reasonable law-making systems are monotonic or none are.[7]

This is not to say that the proofs advanced by axiomatic social choice theory are of no interest. But if our concern is the nature of law-making institutions—electoral systems rather than simply the collective choice rules that are a part of them—we need to exercise great care in extrapolating the findings of social choice theory. For, as Austen-Smith and Banks show, when this wider perspective is taken, what seems an obvious desideratum appears to become a "nonissue."[8]

The notion of a law-making institution involves an important assumption, which ultimately is an idealization. It supposes that we can isolate the issue on which competing judgments arise—for example, whether we should adopt a law prohibiting hard-core pornography—and that individual judgments on this issue are robust, in the sense that an individual's judgment on issue i will not be affected by bringing another issue into consideration (sec. 1.2). This, of course, is not the case. Logrolling is premised precisely on the fact that a legislator's judgment (or at least vote) on a certain issue often will change when that issue is linked with another. It is essentially for such reasons that Arrow has defined individual preferences over entire states of the world rather than particular issues.[9] So the formal problem can be avoided by identifying i as the set of all legislation, though this doesn't seem a helpful way of thinking of legislative institutions. Public opinion polls, candidate debates, press conferences, newspaper editorials, and receptions at philosophy conferences all suppose that it makes sense to ask a person "What is your opinion on issue i?" or to criticize a person's judgment on a specific issue. And this despite the fact that we know that different ways of asking the question or stating the issue—different ways of framing i—may result in different answers. Still, such questions seem much more likely to elicit information than "What is your opinion about the ideal set of all laws?" I shall thus assume for now that we can identify judgments on a particular issue, and consider explicitly the problems raised in practice by being only imperfectly able to do so (sec. 15.4).

13.2 The Political Contract

13.2.1 The Aim of the Contractors

It will be useful to depict the constitutional problem of liberal citizens in hypothetical contractual terms: What type of procedures would all rational citizens, committed to publicly justifying their moral demands on each other, have conclusive reason to accept?[10] Fundamental to any contractual justification is the motivation of the contracting parties. Unless we know what the contractors seek to gain from the agreement, we cannot even begin to speculate about what contract they will endorse. In our case the contractors' prime aim is to honor their commitment to public justification by living under the rule of law. In deciding how they are to adjudicate their disputes, therefore, *the prime motivation of the contractors is to select a law-making institution that, as closely as possible, tracks the publicly justified morality.* As contractors, they are not aiming to advance their values, goals, or ends; at this point their aim is to justify to each other an adjudicative procedure. And a cardinal virtue of an adjudicative procedure is that (in some way yet to be explained) it yields good answers.[11] At this stage, then, Betty cannot justify a particular law-making institution to Alf by showing that it promotes her values, or even that it promotes both of their values. Their current dispute is not what promotes their values, but how to arrive at the best interpretation of the publicly justified morality. It is that question to which they seek an answer.

This is important. We might distinguish two stages of contractual argument: the moral and the political. At the first, moral, stage, we consider individuals committed to public justification yet embracing different values and goals, hence finding themselves at odds. At this first stage they need to justify to each other a basic set of moral principles. Employing the contractual heuristic, each citizen asks the question, "What principles could all rational individuals, committed to public justification, agree upon?" At this first stage, I have argued elsewhere, Alf's aim of advancing his own values is relevant:[12] Like others, he has reason to accept principles of morality that advance his values. My discussion of justified liberal principles (chap. 10) can be understood as a summary of this moral stage of the contractual argument. At the second, political, stage, however, we suppose that each citizen has arrived at his or her own conclusion about the results of the first stage, as well as his or her own view of the best interpretation of these principles in specific cases. But since many of their conclusions are inconclusive, liberal citizens need to justify to each other a procedure to adjudicate their disputes about the demands of the justified principles. My concern here is this second stage, and at this stage liberal citizens' prime concern is, in a broad sense, epistemological.

Of course, their aim is practical, too—their ultimate aim is to get on with life. Thus they seek procedures that are relatively efficient, yield answers that are simple enough to be followed, are fair, and so on. But recall that liberal citizens do not seek a collective choice rule or social welfare function, but a *law*-making institution. And, we have seen, these concerns are part of the ideal of the *rule of law* (sec. 12.1). Consequently, we can say that *within the constraints imposed by the ideal of the rule of law,* the prime concern of our liberal citizens is epistemological—they seek the law-making institution that yields the best answer.

13.2.2 Designed for Whom?

As Rawls rightly points out, hypothetical contractual arguments employing idealizing conditions must distinguish clearly three perspectives: the perspective of the contractors, the perspective of you and me, and the perspective of actual citizens who live under just institutions.[13] In our case, the contractors' perspective is defined by ascribing to them certain ideal motivations: They are solely motivated by the aim of honoring their commitment to public justification. Hence, we can take what they would agree to as an indication of what adjudicative procedures can be publicly justified. The interest of the contractors' perspective to you and me—the second perspective—is that it isolates and dramatizes *our* problem of honoring *our commitment* to public justification. If we imagine ourselves solely motivated by the aim of justifying to each other a law-making institution to adjudicate disputes about justice and the common good, our perspective is the same as that of the ideal contractors. Both perspectives must be distinguished from a third: that of actual people living under the law-making institution. The motivation of the contractors is idealized, so it is not, of course, the same as the motivation of actual citizens in the real world. In the hypothetical contractual account, the motivation of the contractors is determined by what sorts of reasons *justify* an arrangement; we suppose that they are motivated purely by their commitment to justify. But rarely are real people so purely motivated; actual citizens are tempted to be selfish and to ignore what is justified. Our contractors, then, are attempting to justify to each other institutions that will be operated by actual, by no means ideal, citizens. From our perspective—the perspective of you and me—this is the interesting problem: What procedures can be justified, given that actual people do not always honor their commitment to justify themselves to others?

Our aim, and the aim of our ideal liberal contractors, is to design adjudicative institutions that, when operated by real people, lead to decisions that track liberal morality. Fundamental to the design project is, "Just what sorts of people are we designing institutions for?" Famously, Hume provides a clear answer:

It is, therefore, a just *political* maxim, that *every man must be supposed a knave;* though, at the same time, it appears somewhat strange, that a maxim should be true in *politics* which is false in *fact*. But to satisfy us on this head, we may consider, that men are generally more honest in their private than in their public capacity, and will go to greater lengths to serve a party, than when their own private interest alone is concerned. . . .

When there offers, therefore, to our censure and examination, any plan of government, real or imaginary, where the power is distributed among several courts, and several orders of men, we should always consider the separate interest of each court, and each order; and if we find that, by skillful division of power, this interest must necessarily, in its operation, concur with the public, we may pronounce that government to be wise and happy. If, on the contrary, separate interest is not checked, and be not directed to the public, we ought to look for nothing but faction, disorder, and tyranny from such a government.[14]

This general view is close to the heart of Madisonian constitutionalism:

Ambition must be made to counter ambition. The interest of the man must be connected with the constitutional rights of the place. It may be a reflection on human nature that such devices should be necessary to control the abuses of government. But what is government itself but the greatest of all reflections on human nature? If men were angels, no government would be necessary. If angels were to govern men, neither external nor internal controls on government would be necessary.[15]

It is entirely intelligible to accept that politics aims to track justified liberal public morality, yet insist that because *homo politicus* is a knave, political institutions must assume that political actors will have no interest in public justification, but instead be thoroughly devoted to their self-interest. Well-designed political institutions would then aim in Madisonian fashion to channel private interest into policies that track justified morality, operating very much like Smith's invisible hand: People within them would be led to promote a "public good" that was no part of their intention.[16]

It is hard to overestimate the attraction of this picture of political institutions. Indeed, I do not think it is an overstatement to say that contemporary political science has been captivated, not to say captured, by it.[17] Nevertheless, if our aim is a system of laws that respects the core liberal principles of freedom and toleration, and that reliably yields laws that are publicly justified, it is hard to see how this can be achieved with a population of knaves. Although Machiavelli's name is typically associated with this "realist" tradition in politics, he concluded that it is almost impossible to maintain a free state with a corrupt population.[18] This doctrine of civic republicanism has found powerful support in Robert D. Putnam and his colleagues' study of regional government in Italy from 1970 to 1989, which reveals dramatic differences between the performances of regional governments in northern and southern Italy. Although all the regional governments were created at the same time, on almost all measures the governments in the south are worse: they perform badly, they remain undeveloped and relatively unimportant, corruption is pervasive, and the public is unsatisfied. In explaining these differences, Putnam was led to the importance of "civic engagement" in the north—an active participation and interest in public affairs and some devotion to the public good even when the latter is opposed to private interests: "Citizens in a civic community, though not selfless saints, regard the public domain as more than a battleground for pursuing personal interest."[19]

Admittedly, Putnam's research does not show that it is impossible to construct political institutions that direct the activities of relentlessly self-interested people to the public good. But he does show that the political institutions of northern Italy are successful precisely because they are not operated by "knaves," while the institutions of southern Italy, which seem a much closer approximation to self-interested politics, perform badly. So it is not at all obvious that *homo politicus* is necessarily a knave; moreover, we have some reason to suspect that when citizens are knavish, their institutions do not secure the sort of public ends that the republican tradition has upheld as the point of politics.

None of this requires a repudiation of Madisonian constitutionalism. Although Madison certainly believed that political institutions should economize on the need for civic virtue, he did not hold that knaves could operate political institutions that achieve justice:

As there is a degree of depravity in mankind which requires a certain degree of circumspection and distrust, so there are other qualities in human nature which justify a certain portion of esteem and confidence. Republican government presupposes the existence of these qualities in a higher degree than any other form. Were the pictures which have been drawn by the political jealousy of some among us faithful likenesses of the human character, the inference would be that there is not sufficient virtue among men for self-government; and that nothing less than the chains of despotism can restrain them from destroying and devouring one another.[20]

Homo politicus is no angel; political institutions designed on the supposition that they will be operated by angels will no doubt fail. Self-interest, jealousy, and private ambition are common features of political life. But to suppose that *homo politicus* votes or forms political opinions simply on the basis of self-interest first seems wrong as a matter of fact[21] and second, obscures how politics can be understood as a way to achieve justice and the common good.[22] Smith's claim was that if each seeks to maximize his or her individual wealth, the outcome will be the maximization of social wealth. This is not truistic, since sometimes efforts at individual maximization make everyone worse off (as in Prisoner's Dilemma situations), but neither is it miraculous. Since for classical economics "the wealth of any community is the sum of the portions of wealth belonging to the several individuals of which the community is composed,"[23] the claim that the aggregate of individual maximizations maximizes the community's wealth is plausible. Divine intervention really does seem necessary, though, to ensure that the unintentional outcome of each person's single-minded pursuit of self-interest is justice and the common good.

Economic and political life are disanalogous in another way.[24] One engages in market activity in order to satisfy one's preferences or achieve one's personal goals. Smith's claim was that these personal pursuits are not essentially competitive or self-defeating; if each seeks to maximize personal gain, the aggregate gain is maximized. But people do not participate in the market because they aim ultimately to maximize social wealth; they are attracted to it as a path to personal gain. In contrast, our commitment to public justification leads us to political activity as a way to adjudicate our disputes about justice, not as a path to personal gain. Consequently, a political life focused solely on personal gain would be alienating in a way that economic life is not. If the market model of politics is accepted, our ultimate reason for engaging in political activity—to track publicly justified principles—would not be reflected in practice; on this model only appeals to individual interests are recognized in political practice. So we would find ourselves enmeshed in a practice in which we engage in order to publicly justify ourselves, but in which appeals to public justification would be inappropriate. One would find oneself in a polity in which voters appeal only to self-interest in advancing political claims, while one knows that such reasons are not ultimately justificatory, even though good results follow from people's thinking that they are. I hasten to add that this is not logically inconsistent; utilitarian philosophers in particular have stressed the potential gap between the standards for evaluating a practice and the reasons employed by participants in the practice.[25] But for just this reason these practices are typically alienating for those who understand their point—the reasons employed by participants do not reflect the point of the practice. Indeed, so alienating is this self-understanding of one's activity that it invites self-deception. To take the practice seriously, one has to be able to take seriously the sorts of reasons other participants proffer; to do that, it would be best to forget just what the practice is really about.

Liberal political institutions should not be designed for angels, but neither do we have any reason to suppose that they can be successfully operated by knaves. And there is no good reason to suppose that citizens are either.[26] In proposing political institutions designed to track liberal morality, our liberal contractors do best by supposing actual citizens of imperfect virtue. Citizens have opinions about justice that they take seriously,[27] though they are prone to interpret them in ways that coincide with their personal interests. The upshot of all this—and especially of our rejection of a Smithian-inspired invisible hand account of political institutions—is that the aim of contractors is to design procedures that not only track liberal morality, but do so by being in some way *responsive* to the judgments of actual citizens. Absent an invisible hand, responding to what actual citizens (not necessarily all, but at least some) think is justified is necessary if we are to have laws that track what is justified.

13.3 Inconclusiveness, Indeterminacy, and Random Democracy

That the prime aim of our contractors is to justify procedures that track morality by responding to the judgments of citizens distinguishes justificatory liberalism from many contemporary theories of democracy, which understand politics as the confrontation of incommensurable visions of the good life. According to such deeply pluralistic democratic theories, it is for the most part mistaken to describe political views as more or less correct, justified, or reasonable. They are simply divergent, and no standard is available that would allow comparison.[28] From an epistemological point of view, dispute between these contending views is *indeterminate:* Insufficient grounds can be found to adjudicate between these contending views of the good life. No beliefs on these matters are justified. Interestingly, because of this indeterminacy, deeply pluralistic democratic theories are attracted to the idea of lotteries to resolve disputes. Bruce Ackerman, for instance, concludes that "lotteries and majorities have more in common than superficial appearances suggest."[29] As Jon Elster shows, "indeterminancy is a fundamental reason for using lotteries."[30] Although, unfortunately, Elster does not clearly distinguish indeterminacy and inconclusiveness, random decision procedures are particularly attractive when we face indeterminacy.[31] When we confront genuine indeterminacy—when there simply are not enough reasons for choosing one option over another—"we might as well select one at random."[32] After all, *ex hypothesi*, reason cannot instruct us.

If a theory insists on the basic indeterminacy of political disputes and adds a democratic requirement that each person's vote is in some way to count equally (see (14.1), the case for random policy selection begins to look plausible. Robert Paul Wolff writes:

In one sense, majority rule *guarantees* to the members of the majority that their preference becomes law. Hence if a man knows that he is in the minority, he will realize that he has *no* chance at all of effecting his will. This is the characteristic of majoritarian democracy which drives permanent minorities into rebellion, and permits what Mill quite justly called the tyranny of the majority. A system of legislation by lot might therefore be more in accord with the principle of equal chance. Each individual could write his preference on a piece of paper, and the winning law could be drawn from a twirling basket. Then, we might suppose, each citizen could have exactly the same chance that his will would become law.[33]

As Wolff notes, this is not quite right: Betty and everyone else has an equal chance that her or his own bit of paper (with a personal policy preference on it) will be drawn, but the chances of Betty's getting her policy preference depend on the number of other people who write it down on their bits of paper. "Nevertheless," he concludes, "it does seem to come closer to the idea of equal chances than majority rule."[34]

Liberal contractors would reject a policy lottery because they understand their disputes to be for the most part inconclusive, not indeterminate, and inconclusive on only some points. They would concur with Michael Walzer that a policy lottery would be "irresponsible and arbitrary"[35] because it does not seek to track justified morality. It might be objected that liberal citizens cannot be certain that all their disagreements are inconclusive rather than indeterminate. As we saw in section 9.4, some disagreements can aptly be described as cases of nested indeterminacy. Although some law within a certain set of proposals can be justified, there is insufficient reason to prefer one member of the set over another. Sometimes the law simply coordinates action: Although we all have good reason to drive either on the left or the right, no one can form a justified belief that one rather than the other is the publicly justified choice. Here we face a pure coordination problem, and reasoned choice seems impossible. Random devices to determine legislation look plausible. Nevertheless, strong reasons caution against employing such *legislative* devices.[36]

As a rule—and one not open to many exceptions—it seems quite impossible to determine when reasons run out, and so we confront genuine indeterminacy. Recall here our discussion of Greenawalt's claim that in justificatory arguments public reasons are exhausted, and so we are forced to rely on personal reasons to arrive at conclusions (sec. 9.2). I rejected this view; given the costs of epistemic processing and scanning our belief systems for relevant information, our usual epistemic situation is one of too many, rather than too few, reasons. We cannot afford to scan our belief systems for all possible inferences or all relevant beliefs. Because of this, our methodological assumption ought to be that the available reasons rarely run out, and so genuine indeterminacy is rare. Again, indeterminacy is possible, but even in cases in which it seems likely, we are apt to be misled. Consider, for instance, coordination problems, in which indeterminacy really seems likely. Pure coordination problems are rare; the normal coordination problem is the sort of "impure" situation that is modelled by the "Battle of the Sexes" problem in Figure 13.1 (Alf's preferences are in the top right corner of each cell, Betty's in the lower left).[37]

It is Friday night, and Alf and Betty wish to go out together; either coordinated outcome is preferred by both to either uncoordinated outcome. In this politically correct version of the story, Alf prefers the ballet and Betty prefers the wrestling. Although Alf and Betty are engaged in a coordination problem, they are also involved in a conflict: Alf would prefer that they both go to the ballet, while Betty would prefer that they both go to the wrestling. It is not at all clear in this case that the solution is indeterminate rather than inconclusive. Alf may be able to give Betty reasons for going the ballet and not the wrestling, while Betty may advance reasons (that she thinks Alf should accept) for both to go to the wrestling. Again, it is certainly possible that their public reasons run out—for example, no appeals to justice or fairness are relevant. My point here is only that insofar as coordination games are typically impure coordination games, we cannot infer from the existence of a coordination game that the solution is indeterminate.[38] Even in a coordination game the "coordinator" may really be an umpire, adjudicating conflicting public reasons.[39]

Lotteries, it should be noted, are a particularly bad way to resolve inconclusive disputes about the demands of justice and the common good, for they generate perverse incentives for citizens to advance un-

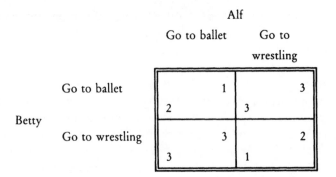

Figure 13.1 An Impure Coordination Problem

justified proposals. In the legislative lottery system, Alf could advance, without harming the chance that his proposal is accepted, the opinion that public morality requires that he be supported in luxury by the state—not a proposal that would seriously be entertained by a procedure that seeks to track what is publicly justified.

13.4 Widely Responsive Procedures

13.4.1 Avoiding Unreasonable Legislation

It may well be wondered: How can liberal contractors justify to each other a law-making institution on the grounds that it "best tracks" liberal morality, when they require procedures just because they disagree about whose judgments "best track" liberal morality?[40] Let me give the simple answer first, adding complexity in section 13.6. First, then, the simple answer: Liberal contractors are able to evaluate law-making institutions in terms of their tendency to yield *bad* laws, namely, legislation that violates fundamental law. Although debates about what are the best specific laws are typically inconclusive, liberal constitutionalism identifies victoriously justified substantive limits on what can be legislated. Consequently, our contractors would choose law-making procedures that are unlikely to violate substantive fundamental law. In the words of Blackstone, they aim at procedures that avoid "unreasonable" legislation.[41] This requirement is clearly fundamental: An umpire who makes decisions that are generally recognized as unreasonable will not perform its assigned task of adjudicating between competing reasonable views. We must, then, reject any proposed method of adjudication that typically yields decisions outside the range of reasonable dispute.

13.4.2 Wide Responsiveness and Self-Protection

It is on this ground that many have advocated democratic procedures; the rights of citizens are more likely to be protected under democratic institutions. As J.S. Mill emphasized, "the rights and interests of every or any person are only secure from being disregarded, when the interested person is himself able, and habitually disposed, to stand up for them." He went on to insist that "human beings are only secure from evil at the hands of others in proportion as they have the power of being, and are, self-*protecting*."[42] Following Mill, liberal democrats have insisted that the chief benefit of democratic government is that the rights of citizens are more likely to be protected against incursion by those holding power. Such responsive government, it is claimed, is more apt to avoid injustice than are those that vest political power in an "enlightened few."[43]

This case for widely responsive institutions is particularly strong, as it supposes that justice and interest typically coincide when one's basic rights are at stake. A government enacting legislation that attacks one's basic rights and civil interests does one an injustice. Consequently, even a citizenry of modest "virtue"—a commitment to uphold justified principles—is apt to oppose these policies. This familiar point is so important it has a strong claim to be deemed the first theorem of liberal democracy: *Law-making procedures that are widely responsive to the judgments of the citizenry have been shown to be the most reliable protectors of basic individual rights.*[44] Admittedly, Millian considerations do not demonstrate in a deductive manner that unresponsive regimes are inferior to more inclusive procedures (such as standard representative democracy or Millian representative government) as ways to resolve disputes about justice. But the record of narrowly based elite regimes as arbiters of liberal morality is unambiguously dismal; neither the Party nor technocrats have given us any reason to doubt Mill's case for significant responsiveness as a condition of a reasonably competent umpire. Law-making procedures that are responsive to citizens' perceptions that their basic rights and interests are being attacked do much better at avoiding "unreasonable" legislation than do narrowly based elite regimes.

This Millian case for wide-responsiveness may seem undermined by the apparent irrationality of self-interested voting. As many economic theorists of democracy have recognized, in an even moderately large election, the chances that any single voter can determine the outcome is, as Loren Lomasky and Geoffrey Brennan put it, "vanishingly small."[45] Now if one is acting purely on self-interest, one has to weigh the potential gains from casting one's vote in a way to bring about an outcome that advances one's interest against the small but nonzero costs of casting a vote (actually going out and voting) and gathering enough information to determine which electoral outcome is best for one's interest. Given that the probability of casting the decisive vote (p) is vanishingly small, even if one's interest would be heavily impacted by one outcome over another (u), the expected payoffs from casting your self-interested vote will also be minute. That is, even for high values of u, the value of p is so low that the value of $p(u)$ will also be tiny; almost certainly less than the expected costs of voting. Consequently, on grounds of self-interest, one almost certainly should abstain from voting: Given the tiny chance that any person's vote will be decisive in determining the outcome in even moderate-sized electorates, it seems that the costs of voting (in terms of inconvenience, and so on) will always outweigh the expected gains. It would thus seem that rational citizens might abstain from voting (see further sec. 15.3). But if so, and if the Millian protective case for democracy depends on the assumption that, when their basic interests are threatened, voters will go to the polls and protect their interests, the Millian argument for wide responsiveness seems to suppose irrational voters.

The argument, however, can be interpreted in a way that avoids this problem. It seems very plausible indeed to suppose that what Judith Shklar called one's "sense of injustice"[46] is most easily aroused when one's basic interests are attacked. Consequently, even supposing that it is irrational for voters cast their ballots to *achieve the outcome of protecting* their interests, voters may nevertheless *express their judgment* that an injustice has been done (see sec. 15.3). If a person's sense of injustice tends to be awakened, and tends to speak unambiguously, when her basic civil interests are threatened, the happy marriage of interest and justice upon when Mill's protective case for democracy depends, is still consummated.

Although this familiar argument is often described as a case for "democracy," it is really a much broader case for systems of law-making in which the mass of citizens exercise enough control over legislation such that, if generally unpopular, it can be overturned.[47] A number of law-making institutions meet this criterion. Mill's plural voting scheme (see sec. 14.2), some corporatist arrangements in which participation occurs within producer groups and trade unions,[48] a regime in which the aristocracy proposes laws but the commoners can reject them, systems characterized by modest property qualifications, either for voters or representatives, as well as standard representative democracy and direct or participatory democracy all incorporate wide responsiveness. Moreover, it is doubtful that a liberal contractor favoring any of the widely responsive systems can show conclusively that it avoids unreasonable legislation more reliably than do the others. For example, despite its unpopularity, Mill's proposal that those with more education should be awarded extra votes is by no means implausible: If we wish to track justified morality, why not accord extra weight to those who have more knowledge and better developed capacities for critical thinking?[49] To be sure, counterarguments suggest themselves: Education is not closely related to political competency, or the rights of those excluded may not receive sufficient protection. But surely these do not decisively defeat (secs. 5.3.1, 9.3.2) Mill's proposal; it remains at least plausible that an educational qualification could increase the reliability of the law-making institution (sec. 14.2).

13.4.3 Why Justificatory Liberalism Selects Widely Responsive Procedures

What I have called the fundamental theorem of liberal democracy rests on an important truth: Ways of making laws that do not respond to the views of most of the citizenry are notoriously unreliable protectors of fundamental rights. Justificatory liberalism, however, provides the basis for an even stronger case for widely responsive law-making institutions. The aim of law-making processes, I have been arguing, is to arrive at laws that track what is publicly justified, and especially to avoid laws that uphold defeated positions. The first part of this book upheld weak foundationalism as the best account of personal justification, according to which what is openly justified for Alf may not be openly justified for Betty. Moreover, I have stressed that our typical epistemic situation is a severe lack of resources to scan belief systems adequately for all possible inferences and inconsistencies. One consequence of this condition of epistemic scarcity is that people are generally better acquainted with their own belief systems than they are with those of others. It is quite impossible to have knowledge of, and properly process the inferences in, the belief systems of many other people; for a number of reasons, most important of which is that one's own belief system is fundamental to living one's own life, one is far better acquainted with one's own system than with others. Consequently, each person is in a privileged, though not unassailable, position when it comes to determining what arguments are victorious or defeated in her or his own system of beliefs. The upshot is that institutions that endeavor to track the publicly justified morality, and in particular to avoid legislating defeated proposals, must draw on the judgments of a wide part of the citizenry.[50]

This is not to say that there are no such creatures as moral experts (secs. 11.2.2, 14.1). But note what sort of knowledge one must possess to be an expert: One cannot claim to have more refined moral insight into the nature of moral reality or God's will, or a superior ability to calculate the general welfare; the claim must be that one has a better grasp of those beliefs that are justified in everyone's system of beliefs, while granting that what is justified in one person's system may not be justified in that of another. Such claims are possible—political vanguards have claimed that they know what the people want better than do the people themselves. But these claims of expertise are typically implausible just because they base their elitism on what we might, in a broad sense, call a "democratic" foundation; what is ultimately justificatory is what the people are committed to accepting. Claims of political vanguards definitely not withstanding, nothing in political history provides the slightest reason to suppose that law-making institutions can track public justification without extensive inputs by the people. Again, this does not justify democracy and its insistence on some sort of political equality; it does, though, justify widely responsive law-making institutions.

13.5 Deliberative Procedures

13.5.1 Deliberation, Consensus, and Justification

Because of pervasive epistemic scarcity, justified law-making procedures must be widely responsive to the judgments of citizens. For much the same reason they must provide ample scope for, indeed encourage, wide deliberation. Victorious justification, it will be recalled (sec. 9.3.3), must meet the publicity condition: Unless an argument has been publicly advanced, and so has been exposed to a wide range of potential defeaters, one cannot be warranted in claiming victory. More generally, I have argued that public discourse is necessary if we are to cope with the scarcity of epistemic resources. One cannot completely scan one's own system, much less those of others; in one respect, at least, public discourse is a cooperative effort in which others help us explore our own commitments. To be adequate, public justifications must be open to, and the subject of, public scrutiny.

All this is in the spirit of much contemporary political theory, which stresses the importance in politics of public dialogue or discourse.[51] But we should be aware that the purpose of public deliberation is not to achieve consensus but to determine what is publicly justified, and the two are not closely tied (sec. 8.2). To be sure, if actual citizens were purely motivated by the commitment to justify themselves, and possessed unlimited cognitive capacities, public deliberation would, perhaps, yield something like consensus. But because these conditions do not obtain, political discourse is more apt to reveal sharp differences than approximate consensus, and so political life is more accurately and appropriately described in terms of conflict than of consensus (see sec. 15.5).

This points to the superiority of justificatory liberalism over Rawls's political liberalism. Political liberalism, it will be recalled, adopts a sort of justificatory populism, according to which the public justification of a principle turns on whether it is the object of consensus of reasonable people (sec. 9.1.2). This leads political liberals to insist that the constitutional fundamentals of a regime, if publicly justified, must be a matter of reasonable consensus.[52] Let us grant for the moment that on basic constitutional issues some sort of approximate consensus can be achieved. The question still arises: If public reason is so closely associated with consensus, in what sense is normal (i.e., nonconstitutional) political discourse governed by public reason? Two options present themselves.

(1) It might be claimed that normal political activity should also aim at consensus. Although some political theorists intimate this, it seems, at best, utopian. The claim that we can achieve consensus on even the most basic of principles is optimistic enough; that reasonable citizens will come to the same conclusions on everyday political matters is, to understate matters, unduly optimistic. It should be stressed that consensus cannot be ensured by unanimity rules. Unanimity rules can ensure that measures are passed only if everyone votes in favor of a proposal; it does not follow that we reach a consensus on the correctness of the judgment (sec. 15.5).[53] A variety of subtle and not so subtle pressures can, and usually are, applied under unanimity rules to induce small minorities to forgo employing their veto. More important, unanimity rules induce side payments or logrolling; Alf, who judges x to be a better law than y on issue i, agrees to vote for y on the condition that Betty votes for z on issue j.[54] But this implies that the law-making procedure is not tracking individual judgments on issue i alone, but j as well. Recall that our aim here is to devise law-making procedures that track individual judgments on a specific issue (sec. 13.1); conse-

quently, a unanimity rule cannot guarantee consensus on the best law relating to issue i.

(2) Because disagreements and conflicts permeate political life, normal politics cannot plausibly be construed as a search for consensus. But if public reason is understood as essentially consensual, how can normal, everyday politics be explained?[55] This leads to a second option, suggested by Bruce Ackerman and Alexander Bickel: To distinguish sharply between constitutional politics and normal politics. On this view, constitutional politics is the realm of public reason and consensus, everyday politics—especially legislative politics—is simply the clash of interests.[56] Insofar as this dualistic theory is not simply a description of actual politics, but is intended in some way to legitimatize it, I have dissented: A policy cannot justly be imposed on some people on the grounds that it advances the interests of others (sec. 12.4.2). I have also indicated that it is dubious even as a descriptive theory of politics insofar as there is little evidence that most people's political opinions or voting behavior are based simply on self-interest.

Rawls, I think, is attracted to this option; whereas Bickel described the Court as articulating basic moral principles, Rawls points to the Supreme Court as an "Exemplar of Public Reason."[57] Moreover, Rawls is quite clear that public reasoning focuses on constitutional essentials, and that "many if not most political questions do not concern those fundamental matters, for example, much tax legislation and many laws regulating property; statutes protecting the environment and controlling pollution; establishing national parks and preserving wilderness areas and animal and plant species; and laying aside funds for museums and the arts."[58] Because of his justificatory populism, however, Rawls is unable to provide a clear account as to what normal politics is really about. Because there seems no hope for consensus, it seems impossible that public justification is the aim, yet Rawls draws back from the view that this sort of everyday politics is simply about the pursuit of self-interest. He grants "that it is usually highly desirable to settle political questions by invoking the values of public reason. Yet this may not always be so."[59] The point of normal political discourse and activity in Rawls's political liberalism remains obscure.

Justificatory liberalism identifies a third interpretation that explains the difference between constitutional and normal politics without adopting a dualistic theory according to which they are about essentially different matters. Constitutional politics concerns what is conclusively justified, and so determines the agenda of normal politics. Widespread consensus is to be expected. Normal politics is about fundamental matters, but is not a search for consensus; it is the confrontation of undefeated, unvictorious judgments about the demands of basic principles. As Amy Gutmann and Dennis Thompson correctly observe:

Acknowledging the moral status of a position that one opposes requires, at a minimum, that one treat it as a moral rather than a purely political, economic or other kind of nonmoral view. This acknowledgement in speech begins with the recognition that an opponent's position is based on moral principles about which reasonable people may disagree (provided that it meets the preclusion conditions for reaching the political agenda).[60]

Normal politics, though, is not constituted by a brute clash of incompatible moral views; it is a confrontation between inconsistent public justifications. Public scrutiny is the test through which proposed justifications must pass; one engaging in public discourse must give serious attention to the opposing views of others, acknowledging that they cannot be rejected without good reason.[61] Normal politics, then, is the arena of moral conflict and argument.

13.5.2 Open Government and Public Reason

Our ideal liberal contractors would thus reject any law-making procedure based simply on the competition or compromise of interests. "The underlying assumption," as Gutmann and Thompson put it, "is that we should be reaching conclusions through reason rather than force, and more specifically through moral reasoning rather than self-interested bargaining."[62] We thus have reason to embrace law-making institutions that induce legislators to "act more like judges" by providing principled justifications for their judgments.[63] Liberal democrats have long defended representative democracy in much these terms. William Nelson, following John Stuart Mill, argues that Mill's case for representative government is, at the core, an argument for "open" and "public government."[64] Consider, for example, Mill's description of representative assemblies:

Representative assemblies are often taunted by their enemies with being places of mere talk and *bavardage*. There has seldom been a more misplaced derision. I know not how a representative assembly can more usefully employ itself than talk, when the subject of talk is the great public interests of the country, and every sentence of it represents the opinion either of some important body of persons in the nation, or of an individual in whom such a body has reposed their confidence. A place where every interest and shade of opinion in the country can have its cause passionately pleaded in the face of the government and of all other interests and opinions, can compel them to listen, and either comply, or state clearly why they do not, is in itself, if it answered no other purpose, one of the most important political institutions that can exist anywhere, and one of the foremost benefits of a free government.[65]

Nelson comments:

Now, it does seem plausible that, when matters of public policy are subject to frequent public debate, and when most individuals are called upon, from time to time, "to exercise some public function," that citizens will attempt to formulate principles in terms of which they will be able to defend their position to others. Similarly, to the extent political leaders must defend their positions publicly, they will formulate principles and conceptions of the common good in terms of which they can justify their position.[66]

Nelson thus maintains that "open" government—which is the heart of democracy—expresses the commitment to publicly justify one's claims; it "encourages both citizens and representatives to think of legislation and policy-making in terms of what can be justified; and it leads them to formulate principles and conceptions of the common good in terms of which they can carry out the process of justification."[67] As a consequence, he maintains, open government "tends to produce morally acceptable laws and policies. *At least, it tends to produce laws and policies within the bounds of the permissible as determined by reasonable moral principles.*"[68] It is important to stress that Nelson does not justify this crucial claim by first identifying basic principles of justice, and then showing that open government respects them; rather, he offers "a very different, though perhaps complementary" argument that the institution of open government encourages citizens to confront each other with public justifications, and in so doing tends to yield results that track the publicly justified morality.[69]

The Millian case for open government is powerful; law-making procedures that encourage citizens and law-makers (whether or not these are distinct groups) to formulate proposals in terms of what can be publicly justified would be selected by our ideal liberal contractors. Although Nelson provides a powerful argument that open law-making procedures are required by theories whose fundamental commitment is to public justification, and that democratic institutions are a species of open law-making procedures, it falls short of showing that only democratic procedures are open in the requisite way. As Mill's own plural voting scheme makes clear, law-making procedures that reject the democratic commitment to political equality can reasonably be described as "open."[70] But though this requirement fails to select democratic institutions uniquely, it does rule out some law-making procedures that satisfied the wide responsiveness condition (sec. 13.3). Importantly, it indicates that the point of acceptable law-making procedures is not simply to translate individual preferences into a social decision. Although the classic axiomatic social choice theorists such as Arrow and Sen did not claim to be evaluating law-making institutions, it has nevertheless become common to interpret social choice theory as equivalent to a theory about law-making procedures or political choice. But social choice theory examines methods of aggregating a set of given individual preferences into a social choice or ordering. The formation of preferences—or, we might say, the ways citizens form judgments and argue with each other—is entirely outside the scope of social choice theory.[71] So even if, *pace* Arrow, we had access to some perfect way to translate any set of individual preferences into a perfectly rational social ordering, no matter how widely responsive such a procedure, it could not in itself qualify as an acceptable law-making institution. On similar grounds, we can reject law-making through public opinion polling. Even if a poll accurately reflected the judgment of citizens, the mere translation of those judgments into law does not pay sufficient heed to openness. Our aim is not merely to track the judgments of citizens on inconclusive issues, but to do so in a way that is most likely to track what is actually publicly justified, and for that purpose openness and deliberation are necessary (see sec. 15.1).

13.5.3 Deliberative Bodies

Madison, as well as Mill, believed that for a law-making institution to respond to public reason it must employ representative bodies. Madison was clear that "it is the reason, alone, of the public, that ought to control and regulate the government."[72] By this he meant that government ought not be controlled by the passions of the public, but also that it ought not be controlled by the unrefined opinion of the public. A properly constituted republic, he argued, would

refine and enlarge the public views by passing them through a medium of a chosen body of citizens, whose wisdom may best discern the true interest of their country and whose patriotism and love of justice will be least likely to sacrifice it to temporary or partial considerations. Under such a regulation it may well happen that the public voice, pronounced by the representatives of the people, will be more consonant to the public good than if pronounced by the people themselves, convened for the purpose.[73]

Today, no doubt, we are apt to be more than a little skeptical of Congress's "love of justice." But the core Madisonian claim remains persuasive: Systems that employ representative assemblies are more apt to encourage refined and enlarged views than those that, for example, always act through plebiscites. This need not be based on a mistrust of public opinion or on an "epistemological elitism."[74] James Fishkin and John Burnheim, both of whom endeavor to increase participation and popular power, argue for the use of deliberative bodies chosen through representative samples of the population.[75] Complex issues call for deliberation in which challenges and responses can be exchanged. Moreover, as Fishkin in particular stresses, the opinions of many citizens on a specific issue may be hastily formed on the basis of inadequate information; deliberative assemblies enhance the quality of public deliberations.[76] In even modest sized polities, representative bodies are indispensable, serving as formal public forums in which debate occurs. They are, as Mill said, places of talk.

Burnheim's and Fishkin's proposals raise an important question: Do the twin requirements of wide responsiveness and wide deliberation call for electoral politics? Fishkin wishes merely to supplement electoral politics with a "deliberative opinion poll" in which a sample of representative citizens meets to evaluate the candidates at the outset of the presidential primaries; Burnheim, in contrast, seeks to do away with electoral politics. On the face of it there is a great deal to be said for a law-making procedure that selects a deliberative assembly through sampling techniques, with the assembly empowered to legislate. With respect to wide responsiveness, this procedure would seem superior to normal electoral systems; even proportional representation systems do not select legislatures that are truly representative samples of the citizenry. So long as voter participation is not randomly related to political positions, electoral politics can be expected to be inferior in this regard. And the representative sampling technique, insofar as it is being used to select a deliberative assembly, appears to meet the deliberative desideratum.[77] At this point, however, Mill's and Nelson's defense of democratic institutions is decisive: In a representative democracy, voting is not simply a way to select deliberative bodies but is an educative experience insofar as it encourages ordinary citizens to think in terms of justice and the common good. Responsive and deliberative procedures that require all citizens to register judgments, if not directly on issues, then on the representatives, encourage all to engage in public debate. Although rational choice theorists typically disparage voting in large elections as a meaningless exercise, the reality is that very large numbers of citizens take their role in electoral politics seriously; the formal occasion of declaring their judgment about common affairs is fundamental to their conceptions of themselves as citizens, as opposed to merely private individuals. We may grant that representative bodies can "refine and enlarge" public opinion, but that is not a reason for failing to encourage public opinion itself to become more refined.

13.6 Non-Neutral Procedures

13.6.1 Public Justification and Two Types of Errors

I have insisted that, when deciding whether a law-making institution tracks the publicly justified morality, liberal citizens can evaluate it in terms of its tendency to yield legislation that violates fundamental law (sec. 13.4.1). Unfortunately, the matter is not quite so simple. If our only goal is to minimize the chance of unjust laws, the obvious solution is to remain in a condition of anarchy, without any laws. Our problem is that we wish simultaneously to avoid two types of errors: "false positives"—laws that the institution enacts which are not publicly justified—and "false negatives"—publicly justified laws that the law-making institution fails to enact.[78] A whole range of possibilities exists—from those that render false positives very unlikely to those that reduce toward zero the possibility of false negatives. Unfortunately, these two goals are often at odds: as we eliminate the possibility of one sort of error, we increasingly leave ourselves open to the other. We can be assured of avoiding false positives if we give negative answers in every case, just as we can avoid giving a false negative by always answering positive. All plausible procedures will entail some risk of both, but an array of possibilities presents itself. And once again it seems that the debate will be inconclusive over a wide part of this range. It is this problem that prompts Nozick's remark quoted at the beginning of chapter 12: "When sincere and good persons differ, we are prone to think they must accept some procedure to decide their differences, some procedure they both agree to be reliable or fair. Here we see the possibility that this disagreement may extend all the way up the ladder of procedures."[79]

False positives (tyrannical laws) and false negatives (justified but not enacted legislation) are not, however, on par. The liberal tradition in politics has been much more wary of overlegislation than underlegislation, of making it too easy to pass laws rather than too difficult. The conjunction of the fundamental liberal principle and the commitment to public justification implies that in order for a law to be justified, every citizen must either (1) already have a justified acceptance of the law or (2) be provided with conclusive reason to accept it. Suppose that liberal citizens have competing inconclusive judgments as to whether there ought to be any legislation at all on issue *i*. One group appeals to some justified principle, insisting that legislation on *i* follows, while another insists that justified principles are not implicated in this issue. This situation may well characterize the recent political controversy about health care in the United States. While followers of the Clintons insist that principles of fairness and justice require radical alteration of the health care system, many opponents insist that no health care crisis exists, at least in a way that implies that an injustice is occurring. Because the onus of justification is on those who would impose legislation, and because this onus is so demanding—to show that the legislation is justified to all citizens—we would expect it to be more difficult to impose a demand on others than to resist it. After all, if each had infallible access to his or her own moral system, and if each was perfectly sincere in reporting the results of his or her own deliberations, proposed legislation would require unanimity. If Betty, and only Betty, was able to show that the legislation was not justifiable in her system of reasons and beliefs, it would be defeated. Of course, people are not infallible and perfectly sincere in these ways, so unanimity is not required.[80] Nevertheless, the stringency of the requirements for justified impositions indicates that a system of adjudication should display a bias against justifying impositions.

It is standardly replied that this liberal-Madisonian doctrine rests on a fundamental error: it supposes that tyranny is more apt to occur through legislation than in its absence.[81] If the status quo is itself unjust, fighting tyranny requires that laws be easy to change; if it is very difficult to alter them, it will be almost impossible to rectify injustices. This is a powerful challenge. To answer it we must first keep focused on our problem: the clash of inconclusive judgments about justice. The paradigmatic situation calling for adjudication is when citizens confront each other with undefeated, but *also unvictorious*, judgments about justice and the common good. Suppose, for a moment, that we could be sure that all the competing judgments fell into this category. In this case, our ideal liberal contractors would endorse a bias against legislation because the onus of justification is on those who would limit the liberty of others. Insofar as all the competing judgments are genuinely inconclusive, no one can claim it is a fundamental injustice if her or his favored legislation is not enacted. And because of an asymmetry in the justificatory position between a would-be imposer and one who resists imposition (sec. 11.2.1), a bias against legislation is justified.

Now let us introduce some erroneous judgments in the population. The Wrong-Headed Reformers believe that proposal *x* is justified, when in reality it has been defeated, and the Wrong-Headed Conservatives believe that proposal *y* is not justified, when it has been victoriously justified. The objection holds that Madisonian procedures protect us against injustice by the Wrong-Headed Reformers but ignores the injustice of Wrong-Headed Conservatives. But this is to overlook the importance of constitutionalism as prior to legislative procedures. The regulative idea of substantive constitutionalism, I argued, is to identify what is victoriously justified, and to shape the political agenda to conform to it. If a principle is victoriously justified, a just constitution will acknowledge it to be so. A just constitution, then, is the chief protector of those upholding victoriously justified principles against those who would ignore, or even overturn, them. If a just constitution is the chief impediment to those who would erroneously ignore or overturn victoriously justified principles, procedures that make it difficult to enact laws are the main defense against those who would mistakenly press defeated or merely inconclusive proposals as eligible for adjudication, thus meriting legislative consideration. Constitutions can and do identify some defeated proposals, but no constitution can anticipate all the possible defeated political positions that might be advanced—procedures that erect barriers to new legislation protect us from these sorts of wrong-headed people.

It may be tempting to reply that this all supposes that the constitution is just and thus protects victoriously justified principles; consequently it fails to speak to the real world of unjust constitutions upholding unjust status quos. This reply calls our attention to two points, one moral, one practical. The moral point is that our commitment to adjudicate our disputes presupposes a just constitution, recognizing fundamental law. In the absence of at least a basically just constitution, revolution may well be a more appropriate path than adjudication (sec. 16.4). But for liberal politics to be a practical as well as a moral possibility, it is necessary not only that the constitution be just, but also that the mass of citizens perceive it to be so: When the constitution is not perceived as basically just, citizens will not be able to agree about what disputes require adjudication, and what is beyond the political (sec. 16.3). Marxists, who believe that private property justifications have all been defeated, and libertarians, who believe that sweeping private property rights have been victoriously justified, cannot even agree approximately about the extent of the political—the range of inconclusive judgments about justice and the common good. If the real world were characterized by such sweeping and intractable disputes about the political, liberal politics would not, I shall argue later, be possible. It is only when the crux of politics is *not* about the nature of political agenda that liberal adjudicative politics can thrive.

Of course, even basically just constitutions may be erroneous. Some victoriously justified principles may not be defended by the constitution as part of fundamental law. But consider the sort of claim being advanced by would-be reformers who hold not simply that a proposal is undefeated, but that it is victorious; they are insisting that the proposal is conclusively justifiable to each and every person (this may involve a claim that a current constitutional provision has been defeated in public justification). This is an ambitious claim: Those advancing it are insisting that they have made their case *beyond reasonable doubt.* An appropriate skepticism toward such claims is manifested by procedures that erect special barriers to their legislative success. Procedures requiring various sorts of extraordinary majorities for constitutional amendments are thus well justified.

13.6.2 Non-Neutral Procedures and the Rejection of Simple Majoritarianism

I conclude that the requirement of neutrality, endorsed by some democratic theorists, is to be rejected.[82] As it is usually interpreted, a procedure is neutral between options x and y if it is no easier or more difficult to enact x than y; it is not biased toward either alternative. It is often said that a procedure that is non-neutral toward the two options is, ipso facto, non-neutral between the people who propose them: If Alf favors x and Betty favors y, and it is easier to enact x than y, then it is said the procedure is biased in Alf's favor. However, the claim that the system is biased against Betty is ambiguous. If it means that the system is biased against Betty just because she is Betty, or because of her personal characteristics, family background, or whatever, then it is false. It is only biased against Betty because she is an advocate of y, and the system is biased against y. It is biased against Betty in precisely the same way the United States constitutional system is biased against Betty if she advocates a constitutional amendment banning abortions. In a way, I suppose, it can be said that the system is biased against her, but such a bias is very different from one that is biased against all of Betty's views, whatever they might be. Although I shall argue that this latter form of bias is indeed unacceptable (sec. 14.2), if Betty can be given good reason to accept a system biased against some *proposals*, then such a bias can be justified to her. And, as I have argued, a system with a general bias against legislation can be justified to all.

On some interpretations, neutrality is one of the defining characteristics of majority rule.[83] Consider Brian Barry's famous, though now somewhat dated, example of five people in a railway compartment—some of whom wish to smoke, some of whom want no smoking—who have not been given any rules by the railway. Barry asks:

Is there any reason why, if the matter is settled by voting, three out of five should not be a sufficient majority to decide? Only, it seems to me, if they had already agreed that there was a presumption of settling the matter one way which should be decisive *unless* a special majority could be achieved.[84]

The basic idea is that any departure from majority rule constitutes a *presumption* in favor of one outcome or another, and so violates neutrality. Because our ideal liberal contractors reject neutrality, they would reject one common understanding of majoritarianism: that disputes should be decided by a simple majority.[85] This is not to say, of course, that procedures employing majoritarian devices are to be rejected; it is only to set aside the idea that the aim of law-making institutions is simply to embody the judgments of the simple majority of the citizens.

In the eyes of some, to reject majoritarianism is to reject political equality and democracy itself. My reply to this charge must await the discussion of political equality in chapter 14. More to the point at present, a number of democratic theorists have recently advocated majority rule on explicitly epistemic grounds; it is, we are told, most likely to give the correct answer to political questions. Drawing on Condorcet's jury theorem, Rex Martin is among those who offers an "epistemic rationale or justification for majority rule":

The argument is probabilistic in form. The argument, put starkly, is that a probability of correctness, for each voter, of greater than half (and for simplicity we assume an equal probability for each voter) would yield a majority rule social decision having an even greater probability of correctness (as to which policies were in the perceived interests of an indeterminably larger number of these voters). And it could be shown, further, that the probability value of the social decision will increase with an increase in any (or in two or in all) of three factors: (1) the absolute size of the difference between the number of voters and the number of minority voters, (2) the probability of correctness of each individual voter, (3) the size of the majority vote, expressed as a percentage of all votes.[86]

If each voter has more than a 50 percent chance of being right (and assume for a moment that each has the same probability of being right), a majority of voters will have greater chance of being correct than any one person. Arthur Kuflik provides some useful illustrations of the principle:

If we can assume that the average voter is only slightly more likely to be correct than not, say 51 percent likely, and if we require only 51 percent of the vote to carry a proposal, then the probability that a 51 percent majority is correct in its judgment when 100 are voting is 51.99 percent. For an electorate of 500, the probability that a 51 percent majority opinion is correct is 59.86 percent. When 1,000 are voting the probability is 69 percent; and when 10,000 are voting, it is 99.97.[87]

A number of considerations defeat this epistemic justification for simple majority rule. First, and by far most important, it is not an argument for simple majority rule at all. I have argued that false positives (enacted legislation that violates the justified principles of the social contract) are more serious problems than false negatives (justified proposals that are not enacted). The political contractors will choose procedures that tend to avoid false positives, even at the cost of allowing false negatives. Given this, let us characterize a "correct answer" as "the legislation does not violate the constitution." In the first example given by Kuflik of 100 voters, each of whom is correct 51 percent of the time, under a simple majority principle (51 percent required for passage) the probability of a correct answer is 51.99; if a special majority of 60 percent is required for passage, the probability of a correct answer is 69 percent; if the voting population in increased to 1,000, a 60 percent rule gives a correct answer 99.97 percent of the time (as compared with 69 percent under a simple majority formula).[88] Under these conditions, the jury theorem supports extraordinary majorities,

Second, however, democratic theorists should be cautious in appealing to the jury theorem, as it is not clear that it endorses widely responsive procedures. The probability of a correct answer plunges just as dramatically *downward* if the average voter is more likely to be wrong than right. Thus, whether the argument endorses or condemns wide responsiveness depends on whether the average voter is more or less likely to be correct, and it seems very hard to be sure about this.[89] It is important to stress that the core claim of this argument is much stronger than those that I have advanced: I have argued that widely responsive procedures tend to violate basic rights and important interests less often than narrowly responsive ones, and that deliberative procedures tend to make fewer errors, and to track public justifications better, than nondeliberative ones. Whether or not the average citizen is more or less apt to make a mistake on most political issues is, however, a much more difficult matter to decide. And it is absolutely fundamental to this Condorcetian epistemic case for democracy.

But suppose we could develop a reliable test of citizen competency.

Under these conditions, the argument tends to support the disenfranchisement of the least competent. This is clearly so for those more likely to be wrong than right, but it also applies to those who are more likely to be right, but who are below the median competency. Just how many would be disenfranchised depends on a number of factors (e.g., how inferior they are to others, the total population remaining), but the analysis easily leads to significant disenfranchisement.[90]

Finally, the argument is most plausible when two "natural" choices confront each other, such as whether the defendant is guilty or not guilty. But in politics we are almost always confronted with a wide variety of choices, and any method employed to narrow the choice leads to the possibility of agenda manipulation.[91] Given that the choices confronting citizens will be significantly determined by various sorts of agenda manipulations—not only by leaders, but by voters—the claim of any voting system to produce the "best" or "correct" answer is suspect. At best—leaving aside these problems—it might be claimed that a majoritarian (not a simple majoritarian) procedure selects the best of the available alternatives, where what is available is going to depend on the voting procedures employed and the ways that the agenda has been manipulated.[92] But, as we shall see in section 15.1, even that claim is too strong.

13.6.3 Justice and the Common Good

The strength of a widely responsive law-making institution is that it draws on citizens' interests to alert law-makers to harms to basic civil interests, deprivations of rights, and opportunities to promote the common good. As Dewey put it, as a rule each is a good judge as to "where the shoe pinches."[93] In this way, responsive institutions economize on virtue by drawing on the interests of citizens to track the publicly justified morality. The danger is that citizens advancing claims based on interests may secure legislation that does not express a publicly justified claim, but a sectarian or factional interest. That danger is the most important justification for a non-neutral law-making institution, whether this is achieved through requirements of extraordinary majorities, bicameralism, legislative rules that require approval of a number of committees, or other legislative barriers. In some way, the liberal state must seek to impede those advancing sectional claims from legislating norms that impose on all citizens.

James Buchanan's distinction between the protective and productive states has much to recommend it in this regard. Very roughly, in public choice theory the task of the protective state is to protect the freedom of citizens against invasions by others.[94] The heart of the protective state, according to Buchanan, is a "third-party adjudication" institution—individuals who disagree about the requirements of the social contract require an "umpire" to resolve their dispute. The protective state, he says, aims at "truth-judgments" about individual rights.[95] The essence of the protective state, then, is very close to what I have called the juridical state, especially concerning disputes about justice. In addition to the protective state, Buchanan proposes a "productive state" to secure public goods that are not being adequately produced by the market. Buchanan is adamant that the adjudicative nature of the protective state is not shared by the productive state—its aim is to increase efficiency, not adjudicate disputes about rights. Although I have argued that the adjudicative function of the state carries over into disputes about the common good—after all, citizens are making claims that certain policies advance the common good—the two sorts of disputes should nevertheless be distinguished, for (1) disputes about policies that promote the common good are much more likely to be articulated simply in terms of the interests of citizens rather than an appeal to basic principles, and (2) cases for policies in terms of the common good will often be economic arguments about how to promote efficiency and achieve public goods—the sorts of concerns that define the productive state.

Public choice theory has argued that radically non-neutral procedures are appropriate in disputes about the common good, procedures that tend toward unanimity. Recall that arguments based on the common good hold that everyone's interest will be advanced by a certain policy (sec. 12.4.2). Although, as Mill recognized, people can be wrong about their interests, he also thought that the best general presumption was that one is the best judge of one's own interest.[96] Consequently, while there are good reasons for not insisting on strict unanimity, proposed policies justified on the grounds that they advance a common good are properly subject to very demanding requirements. That even a significant minority oppose the policy is strong reason to doubt that it is publicly justified. If common good–based proposals are not subject to severely non-neutral requirements, it is all too likely that they will become a pretext for groups pressing sectional interests and obtaining illicit transfers from others. There thus is great merit in Geoffrey Brennan and James Buchanan's proposal that the Wicksellian unanimity rule be taken as a "benchmark on which analysis and discussion of constructive constitutional reform must be based."[97]

However, with regard to disputes about basic rights—the "protective state"—less severely non-neutral rules are justified. We have seen that on these matters citizens have inconclusive competing judgments; because deep disagreement is to be expected about these issues, a significant dissenting minority is not as strong evidence that the proposal is not justified. Liberal citizens require an umpire precisely because they regularly find themselves disagreeing about the demands of justice. Too strongly non-neutral procedures would drive them back into a situation akin to the "wait and see strategy" in the state of nature, in which no specific demands can be justified. Even here non-neutral procedures are justified, but unanimity rules are not even properly the benchmark of discussion (sec. 15.5).

Claims based on justice and rights ought to be institutionally distinguished from those based on the common good (which will often be public good arguments). What is required by our sense of justice is to be distinguished from what aims at mutual benefit. The law-making institution properly responds differently to such claims, based on the sorts of claims they are as well as on the dangers of sectional legislation attending each. Admittedly, the boundaries between the two are not always sharp. But neither are the boundaries between supply (money) bills and other legislation, yet legislative systems often employ different procedures for the two.

CHAPTER 14

Political Equality

14.1 The Limits of the Consequentialist Justification of Democracy

It will be helpful to summarize the desiderata for law-making institutions, and to review briefly what sorts of procedures are excluded and what remains.

Nonrandomness. Ideal liberal contractors would not choose to resolve policy disputes through policy lotteries, no matter how fair or egalitarian such lotteries may appear. This desideratum does not exclude law-making by deliberative assemblies chosen by lot; it excludes only selecting policies directly by random devices.

Wide Responsiveness. What I have called the "first theorem of liberal democracy" is that widely responsive law-making institutions are the most reliable protectors of basic individual rights. First and foremost, liberals are democrats because democracy tends to respond to the judgments of citizens that the government is violating their rights, and so is a reliable protector of rights. Law-making restricted to the few and not responsive to the judgments of the many—whether it is called aristocracy, oligarchy, or rule by the vanguard party—is thus rejected.

Deliberative Procedures. The case for wide responsiveness acknowledges that, because citizens have a fundamental interest in protecting their rights, each is generally a good guardian of her or his own rights. So our ideal liberal contractors would certainly acknowledge that all actual citizens sometimes, and perhaps some all of the time, are driven by self-interest. But we have no good reason to suppose that political life is ruled only by self-interest, and good reason to believe it is not. Moreover, it seems implausible that a political life dominated by self-interest will reliably track what is publicly justified. Given our basic situation of epistemic scarcity, public justifications are only to be relied on when they have passed through the filter of public debate. Following Mill (and a host of others), I have argued law-making institutions must provide ample scope for wide deliberation, encouraging debate and deliberation among ordinary citizens. Susan Hurley puts it well: "A cognitive conception of democracy . . . makes demands on citizens; voters and other decision makers must strive to avoid arbitrariness, and must be encouraged to express thoughtful and reasoned opinions through their votes."[1] Moreover, in even modest-sized polities a formal deliberative assembly, in which proposals are publicly debated, is required. This deliberative desideratum excludes "plebiscitary democracy"—a method that builds in a sort of wide responsiveness but discourages deliberation. Indeed, it seems to require some sort of electoral politics, with a formal role for an opposition that focuses debate on the government's legislation. We have no evidence for the belief that in modern states deliberative procedures can thrive in single-party systems.

Non-neutrality. In a basically just constitutional regime, I have argued, law-making procedures should not be neutral between enacting and blocking legislation; given the onus of justification on those who would impose their norms on others, barriers to legislation are appropriate. Thus I have argued that ideal liberal contractors would reject simple majority rule. More controversially, I have maintained, arguments based on claims about the demands of justice and those seeking to establish that some policy benefits everyone are to be distinguished; the latter should be subject to more severely non-neutral requirements than the former.

Because of the primary role accorded to these "tracking desiderata," justificatory liberalism offers a basically consequentialist justification of law-making institutions. But it would be wrong to interpret this as consequentialist justification of democracy, for the tracking desiderata do not uniquely select democratic institutions.[2] It is, I think, manifest that the familiar varieties of constitutional representative democracy are within the set of law-making institutions that satisfy the four desiderata. But also belonging to the set is, for instance, Mill's conception of representative government, which includes a scheme for unequal weighting of votes. Mill insists that each person should have a voice in government (hence satisfying wide responsiveness), and we have seen that Mill is one of the foremost proponents of deliberative government. But all this is consistent with differential weighting of votes by, for example, education. Mill, in fact, provides a plausible epistemic case for inequality. If our regulative concern is to track public morality as well as possible, it is reasonable to suppose that we ought to seek out political wisdom and give it special weight. Mill believes that all reasonable people would acknowledge that the political judgment of some is superior to that of others. "No one but a fool, and only a fool of a peculiar description, feels offended by the acknowledgment that there are others whose opinion, and even whose wish, is entitled to greater consideration than his."[3] Mill thus suggests that our common concern with the most reliable institution would lead us to reject political equality—hence his plural voting scheme.

We can distinguish a strong and a weak Millian claim. The strong claim is that the tracking desiderata victoriously justify his plural voting scheme over democratic institutions that, in some way, insist that all votes be weighted equally; in other words, epistemic considerations eliminate democratic equality. The weak Millian claim is that, even if tracking considerations do not select plural voting over one person, one vote, they certainly do not do the opposite; in other words, they do not select democratic equality over plural voting. According to the weak claim, epistemic considerations do not rule out plural voting.

I shall argue presently that the strong Millian claim fails. However, the weak claim seems unassailable. Mill presented his plural voting proposal not only as a way to give extra weight to political expertise, but to accord extra political influence to the (educated) minority for resisting majoritarian demands. His aim was to deprive both the uneducated masses *and* the educated minority of power to dominate and oppress the other. Thus, in Mill's eyes, his proposal simultaneously gives the proper additional influence to epistemic competence while achieving the liberal end of nondomination. I see no convincing argument that one person, one vote is manifestly a better tracking procedure than awarding votes according to, say, education, with perhaps a 5:1 ratio between the top and the bottom of the scale.

14.2 The Principle of Equality and Political Equality

14.2.1 Two Views of Political Power

Charles Beitz criticizes Mill's proposal as deeply unfair, and believes it points to a defect with all attempts to justify democratic institutions in essentially consequentialist terms. Mill, Beitz indicates, takes the perspective of "society as a whole"—what system would lead to the best overall results—rather than focusing on the perspective of each citizen. Taking up the individual perspective, Beitz believes, makes us sensitive to the way an unequal system of votes attacks the self-esteem of those who are "disadvantaged by the scheme."[4] As I shall argue below, I think Beitz is quite right that Mill's scheme is unfair. But Beitz's analysis of this unfairness is, I believe, mistaken; more important, it calls our attention to two very different understandings of political power. Underlying Beitz's theory of political equality is the supposition that political power is primarily to be understood as a personal good; those denied their share have a grievance based on fairness or distributive justice. "The poorest and richest," he tells us, "are equally responsible for the conduct of their own lives and the choice of an individual good and should have equal authority over the public decisions that affect them."[5] Beitz is by no means alone in proposing this view. Any Gutmann makes a similar point when arguing that "the right to participate as an equal in democratic politics is a particularly important interest of citizens in any society committed to the idea of human equality."[6] Thomas Christiano has applied this analysis most clearly to decision rules and political equality. Christiano argues that collective decision procedures "assign the participants resources for determining the outcome."[7] Once we understand collective decision procedures as distributing resources, we can then apply principles of just distribution. He writes:

Now, the question is, Is there an intrinsic argument for democratic control over these procedures? Principles of economic justice provide the solution to the problem of the division of benefits and burdens in a society when there is a scarcity of goods. The way such scarcity comes about is when the interests of individuals are such that they conflict as a result of there not being enough resources to satisfy them all. . . .
     I claim that for collective properties there is an analogy to the problem of economic scarcity. . . .
     . . . The idea of political equality is to distribute power so as to have a just resolution to the conflict over collective properties.[8]

Applying the principle of equality of resources to this distributive problem, Christiano endorses political equality as a requirement of distributive justice.[9]

     Justificatory liberalism proffers a very different account of political power and, therefore, of political equality. I stressed that the aim of the political contract is to arrive at adjudicative institutions that track public justification. Political institutions, I have been arguing, have a point: to resolve our disputes about justice and the common good in a way that, so far as we can tell, is consistent with the justified liberal morality. Political institutions thus are not to be understood as distributing an essentially personal good—political power—to which each person has a legitimate claim. No one, I have been supposing, has a basic moral right to impose norms on another through legislation. The imposition of norms requires justification—good reasons must be provided to show that the imposition is justified. This can be accomplished in two ways. First, one can advance a substantive reason that the norm is justified; the possibility, and limits, of such justification occupied us in part II. Alternatively, one can maintain that one's proposal is a legitimate interpretation of a substantively justified norm, and though one's interpretation is inconclusive, it has been selected by a reliable publicly justified procedure. Suppose that Alf did make this claim, but Betty resisted it, and indeed is able to establish that her procedure tracks public justification better and thus rejects Alf's favored interpretation. Alf's claim to have publicly justified himself would be undermined; he has claimed to speak for public morality but has been shown that Betty's institution speaks in a truer voice. On what grounds can he justifiably still insist on his interpretation?

Perhaps, à la Beitz, Alf points out that his egalitarian procedure does not tarnish the self-esteem of those—Charlie, the less competent—accorded less influence in Betty's more reliable procedure. But Betty's rejoinder is decisive. The difference in the reliability of the two institutions stems from giving Charlie's vote an equal weight; his judgment is less competent. If taking account of Charlie's opinion clearly decreases the reliability of the entire institution, the most plausible hypothesis is that he has unsound opinions. But Betty quite rightly will object that Charlie has no right to impose unsound opinions on her. Charlie has no grievance if his proposed public justifications are excluded from consideration because they are unsound, because he has no moral claim that his proposed justifications, just because they are his, must be accorded weight. We can now see that even if we reject the hypothesis that the epistemic inferiority of Alf's procedure stems from Charlie's incompetence, neither he nor Charlie can justifiably demand that Betty submit to it. Regardless of why Alf's is inferior, if Betty can show that her procedure more reliably tracks liberal morality, she can victoriously justify it as a superior umpire. If so, she can show that both Alf's and her commitment to making only publicly justifiable demands on others is better honored by relying on her procedure. That Charlie is excluded would not show that the procedure is not justified to him; for he also is committed to public justification, and so he too has conclusive reason to embrace Betty's procedure over Alf's.

A claim to political power is a claim to political authority over others—a public office—rather than a claim to a resource that is personally beneficial. To be sure, because political rights allow one to protect one's basic rights, and because that increases the reliability of a law-making institution, there is something in Beitz's argument. But even here one's claim is not simply that one has a right to political power because it benefits one, but because it promotes the *telos* of government—to secure justice.

14.2.2 The Principle of Equality

Anyone taking part in a law-making institution is claiming political authority over others. To be a voter is to occupy a political office.[10] I argued in section 12.2 that fundamental to the rule of law is the principle of equality. Unlike private citizens, public officials are under a standing obligation to justify themselves: If they are to rule through law, they must be able to justify any differential treatment of citizens. A public official who disadvantages one person vis-à-vis another must be able to provide publicly accessible reasons for this difference in treatment. If the official is unable to do so, the suspicion is that she rules through personal preference rather than law.

Consider in light of this Mill's claim on behalf of plural voting. As a voter with additional votes, Mill would be challenged to justify this differential treatment. Unless he can advance public reasons, the difference violates the principle of equality, and so is unjust. Of course, as we saw above, Mill sought to provide such reasons. But although these reasons are not obviously defeated, neither are they conclusive. To see why, let us grant Mill's first claim: that those who are more competent merit additional political authority. I have already accepted that there might be moral-political sages (sec. 11.2.2); if any are to be had, it seems appropriate that they (or even quasi sages) be accorded a more influential voice. But Mill's proposal fails here for the same reason that appeals to sages could not solve the problem in the state of nature: Victorious justifications about who are the sages seem quite impossible. As David Estlund asks, "who will know the knowers?"[11] Mill might propose an educational standard, but it can reasonably be claimed that eggheads have little practical experience. After all, not even many philosophers believe that philosophers ought to be kings. But in the political contract philosophers will have reasonable objections to the special claims of the more worldly, who will have plausible objections to the special claims of the religious, or the old, and so on.

When faced with a demand to justify differential treatment, an advocate of plural voting can only provide an inconclusive justification. But this is not sufficient. The aim of the political contract is the justification of one umpiring procedure rather than another; unless one can provide a conclusive justification for an adjudicative procedure, insisting that others submit to it is mere browbeating—one is trying to override their epistemic authority, to subjugate them by replacing their reasonable judgments with one's own. Consequently, for a Millian to insist on an adjudicative procedure incorporating plural voting would be inconsistent with the rule of law, for it would entail burdens and privileges for which sufficient public reasons have not been advanced. Those granted a lesser voice would justifiably conclude that they are subject to the will of men, not the impartial rule of law. The proposal is thus inadequately justified: It does do not meet the requisite standard at this contractual level. An inconclusive justification of constitutional political inequality, then, violates the principle of equality, which is fundamental to the rule of law. To use Richard Arneson's colorful phrase, this accounts for the "bad smell of Mill's plural voting scheme":

The mechanical rule that determines who gets the extra votes is bound to use at best a very rough proxy for the qualities of superior competence and public-spiritedness that are supposed to justify the procedural benefits conferred. (If it were attempted to avoid this problem by allowing the authority that issues plural votes wide discretion in the use of its authority, this would guarantee arbitrary and inconsistent determinations.) In this setting those denied plural votes would be very likely to perceive the denial as an official insult issued by public authority. "Why them and not me?" is a question bound to rankle in the mind of the nonplural voter.[12]

The ideal of umpiring through law, then, leads to what I shall call the principle of political equality (PE):

PE: All inequalities of political authority must be justified; inequalities within the law-making institution must be conclusively justified. Inadequately justified differences in political authority are unjust. Differential political power granted on the basis of superior moral or political competence cannot be publicly justified.

The key to the argument for PE, and therefore for democratic adjudication, is that the justification of the law-making institution—the legislative umpiring procedure—is not part of normal political dispute but a matter of fundamental law. This seems manifestly correct. Normal politics—the clash of inconclusive judgments about justice and the common good—presupposes that an adjudicative procedure is victoriously justified. If the fundamental features of the law-making institution are themselves part and parcel of normal politics, some inconclusive views about the best umpire will be imposed on others. But that clearly is to abandon the ideal of a publicly justified political life. Because, then, the main features of the law-making institution are necessarily a matter of constitutional fundamentals, PE demands that differential burdens and privileges be conclusively justified.

The political contract, then, endorses a mixed, consequentialist-fairness argument for democracy. Consequentialist considerations do a great deal of the work, excluding a number of proposals, including those such as the policy lottery that themselves articulate a conception of political equality. But the primary, tracking, desiderata do not uniquely select democracy. Democracy is justified because, of all the law-making institutions that meet the tracking requirements, it is fair in the sense that it does not violate the principle of equality, and so is uniquely consistent with the rule of law as applied to the constitution. The fairness of democracy does not lie in the claim that it is a fair compromise among citizens, each of whom would like a larger share of the decision-making resources, but end up settling for an equal share.[13] Rather, its claim to be fair is the claim of all nonarbitrary governments to be fair: Citizens are treated the same unless good public reasons can be advanced for deferential treatment.

14.3 On Political Inequality

A justified law-making institution cannot violate the principle of political equality, though it can admit justified inequality. It must be stressed tha the principle does not prohibit political inequality: It requires that differences in political power be publicly justified. To apply PE, however, we must identify the boundary conditions for a law-making institution. How do we identify precisely what constitutes a law-making institution?

I have argued that law-making institutions that satisfy the tracking desiderata involve four elements: (1) voters form judgments on issues and candidates, (2) electoral rules translate their judgments into representative assemblies, (3) legislators form judgments about various proposals that (4) are then translated into laws through voting rules. These four steps must characterize at least some legislation, although referendums may be employed to decide some issues, which, essentially, skip steps (2) and (3). And, as we shall see, judicial review can add yet another step (sec. 16.2). In trying to specify the boundary of a law-making institution, a simple proposal is that we count anything that affects any of these four stages as part of it. Any factor that influences one of the steps, we might say, constitutes an input to the law-making institution, and so is part of that institution. After all, if some factor determines the final result of the institution, in a pretty straightforward sense it is part of the process. This simple proposal contains an important insight: A political institution cannot be sharply distinguished from the various factors that determine its outcomes. Those theorists who insist that formal procedural equality is the alpha and the omega of political equality, and thus take no account of the way in which "background" factors affect the procedure, presuppose an implausible account of the boundary conditions of the procedure itself; the procedure, they say, is simply the rules, and has nothing to do with the sorts of inputs that affect the outputs.

That wider background conditions are relevant to the justification of a law-making institution is an insight; that there is no important distinction between the institution and wider social conditions with which it interacts is a mistake. In designing and evaluating institutions that translate individual judgments into law, we need to be aware that institutional structures are important in determining the resulting decisions, but that the final outcome is not simply an artifact of the institution; other inputs also affect the outcome. Consider, for example, R. Kent Weaver and Bert A. Rockman's model of the role of institutions in determining policy outcomes in Figure 14.1.

Institutional features affect the decision-making process, and ultimately the policy outcomes, but the relation is mediated by a number of factors. Although institutional designers must be cognizant of the wider influences, the task of our political contractors (sec. 13.2) becomes unmanageable if they seek to evaluate and control all such influences. The task of institutional design, though critical, is more limited: to justify political structures that yield laws that respond to the judgments of citizens. The institutional structures involve various levels of generality, but certainly include electoral laws, legislative procedures, including norms involving government formation, the extent of bicameralism, and independence of legislative committees, as well as the extent of judicial review.[14] These matters are constitutive of law-making institutions. As such, they are matters of fundamental law, and inequalities inherent in their operation stand in need of conclusive justification.

This, again, is not to deny that the wider social, political, and economic factors that affect the outputs of an institution are relevant to its justification. But the ways that wider social conditions impact on political institutions are complex and contentious matters; moreover, whether or not the political inequalities arising from these broader social conditions are justified depends on the judgment whether or not they are legitimate consequences of justified principles. Consider, for example, one of the most controversial issues in contemporary demo-

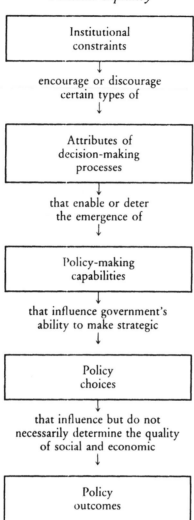

Figure 14.1 The role of institutions in determining policy outcomes. (Weaver and Rockman, "Assessing the Effects of Institutions," 1993, p. 9.) Copyright The Brookings Institution. Used with permission.

cratic theory: the link between political equality and economic equality.[15] Christiano, among others, stresses that his "notion of democracy is not purely formal in that it requires the equal distribution of all resources that go into collective decision making. Hence, information, and resources for coalition building, must be distributed equally along with votes and other formal devices."[16] In the eyes of some, political equality requires a limit on economic inequalities; more radically, it is sometimes insisted that political equality is inconsistent with capitalism and private property. Robert Dahl, perhaps the preeminent political scientist writing on democracy, suggests that capitalism tends "to produce inequalities in social and economic resources so great as to bring about severe deprivations of political equality and hence of the democratic process."[17]

It is certainly true that inequalities in wealth, income, and access to information affect the outcome of law-making institutions. And it also seems right that the ideal of political equality cannot be fully articulated simply in terms of formal, procedural, equality; a system that assured one person, one vote, but allowed debate to be controlled by one powerful group would not meet the ideal of political equality. Effective political authority would be unjustifiably unequal: The judgments of some would have an advantaged political role that could not be justified. However, according to the principle of political equality an inequality of political power can be justified. And it often is, for example, by appeal to the effects of basic liberal liberties. A system of individual liberty will result in some being more popular and articulate; the resulting political inequality can thus be publicly justified, and so is not arbitrary. So, too, supposing that a system of private ownership is publicly justified, resulting inequalities of wealth that lead to political inequalities can be justified. Again, private ownership of newspapers certainly results in political inequality—those who own the newspaper have a significantly more important role in public debate than do most citizens. But this inequality also stems from the right to free speech. Now this sort of conflict of principles—between victoriously justified liberal principles and the prima facie demands of political equality—is precisely the sort of dispute on which conclusive answers simply are not forthcoming: It is the type of dispute that is definitive of the political. Because the justification of political inequality arising from these diffuse background conditions invokes contentious claims about liberal principles, such justification involves political issues, and must be resolved by political institutions. Thus, for instance, regulation of media ownership, campaign financing,[18] and controlling the behavior of interest groups seem essentially political issues; the precise nature of the problems they present cannot be anticipated ahead of time, nor are conclusive justifications for particular policies forthcoming.

Now no doubt some will insist that the distinction between an institution and its background conditions is untenable and unreal. It is all-too-common to insist that where no clear distinction can be made, none at all is to be found. Surely this is wrong. The democratic tradition has insisted that law-making procedures that exclude or discriminate against some citizens are unjust. On issues such as apportionment and voting rights—matters intimately associated with the four stages of the law-making institution—democrats have been devoted to equality. On these matters inequality cannot be justified through the political process, and so in the United States the protection of institutional equality has been the purview of the courts (sec. 16.2.3). And in regulating these issues the court has often focused on due process and equal protection of the law—both expressions of the principle of equality before the law, the source of the principle of political equality. In contrast, broader disputes about the level of economic and social equality required for a democratic political order have been—quite properly— subject to political adjudication.

CHAPTER 15

Challenges to Adjudicative Democracy

15.1 The Challenge from Social Choice Theory

Before completing the account of adjudicative democracy by considering the place of the judiciary and the problem of political obligation, it is necessary to consider some likely objections to the essentially epistemic conception of democracy defended in the previous chapter. The most obvious objection emanates from social choice theory. I have defended representative democratic law-making institutions on the grounds that they are at least as reliable at tracking what is publicly justified as are alternative systems and, in addition, satisfy the principle of political equality, and, thus, are consistent with the rule of law. But social choice theory would seem to show that this cannot be so. Let me explain.

The notion of a law-making institution that tracks the judgments of citizens seems to suppose that, given a set of individual judgments on an issue, some law tracks them best. Call this the optimal law. For there to be an optimal law, there must exist some function f that is (1) uniquely justified, and that (2) yields a unique law for any set of individual judgments. If there is such a function, then in principle a law can be generated that best tracks the judgments of citizens. It is important to stress that f need not be an actual voting system; it could be that f can be identified, but that no actual system of voting (v) duplicates f.[1] This might be the case if f were a uniquely justified way of identifying the law that best tracks individual judgments, but since almost all actual systems of voting are subject to strategic manipulation[2]—people not sincerely expressing their judgments when voting—it easily could follow that no v perfectly tracks f. If social choice theory merely established that no v perfectly tracks f, this would be of interest, but it would not show that voting is "meaningless."[3] It would only show that voting is an imperfect procedure, but probably no one really doubts that anyway. If social choice theory—and, in particular, Arrow's theorem—shows that voting qua tracking is meaningless, it must show that no f exists—there simply is no unique function that transforms a set of individual judgments into the "true" or "best" social choice.

Arrow's theorem certainly provides some support for this last claim. Arrow, of course, shows that given a choice between three or more options, there exists no social welfare function (very roughly, a way of producing a complete, transitive social ordering out of complete, transitive, individual orderings) that satisfies a set of apparently reasonable conditions.[4] If all these conditions are necessary for a reasonable f—and if a reasonable f aims at a social ordering rather than simply a social choice[5]—then Arrow shows the impossibility of a reasonable f. And if the aim of voting is somehow to approximate f, but there is no reasonable f, it does all begin to look pretty meaningless.

The most obvious and well-worn way to resist this conclusion is to question Arrow's conditions. If some of Arrow's conditions are not necessary for a reasonable f, that no f can satisfy them all does not show that no reasonable f is to be found. And although well-worn, this approach has great merit. In our analysis of law-making institutions we have seen, for example, that conditions such as monotonicity[6] that seem straightforward when applied to voting rules are of dubious value when we evaluate electoral systems.[7] More generally, what conditions it is reasonable to impose on a social choice mechanism seem dependent on what we aim for it to do.[8] Thus the condition of neutrality is often thought to be fundamental to majority rule, but we have rejected it. The same lesson applies, for example, to the controversial Arrovian Independence Condition and even the Pareto condition.

I shall not pursue this response, however meritorious. Another point is more fundamental for our analysis. As has been noted by others, social choice theory does not show that an epistemic conception of voting is meaningless.[9] The conception of democratic adjudication offered here is epistemic insofar as the ultimate goal is to arrive at laws that are consistent with, and express, the publicly justified morality. Tracking the judgments of individuals is only a proximate aim; we are not interested in tracking them because (as in Riker's notion of "populist democracy") the expression of the popular will is an end in itself,[10] but because they are reliable indicators of what is publicly justified.

The point, then, is that the function f, which translates individual judgments into a collective choice, is intended as an approximation of LM, the justified liberal morality. So v approximates f, which in turn approximates LM. Suppose that we grant that no perfect f is to be discovered; there is no function that best transforms a set of individual judgments into a social choice. But this is no more troubling to justificatory liberalism than the claim that no v perfectly corresponds to f is troubling to William Riker's notion of populism. That is, Riker's populist in interested in voting as a way to express the popular will; let us say that a populist has discovered the perfect f. As I said above, populism would not be shown meaningless or empty if no voting system perfectly tracked f. Indeed, Rousseau—assuming for now that Riker is correct that he was a populist—recognized this. Voting, said Rousseau, does not always reveal the general will; sometimes the results do not track the general will, but instead reveals the "will of all."[11] As long as a general will exists—as identified by f—this only shows that voting is an imperfect procedure for expressing the general will. Returning to justificatory liberalism, if the expression of popular opinion is itself only a way of identifying the publicly justified morality, the fact that there is no uniquely best function to translate individual judgments into a social judgment is a problem of the same order: It shows that the world is imperfect, and that there is no unique answer to the question, "What do the people think?" But since we only care what the people think because it is a guide to answering "What morality is publicly justified?" social choice theory cannot show that epistemic voting is meaningless or empty, only imperfect.

The case for democracy, then, is that voting systems based on a universal franchise and political equality are justified, partially because they are responsive to the judgments of citizens, and this responsiveness in turn is, of the alternatives, a reasonably reliable way to track public morality. The case for democracy is based on two tracking claims: that voting adequately but imperfectly tracks popular opinion, and that popular opinion adequately but imperfectly tracks the publicly justified morality.

15.2 The Charge of Public Incompetence

Voting, then, is not justified simply as a way to express the people's will, but as a way to tap public opinion that in turn indicates what is publicly justified. To many, this is naive: Public opinion is typically described as shallow, ignorant, or perhaps even malicious. Even James Fishkin, who seeks to devise new participatory institutions, insists that "the deliberative competence of mass publics is suspect. It is a dubious accomplishment to give power to the people under conditions where they are not really in a position to think about how they are to exercise that power."[12] And a good deal of research on public opinion seems to bear this out. Philip E. Converse and Gregory B. Markus report panel studies of Americans from 1956–60, and again from 1972–76. These studies interviewed the same group of subjects (within, not between, each period), asking for opinions on issues, candidates, and political party affiliations. The studies reveal that opinions on issues are extremely variable—the same person, interviewed over several years, is apt to change his opinions on matters such as whether the United States should give economic assistance to poor countries, whether the government should guarantee jobs, or whether schools should be desegregated (opinions about abortion tended to be considerably more stable.).[13] The overall picture is clear: People seem to change their opinions amazingly often, while retaining their political party identification.

Not only did Converse find great variation in the same person's opinions from one interview to another, but he found no obvious rationale for the changes—they seemed random and meaningless.[14] Fishkin's suspicion of the competency of mass publics seems well grounded. More important, it seems most dubious that public opinion could track anything, since it appears to fluctuate so wildly.

One response is that of Brennan and Lomasky: "On the whole, people are better judges of other people than they are of rival policies."[15] Converse's studies support this proposal, at least insofar as people's attitudes toward candidates are more stable than their attitudes toward polices.[16] This suggests a conception of representative democracy according to which citizens are selecting trusted deliberators, not seeking to express their opinions about discrete issues. And to some extent this must be right; after all, in representative democracies citizens typically vote for candidates, not directly on issues. Yet if I am right that a desideratum of a justified law-making institution is that it responds in some way to the judgments of citizens about what the government is doing, it seems deeply disturbing that citizens' attitudes toward policies fluctuates widely. What is there for voting to track?

In their magisterial study of American public opinion over the last fifty years, Benjamin I. Page and Robert Y. Shapiro provide a very different response to Converse's work. Collective public opinion, they show, has properties distinct from individual opinions:

If individuals' real opinions, or measurements of those opinions, are subject to *any* sort of random variation—whether from transient scraps of information that temporarily change beliefs and preferences, or from question ambiguity or interviewing mistakes or keypunch errors, or from "top of the head" sampling of conflicting considerations, or from mood swings, or any other factor that is independent from one citizen to another—then simple statistical reasoning indicates that those errors will tend to cancel each other out when the opinions of individuals are aggregated. Collective measurements—averages (means or medians), majority or plurality choices, marginal frequencies of response—will tend accurately to reflect the "true" underlying or long-term opinions of individuals.

That is to say, even if individual opinions or survey responses are ill-informed, shallow and fluctuating, collective opinion can be real, highly stable, and . . . based on all the available information. . . .[17]

To examine this hypothesis, Page and Shapiro analyzed public opinion polls over the last fifty years on social issues such as racial equality, civil rights, woman's rights, economic issues (including regulation of the economy, welfare, and industrial relations), and foreign policy. Four of their conclusions merit emphasis.

(1) *Collective policy preferences are highly stable.* In their analysis of policy preferences Page and Shapiro analyzed 1,128 questions that were repeated in different surveys. They found that 58 percent of the responses show no significant change at all; when foreign policy issues are removed, the stability rises to 63 percent.[18] Moreover large swings in public opinion—which they characterized as a change of 20 percent or more—were rare: Only 13 percent of the changes in public opinion were of that magnitude.[19] Changes in public opinion are generally gradual, although abrupt movements, especially in foreign affairs, are not unusual.[20]

(2) *When collective policy preferences change, there is typically a plausible explanation.* For instance, Page and Shapiro note that a movement in public opinion toward a more permissive attitude to abortion was associated in the early 1960s with the rubella epidemic and widespread publicity about the birth defects resulting from thalidomide.[21]

(3) *Collective opinion responds reasonably to information.* Page and Shapiro argue that collective public opinion responds more efficiently to a greater amount of information than does individual opinion. To a large extent they credit the epistemic benefits of discourse and the exchange of ideas; they also credit what might be called the Condorcet jury theorem effect (sec. 13.6.2).[22] "Collective opinion has responded rapidly and in sensible ways (given the information provided) to international events, wars, crises as well as to more subtle gradual trends in technology, the economy and society."[23]

(4) *Americans' policy preferences are coherent and sophisticated.* Page and Shapiro find that collective opinion yields consistent policy preferences; what is often taken to be evidence of inconsistency, they argue, actually indicates sophisticated distinctions in policy matters. For example, public opinion polls revealed different answers to differently phrased survey questions about euthanasia. Consider the following two questions:

"When a person has a disease that cannot be cured, do you think that doctors should be allowed to end that patient's life by some painless means if the patient and his family request it?"

If a person has a terminal disease, should the patient be allowed to tell the doctor to let him die?[24]

Public opinion is significantly more apt to respond positively to the second question than to the first. As Page and Shapiro note, the second question refers to a "terminal" illness rather than a merely "incurable" one, and asks whether the patient should be "allowed" to die rather than asking whether the doctor to be allowed to "end [his] life"—the latter suggests an active intervention. "Whatever one's own views may be of the moral and other issues involved," Page and Shapiro conclude, "this kind of differentiation fits well with our view of collective public opinion as coherent and sophisticated."[25]

15.3 Politics, Self-Interest, and Adjudication

I have already responded to the general claim that political opinions and behavior are thoroughly self-interested (sec. 13.2); I shall not repeat myself. I wish to consider the more specific claim that adjudicative democracy is threatened by the predominance of self-interest in politics.

In *Federalist 10* Madison recognized both the juridical nature of legislation and the dangers facing it:

No man is allowed to be a judge in his own cause, because his interest would certainly bias his judgment, and, not improbably, corrupt his integrity. With equal, nay with greater reason, a body of men are unfit to be both judges and parties at the same time; yet what are many of the most important acts of legislation but so many judicial determinations, not indeed concerning the rights of single persons, but concerning the rights of bodies of citizens?[26]

Madison's worry seems applicable to the adjudicative roles of both voters and legislators. Turning first to the voters, if each voter has some "virtue" but is not immune to self-interest, it appears that the voters are apt to use the suffrage as a means to advance self-interest rather than the public good; "it is unreasonable for Men to be Judges in their own Cases. . . . Self-love will make men partial to themselves and their Friends"[27] And, if so, the juridical conception of democracy is undermined: It assigns voters a judicial role precisely in the situation in which judicial roles are inappropriate.

One solution is suggested by both Page and Shapiro's work and Rousseau's analysis of democratic deliberation. If, on any specific issue, self-interest affects people's decisions in a random way, then in the very process of aggregating judgments we can expect these biases to "cancel one another, and the General Will remains as the sum of the differences."[28] However, the development of factions appears to undermine the "canceling out" solution; they organize their interests, and so interests are no longer randomly distributed. Since they are no longer random disturbances, the aggregation process will not cancel them out. Rousseau seems able to recommend the "canceling" solution because he seeks to do away with "intrigues" and "partial associations."[29] Famously, Madison rejects this option in Federalist 10. There are, he tells us, only two ways to remove faction: "the one, by destroying the liberty which is essential to its existence; the other, by giving to every citizen the same opinions, the same passions, and the same interests."[30] The latter is impossible, and of the former remedy, "it could never be more truly said . . . that it was worse than the disease."[31] For Madison, what remains is controlling the effects of factions, for example, through a balance of power.

I shall not try to improve on the Madisonian prescription; the desideratum of non-neutral procedures was intended, in part, as a response to the problem of factions. However, without in any way siding with Rousseau against Madison, there is reason to think that the problem of self-interested voting may be less of a threat to adjudicative democracy than Madison fears. As we saw (sec. 13.4.2), in even moderately large elections it is dubious that casting a vote to advance one's interests is rational: the expected benefits almost surely are outweighed by the costs. Now suppose, as I have argued seems empirically the case, voters are not simply self-interested, but also have a commitment to justice and the public good. If so, the irrationality of self-interested voting produces what Brennan and Lomasky nicely describe as a "veil of insignificance."[32] As with Rawls's "veil of ignorance" which, by taking away all knowledge of specific facts about oneself or one's society, makes it impossible for parties in the original position to base their decision on these factors, the insignificance of one's vote as a way of advancing self-interest removes self-interest from one's deliberations, and so allows one to consider disinterested reasons for casting one's ballot one way or another. If people are both virtuous and self-interested, the veil of insignificance explains why voters can be relied upon to be judges in their own case. At least for fully rational voters, self-interest is not relevant.

I hasten to add that Brennan and Lomasky are skeptical of this benign account of the veil of insignificance. As they point out, it also allows people to vote on the basis of prejudice and malice against their better interests. Whether we are to welcome or worry about the veil of insignificance depends ultimately on political psychology. Brennan and Lomasky are clear descendants of those who believed that the passions are a threat to social order; peaceful social life, on this view, depends on enlisting the interests and quieting the passions.[33] The alternative view, closer to the spirit of Kant, is that self-interest tends to corrupt the moral judgment; when self-interest can be held in abeyance, the likely outcome is more apt to be moral than either malicious or martial. Manifestly, the case for adjudicative democracy depends on Kant's view being nearer to the mark. Happily, I see no reason to doubt that it is.

It might be thought that the conclusion changes when we examine factions rather than individual voters. Individual voters, it may be argued, have nothing significant to gain by voting on self-interest, but as members of factions, which can reap large benefits, things are very different. However, the rational nonparticipation of the self-interested voter in large elections is reproduced as his rational free-riding in large coalitions.[34] As a member of a faction, the rational self-interested strategy would seem to be to let the other faction members advance one's interest while you, seeing that your own participation is not critical, act on the basis of justice and the common good. Supposing this is the rational strategy for each faction member, the veil of insignificance once again does its work. Of course, citizens do cast ballots, write letters to the editor, and give money to Greenpeace. That they do so consistently, and that so much of this behavior is manifestly irrational on self-interested grounds, points to the hypothesis that other reasons must move citizens in politics.[35]

Madison was worried about factions in the legislature. And the veil of insignificance is not drawn in the legislature. Legislatures are small enough that one can significantly advance one's interest by voting one way rather than another. Again, Madison stresses the division of powers as an effective check, and we shall consider presently whether a system of judicial review is justified to check legislative self-interest. But it is worth noting here that the empirical evidence does not indicate that legislators act in a relentlessly self-interested way.[36] And, of course, the essence of representative democracy is to harmonize at least partially the self-interest of legislators and public opinion. Not that legislators always follow their constituents' wishes. But it is interesting that they seldom diverge from those wishes without being able to offer some explanation for their unpopular stance. And, as John Kingdon points out, this "explanation is neither superfluous nor a mere political cover; it is part and parcel of the decision."[37]

Legislative politics is not essentially unprincipled. Alexander Bickel is among those who disagree—he stresses the importance of attending to the principled features of politics, and thinks that the problem with "legislative assemblies" is precisely that they do not:

> There, when the pressure for immediate results is strong enough and emotions ride high enough, men will ordinarily prefer to act on expediency rather than take the long view. Possibly legislators—everything else being equal—are as capable as other men of following the path of principle, where the path is clear or at any rate discernible. Our system, however, like all secular systems, calls for the evolution of principle in novel circumstances, rather than only for its mechanical application. Not merely respect for the rule of established principles but the creative establishment and renewal of a coherent body of principled rules—that is what legislatures have proven ill equipped to give us.[38]

It is on Bickel's—and apparently Rawls's (sec. 13.5.1)—view that the Supreme Court is the definitive voice of public reason. Although this view has, understandably, great popularity among jurists, it relies on a selective reading of American political history. One sort of familiar history of principled political decisions in the United States is to focus on the great Court decisions, particularly those such as *Brown v. Board of Education* that upheld basic civil rights; yet equally momentous as a principled political decision was the Civil Rights Act of 1964.[39] As Stephen Macedo observes, the bifurcation of legislative politics as the arena of interests and judicial politics as the forum of principle not only is inaccurate, but encourages an illiberal understanding of political life as a sort of "game in which players compete to advance their interests."[40] Legislative politics not only can be, but often has been, a fundamental part of the practice of liberal citizens to publicly justify their principled demands on each other.

Although Macedo concurs with justificatory liberalism in rejecting the idea that politics is simply the arena of conflicting interests, he indicates that it falls into the opposite error:

> At the opposite pole from the cynical [i.e., interest theory of politics] is a highly moralized conception of politics. Legitimate political activity, it may seem right to insist, should not only be constrained by principled considerations, but should aim only at impersonal moral ends, such as the protection of rights and the good of all. . . . To make this move, to define legitimate liberal politics in terms of moral purposes, is to insist on a complete fusion of policy

and principle and to elevate our expectations about the virtue of the participants.[41]

This certainly seems to describe the conception of politics I have advanced, though on the same ground it also seems to characterize the view of the *Federalist Papers* that justice and the common good are the end of government (secs. 12.4.1–2). In any event, I have certainly argued against the view that liberal principles merely "constrain" legislative decisions (sec. 13.4.1). Laws are impositions of norms on citizens; for these impositions to be justified, it is not enough that they do not violate some fundamental principle, for that leaves unanswered the question of why the imposition is justified. I have insisted that only a law that is the result of a publicly justified law-making institution can meet the test of public justification, a test with which Macedo himself concurs.

Justificatory liberalism, then, is by no means a philosophical justification of the current understanding of political life. On the view I have been defending in this book, contemporary political institutions regularly make coercive impositions that are unjustified—those done in the name of a variety of "policy" objectives, which further the goals of some citizens by conscripting others into their projects without public justification. This does not render the theory libertarian, for it allows the state to impose redistributive laws, to institute policies that secure basic needs, and so on, but only on the grounds that justice or the common good requires them. Neither does it mean that interests have nothing to do with political life or legislative politics. Liberalism, it will be recalled, seeks to protect the basic civil interests (sec. 11.3.1) and rights of all citizens; representative democracy is a justified adjudicative procedure because it is widely responsive to the views of citizens, particularly to their judgments about harms to their civil interests and deprivations of basic rights. Representative democracy economizes on virtue by enlisting this concern of citizens with protecting their basic interests into the aim of tracking the justified morality. Moreover, insofar as citizens can show convincingly that certain policies promote not simply the interests of some, but of all, they are appropriately adopted by the "productive state."

15.4 Vote Trading

I have been supposing throughout that citizens and legislators vote sincerely, that they express their actual judgments on each issue. That this is indeed an assumption, and a controversial one at that, is brought out through an analysis of vote trading. Consider the following imaginary example (based on Riker's Display 6–5).[42] Assume that we have two issues to be decided in a legislature split into three factions:

    x: to provide increased federal funds for urban renewal projects, which will mostly benefit the Rustbelt states. Someone against this we can say is for not-*x*, which will be designated ~*x*.

    y: to increase expenditure for defense. Those in the Sunbelt states will primarily benefit from this. Someone against this is for ~*y*.

Our three groups, then, are Rustbelters, Sunbelters, and Others. Each has 100 votes in our imaginary legislature. Their judgments are ordered as shown in Table 15.1.

Rustbelters would prefer the urban aid, but do not want increased defense spending; perhaps they hope to fund the aid to urban areas with defense cuts. But they would prefer both the urban aid and increased defense spending to no urban aid at all. If they cannot get their urban aid, they want at least to hold the line on federal spending so that their economies might improve. The last thing they want is increased federal spending and no urban aid.

The *Sunbelters* wish not only to resist defense cuts, but want some increases in defense spending to spur growth in their states, many of which rely on defense contractors. They would prefer not to increase the federal deficit with urban renewal expenditure; however, they would prefer both urban renewal and increased defense spending to no increase in defense spending. But if they cannot get the increase in defense spending they want, they certainly want at least to hold the line on other new expenditures, so they can go back to their districts arguing that they were in favor of keeping the lid on federal expenditure. The worst thing that could happen for them is for the Rustbelters to get their urban renewal aid, and so increase the deficit but leave them emptyhanded.

The *Others* are not enamored of either project; they are worried about the deficit, and see no good justification for either expenditure. If there has to be expenditure, it always sits better with their constituents if it is for defense. But they don't want to fund both projects at the same time—that would lead to terrible strains on the budget; so they prefer to fund either the Sunbelters or Rustbelters alone than to pay for both projects.

If we suppose (1) the issues are identified in such a way that *x* and *y* are distinct, and (2) people vote according to their preferences, then both *x* and *y* will be defeated, leaving us with ~*x*,~*y* (*x* v.~*x*: ~*x*

Table 15.1

Rustbelters	Sunbelters	Others
x, ~y	~x, y	~x, ~y
x, y	x, y	~x, y
~x, ~y	~x, ~y	x, ~y
~x, y	x, ~y	x, y

wins, 200 to 100; y v. $\sim y$: $\sim y$ wins, 200 to 100). However, there is a clear possibility here for vote trading. The Rustbelters will agree to vote for the defense spending when that vote comes up (even though they prefer $\sim y$ to y). And the Sunbelters agree to vote for urban aid when that vote comes up (even though they prefer $\sim x$ to x). By trading their votes in this way, each group will secure its second preference (x,y) rather than the third preference $(\sim x, \sim y)$ that would be obtained without vote trading.

Our story can be interpreted in two ways. One is that the Sunbelters and Rustbelters have redefined the issue. As they understand it, there are not two issues—"Should we give aid to urban transportation?" and "Should we increase defense expenditure?"—but rather one—"Should we have both aid to urban transportation and increased defense spending or neither?" How we describe a person's opinions on various issues apparently depends on how they are bundled together. All this is true; unfortunately, I have very little to say about how to resolve it. Formal theorists have explored various "independence conditions" that arrive at social decisions in ways that are not sensitive to infeasible or irrelevant options, but these conditions themselves are highly contentious.[43] And I have no formal insights to offer. Instead, I wish to advance an apparently pedestrian but still, I think, important thesis: Although issues are not what philosophers call "natural kinds" but are themselves contested in, and emerge through, politics, this by no means implies they are arbitrary and that anyone can call just anything "an issue."

The first part of the thesis—that the definition of an issue is itself a matter of political dispute—is fundamental to William Riker's analysis of disequilibrium in politics. Riker narrates a sweeping story of nineteenth-century American politics in which losers continually sought to redefine issues, so that political contests would take place on dimensions—issues—on which they would be winners. Precisely what constitutes an issue is determined by the political process itself; as Riker puts it, a process of natural selection operates, weeding out issues (and their formulations) that fail to provide electoral success, leaving those that work, for a while.[44] We thus confront the limits of the idea of tracking; the law-making institution not only tracks individual judgments but, through the debate and electoral competition intrinsic to the institution, shapes what the issues are and they way they are defined.

Issues, we might say, are political kinds, not natural kinds.[45] But that does not mean they are whatever you say they are. Perhaps, in our example, a Rustbelt legislator could convince the public there was only one issue involved here, but certainly some work would need to be done. One attempt might be to recast the votes as economic stimulus votes, or jobs votes. But saying so does not make it so. And surely simply saying that "urban aid and defense or neither" is a political issue is strikingly unpersuasive. This is not to say that the legislator might not justify her voting by saying that she was confronted with a choice between both and neither, and so vote trading was justifiable. This leads us to the second interpretation of the example: that the legislators identify these as distinct issues, but trade their votes in order to obtain the favored result on the issue with which they are more concerned. Traditionally we have been taught that logrolling of this sort is a threat to good democratic government,[46] but a number of contemporary democratic theorists see it as a positive virtue.[47] Which is it?

I suggest that the distinction between the "protective" and the "productive" state points to a complex answer. Insofar as our focus is on adjudicating disputes about justice—such as the extent of civil or welfare rights—vote trading is indeed a danger. Suppose that our example was not Rustbelters, Sunbelters, and Others, but parents against pornography, welfare recipients, and others. The parents against pornography wish to close down the adult bookshops (call that x), while the welfare recipients want an increase in their benefits (call that y). Given the same profile of preferences as in Table 15.1, both measures will be defeated; neither pass the legislature's test of public justification. Suppose now the two groups trade votes as they did in the example; both measures pass. But here the claim that representative democracy tracks public justification is implausible; making both groups happy—or even giving them the polices to which they are deeply committed—is not a proxy for public justification of the laws. Of course, that vote trading—and, in general, strategic voting—is to be discouraged in legislation about justice does not mean that it can be prevented. Nondictatorial, nonrandom procedures over three options are inherently open to strategic manipulation.[48] Nevertheless, some voting procedures, such as approval voting, are relatively immune to strategic voting; we have good reason to adopt them in certain situations.[49]

In contrast, vote trading aiming at policies based on the common good is less subject to this criticism. If the aim of the "productive" state is to secure goods in the interest of all, then allowing vote trading in principle broadens the packages and the beneficiaries. This seems especially appropriate given the strongly non-neutral procedures that properly characterize common good–based proposals. If it is difficult to enact such polices without very wide appeal, measures that broaden the appeal are reasonable. But even if the principled objection to vote trading does not apply to common good proposals, objections still arise. Most obviously, in the absence of Wicksellian rules that tie expenditure and revenue proposals, vote trading is apt to lead to polices that provide visible benefits to some groups while dispersing costs over the entire population.[50] However, supposing a severely non-neutral law-making institution conjoined with Wicksellian rules, vote trading may be unobjectionable or even beneficial.

15.5 Adjudication versus Mediation

Throughout most of the second and all of the third parts of this book I have maintained that liberal citizens have powerful reasons to adjudicate their disputes about the proper interpretations of public morality. Politics has thus been depicted as properly juridical, focusing on the adjudication of competing views about justice. But it may be objected that this is too confrontational and adversarial a doctrine;[51] successful political systems mediate disputes, finding compromises that leave all parties more or less satisfied rather than declaring winners and losers.[52] Vote trading might itself be understood as a mediating device.

To formulate a reply, we need first to distinguish two ways of achieving agreement, what Fred D'Agostino has described as the consensus and the convergence models.[53] If both Alf and Betty share a reason R that justifies to them a law l, the justification is grounded on rational consensus; if the law is justified to Alf on the basis of his reason R_A and to Betty on the basis of her reason R_B, the justification is grounded on the convergence of their belief systems. Both are bona fide modes of justification: to show that others share your reason justifying l, and that they possess a different reason justifying l, both justify l (assuming the principle of sincerity is met; see sec. 9.2.2). We need to distinguish, however, two phases of adjudication—argument and verdict. The argumentative phase concerns the sort of reason giving we examined in part II. People offer justifications for proposals, others question those reasons, and so on. Political debate and deliberation is argumentative in this way. But because, as I have maintained, this sort of argumentation is typically inconclusive, we need a way to end the dispute, to bring it to practical closure even though we are still confronted with an open question. At that point we require a *verdict*—an authoritative judgment as to whether a proposed justification has succeeded, on the basis of either consensus or convergence.

At the level of verdict, convergence arguments are inappropriate. As with a jury, the ideal is *consensus of rational belief* either that the case has been made or that it has failed. Consider a jury in which some jurors vote for the verdict because they believe the accused innocent, others because the are racially prejudiced toward the prosecution attorney, others because they have racial sympathy with the accused, and yet others because they wish to get out of the jury room as quickly as possible. Without doubt, such convergence of reasons plays a role in jury verdicts, but in a very obvious way such reasoning is inappropriate. Jurors delivering a verdict are not supposed simply to be happy with it and willing to support it for their own personal reasons. Rather, they occupy a public office, and as officials they are expected to give a judgment as to whether a case for guilt has been made to the required standard of proof; it is a consensus of belief on that matter, not simply a convergence of reasons for voting one way or another, that justifies a jury verdict.

Turn now to a legislature. If the *telos* of legislative politics is to find compromises that leave almost all parties satisfied with the outcome, convergence voting is certain to predominate. *Ex hypothesi* we disagree about the merits of the arguments; if legislative politics aims at widespread support for all measures—in the sense of trying to keep the overwhelming majority happy with every bill—the parties will have to be given different reasons for supporting legislation. Instead of delivering a verdict on whether the proposed law is justified—as Rousseau might say, whether it expresses the general will—legislators will vote on the basis of whether *they have reasons to endorse the bill*. As Rousseau recognized, if law-makers ask this question, they are led to coalitions and factions to press bills that advance their interests. Of course, those left out of the coalitions have no reason to support these bills; this may be so clear—they may find themselves so disadvantaged—that the proposed law, even if endorsed by a large majority, is clearly defeated from the standpoint of public justification. It articulates the will of all, not the general will.

Once again, this may seem hopelessly naive; legislators vote for bills that appeal to their own reasons, not ones that they think can be justified to all. As I think Rousseau recognized, democratic politics can often promote justice and the common good even when many act solely on the basis of their own concerns. That, I think, is the significance of Rousseau's idea that the "pluses and minuses cancel each other out" (sec. 15.3): to a large extent, these nongeneral reasons offset each other. This is one of the ways in which democratic politics economizes on virtue: We do not need to suppose that citizens and politicians are thoroughly virtuous in order for them to enact just laws. But as Rousseau and Madison both realized, it does not follow from this that a just order can do totally without virtue, or that its institutional structures should not encourage it. The great error of naive pluralism is in supposing that the public interest is simply the "diagonal of the forces that constantly struggle for advantage."[54] As Mill perceived, political institutions should encourage each citizen and official to "weigh interests not his own; to be guided, in case of conflicting claims, by another rule than his private partialities."[55] Political institutions that aim to please all parties, and so stress convergent verdicts, discourage taking up the wider perspective Mill had in mind. Each is encouraged to ensure that the law is acceptable from *his or her* perspective rather than the *public* viewpoint.

The difference between the protective and productive state looms large here. In deliberating about laws that articulate the demands of justice, I have been arguing, discussion should stress the various reasons justifying the law, but the final verdict should concern whether the law is publicly justified. Consequently, institutions and procedures that encourage convergent verdicts are to be discouraged. To some extent the same holds true for deliberations about policies that advance the common good; there, too, the vote should constitute a verdict on whether the common good is advanced by the policy in question. Nevertheless, in such deliberations interests come to the fore; each is well acquainted with the interests of his or her own faction, and a major test of whether a policy is in the interest of all is whether all factions find some reason to support it. In such debates convergent verdicts are very likely—each group evaluates the policy from the perspective of its own interests. And because this is so, and because convergent verdicts are apt to leave out of consideration the minority who may not have an interest advanced, strongly non-neutral procedures are appropriate as a way to ensure that the convergence is universal. In contradistinction, the institutions of the protective state, though properly non-neutral, ought not to be as rigorously so. Procedures that, for example, require large extraordinary majorities encourage convergent verdicts, since to ensure passage of almost any piece of legislation those who disagree with it must be enlisted, and this is accomplished by giving them convergent reasons to support it. Thus procedures requiring unanimity are not even a regulative ideal with regard to controversies about justice; at some point, the upshot of increased barriers is to make consensus verdicts impossible, driving legislators to convergent ones, and so abandoning the public perspective in favor of a coalition of private wills.

CHAPTER 16

The Judiciary and the Limits
of Legislation

16.1 Judges as Umpires

In order to resolve the clash of private judgments characteristic of the state of nature, argued Hobbes, Locke, and Kant, we require an umpire who resolves disputes through the rule of law, the definitive voice of public reason. Thus far I have been dealing with the umpire that formulates general rules; I now turn to the application of those rules to specific cases.

While some readers may have resisted the conception of a lawmaking institution as an umpiring procedure, understanding judges as umpires or officials in a game is hardly revisionary. Consider, for example, H.L.A. Hart's account of the finality of a supreme tribunal, which analyzes the role of judges as akin to that of scorers in cricket.[1] Imagine a scorer who came to a game of cricket and announced: "The score is whatever the scorer says it is." Hart comments:

> It is important to see that the scoring *rule* remains what is was before and it is the scorer's duty to apply it the best he can. "The score is what the scorer says it is" would be false if it meant that there was no rule for scoring save what the scorer in his discretion chose to apply. There might indeed be a game with such a rule, and some amusement might be found in playing it if the scorer's discretion was exercised with some regularity; but it would be a different game. We may call such a game the game of "scorer's discretion."[2]

In both cricket and scorer's discretion the scorer's judgment might be final, in the sense that it cannot be appealed. This is one sense in which the score is what the scorer says it is. But in cricket, unlike scorer's discretion, the scorer can be wrong; since he does not make up the scoring rules, he can make errors in applying them. In contrast, in scorer's discretion the scorer is infallible; the score simply is what the scorer says it is.

The application of law by judges is to be understood on the model of cricket, not scorer's discretion: Judges are applying rules not of their own making and, like any umpire, they can make errors. Once again we see the complicated mix of epistemological and practical elements that characterizes umpiring. We expect the umpire to do her best to track the merits of the case—to give a correct answer—and yet the finality of the umpire's call does not depend on the correctness of the decision. The umpire's calls are final (but see secs. 16.3–16.4) but by no means infallible.

Because umpires are expected to track the epistemological merits of the case as best they can (given practical constraints), expertise is valued in their selection. Now in the case of disputes about the demands of the publicly justified morality, I have argued that claims to expertise could not be made out; liberalism, as Jan Narveson says, recognizes "no high priests of morals" (sec. 11.2.3). But when we switch focus to the application of laws to specific cases, claims of expertise can be validated; the bone of contention at this phase of the dispute is not the requirements of liberal principles, but the requirements of a system of laws designed to express them. Judges have a publicly justifiable claim to have their decisions enforced by law because they have a valid claim to be experts at applying the law. "Hence it is that there can be but few men in the society who will have sufficient skill in the laws to qualify them for the stations of judges."[3] The authority of judges derives in part from their epistemological competence: Those who do not know the law are unsuited to judicial office. To be sure, some law school professors may know more law than many judges—just as some fans may have a far deeper knowledge of baseball than most umpires. Yet neither law school professors nor baseball fans have the requisite authority, which serves to remind us that the authority of umpires does not *simply* derive from their status as *an* authority.

If judges are umpires regarding the law (and not about the requirements of liberal morality), their job is not to express their own moral judgments but to form and enforce opinions about the demands of the system of laws.[4] If the occupant of a judicial office simply seeks to enforce her own controversial views about the demands of liberal morality, she claims a privileged position for her moral views—that they can be judicially enforced—that cannot be publicly justified. Such a judge properly is charged with subverting the function of the citizen and the legislator, and illicitly elevating herself as a privileged interpreter of liberal morality.

The analysis of hard cases in the law, however, seems to show that this conception of the judicial task fails to appreciate the "open texture" of legal rules. As Hart famously observes,

Particular fact-situations do not await us already marked off from each other, and labelled as instances of a general rule, the application of which is in question; nor can the rule itself step forward to claim its own instances. . . . [In applying a law, e.g., one prohibiting vehicles in the park] [t]here will indeed be plain cases constantly recurring in similar contexts to which general expressions are clearly applicable ("If anything is a vehicle a motor-car is one") but there will also be cases where it is not clear whether they apply or not. ("Does 'vehicle' used here include bicycles, airplanes and roller skates?")[5]

Thus Hart insists that the application of rules is inherently subject to "indeterminancies."[6] Even if we accept Hart's claim that, within a certain range, the application of laws is indeterminate, this would not, as Hart rightly insists, turn the law into a game of judges' discretion. Hart does not think the law is thoroughly indeterminate—in many cases its requirements are clear, and judges can manifestly err in applying it.

The question arises, however, whether in hard cases the law is genuinely indeterminate. Three possibilities are worth exploring:

1. In hard cases legal rules are *publicly indeterminate*. In hard cases public reasons are insufficient to justify a legal proposition, and a judge must rely on her own merely personally justified beliefs.
2. In hard cases legal rules are only *legally indeterminate*. In hard cases legal reasons are insufficient to justify a legal proposition, but sufficient public reasons are available to at least inconclusively justify a finding.
3. In hard cases legal rules are *legally inconclusive*. In hard cases judges cannot provide conclusive justifications of legal propositions, but sufficient legal resources are available to justify an inconclusive belief based purely on legal reasons.

The first option is in the spirit of Greenawalt's analysis of voters who find that public reasons run out, and so can only form justified beliefs by appealing to personal reasons (sec. 9.4.2). To the extent the law really is publicly indeterminate, the rule of law is an unattainable ideal. Basic to the rule of law is the principle of equality, according to which state officials must justify their decisions through public reasoning (sec. 12.2). Judicial opinions not only resolve disputes but provide *justifications* for legal conclusions.[7] Insofar as a judge is *publicly justifying* a conclusion, she cannot appeal to personal or idiosyncratic reasons, for they do not provide the requisite public reasons. Judges who rely on merely personally justified beliefs in imposing burdens would thus manifest the rule of men, not of laws. Happily, there is little reason to think legal rules are ever publicly indeterminate. Throughout I have stressed the abundance and complexity of public reasons. That judges would be faced with hard cases in which all the public reasons run out is most unlikely.

The real debate, then, is between those who hold that, because the law is indeterminate, judges must appeal to nonlegal public reasons, and those who insist that the legal reasons do not run out, though legal findings are often inconclusive. Given the complexity of legal systems, the latter seems much more likely. The very complexity of the law is what generates hard cases—both sides to the dispute are able to marshal plausible legal arguments to support their claims. If the legal system is so complex that both parties can employ it to form reasonable competing views, it would be surprising indeed if a judge had to go outside the law to decide the issue. The law is sufficiently rich for competing views to be justified; consequently, the judge, too, has the resources to form an opinion on legal reasons alone. As in analyses of conflicting public justifications, analyses of hard cases in the law go wrong when they suppose that, if a system of belief provides the basis for competing conclusions, a rational believer must go outside the system to form a justified belief. If the dispute arises from the very complexity of the system, bringing in new reasons—increasing the complexity of the dispute—is as unnecessary as it is unwise.

However, the distinction between options (2) and (3) is not quite so stark as I have presented it, for the line between legal and moral reasons is not well-defined. I have argued that a *telos* of the law is to secure justice by tracking the publicly justified morality, and that laws that violate publicly justified principles fail *as laws* (sec. 12.3). Consequently, the determination of a legal proposition cannot be entirely divorced from a judge's opinion about what is publicly justified. But though this blurs the distinction between (2) and (3), it does not obviate it. That a judge must appeal to her understanding of public morality to determine what is the law is not to say that the law is silent, and therefore the judge must simply impose her own views about public morality.

Ronald Dworkin's analysis of hard cases has much to recommend it here. Dworkin's Herculean judge "must develop a theory of the constitution, in the shape of a complex set of principles and polices that justify that scheme of government." [8] To justify a legal proposition in a hard case, then, a Herculean judge must develop a theory of the constitution, which of course includes theory about the political principles that the constitution protects and articulates. Dworkin's coherentist leanings are indicated here by his strong disposition to justify particular judgments by showing that they are part of a best theory of the practice. [9] The justification of a legal belief β is its status as a member of a coherent set of beliefs and principles. Clearly, we do not want to follow him all the way down that road (chap. 6). However, as I argued in section 8.1, one of Dworkin's great insights is the way in which systemic considerations support some interpretations of rules and defeat others. This does not drive us to global coherence; to say that other elements of a system of reasons can justify an interpretation of a rule need not appeal to what renders that system most coherent (we may have no idea what that would be). It is, rather, to recognize that the justification and interpretation of one belief impacts on others. Consistent with our general account of justification, judicial reasoning is best understood (as indeed it is) as a series of local inferences and specific arguments, with due allowance made for the fact that any inference is part of a system of beliefs, and so its validity is dependent on the way it meshes with other inferences in one's system, in particular whether there are defeaters for any given justification within one's system. Because legal claims are indeed part of a system of moral and political principles, Dworkin's thesis that legal, political, and moral reasoning overlap is a genuine and important insight.

16.2 Judicial Review

16.2.1 The Court and Moral Expertise

That judges must appeal at times to their moral and political beliefs when making legal determinations may seem to help justify the institution of judicial review, the authority of a Supreme or High Court to rule that acts of the legislature are unconstitutional. I shall argue here that a proper interpretation of the role of judges justifies a limited form of judicial review. I begin by considering two popular cases for a stronger—more "activist"—judicial review, and showing why they fail.

We have already encountered the first case for strong judicial review, implicit in the view of legislative politics as the hotbed of competing interests (secs. 13.2, 15.3). Alexander Bickel famously insisted that judicial review, especially as practiced by the Supreme Court of the United States, brings principle or morality into law.[10] Because, as Rawls says, "it is the only branch of government that is visibly on its face the creature of that [i.e., public] reason and of that reason alone," the Court is the "exemplar" of public reason.[11] If, then, the Court is the exemplar of public reason and justification, it is appropriate to accord it a preeminent role in public disputes about the dictates of public morality. And this, of course, is essentially the view of many Americans: On the great moral issues of the day—racial and sexual equality, the protection of the poor—it is the Court that speaks for principle and morality. That legislative institutions have little regard for basic rights makes judicial power to restrain them imperative.[12]

Throughout part III of this book I have argued against the conception of political life from which this popular understanding of the Court arises. As a matter of fact, legislative politics is not simply the arena of clashing interests, and a political theory whose fundamental commitment is to public justification aims at a legislative politics in which principle is increasingly important. To allow that principled deliberation is in some way the special purview of the judiciary is to accept, and encourage, the corrupted understanding of politics as a battle among interest groups, each claiming to impose its favored policies on the rest with no better justification than that it has marshaled the numbers to do so. A justified liberal polity, I have argued, provides no space for such political life.

Stephen Macedo's position is certainly to be preferred: Macedo agrees that the interest group theory of politics is at odds with liberal public justification, and that a liberal political life requires that the legislature engage in public justification (sec. 15.3). Macedo, then, is himself a critic of the dichotomy between legislative selfishness and judicial principle. Yet he, too, argues for a strong version of judicial review. The Court and legislature, he maintains, are coordinate interpreters of the Constitution;[13] both engage in public reasoning about the demands of basic liberal principles. Having multiple institutions interpreting liberal morality, he tells us, is part of the ideal of limited government.[14] In my terms, it can be argued that judicial review is part of a non-neutral justified umpiring procedure. We need, however, to distinguish two questions: Are strongly non-neutral (i.e., antimajoritarian) institutions justified? Would judicial review by a Supreme or High Court be justified as one such institution?

Regarding the first, I have argued in the affirmative (sec. 13.6). But it seems doubtful that an institution such as the Supreme Court can be justified as such an institution, for at least three reasons.

1. First, it is at best only minimally responsive. Although we have good reason to embrace political institutions that are not responsive to the simple majority, that is a long way from accepting an institution to which a tiny group of people—people who are not particularly representative of the citizenry—are appointed for life. Justified umpiring procedures, I have argued, seek in some way to track the views of the citizenry. That an umpiring institution should accord such weight to

the views of nine people selected for life seems at best of dubious value in tracking the views of citizens.

2. Because they are occupying legal offices, Supreme Court justices' claim to authority derives in important ways from their legal qualifications (sec. 16.1). But if they claim authority partly because they know the law, this gives them no special claim to be interpreters of liberal morality on disputed issues. That liberals recognize no high priests of morality (sec. 11.2.3) also implies that they recognize no high court of morality, and so no high court justices to sit on it. Claims by defenders of the Supreme Court that it is a definitive interpreter of liberal morality thus confuse us about the grounds for its authority: Are the justices of the Court legal or moral experts?[15] If they are supposed to be especially wise moralists, Robert Dahl's remark that judicial review amounts to a weak version of rule by Platonic guardians is apropos.[16]

3. As I have acknowledged, the political inequality required by expert rule can be justified if (a) it can be shown that expert rule tracks liberal morality better and (b) such experts can be publicly identified. Supporters of judicial review usually assume that (a) is the case—that political procedures including judicial review protect individual rights better and so track liberal morality better than alternative arrangements. As Dahl observes, however, there seems little evidence that this is so. Of the twenty-two democracies considered by Arend Lijphart, thirteen possessed judicial review.[17] As Dahl concludes, it has not been shown that systems that employ judicial review protect rights better than those that do not.[18] Moreover, Americans who tend toward the heroic vision of the Court often emphasize decisions such as *Brown v. Board of Education* that upheld minority rights, while minimizing the impact of those such as the Dred Scott decision or *Plessy v. Ferguson*, which reinforced oppression of the minority.

16.2.2 The Court and Legal Expertise

It might be objected that I have laid too much stress on justifications of judicial review in terms of a special *moral* competence of high courts. The very idea of fundamental *law* or a constitution (sec. 12.4.1), one may argue, requires the institution of judicial review. If fundamental law limits the authority of the legislature, then who is to interpret fundamental law? But even accepting that fundamental law limits the authority of the legislature, a number of possibilities present themselves. In her study of the development of judicial review in the United States, Sylvia Snowiss identifies three possibilities, corresponding to three phases in American judicial review.

1. The first possibility, reflected in Blackstone's writings and important in American legal thought up to *Federalist 78,* holds that while the existence of fundamental law clearly implies that the legislature is not *omnipotent,* the legislature may still be *supreme* in the sense that no body is entitled to enforce fundamental law against the legislature. Fundamental law may be held to limit the legislature's authority by speaking *to* the legislature. Insofar as the courts did undertake to review legislative enactments in this period, they were viewed as extraordinary political interventions, "a judicial substitute for revolution." [19]

2. In the second phase identified by Snowiss, from *Federalist 78* to *Marbury v. Madison,* the courts regularized their role as enforcers of fundamental law, but judicial review was still understood as a political rather than a legal act. In overturning a legislative enactment, the courts, on this view, were appealing directly to the fundamental law and the social contract, charging the legislature with a manifest violation of the terms of political association. The appeal in such review was not to a legalistic analysis of a written text, but to a "publicly verifiable" charge that the legislature had engaged in a "concededly unconstitutional act" violating fundamental law. [20]

3. Last, Snowiss argues that under the influence of Justice Marshall the Supreme Court converted judicial review into a regular exercise of legal interpretation of a written text, relying for its authority on its status as definitive interpreter of written laws. All three theories recognize that legislatures are bound by fundamental law, and American judicial practice in particular has vacillated between proponents of versions of (2) and (3). [21] But most American "liberals" believe that something along the lines of Marshall's doctrine is fundamental to liberalism and the rule of law. Advocating "judicial restraint" is often perceived as paramount to endorsing brute majoritarianism.

Nevertheless, justificatory liberalism points toward a justification of judicial review along the lines (2)—the "concededly unconstitutional act" rule—and not (3), Marshall's doctrine that because the constitution is a legal text, the Court has special expertise in interpreting it. "The judiciary's power to invalidate the decisions of other institutions should be reserved for those special occasions when some aberrant governmental action is emphatically inconsistent with constitutional theory, text, and public understanding as expressed in prolonged practice." [22] This follows from the fundamental problem of politics: the necessity of adjudicating how best to apply inconclusive political principles. As I have repeatedly stressed, rights to free speech, association, privacy, and so on, are abstractly justified, but their application is in dispute. The task of liberal politics is to adjudicate disputes about the application of fun-

damental law. If that is true, to accord the Court's inconclusive interpretation of these principles priority over the responsive institutions'
judgments is indeed to erect the Court into a quasi–guardian. As pre-
(and a good deal of post-) Marshall jurisprudence recognized, the interpretation of fundamental law is a *political* issue; for the Court to claim
a privileged position in interpreting fundamental law is for it to claim a
privileged *political* role.

Because the stuff of liberal politics is the confrontation of competing
inconclusive claims about the demands of liberal morality as articulated
by fundamental law, the inconclusive opinions of judges about the demands of fundamental law ought not to be accorded a special status.
However, when the legislative institutions adopt an act that, in the
opinion of the high court, is manifestly contrary to fundamental law,
the court rightly has the power to overturn it. And it has the power
because the authority of the legislative institutions is, according to liberal constitutionalism, restricted to the adjudication though law of
competing inconclusive disputes about justice and the common good.
If the legislative institutions manifestly violate fundamental law, they
are acting to impose a defeated proposal on some citizens and so are
acting outside the scope of their legitimate authority. And since acts
that are manifestly contrary to fundamental law fail *as law* (sec. 12.3.3),
the courts cannot enforce them.

Judicial review is justified, but in general courts ought to be deferential to legislatures. It should be obvious that this does not derive from
a majoritarian commitment, since I have advocated legislative procedures that are significantly nonmajoritarian. Judicial deference to the
legislative branches is properly based on a recognition that the resolution of disputes about basic principles is quintessentially political, and
the legal expertise of judges does not justify a privileged position for
their political opinions over those of their fellow citizens. From this
perspective—as, I think, from most perspectives—the U.S. Supreme
Court's decision in a case such as *Roe v. Wade* was manifestly political,
and so inappropriate. The Court's interpretation of the right to privacy
is plausible, but certainly not compelling. This style of judicial review
selects an inconclusive judgment about the demands of a basic political
principle as decisive, and to be embodied in law. That is to say, it
performs the task of politics. This is not to say the Court's decision
about the right to privacy was wrong; it was wrong about its authority
to decide reasonable disputes about fundamental law.

Like most proposals that draw lines, this doctrine of judicial review
is subject to the criticism that the lines are not clear. In matters concerning the demands of basic principles in which the legislature's opin-

ion is not manifestly contrary to the Constitution, the Court should defer to the legislature, but in applying "normal" law, courts must often insist on their inconclusive judgments about what the law requires (sec. 16.1). But the lines between manifestly unreasonable enactments and inconclusive but reasonable laws, and between fundamental constitutional issues and the application of ordinary legislation, are themselves contentious matters. A doctrine of judicial review does not provide an algorithm for deciding what cases a court should consider. It is, however, a justification for one sort of critical judicial attitude rather than another. For a judge to accept that disputes about the contours of basic rights are a political issue, and for the most part outside the legal competence of judges to resolve, is itself important, even if what such acceptance requires is, like so many matters, open to doubt in many cases.

16.2.3 Procedural Review

Legal theorists sometimes write about *the* problem of judicial review. It seems, though, that the problems posed by judicial review of legislative acts as unconstitutional differ depending on whether the acts under consideration are interpretations of substantive fundamental principles or involve the integrity of the political and legal process. Thus far I have concerned myself with the former—judges upholding their interpretations of fundamental law over that of the legislative branch. However, as John Hart Ely has shown, a basic function of courts is to serve as "gate keepers," ensuring that the competition for political offices and the legal process itself remain fair. Indeed, according to Ely, American judicial review is overwhelmingly concerned with processes rather than substantive principles because the Constitution is: "The original Constitution was principally, indeed I would say overwhelmingly, dedicated to concerns of institution and structure and not to the identification and preservation of specific substantive values."[23] Ely insists that even the Bill of Rights is concerned with process values as well as substantive principles. While Ely's critics are no doubt correct that he squeezes too much of the Constitution into a procedural interpretation,[24] his general approach, involving judicial deference to the legislature on substantive values while endorsing nondeferential interpretation of process requirements, seems essentially correct.[25] Here the dictum that one cannot be judge in one's own case (sec. 15.3) really is applicable. The legislative branch cannot be relied on to ensure that excluded groups have an opportunity to challenge those who presently hold sway in the legislature; as Ely puts in, in these cases the Court is needed to act as a "referee."[26]

The approach to constitutional adjudication recommended here is akin to what might be called an "antitrust" as opposed to a "regulatory" orientation in economic affairs—rather than dictate substantive results it only intervenes when the "market," in our case the political market, is systemically malfunctioning. (A referee analogy is also not far off: the referee is to intervene only when one team is gaining unfair advantage, not because the "wrong" team has scored.) Our government cannot fairly be said to be "malfunctioning" simply because it sometimes generates outcomes with which we disagree, however strongly (and claims that it is reaching results with which "the people" really disagree— or would "if they properly understood"—are likely to be little more than self-deluding projections). In a representative democracy value determinations are to be made by our elected representatives, and if in fact most of us disapprove of them we can vote them out of office. Malfunction occurs when the *process* is undeserving of trust, when (1) the ins are choking off the channels of political change to ensure that they will stay in and the outs will stay out, or (2) though no one is actually denied a voice or a vote, representatives beholden to an effective majority are systematically disadvantaging some minority out of simple hostility or a prejudiced refusal to recognize commonalities of interest, and thereby denying that minority the protection afforded other groups by a representative system.[27]

As Ely notes, this conception of judicial review does not suppose that judges are high priests of morality. However, "lawyers *are* experts on process writ small, the process by which facts are found and contending parties are allowed to present their claims."[28]

The obvious objection to Ely's (and my) distinction between substantive disputes and issues of procedural fairness is that the determination of the latter may require appeal to substantive principles. For example, to determine whether an electoral arrangement leads to malapportionment, it seems necessary to develop a theory of political equality, including justifications for departing from political equality. And this seems to require the Court to examine controversial interpretations of basic substantive principles.[29] This may be a more serious problem for Ely, who evinces a sort of value skepticism, or perhaps a sort of majoritarian conventionalism.[30] A skepticism about moral principles is no part of my case for judicial deference; the crux of that case is that adjudicating disputes about the implications of basic principles is the political task par excellence, which judges should not seek to usurp. But appeal to controversial interpretations of substantive principles is not usurping the political process if the justification for the appeal is that the decision-making institution has been corrupted.[31] Once again, justification for the decision is crucial. As Ely notes, if the Supreme Court appeals to substantive principles on the grounds that the legislature has given an erroneous interpretation of the rights of citizens, this is almost certainly inappropriate (given the clear mistake rule). But if the justification is that the umpiring procedure is not operating according to its constitutional provisions and is violating political equality, appeal to basic principles serves a very different function. Again, no algorithm is to be had for distinguishing the two, but a judicial review that seeks to distinguish them will have a very different character from one that does not.

16.3 The Moral Obligation to Obey the Law and Its Limits

The umpire, I have argued, is to adjudicate a certain set of moral disputes, namely, those in which competing undefeated public justifications confront each other. Judges are properly deferential to laws that lie in this area. Thus, in 1973 a Supreme Court justice such as Harry Blackmun[32] rightly should have deferred to the judgments of state legislatures, despite his belief that a woman's right to privacy included a right to abort fetuses (during some periods in the pregnancy). But this means that such a judge would be bound to act contrary to his own moral conviction, perhaps upholding statutes that he believed wrongly restricted the right to privacy.

This is not simply an occupational hazard of a judicial career; it is the normal situation of citizens in a liberal state. No matter what the umpire decides, some citizens will be justified in believing that the decision is wrong. As I have stressed throughout, to accept rule by an umpire is to acknowledge that the umpire's decision that you should Φ gives you a moral reason to Φ even if you believe that Φ-ing is wrong. That is, although on your best evaluation of the merits of the case, $\sim\Phi$ is the thing to do, if the umpire says that you should Φ, this gives you a moral reason to exclude acting on your own evaluation and to do what the umpire says. Unless one is prepared in this way to act contrary to one's own evaluation, one is not really submitting the dispute to arbitration. And if one has a moral obligation to abide by the umpire's ruling, then one must have a moral obligation to obey the law, in the sense that one has a moral obligation to Φ just because the law says to Φ even though one thinks Φ-ing is wrong. Contrary to much current thought, it is therefore no "fetish" to accept that "illegality per se is a reason for doing what the law requires or not doing what it forbids."[33] Those who are not prepared to accept this are justly accused of the vice of arrogance—of insisting that their own unvictorious reasonable beliefs about morality are definitive.[34] Because we have a reason to submit disputes to a judge or an umpire, we have a moral reason to accept the decision of our umpire, even when we disagree.[35]

However, the liberal theory of law does lead us to reject one very strong interpretation of the moral obligation to obey the law, namely, that one has a moral obligation to obey *all* purported laws.[36] The obligation to obey the umpire holds only for inconclusive disputes. If a citizen judges that the umpire is making calls contrary to victorious justifications, he must conclude that the umpire is seeking to enforce an unreasonable view, and is acting outside the bounds of the rule of law. It is here that R.E. Ewin's essentially Hobbesian account of the umpire goes astray. Though Ewin believes that the decisions of a procedurally unfair umpiring procedure do not bind citizens, he follows Hobbes in insisting on the inappropriateness of citizens' making obedience contingent on their judgment of the substantive merits of the decision.[37] Ewin's proposal would be compelling if we submitted to an umpire solely because of practical problems that result from brute disagreement; in that case, *any* disagreement may be thought to be a matter for adjudication. On the more Lockean account I have defended in this book, however, our commitment to adjudication follows from our fundamental commitment to public justification. It is when Alf is unable to victoriously publicly justify his reasonable views about justice that he is led to arbitration, but he has no reason to submit his publicly justified principles to the umpire. He has (he believes) publicly justified them, so he cannot see how *his commitment to public justification* could give him a reason to submit them to an umpire; he has no conceptual resources that could allow him to recognize such a reason. Certainly the mere fact that others disagree cannot show that he has failed to justify his claim, any more than the dissents of creationists show that evolutionary biologists have failed to justify their views.

Although it leads to a much messier account, Locke, not Hobbes, is right: The moral obligation of citizens to obey the law depends on the substantive merits of the law. A citizen has no obligation to obey a law if the umpire is enacting defeated proposals.[38] A Hobbesian might object that a citizen at best *thinks* that a principle has been victoriously justified, while the umpire and other citizens obviously *think differently*. If Alf has judged that a particular moral claim has been victoriously justified, while Betty thinks that it is within the set of inconclusively justified (undefeated unvictorious) proposals, doesn't this dispute need adjudication? Aren't we back where we began?

From Alf's perspective, or from the perspective of any other liberal citizen, we are not. From any particular perspective, a citizen's commitment to public justification can lead him to submit to an umpire, but this very same reason will lead him to resist an umpire who, in his judgment, is seeking to impose defeated—publicly unjustified—proposals on him. Any citizen can and will distinguish what is fundamental and justified from what is reasonably disputed; that he will submit the latter to arbitration will not lead him also to submit the former. Indeed, for liberals to submit *all* moral disputes to the umpire is to allow that, if challenged by an illiberal citizen, fundamental liberal principles themselves might legitimately be overturned by the umpire.

The problem arises when Alf's judgment about what has been victoriously justified and what has not differs radically from Betty's. When that happens, Alf and Betty disagree not simply on what is the correct outcome of political dispute; they disagree on what should be on the political agenda. Liberal politics will be, at best, imperfect in a community so divided, for one or the other will refuse to admit that a political resolution of some issue is morally legitimate. If the division is restricted to a small number of issues, perhaps devices such as gag rules will allow liberal politics to function by insulating it from those conflicts that cannot, from a practical point of view, be successfully adjudicated.[39] However, if the community is deeply divided in this way on a wide range of issues, the practical resolution of moral disputes through the rule of law will be precarious, for whatever the umpire decrees, some will declare that it is a violation of fundamental law. In such a society the law may still usually be complied with, but most will not perceive themselves to be obligated to obey, and a gnawing cynicism seems inevitable.

16.4 Revolution and Utopian Aspirations

Alf's commitment to public justification, I have argued, does not provide him with a reason to obey a manifestly immoral law that he Φ when $\sim\Phi$-ing is publicly justified. A qualification is in order: It may provide such a reason if obeying that law is necessary to preserve a basically just system of adjudication from collapse. In such an unlikely situation, we need to distinguish Alf's global commitment to public justification from the specific commitment to $\sim\Phi$. If it arose that honoring his commitment to $\sim\Phi$ brought about the collapse of an umpiring procedure that was generally reliable, and this umpiring procedure would not be replaced with one that was generally reliable, Alf's specific and global commitments to public justification conflict. Although what Alf should do here depends on the details of the case, including just what Φ is, we can envisage situations in which the thing for Alf to do would be to Φ, despite its *manifest* immorality. Living under a reasonably just umpiring procedure is a great moral good; it allows a social life in which our relations with each other are informed by respect, and in which we can honor our commitment to justify our demands. This good is not to be lightly discarded.

While the above situation seems somewhat fanciful,[40] it aids in thinking about a less fanciful question: When is Alf justified in taking up arms against a regime or, more moderately, taking measures designed to overthrow (though extralegal measures) an umpiring mechanism? Again, much depends on the details: What sorts of costs are associated with opposition? What is the chance that a better regime will come about? Yet one general point can be made: A basically just umpiring procedure is such a great good that it is very difficult to make out a case for overthrowing it, especially if its overthrow involves violence. Revolution becomes a plausible option when a regime loses its character as basically just, and no longer serves the ends for which is was instituted:

That whenever any Form of Government becomes destructive of these ends, it is the Right of the People to alter or to abolish it, and to institute new Government, laying its foundation on such principles, and organizing its powers in such form, as to them shall seem most likely to effect their Safety and Happiness. Prudence, indeed, will dictate that governments long established should not be changed for light and transient causes; and accordingly all experience hath shewn, that mankind are more disposed to suffer, while evils are sufferable, than to right themselves by abolishing the forms to which they are accustomed. But when a long train of abuses and usurpations, pursuing invariably the same Object, evinces a design to reduce them under absolute Despotism, *it is their right, it is their duty,* to throw off such Government, and to provide new Guards for their future security.[41]

Utopian aspirations—hope for an even more just, even better tracking law-making institution—are unlikely to justify rebellion against a basically just umpire. This, of course, is especially true of basically just governments that build into the adjudication procedure ways to amend the procedure itself. This insight allows us to respond to an objection to the argument of part III, namely, that the argument for a justified umpiring procedure is itself essentially inconclusive. I have argued that the political contractors will choose a nonrandom, widely responsive, deliberative, non-neutral law-making institution that satisfies the principle of political equality, distinguishes the protective and productive functions of government, and allows limited judicial review. This may seem a disappointingly general result. It is certainly general when compared with K.O. May's theorem, which shows that, given two options, only simple majority decision making satisfies a small set of reasonable criteria.[42] The desiderata I have defended here can be met by diverse systems. Given this, it appears that we have not really solved the problem of the state of nature. In the state of nature we are confronted by diverse and competing demands, most of which are inconclusive. Hobbes, Locke, and Kant all argue that, to solve the problem of competing private judgments, we require an umpire to provide public, definitive laws. But this only solves our original problem of honoring the commitment to justify ourselves if we can at least victoriously justify the umpire; if our opinions about the justified umpire are inconclusive, it seems that we are back where we began.

Happily, we are not. We have been able to identify a set of desiderata that serve to eliminate many possible umpiring procedures (including the ancient one of selecting a single person as the umpire and the modern one of appointing the majority). We have been able to identify the set of justifiable law-making institutions, and these are well described as the family of representative democracies. Moreover, we have seen that law-making institutions must not be characterized by political inequalities unless they can be conclusively justified.

Yet we have not selected a unique procedure, so it seems that a modified version of the problem of the state of nature confronts us. Alf advocates a system similar to that designed by the constitutional convention in Philadelphia; Betty supports a justified system closer to that arrived at by the National Australian Convention of 1897–1898. Assume both are within the set of justified procedures; unfortunately, Betty lives in New York, not Sydney. Why should she be forced to live under the U.S. Constitution of 1789 rather than the Australian Constitution of 1900?

Utopian aspirations are to be restrained. If Betty lives under a just system of government that meets all the publicly justified desiderata, she has a great moral and practical good, a good that merits protection. The adjudication procedure deserves her allegiance. True, in an important sense Alf has received more than Betty: He not only has a just system of government, but one that he believes is best justified. We might even say that, to this extent, the arrangement between Alf and Betty is not entirely fair. But such fairness is utopian, a system in which even the smallest procedural details can be conclusively justified to all. Because of the limits of our ability to reason publicly, this really is utopian. All possible political systems will include features that cannot be conclusively publicly justified on their merits. Their justification is that, of the possible arrangements that meet the desiderata, they exist; because of that, they solve an impure coordination problem (secs. 9.4.3, 11.2.3, 13.3).

This is not a justification for embracing the status quo, for no existing political system fully meets all the desiderata. The protective and productive functions of government are often confused; more seriously, politics often degenerates into the mere competition of private interests, and the principle of political equality is regularly compromised. When a government fails to meet basic requirements of a just umpiring procedure, it can be at best nearly just; when it departs radically, it is simply unjust. So Betty's problem—the problem of living under an umpiring procedure that meets all the publicly justified desiderata but is not the one she thinks is best—is not a problem any of us are lucky enough to have. Our problem is the more serious one of citizens living in partially just states, and we must determine whether they are just enough to merit our allegiance.

CHAPTER 17

Conclusion: Justificatory Liberalism and Its Rivals

Liberal politics has both a moral and an epistemological basis. Liberal politics requires, first, that citizens recognize their moral commitment to justify their demands on each other, and second, that citizens understand what is involved in such justification. In *Value and Justification* I tried to show that liberal citizens are indeed committed to the justification of their demands; parts of this book, especially chapter 8, were also devoted to supporting this claim. The rejection of this moral supposition leads to a corrupted political life. Unfortunately, this corrupted conception is widely embraced. If political demands on others need not be justified to those others, political life becomes a matter of simple imposition by the powerful on the weak. Some variants of this conception, associated with majoritarian democracy, insist that those with the numbers get to impose on those without the numbers. Others, more closely associated with interest-group pluralism, believe it is simply obvious that politics is about one group imposing its will on others. To be sure, such political theorists typically have modest sorts of impositions in mind—taxing their fellow citizens to promote their favorite projects rather than sending them to the gulag. Yet for all that, politics is understood as the institutionalization of unjustified impositions. Public choice theorists have studied this sort of politics under the description of "rent seeking"—though they are wont to use this term for almost any expenditure of which they do not approve. Institutionalized aggression might be another name.

This is strong language. But given the easy and wide acceptance of the idea that politics is properly understood as the competition of relentlessly self-interested groups furthering their aims by enlisting government support, strong language seems necessary at least to signal that this popular view manifests an easy acceptance, perhaps approval, of some imposing on others without justification. And that sounds like a form of aggression; it is certainly browbeating (sec. 8.4). It is almost as if a number of political scientists and theorists have interpreted Madison in *Federalist 10* as telling us that politics is simply the war between factions and can never be anything else. To be sure, such a politics may have a purpose; the institutional war we call politics may still be superior to the war of all against all in the state of nature, but few explicitly endorse such a conception of politics as a good thing. Typically, those who depict politics as institutionalized aggression present themselves as hardheaded students of the political world, simply observing the way politics operates. One of the things I have tried to show in part III of this book is that the evidence for this empirical claim is amazingly thin. Neither voters nor politicians seem to act as the theory predicts. Self-interest is an important motive in politics; there is, though, very little evidence that politics can be adequately explained as purely self-interested.

Although rejecting the commitment to justification leads one away from a genuinely liberal political life toward the politics of self-interest, accepting the commitment to justification does not assure a liberal politics. In this book I have attempted to show that we also must have some idea of what constitutes an adequate justification. Rawls's theory, and political liberalism generally, is indicative of the problems of embracing the commitment to justify while at the same time forgoing epistemological commitments. Political liberalism is driven to a sort of populist consensualism because it deprives itself of the resources on which to ground the claim that liberal principles are justified in the face of sustained dissent by reasonable people. Any reasonable person who does not accept its claims becomes a counterexample. Pushed by its populism, political liberalism moves to modify and weaken its liberal commitments in search of an ever wider and thinner consensus. Ultimately, I think, it loses its character as a liberal doctrine, for little, if anything, is the object of consensus among reasonable people. Reasonable people, we have seen, are very often wrong, and very often resist changing their views even when their errors are pointed out to them. The project of securing a consensus of all reasonable people leads to the undermining of political liberalism's liberalism, which is to say that it leads to self-destruction.

On reflection, this should not be at all surprising. The conjunction of (1) the idea that, to use Stephen Macedo's formulation, the "moral lodestar of liberalism is . . . the project of public justification"[1] (sec. 1.1) and (2) a theory that, for all practical purposes, is highly skeptical about any controversial justificatory claims, leads to (3) a skeptical politics: Combining the two leads to the motto: Justification is everything. Little can be justified.

Like many important mistakes in philosophy, this one has its basis in a deep truth. *Justification is of fundamental importance, yet it really is hard to conclusively justify much.* My aim in this book has been to show how an adequate theory of justification shows not only why it is so hard to conclusively justify much, but also demonstrates how that very inconclusiveness can lead us to justify adjudicative institutions to carry on the justificatory project. Politics, we might say, is the continuation of ethics by other means. The juridical state provides the framework for citizens to adjudicate their inconclusive views as to what impositions are publicly justified.

If a type of populist consensualism that ultimately undermines liberalism is the consequence of trying to forgo justificatory commitments, another threat to a liberal political order is overconfidence in one's justifications. Consider those who accept that politics is about what can be justified, but also insist (as most ordinary reasoners do, see sec. 9.1.2) that what is justified for them is necessarily conclusively justified. From this once again arises a politics of imposition—not the imposition of our self-interested projects on the rest, but the imposition of all our moral opinions on each other. This is no fanciful picture; it is all too common in our political life. On numerous issues—abortion, gun control, AIDS research, welfare policy—citizens not only advance definite opinions about complex issues, but do so utterly confident that they are correct beyond a doubt, and that their opponents are either pigheaded or simply evil. When this condition obtains, politics is the continuation of moral war by other means, and is characterized by the shrill protesting of those who have lost, proclaiming the corruption of the political institutions controlled by their foes.

A liberal political life, if not precisely precarious, depends on citizens' recognizing several not-all-that obvious principles:

1. *The Commitment to Public Justification.* The aim of the political order is not to provide the means for some to coerce others to assist in favored projects, but to provide a rule of laws that articulate the justified demands that citizens can make on each other. This principle is violated by "interest-group liberals."

2. *Confidence in the Basic Principles of a Liberal Regime.* If liberalism is to avoid the populist consensualism of political liberals, citizens must be able to have a justified belief that liberal principles are publicly justified, even in the face of opposition by many reasonable citizens. As we have seen (sec. 16.4), a commitment to public justification is not inconsistent with disobedience and even revolution. Liberalism has been a doctrine upholding the right to revolt as well as the obligation to obey, because liberals have grounds

for standing up for some principles and refusing to adjudicate or compromise them. Justificatory liberalism accounts for this. It also shows why, as Locke put it, *"every Man is Judge* for himself"[2] when deciding when revolution is appropriate. Each citizen's obedience to the umpire is based on his or her belief that the umpire is resolving disputes in a publicly justified way. When a citizen concludes that the umpire no longer is performing that function, his or her commitment to public justification can no longer bind to obedience.

3. *Willingness to Accept and Comply with Laws with Which One Morally Disagrees.* A self-interested conception of politics would seem to have one great advantage over a moralized vision: One can reconcile oneself to losing out over interests, but to lose on morality seems intolerable. How can one abide a law that one believes is morally wrong? Many if not most contemporary political philosophers seem to take it for granted that a moral being could never allow herself to be bound by such a law; thus, as we saw, the moral obligation to obey a law simply because it is a law is sometimes described as a "fetish." Justificatory liberalism shows how we can have a moral obligation to obey a law we believe to be immoral: If our judgment of its immorality is inconclusive, we have an obligation to submit the dispute to a justified umpire, and abide by the verdict. If, on the other hand, we conclude that the law is conclusively immoral, we are apt to have no obligation to obey.

Even putting aside the errors of the self-interested conception, and accepting the commitment to justification, liberal politics requires that we avoid the Scylla of supposing that what we reasonably believe is conclusively justified—and therefore can demand as a matter of justice that it be embodied in legislation—and the Charybdis of fleeing from ever standing up for our fundamental principles when reasonable people disagree with us, compromising on every issue or always seeking consensus. The rivals of justificatory liberalism fall into these errors because the fail to take seriously the moral-epistemological basis of liberal politics.

APPENDIX

Liberal Principles in a World of States

Liberal Universalism and State Sovereignty

One of the most perplexing aspects of liberal theory is its account of the relations between sovereign states. On one hand, liberals have traditionally been drawn to moral universalism: Basic rights, liberals have insisted, are genuinely human rights—all humans have valid claims to such rights. Thus, universalism inclines liberals toward a cosmopolitan view. All people have the same basic rights, and so perhaps they should live under the same political institution—a world state. At a minimum, liberal universalism appears to endorse an interventionist foreign policy. If we assume a world of multiple states (umpires), liberal cosmopolitanism apparently sanctions one state in interfering in the "internal" affairs of another if the latter is violating the basic rights of its own citizens. In this vein, L. T. Hobhouse praised William Gladstone—perhaps the greatest liberal statesman of all—for his moralism and cosmopolitan perspective; as Hobhouse put it, in Gladstone's eyes there was "no line drawn beyond which human obligations cease."[1] More recently, Stanley Benn has pointed to Gladstone to show that "the liberal tradition includes a strong vein of universalistic, humanitarian moralism, even in its approach to international relations."[2] This commitment, Hobhouse held, led Gladstone to abandon Cobden's strict principle of nonintervention.[3]

Yet the history of liberal theory also manifests a respect for state sovereignty and adherence to a principle of nonintervention. "Self-determination" has been a basic liberal principle. According to Ludwig von Mises:

The right of self-determination in regard to the question of membership in a state thus means: whenever the inhabitants of a particular territory, whether it be a single village, a whole district, or a series of adjacent districts, make it known, by a freely conducted plebiscite, that they no longer wish to remain united to the state to which they belong at the time, but wish either to form an independent state, or attach themselves to some other state, their wishes are to be respected and complied with.[4]

This, however, leads to supporting a principle of nonintervention: If some groups have a right to form their own state, then others should not meddle in their internal affairs once they have done so. And examination of Gladstone's own career reveals that, while championing an obligation to assist foreigners in need, he also upheld a conception of international society based on a strong, though not absolute, principle of nonintervention.[5]

These commitments seem at odds. Like many other contemporary students of international relations theory, Charles R. Beitz insists that moral universalism is inherently opposed to any notion of state sovereignty that upholds a strong principle of non-nonintervention.[6] As Beitz understands it, to accept what is often called external sovereignty is to affirm that states are "morally free to arrange their internal affairs as their governments see fit."[7] The worry, then, is that genuine moral universalism cannot admit a principle of noninterference in the internal affairs of other states. We might reason as follows: (1) according to liberalism, the legitimacy of any state depends on whether it respects the basic rights of its citizens; (2) according to universalism, all humans possess the same basic moral rights; so (3) a state that attacks the basic rights of its citizens is illegitimate and, consequently; (4) other states are in no way committed to refrain from interfering with the internal affairs of such a state. But (5) this seems inconsistent with a strong principle of noninterference, which grants states great leeway as to how they arrange their internal affairs.

The umpire account of political authority defended in this book shows that this conflict is illusory: Moral universalism is consistent with a world of sovereign states based on a strong principle of noninterference. Suppose that the basic liberal principles described in sections 10.2 to 10.4 are universally victoriously justified: They are justified to each and every person in the world. This would yield a universal morality. We have seen, though, that these principles are abstract and their application inconclusive. An umpire is thus required to select one of the competing inconclusive interpretations of each universal principle. So long as the government of state B does not violate the manifestly justified principles, or enact manifestly defeated ones, the government of state A has no authority to demand that B follows A's interpretation of the universal morality. This points to the principle of nonintervention (NI):

NI: The government of state A has no authority to demand that the government of state B follows its own interpretation of liberal morality if:

1. The umpiring mechanism of B is publicly justified among the citizens of B and;

2. The policies of the government of B do not manifestly (a) violate publicly justified morality or (b) enact defeated proposals.

Suppose that state A criticizes state B's policies toward its own citizens, arguing that they are immoral. But if A acknowledges that opinions on this matter are inconclusive, it must accept that according to NI it has no authority to demand that B follows its interpretation. Consequently, it would be merely international browbeating for A to demand that B do as it wishes on this matter. If the government of A respects its commitment to public justification, it is committed to respecting B's authority on this matter. This is a genuine principle of nonintervention. Moreover, given that most of our disputes about justice are indeed inconclusive, NI will often be applicable. When, on the other hand, the government of B is violating the publicly justified rights of its citizens, B's government acts without authority. In this case, A can make a moral demand that B desist and, with public justification, act to protect these rights. Under what conditions A has a duty to so act I leave aside for now. For present purposes the important point is that NI provides no protection for the government of B in such cases.

It is, I think, remarkable that this analysis—which is a clear implication of the umpire account of political authority defended in this book—converges with Hugo Grotius's classic doctrine of the right to intervene. Grotius acknowledges the justice of a military intervention against a sovereign who has wronged its own subjects.[8] It is essential to notice, though, that Grotius defends (1) the rights of the sovereign to punish its subjects, but then adds (2) "these rights [only] have force in cases where the subjects are actually in the wrong, *and also, you may add, where the cause is doubtful.*"[9] Grotius thus concludes that the rights of the sovereign cannot protect it when it has wronged its citizens in obvious—and from his examples, terrible—ways. As an example of a sovereign who has wronged his subjects in such a way as to open the door to external intervention, Grotius points to, among others, Phalaris, who was legendary for his cruelties. One translation suggests that it is only when sovereigns have provoked their people "to despair and resistance by unheard of cruelties, having themselves abandoned all the laws of nature" and have thus lost "the rights of independent sovereigns" that intervention if justified.[10] It thus would appear that until the sovereign abandons universal morality it has a special status vis-à-vis its citizens, to the extent that in "doubtful" cases the sovereign is authorized to render publicly definitive judgments, and so other sovereigns have no right to intervene.

The Extent of the State

It might be objected that my analysis of the umpire's authority does not so easily fit into a world of independent states, each with extensive rights of sovereignty. I argued in section 11.2 that individuals committed to public justification have conclusive reason to quit the state of nature, and submit their disputes to the judgment of an umpire. But Kant is clear that the problem of the state of nature—that each acts on his own judgments about justice—applies not only to a state of nature among individuals, but among "nations and states" as well.[11] And because Kant also argues that one would be justified in forcing another individual to leave the state of nature and enter a "juridical state," we might extend Kant's argument by holding that one government would be justified in interfering with the affairs of another if doing so helped bring about a "cosmopolitan" constitution with a legal system capable of producing a single definitive answer to all disputes.

As Kant himself recognized, a single world state could itself pose a threat to justice.[12] It is anything but obvious that a world umpire— which, if it turned tyrannical, may well be beyond challenge—is the best way to resolve our disputes about justice. Leaving this worry aside, another problem is that a universal umpire may *decrease* the scope of public justification. To see how this may occur, suppose that in population O_1 law l has been proposed. Now l is defeated if, in any persons's system of reasons and beliefs, he has conclusive reason to reject it. If l is clearly defeated in anyone's system, then it cannot be the case that the public justification endorsing l is inconclusive. Now, suppose that in O_1 we conclude that l is not defeated. But it may well be the case that within a group $\{O_1 \& O_2\}$ there will exist some person in whose system of reasons and beliefs the law is decisively defeated. So in the larger group l is a defeated proposal, where in O_1 it was a reasonable view that could be selected by the umpire. This, of course, is especially true if the larger group includes those from very different cultures, who may have different sets of justified beliefs (see secs. 3.4 to 3.5).

The set of publicly justified proposals is apt to be richer in smaller than larger groups. What demands are justified in one's family may be extensive, while what demands one can justify to every other human may be exceedingly modest. From the perspective of resolving our disputes about justice and the common good, as we enlarge the size of the population subject to the same umpire we gain insofar as we do not have conflicts among independent umpires. But we lose insofar as less can be justified within the larger group. The "optimal" size of the population subject to an umpire thus depends on a variety of factors. Suppose for example we wish to know whether population O_1 should have its own umpire, or share an umpire with O_2. The following are all relevant variables:

1. How much more can be publicly justified within O_1 as compared with the combined group, $\{O_1 \ \& \ O_2\}$?
2. How much do the people in O_1 interact with O_2? How often do they make moral demands on each other?
3. What is the evidence that unresolvable disputes will arise between the umpires of O_1 and O_2?
4. Is there a possibility for an institutionalized way for the umpires of O_1 and O_2 to resolve their disputes? (How effective are international law and international organizations?)
5. Will including the population of O_2 drastically reduce the reliability of the umpiring procedure?

Much more could be said. The point is that there is no obvious argument that a universal umpire is the most effective way for people to resolve their disputes about justice and the common good.

Is Justificatory Liberalism Universalistic?

I have been supposing that the basic set of liberal principles is indeed universally justified, thus giving rise to the apparent (but ultimately illusory) tension between universal principles and state sovereignty. But does justificatory liberalism uphold the universality of liberal principles? Two questions, which may seem almost identical, must be distinguished:

1. Is it possible that there is some population O_1 in which nonliberal principles are justified?
2. Is it possible that there is some population O_1 on which demands based on liberal principles cannot be justified?

The first question probably should be answered in the affirmative. We can imagine a small group of like-minded people among whom, for example, establishment of a religion can be justified. Perhaps this group is characterized by devotion to a religious creed. Because all of the population may actually assent to the religious creed, a lower level of justification will suffice since its establishment does not require overriding anyone's epistemic authority (sec. 9.2). However, problems will confront such an illiberal umpire: As children mature into adults, they may come to reject their parents's orthodoxy, and so contend that the illiberal norms are no longer publicly justified. Although in principle we can suppose that a small group of like-minded people may be able to honor their commitment to public justification through illiberal norms, this seems dubious in any significantly sized group in the modern world. Societies deemed "religious" or "traditional" are not purely traditional or religious: in any but the smallest groups it is a practical certainty that some will possess systems of reasons and beliefs that defeat establishment proposals, thus paving the way for liberal toleration.

Even if we grant that the first question might in some cases be answered in the affirmative, this by no means shows the second will be so answered. Suppose that O_1 is sufficiently homogenous that an establishment proposal can be publicly justified within it. But when members of this closed society confront outsiders, they will encounter the diversity of perspectives that defeats their establishment proposal. That is, the members of O_1 will not be able to justify their illiberal norms to outsiders. If the members of O_1 are indeed committed to public justification, and if they understand themselves to be self-directed—people whose actions properly reflect their own beliefs and values rather than the beliefs and values of others—then, as I argued in *Value and Justification*, their commitment to public justification will lead them to embrace basic liberal principles such as noninterference. But, as acknowledged in *Value and Justification* (pp. 383 ff), it may be that some cultures such as the Balinese do not entertain this conception of themselves, and so liberal demands on these people cannot, perhaps, be justified.

Liberal principles will be justified among strangers, conceiving of themselves as agents who direct their own lives, and who share with each other very little in the way of common religious beliefs, ideas of the good life and so on. It is these sorts of relations—the relations that obtain among the members of what F.A. Hayek calls a "Great Society"[13]—that properly are regulated by liberal political principles.

NOTES

CHAPTER 1

1. Macedo, *Liberal Virtues*, 78. I, too, have argued for this fundamental liberal commitment in Gaus, *Value and Justification*, chap. 19.
2. Waldron, "Theoretical Foundations of Liberalism," 36–37.
3. Larmore, "Political Liberalism," 349.
4. Rawls, *Political Liberalism*, 44. Cf. Larmore's claim that "the reasons for the ideal of neutrality are not primarily *epistemological*. . . . [t]hey are instead basically *moral*"; "Political Liberalism," 342.
5. See Rawls, "Priority of Right and Ideas of the Good," 256, 267; Rawls, "Domain of the Political and Overlapping Consensus," 242–43. See also Introduction to *Political Liberalism*, in which Rawls characterizes the moral epistemologies of Kant and Hume as "comprehensive" doctrines, i.e., ones that cannot be justified to everyone.
6. Rawls, *Political Liberalism*, 9 ff.
7. I have argued so in Gaus, *Value and Justification*, pt. 2.
8. Traditionally, epistemology concerns not only the theory of justified belief, but also a theory of knowledge. My concern here is only with the former.
9. See Raz's criticism of political liberalism in "Facing Diversity: The Case of Epistemic Abstinence." While I am in sympathy with much of Raz's essay, there is much with which I disagree. Two differences stand out: (1) Raz draws no consistent distinction between justified belief and true belief, a distinction that I see as crucial; (2) like the political liberals, I, too, seek to draw epistemological boundaries between different sorts of issues, a task of which Raz is critical. On the first point, see Raz's long footnote on p. 15.
10. D'Agostino, "The Idea and the Ideal of Public Justification," 158. For a similar charge, see Herzog, *Without Foundations*, 18 and "Conclusion," 218–43.
11. D'Agostino, "The Idea and the Ideal," 156. D'Agostino cites Bruce Ackerman as a liberal who believes that such justificatory neutrality can be achieved. See Ackerman's "What Is Neutral About Neutrality?" Because the idea of neutrality is itself so complex, I shall not employ it here. For useful discussions, see Larmore, *Patterns of Moral Complexity*, 42–48; Arneson, "Neutrality and Utility"; Jones, "The Idea of the Neutral State"; and Waldron, "Legislation and Moral Neutrality."
12. D'Agostino, "The Idea and the Ideal."
13. Somewhat surprisingly, D'Agostino endorses Rawls's theory because it articulates his own political preferences.
14. I run the risk here of offending those who insist on a sharp distinction between metaethics and normative ethics. A good example of the way essentially metaphysical and normative doctrines can be woven together is Mackie's *Ethics: Inventing Right and Wrong*.
15. There are obviously exceptions to my broad claim that contemporary ethics pays scant attention to justified belief. Alan Gibbard's recent work is perhaps the first that comes to mind. See his *Wise Choices, Apt Feelings*.
16. See Rawls, *Political Liberalism*, Lecture III. sec. 8, Lecture IV, sec. 8. This is an implication of Rawls's idea of "overlapping consensus." See Lecture IV.
17. I argue this point in more detail in Gaus, *Value and Justification*, 404–7. See also D'Agostino, "Some Modes of Public Justification," 400 ff.
18. Brink, *Moral Realism and the Foundations of Ethics*, 17. Brink acknowledges that these are not sufficient conditions for moral realism.

19. See Brink's discussion of moral constructivism, *Moral Realism and the Foundations of Ethics*, 19 ff. Brink maintains that a belief in moral realism is required by coherence, so in this broader sense he does not think that coherence is consistent with nonrealism. My point is that either a realist or a nonrealist can be a coherence theorist, though of course they will disagree about the system of beliefs required by coherence. I criticize coherence theories in chap. 6 below.

20. See Bonjour, *Structure of Empirical Knowledge*, e.g., 88.

21. This is noted by Bonjour. I develop this point in Gaus, "Green, Bosanquet and the Philosophy of Coherence."

22. See Rawls, "Justice as Fairness," 230; Larmore, "Political Liberalism," 354–55.

23. Francis Snare, for instance, characterizes noncognitivism as the claim that "No judgment just *is* a (true or false) statement of fact"; *Nature of Moral Thinking*, 76.

24. I say "sometimes" here in order not to prejudge the issue as to whether some judgments are self-justified. See chap. 7.

25. For views that hold that ethics is cognitive in this sense, though not about truth or falsity, see Toulmin, *An Examination of the Place of Reason in Ethics*; Habermas, *Moral Consciousness and Communicative Action*, 43 ff.

26. The qualification "much" relates to the analysis of public justification in part II, where the account departs from emotivism.

27. See Brandt, "Emotive Theory of Ethics," 305–9; Brandt, "Stevenson's Defense of the Emotive Theory."

28. See Ewing, *Ethics*, chap. 7; Urmson, *Emotive Theory of Ethics*, chap. 7.

29. I have argued that value judgments do indeed have this structure; see Gaus, *Value and Justification*, pt. 1. See also Gibbard, *Wise Choices, Apt Feelings*, and Mabbott's discussion of emotivism in his *Introduction to Ethics*, chap. 8. For a survey see Deigh, "Cognitivism in the Theory of Emotions."

30. More interesting sorts of mistakes are also possible—e.g., one who claims to fear something recognized as harmless. I examine such errors in depth in Gaus, *Value and Justification*, see esp. 165–72.

31. I analyze inferential reasoning in part I.

32. For defense of this claim, see Gaus, *Value and Justification*, 74–79.

33. See, e.g., Brandt, "An Emotional Theory of the Judgment of Moral Worth."

34. It is perhaps worth noting here that although contemporary moral philosophers find it difficult not to talk about reflective equilibrium, it was introduced as a general justification of deductive and inductive inference rules. There is, then, some tradition of bridging the gap between empirical and normative justification. See sec. 7.4 below.

35. Habermas, *Moral Consciousness and Communicative Action*, 68. I am not claiming here that the details of Habermas's conversational theory are embraced by political liberals. For critical discussions, see Larmore, *Moral Complexity*, 55–59; Moon, *Constructing Community*, chap. 4.

36. See Ackerman, "Why Dialogue?"

37. Benn, *A Theory of Freedom*, 19, 2.

38. Rawls, *Political Liberalism*, Introduction, Lecture II, secs. 2–3; Cohen, "Moral Pluralism and Political Consensus."

39. Benn, *A Theory of Freedom*, 19.

40. For Habermas, see his distinction between deontological issues and questions of the good life in *Moral Consciousness and Communicative Action*, 104; for myself, see sec. 9.2.

CHAPTER 2

1. We can put aside the chicken or the egg problem: which comes first, interpersonal justification or personal reasons? I see no reason to worry about that problem here (or proba-

bly anywhere). My point is that a participant in any given discourse enters with a conviction that he has reasons for what he believes.

2. Habermas, I believe, agrees. See his *Theory of Communicative Action*, 1:12–15.

3. I am characterizing inferential justification very broadly; I am not supposing that a conscious reckoning through several steps is necessary for an inferential justification. As I understand it, inferential justification is essentially the same as believing for a reason. See Audi's distinction between the "structurally inferential" and the "episodically inferential" in *Structure of Justification*, 238 ff.

4. See Freud, "Inhibitions, Symptoms and Anxiety," 256.

5. This example is a modification of Pollock's in *Contemporary Theories of Knowledge*, 81. For a similar example see Swain, "Justification and the Basis of Belief," 25. See also Audi, *Structure of Justification*, 6 ff.

6. See Williams, "Deciding to Believe."

7. Unless it is confusing to do so in a particular context, I shall employ β (and α) to designate both belief states and sentences. If we wanted to be very careful, we could use β to designate a belief state and b to designate the statement that is believed.

8. The so-called Gettier problem encouraged this. Despite the disagreements with Stephen Stich that will emerge in this book, I concur wholeheartedly with his evaluation of this reliance on eccentric counterexamples. See Stich, *Fragmentation of Reason*, chap. 1. For a review of contemporary epistemology with special reference to the Gettier problem, see Shope, *Analysis of Knowing*.

9. Pappas, "Basing Relations," 57. Typically, the bizarre example is offered as an argument sufficient for rejecting a proposal. I should note that the fixation of analytic philosophers with specifying necessary and sufficient conditions—be it for knowledge, justification, or whatever—has spawned this counterexample industry. Except when giving technical definitions, I make no claim to giving the necessary and sufficient conditions for reasonable use of any terms. It seems prima facie implausible that such conditions exist, so it isn't surprising that they are so difficult to state.

10. Elster, "Belief, Bias and Ideology," 140.

11. Benn, *A Theory of Freedom*, 26. See Williams, "Deciding to Believe," 141–42.

12. Armstrong, *Belief, Truth and Knowledge*, 80.

13. For a much more sophisticated development of this view than I offer here, see Swain, "Justification and the Basis of Belief." On overdetermination see also Audi, *Structure of Justification*, 239–40.

14. For summaries, see L. Ross and C.A. Anderson, "Shortcomings in the Attribution Process," 144 ff. See also Nisbett and Ross, *Human Inference*, chap. 8.

15. L. Ross and C.A. Anderson, "Shortcomings in the Attribution Process," 147–48.

16. However, the worry discussed in the text does alert us to the dangers of combining the sustaining analysis with a Freudian notion of unconscious beliefs: Such a combination may well be immune to any possible counterexample. But this is a more general problem of Freudian theory.

17. I put aside here the question of the falsification of "theories" or various sorts of law-like statements; considering these issues would take us too far afield in the philosophy of science. See, e.g., Fetzer, *Scientific Knowledge*, pt III.

18. This may be a natural response—and it is certainly the response of the investigators—but it is not, as I understand him, the lesson drawn by Stich in *Fragmentation of Reason*. See below, sec. 4.6. For Gilbert Harman's interpretation, see his *Change in View*.

19. See Armstrong, *Belief, Truth and Knowledge*, 82–85.

20. Lehrer, *Theory of Knowledge*, 169–70.

21. See Kohlberg, *Philosophy of Moral Development*, 17–19, 115 ff; Piaget, *Moral Judgment of the Child*, chap. 1.

22. See Kagan, *Nature of the Child*, 139 ff.

23. See, e.g., Freud, *The Ego and the Id*. For a recent sympathetic explication of Freud's view, see Scheffler, *Human Morality*, 80 ff.
24. Lehrer considers the possibility that Mr. Raco might become entirely deranged if he were transformed into a decent fellow, and so would be incapable of any beliefs about medicine. Even so, Lehrer argues, his current beliefs would be justified. Much depends here on how we interpret the counterfactual test. Say the loss of his racist beliefs would produce a chain of events that caused Mr. Raco's death. Does this show that the scientific beliefs were not sustaining the medical beliefs, and so his medical beliefs were not overdetermined? Only if the counterfactual test requires taking account of the psychological and physical consequences of a person's losing a certain belief. Though arguing this would take us too far into the analysis of counterfactuals, Lehrer's interpretation is not, I think, particularly plausible. After all, that Mr. Raco would go mad without his racist beliefs does not show that the scientific evidence was not sustaining the medical beliefs. Lehrer also posits that the racist beliefs are so strong, nothing else could add to the strength of his medical beliefs. But as far as I can see, this is not relevant to the question of overdetermination. See Lehrer, *Theory of Knowledge*, 171.
25. See Elster, "Belief, Bias and Ideology"; Armstrong, *Belief, Truth and Knowledge*, 95–96.
26. Cf. Foley's defense of "epistemic luck" in *Theory of Epistemic Rationality*, chap. 4.
27. Reliabilism is a form of externalism; I consider externalism in general in chap. 3.
28. An elaboration of such a view is Alvin I. Goldman's "historical reliabilism"; see his "What Is Justified Belief?" See also Nozick, *Philosophical Explanations*, 264 ff.
29. See Lycan, *Judgment and Justification*, 106; Nozick, *Philosophical Explanations*, 172; Rawls, *Political Liberalism*, 116–18, and the references given in Rawls's note 21, 117.
30. This is not a statement of Nozick's view. See *Philosophical Explanations*, 317 ff.
31. See Meinong, *On Emotional Presentation*, chap. 12. See also Findley, *Meinong's Theory of Objects and Values*, chaps. 9–10.
32. Ideal observer theories in ethics may be understood in a similar way.
33. Some versions of reliabilism allow for some, though not a majority, of false justified beliefs. See Foley, *Theory of Epistemic Rationality*, 155–62.
34. Ibid., 162 ff.
35. Goldman proposes a reliabilist theory that avoids these problems. For a discussion, see Pollock, *Contemporary Theories of Knowledge*, 177.
36. See Rorty, *Philosophy and the Mirror of Nature*, 360 ff, and "Science as Solidarity."
37. Cf. Raz, "Facing Diversity." The extent to which Raz's view departs from that advanced in this book is not clear; though Raz often insists that the question of "truth" cannot be put aside, his real concern may be that the notion of justified belief cannot be ignored (see 15, n. 34). If so, then I entirely concur with Raz.
38. On the general idea of externalism, see Pollock, *Contemporary Theories of Knowledge*, chap. 4; Lehrer, *Theory of Knowledge*, chap. 8. See sec. 3.2 below.
39. See Armstrong, *Belief, Truth and Knowledge*, p.79.
40. See Pollock, *Contemporary Theories of Knowledge*, 19. On noninferential justifying reasons, see sec. 7.1.
41. See Chisholm, "Foundation of Empirical Statements."
42. This is parallel to an internalist epistemological theory according to which sensations can be reasons for beliefs though not themselves beliefs. See Pollock, *Contemporary Theories of Knowledge*, chap. 5.
43. Lycan, *Judgment and Justification*, 95. Emphasis in original. Cf. Armstrong, *Belief, Truth and Knowledge*, 77 ff.
44. I have defended the existence of basic affects in Gaus, *Value and Justification*, chap. 2.
45. See Gaus, *Value and Justification*, pt. 1.
46. I made this mistake in Benn and Gaus, "Practical Rationality and Commitment."

CHAPTER 3

1. Pollock, *Contemporary Theories of Knowledge*, 37.
2. See Freud, "Inhibitions, Symptoms and Anxiety," 245 ff. See Gaus, *Value and Justification*, 75–76.
3. This is familiar in the literature on reasons for action; see Williams, "Internal and External Reasons." See also Benn, *A Theory of Freedom*, chap. 2; Darwall, *Impartial Reason*; T. Nagel, *View from Nowhere*, 140–42.
4. This distinction is similar to that between subjective and objective justification. However, as should become clear momentarily, I believe these are rather misleading labels. See Pollock, "A Plethora of Epistemological Theories,"109–10; Gibbard, *Wise Choices, Apt Feelings*, chap. 1.
5. This is often thought to support coherence accounts of justification; Pollock shows why this is not so in *Contemporary Theories of Knowledge*, 67–71. On coherence theories, see chaps. 5–7 below.
6. See Ellis, *Rational Belief Systems*, 4.
7. Open justification is related to Brandt's use of "rational" "to refer to . . . moral systems which would survive maximal criticism and correction by facts or logic"; *A Theory of the Good and the Right*, 10.
8. Here and throughout I will use "belief system" as a shorthand for system of reasons and beliefs.
9. Raz, *Practical Reason and Norms*, 17. Cf. Darwall's remark that "When we look to see what reasons there are to believe a proposition we do not simply reflect; we look outward to see what might bear on it. It would seem, therefore, that we must think that reasons to believe propositions are not provided simply by what we already believe." Darwall, *Impartial Reason*, 44. This, of course, is an apt description of open justification.
10. Cf. Raz, *Practical Reason and Norms*, 15 ff.
11. Benn and Gaus, "Practical Rationality and Commitment."
12. For the permissive view, see Gibbard, *Wise Choices, Apt Feelings*, 46, 89; Pollock, *Contemporary Theories of Knowledge*, 124 ff. On epistemic commitments, see Foley, *Theory of Epistemic Rationality*, 17 ff.
13. See Dennett, *Intentional Stance*, 55–56.
14. Doyle, *A Study in Scarlet*, 21.
15. For a good discussion, see Lycan, *Judgment and Justification*, chap. 3.
16. "Jim finds himself in the central square of a small South American town. Tied up against the wall are a row of twenty Indians, most terrified, a few defiant, in front of several armed men in uniform. A heavy man in a sweat-stained khaki shirt turns out to be the captain in charge and, after a good deal of questioning of Jim which establishes that he got there by accident while on a botanical expedition, explains that the Indians are a random group of inhabitants who, after recent acts of protest against the government, are just about to be killed to remind other possible protestors of the advantages of not protesting. However, since Jim is an honoured visitor from another land, the captain is happy to offer him a guest's privilege of killing one of the Indians himself. If Jim accepts, then as a special mark of the occasion, the other Indians will be let off. Of course, if Jim refuses, then there is no special occasion, and Pedro here will do what he was about to do when Jim arrived, and kill them all." Williams, "A Critique of Utilitarianism," 98.
17. See Cherniak, *Minimal Rationality*, chap. 3.
18. See Lycan, *Judgment and Justification*, 55 ff.
19. Ibid.
20. Field, "Mental Representations."
21. Newton-Smith, "Relativism and the Possibility of Interpretation," 110. The names of the variables have been changed.

22. Ibid. Again, the names of variables have been altered.
23. See Audi, *Structure of Justification*, 145 ff.
24. Another grounding for the objection might be the absolute idealist thesis that in a perfectly coherent system every truth implies every other truth. On this view, a belief system with even one true belief would be rationally flawed if it had any false beliefs (since that would be to ignore some implications of its own beliefs). And, since there is but one truth, perfectly coherent systems must be identical. I shall defer detailed examination of this view until later (chap. 6), but it should be manifest that it is an exacting, indeed hopelessly exacting, ideal of rationality. Relying on such exacting ideals of rationality only leads us astray, since we have no idea how they can be applied. In any event, a traditional objection to coherence theories of truth is that there can indeed be two systems of belief, inconsistent with each other, but each coherent. Thus it has long been argued that a coherence view of truth actually leads to a relativism of reasons. See, e.g., Alan H. Goldman, *Empirical Knowledge*, 80–87.
25. Ellis, *Rational Belief Systems*, vii.
26. Ibid., vii–viii. Peter Gärdenfors agrees that *"epistemic attitudes* such as 'acceptability' are more primitive notions for a semantical theory than 'truth' "; *Knowledge in Flux*, 19.
27. See also Forrest, *Dynamics of Belief;* Gärdenfors, *Knowledge in Flux*. I provide a very basic sketch in the text, roughly following Ellis's static and nonprobabilistic analysis of rational belief systems.
28. I have altered Ellis's notation. See *Rational Belief Systems*, 7–8.
29. See chap. 2, n. 7.
30. See XV above for meaning of symbols. Some notations have been altered.
31. The idea behind completability is that there is a way to replace X evaluations with either A or R evaluations. See Ellis, *Rational Belief Systems*, 9 ff; Gärdenfors, *Knowledge in Flux*, 26.
32. Ellis, *Rational Belief Systems*, 22 ff; Forrest, *Dynamics of Belief*, 21 ff; Gärdenfors, *Knowledge in Flux*, 39 ff.
33. I am focusing here on acceptance of beliefs. *Mutatis mutandis* this can be applied to rejection. See Forrest, *Dynamics of Belief*, 21 ff.
34. Forrest makes a similar observation; *Dynamics of Belief*, 21. See also Pettit, *Common Mind*, 244 ff.
35. See Lawson, "Proving the Law."
36. It has been suggested to me that these issues can be resolved in a uniform way by appeal to an expected utility model. It is tempting to think that a strategy that yields the highest expected payoff in terms of true (or justified) beliefs should be adopted. But this will not do. For one thing, we cannot identify a single maximand—true beliefs—for we are interested in both obtaining true beliefs and avoiding false ones. If our only goal was securing true beliefs, we would do well to believe everything. Because we are simultaneously seeking two ends—securing truth and avoiding error—no single epistemic maximand presents itself. (See sec. 14.5 below.) The only way to create a single maximand is to go outside epistemic considerations, for example, by appealing to a general expected utility model. But that, too, seems wrong, for it indicates that belief acceptance should be guided solely by its good consequences and not in particular by its truth or justification. I argue against this view in Gaus, "The Rational, the Reasonable and Justification." Cf. Foley, *Theory of Epistemic Rationality*, chap. 5. For explorations of probability models, see the references in n. 31 above.
37. See Forrest, *Dynamics of Belief*, 27.
38. An upshot of this is that one can be justified in believing α but not justified in employing it as a premise in an argument justifying a further belief, β. See Foley, *Theory of Epistemic Rationality*, 57 ff. This limits the extent of our belief commitments.
39. See Braine, "On the Relation Between the Natural Logic of Reasoning and Standard Logic."

40. Ellis, *Rational Belief Systems*, 31, chap. III.
41. See Lukes, "Some Problems About Rationality," 208 ff. See also MacIntyre, *Whose Justice? Which Rationality?*
42. See Williams, "*Ought* and Moral Obligation."
43. From Williams, "Ethical Consistency," 180, notation slightly altered. See also Hurley, *Natural Reasons*, 125 ff.
44. Williams, "Ethical Consistency," 181–82. Notation altered, emphasis in original.
45. Williams and others take this as indicating that moral conflict is very different from cognitive conflict. I consider this in sec. 5.4.

CHAPTER 4

1. Stich, *Fragmentation of Reason*, 13. Emphasis in last sentence added.
2. I apologize to the reader not only for "openly justified," but even more for "closedly justified."
3. For the present purposes, I do not distinguish the idea of a belief system from a cognitive system, though there are clear differences (e.g., some of those who refer to cognitive systems may reject the concept of belief, which constitutes no small difference.) Remember that I include in belief systems not only beliefs, but norms regulating inference.
4. See Piaget, "Growth of Logical Thinking from Childhood to Adolescence," 440–41. See also Habermas, *Moral Consciousness and Communicative Action*, 116–88.
5. See D'Agostino, "Transcendence and Conversation." More generally, see Rorty, *Philosophy and the Mirror of Nature.*
6. See Quine's distinction between "sectarian" and "ecumenical" attitudes to rival theories; *Pursuit of Truth*, 98–101. I have been arguing for a combination of sectarian devotion to your perspective with a dash of ecumenicalism when deciding what reasons others have.
7. Mill, *A System of Logic*, 4. See also Mill, *An Examination of Sir William Hamilton's Philosophy*, chap. 20; Ellis, *Rational Belief Systems*, v, chap. 2.
8. Even P.N. Johnson-Laird, a critic of mental logic theory, acknowledges this in "Reasoning Without Logic." This supposition, of course, characterizes Piaget's thought; see, e.g., his "Logic and Psychology." For a criticism of Johnson-Laird, see James H. Fetzer, "Argument for Mental Models is Unsound."
9. Rips, "Cognitive Processes in Propositional Reasoning," 40. A conflicting view is supported by Johnson-Laird's more recent work. He has argued in favor of a theory of reasoning that focuses on access to the truth conditions of the connectives rather than on inference rules, an approach that he claims has advantages over mental logic theories ("Reasoning Without Logic"). However, the notion of "semantic information," which is fundamental to his analysis, seems to be derived from analyses of truth tables. Though he argues that "Most people have an intuitive grasp of these [semantic] differences" (ibid., 19), his earlier work concluded that people do not employ truth tables in reasoning. Wason and Johnson-Laird, *Psychology of Reasoning*. See also Braine, "Natural Logic of Reasoning and Standard Logic."
10. See, e.g., Wason and Johnson-Laird, *Psychology of Reasoning*, chap. 8; Braine, "Natural Logic of Reasoning and Standard Logic," 5 ff. See sec. 4.5 below.
11. See Braine, "Natural Logic of Reasoning and Standard Logic;" Rips' "Cognitive Processes and Propositional Reasoning." For supporting evidence see Braine and Rumain, "Development of Comprehension of 'or': Evidence for a Sequence of Competencies."
12. Rips, "Cognitive Processes and Propositional Reasoning," 64 ff.
13. Developmental theory, characteristic of Piaget, avoids the extremes of a strictly innate or strictly learned account of mental logic. I have considered the contrast between these types of psychological theories at some length in Gaus, *Modern Liberal Theory of Man*, chap. 4.

14. Johnson-Laird, "Reasoning Without Logic," 15–16.
15. On being "deductively driven," see Schick, *Understanding Action*, 15. For a defense of the claim that commitment to norms of rationality is "substantive" and rejectable, see Galston, *Justice and Human Good*, 90 ff, and *Liberal Purposes*, 50. I have criticized Galston's view in Gaus, *Value and Justification*, 313–15.
16. See further Davidson, "A Coherence Theory of Truth and Knowledge," 129 ff; H. Putnam, *Reason, Truth and History*, 119 ff.
17. Hollis, "Limits of Irrationality," 214–15. For Hollis this is a necessary presupposition of translation; Lukes views it as an empirical fact to be discovered. Cf. Hollis, "Limits of Irrationality," and Lukes, "Some Problems About Rationality" and "Relativism in Its Place."
18. Hollis, "Reason and Ritual," 232. Notation altered. Cf. Davidson, "Radical Interpretation," 136; Hookway, "Indeterminacy and Interpretation," 26–27.
19. See Williams, "Truth in Relativism," 133.
20. Davidson, "Radical Interpretation," 137. Cf. Grandy, "Reference, Meaning and Belief"; Lukes, "Relativism in Its Place."
21. Hollis, "Social Destruction of Reality," 73–74.
22. However, if the bridgehead interpretation is seen as easily revisable in light of later interpretive problems, then extreme charity may be more easily achieved; rather than conclude that β is irrational, we can go back and revise our translation of the bridgehead to rationalize β. See Lukes, "Relativism in its Place," 272.
23. In what follows I employ the idea of an inferential norm widely, to include rules about causal attributions. This follows the use by investigators such as Nisbett and Ross, *Human Inference*.
24. Quoted in Mill, *A System of Logic*, 766. See also Nisbett and Ross, *Human Inference*, 116.
25. Quoted in Mill, *A System of Logic*, 767.
26. As James George Frazer observed of magical acts, "by imitating the desired effect you can produce it." Quoted in Jarvie and Agassi, "Problem of Rationality in Magic," 173.
27. Cf. Winch, *Idea of a Social Science*.
28. "Thus, the psychoanalyst proceeds from the conviction that symptoms and causes will seldom prove unrelated in their distinctive external features and from its corollary that overt symptoms may have features either identical to or opposite to their psychic causes." Nisbett and Ross, *Human Inference*, 117.
29. Grandy, "Reference, Meaning and Belief," 446.
30. For a different line of argument for placing limits on eligible interpretations, and thus limiting our charity in interpretation, see Hurley, *Natural Reasons*, esp. chap. 5.
31. Cf. Lukes, "Relativism in Its Place," 282 ff. On the general idea of "contextual" reasons, see Lukes, "Some Problems About Rationality," 211–13. Cf. S.K. White, *Recent Work of Jürgen Habermas*, 13–22.
32. Of course, many atheist philosophers have argued that religious belief is unjustified in this way, e.g., because it is based on insufficient evidence. For a reply, see Plantinga, "Reason and Belief in God." This relates to my comments on standards of proof in sec. 3.4.
33. On taming *moral* relativism with Davidsonian arguments, see Cooper, "Moral Relativism."
34. Cherniak, *Minimal Rationality*, 30. Notation altered.
35. Stich, *Fragmentation of Reason*, 42–43. Reference to Cherniak deleted.
36. Davidson, "Coherence Theory of Truth and Knowledge," 132. I am not maintaining here that meanings are in the head, though obviously something is—if not meanings, then contents. We would expect a community of inverse feasibility beings to have a rather different form of life; their jokes would be different, as would their stories to their chil-

dren. ("Tell us again about the independence of the axiom of choice," said the kindergartner. But what would be meant by describing this as a kindergartner?)

37. Davidson, "Radical Interpretation," 139.
38. These are approximations of Rips's statements of the standard rules. Notations have been altered. For his precise statement of the standard rules, as well as the analogs in his theory of reasoning, see Lance J. Rips, "Cognitive Process in Propositional Reasoning," 45.
39. Mill, *System of Logic*, 2:736–37.
40. Ibid., 765.
41. See Nisbett and Ross, *Human Inference*, 115 ff.
42. Tversky and Kahneman, "Judgment Under Uncertainty: Heuristics and Biases," 6.
43. Tversky and Kahneman, "Belief in the Law of Small Numbers," 26.
44. Ibid., 27–28.
45. See Kahneman and Tversky, "On the Psychology of Prediction"; Nisbett and Ross, *Human Inference*, chap. 7.
46. Nisbett and Ross, *Human Inference*, 25.
47. See Kahneman and Tversky, "On the Psychology of Prediction."
48. Tversky and Kahneman, "Belief in the Law of Small Numbers," 25.
49. Nisbett and Ross, *Human Inference*, 27.
50. Cherniak stresses the importance of quick but dirty reasoning to cope with computational complexity; *Minimal Rationality*, e.g., 81 ff.
51. On availability, see Tversky and Kahneman, "Availability: A Heuristic for Judging Frequency and Probability."
52. Nisbett and Ross, *Human Inference*, 55.
53. Quoted in Nisbett and Ross, *Human Inference*, 15.
54. See Stich, *Fragmentation of Reason*, chap. 1. Stich supports his position by citing Tversky and Kahneman's work.
55. Stich and Nisbett stress that people are often quite satisfied with their normatively faulty inferences. If so, this casts doubt on the adequacy of a subjective theory of justification, such as some interpretations of reflective equilibrium. See Stich and Nisbett, "Justification and the Psychology of Human Reasoning." On reflective equilibrium, see sec. 7.4 below.
56. Wason and Johnson-Laird, *Psychology of Reasoning*, 237.
57. Ziva Kunda and Richard Nisbett, for example, show that people understand the law of large numbers only partially, a norm relevant to Case A; "Prediction and the Partial Understanding of the Law of Large Numbers."
58. See Nisbett, Fong, Lehman, and Cheng, "Teaching Reasoning"; Lehman and Nisbett, "A Longitudinal Study of Undergraduate Training on Reasoning"; Nisbett, Krantz, Jepson, and Kunda, "The Use of Statistical Heuristics in Everyday Reasoning."
59. Lehman and Nisbett, "Longitudinal Study of Undergraduate Training on Reasoning," 959. That rules of inference can be taught does not contradict the claim that they are the laws of thought; training can improve all sorts of natural abilities and tendencies. It does, however, lead to questioning a strict stage-developmental approach as advocated by Piaget. See Nisbett et al., "Teaching Reasoning," 626 ff.
60. "Most readers will be able to provide their own anecdote of a person involved in a game of chance like roulette who has been losing heavily while betting on a certain number. In some circumstances it might be reasonable for the subject to infer that the game is crooked. In other circumstances, where the hypothesis of a dishonest game can be ruled out as extremely unlikely, the reasonable expectation is that the chance of hitting the favored number after a long losing streak is exactly the same as the chance of hitting the number at any other time. But the subject of our anecdote makes neither inference. Rather, his losing streak leads him to stick all the more doggedly to his favored number,

in the beliefs that the chance of hitting that number increases as the number of turns in which it fails to win increases.

"The principle of inference involved by our misguided subject would seem to be something like the following:

> In fair game of chance, the probability of a given sort of outcome occurring after $n + 1$ consecutive instances of non-occurrence is greater than the probability of its occurrence after n consecutive instances of non-occurrence."

Stich and Nisbett, "Justification and the Psychology of Human Reasoning," p. 192.
61. Ibid., 197. Emphasis added.
62. Ibid., 198 ff.
63. Stich, of course, has a good deal more to say on all this, but continuing the argument would constitute a book in itself; see esp. chap. 4 of *Fragmentation of Reason*. I shall not answer here Stich's charge that Quinean-like strategies of interpretation do not really allow for any significant inferential errors (ibid., chap. 2). I have indicated why error is possible on a bridgehead account in sec. 4.3.

CHAPTER 5

1. I defended a commitment view in sec. 3.3.
2. Larmore, "Beyond Religion and Enlightenment," 813. Emphasis added. See also Harman, *Change in View*, 29–30.
3. Some might object to this principle on grounds of "epistemic clutter"—we cannot believe all manifestly credible beliefs because there are an infinite number of them. But Axiom 4 does not require that we explicitly or consciously hold all the justified beliefs. See sec. 3.3 above.
4. See Gaus, "The Rational, the Reasonable and Justification," where I criticize Nozick's alternative epistemic rule that one does not have to believe extremely credible statements if doing so sets back one's utility.
5. In either the closed or the open sense. We can assume either an internal or external perspective on whether a reason is a defeater for Alf.
6. Pollock, *Contemporary Theories of Knowledge*, 38. See also Foley, *Theory of Epistemic Rationality*, chap. 1.
7. It might be objected here that an inconsistency within a triplet can be resolved by rejecting any one of them—so why do I insist that it is the conclusion, β, that must be given up? Remember, though, that R_1 and R_2 are already justified parts of one's belief system, whereas the justification of β (and whether it should be included) is in question. From that perspective, the onus of justification, as it were, is on β. The claim being evaluated is that β follows from one's belief system, and so is justified; but if R_2 defeats it, then it does not follow. It is important to note here that R_1 and R_2 are not only both already justified, but are themselves logically consistent. Nevertheless, based on coherence considerations, one could reorganize one's belief system so that R_2 was eliminated; then, of course, the inference from R_1 to β would not be defeated. On the relation between such coherence considerations and inferential chains, see secs. 7.2 to 7.4 below.
8. Pollock, *Contemporary Theories of Knowledge*, 38. Compare Benn's analysis of overriding reasons in *A Theory of Freedom*, and Raz's analysis of stronger reasons in *Practical Reason and Norms*.
9. The detective provides a new explanation of the particular beliefs, and this new explanation shows that they do not support the inference that Betty is cheating. On such explanatory hypothesis and their role on justification, see sec. 7.4.1.
10. See here Schauer, *Free Speech: A Philosophical Inquiry*, 181–84.

11. See Pollock, *Contemporary Theories of Knowledge,* 46 ff.
12. We also can speak of justifiable beliefs in either the open or closed senses. See sec. 3.1.
13. Hurley's case is supported by the usage of many epistemologists, who also employ the idea of *prima facie* reasons when, for example, specifying the notion of a defeater.
14. Hurley, *Natural Reasons,* 133.
15. Ibid., 133–34. Citation omitted.
16. See ibid., chap. 8.
17. Ibid., 137.
18. See here Benn and Gaus, "Practical Rationality and Commitment." Cf. Habermas, *Knowledge and Human Interests,* esp. Appendix.
19. Hurley, *Natural Reasons,* 98.
20. T. S. Kuhn, *The Structure of Scientific Revolutions,* 185.
21. Berlin, "Two Concepts of Liberty," 167.
22. For more on the similarity of *akrasia* of belief and action, see Benn and Gaus, "Practical Rationality and Commitment."

CHAPTER 6

1. For examples and analyses of the argument, see Quinton, *The Nature of Things,* 119–23; Chisholm, *The Foundations of Knowing,* 128 ff; William P. Alston, "Two Types of Foundationalism," pp. 171–79; Lewis, *An Analysis of Knowledge and Valuation,* 186 ff; Armstrong, *Belief, Truth and Knowledge,* 152 ff; Pappas and Swain, Introduction to their *Essays on Knowledge and Justification,* 31–32; Brink, *Moral Realism and the Foundations of Ethics,* 104 ff; Laurence Bonjour, *Structure of Empirical Knowledge,* 17–25; Audi, *Structure of Justification,* 125 ff.
2. See Pollock, *Contemporary Theories of Knowledge,* 74–75.
3. Bonjour, *Structure of Empirical Knowledge,* 232, n. 10.
4. Ibid., 14.
5. Cf. Sosa, "The Foundations of Foundationalism."
6. See Bonjour, who describes this as a very weak form of foundationalism; *Structure of Empirical Knowledge,* 28. I defend a version of weak foundationalism in chap. 7 below.
7. Brink, *Moral Realism,* 103. But see Audi's discussion of coherentism as relying on noninferential justification; *Structure of Justification,* 140 ff. Much depends here on just what one understands by "inferential." See chap. 2, n. 3, above.
8. Brink, *Moral Realism,* 103. Citations omitted.
9. Cf. the discussion of the basing relation in sec. 2.1.
10. Bonjour, a coherence theorist, is clear about this; *Structure of Empirical Knowledge,* 24–25.
11. See Audi, *Structure of Justification,* 138.
12. For an overview see Gaus, "Green, Bosanquet and the Philosophy of Coherence." See also Crossley, "Self-Conscious Agency and the Eternal Consciousness: Ultimate Reality in Thomas Hill Green."
13. Foley, *Theory of Epistemic Rationality,* 94. Note to the phrase "there is no exit from the circle of one's beliefs" (attributing it to Keith Lehrer) deleted. Pollock shows that the idea behind this maxim is not specially bound up with coherence theories; *Contemporary Theories of Knowledge,* 66–71.
14. Absolutist idealists may have depicted religious convictions along these lines, as truths of the Absolute that we can only accept on faith. Religion, said Bernard Bosanquet, is "the normal attitude of the healthy finite mind," seeking, as it were, to get outside of itself and touch the Absolute; *The Value and Destiny of the Individual,* 27.

15. See Pollock, *Contemporary Theories of Knowledge*, 82; Pollock, "A Plethora of Epistemological Theories," 103–4.
16. Foley, in his argument for the possibility of epistemic luck, argues against requiring the right kind of "causal history, where causal history is understood broadly to include not only what causally originates but also what causally sustains the belief"; *Theory of Epistemic Rationality*, 177. My claim here is that the sustaining view is not really concerned with causal histories at all, but with whether at the current time the person connects his beliefs with their grounding reasons.
17. The first distinction is Brink's, *Moral Realism*, 123; the second is Bonjour's, *Structure of Empirical Knowledge*, 91. Lehrer makes a related distinction based on pragmatic justification; *Theory of Knowledge*, 89.
18. Blanshard, *The Nature of Thought*, 2:264.
19. Bonjour, *Structure of Empirical Knowledge*, 98.
20. Ibid., 95 ff.
21. For example, a system containing β and the belief that β was terribly improbable would not violate consistency but would violate probabilistic consistency.
22. Russell Hardin, a utilitarian, is very clear about this. See his *Morality Within the Limits of Reason*, esp. chaps. 1, 3.

CHAPTER 7

1. Brink, *Moral Realism*, 120.
2. Quine and Ullian, *The Web of Belief*, 18.
3. Ibid., 16.
4. For a different argument for this conclusion, see Lycan, *Judgment and Justification*, chap. 8.
5. Goodman, "Sense and Certainty," 162–63.
6. See ibid., 165 ff.
7. Brink, *Moral Realism*, 116–17.
8. Lycan, *Judgement and Justification*, 165. Cf. Rorty, *Philosophy and the Mirror of Nature*, 106.
9. See Foley, *Theory of Epistemic Rationality*, 68.
10. This, I think, is the truth in Harman's coherence theory. See his *Change in View*.
11. For a discussion of such claims, see Quinton, *Nature of Things*, chap. 6; Alston, "Self-Warrant: A Neglected Form of Privileged Access." For criticism of the claim to incorrigibility, see Lehrer, *Theory of Knowledge*, chap. 3, as well as Brink, *Moral Realism*, 104 ff.
12. See Pollock, *Contemporary Theories of Knowledge*, esp. chap. 5.
13. One of the fascinating features of Don Herzog's recent critique of foundationalism is that he refuses to identify explicitly what the doctrine maintains—though he certainly believes that it is wrong; *Without Foundations: Justification in Political Theory*.
14. This is a modification of Triplett, "Recent Work on Foundationalism," 96. See also Van Cleve, "Foundationalism, Epistemic Principles and the Cartesian Circle," 74; Haack, "Theories of Knowledge: An Analytic Framework"; Pollock, "Plethora of Epistemological Theories."
15. See Bonjour, *Structure of Empirical Knowledge*, 26 ff; Pastin, "Modest Foundationalism and Self-Warrant," 279–81; Audi, *Structure of Justification*, pt. 1; Lehrer, *Theory of Knowledge*, chaps. 3 and 4. See also the references in the previous note.
16. Foley, *Theory of Epistemic Rationality*, 49–50.
17. This is not to say that they are incorrigible. See ibid., 59.
18. See Pollock, *Contemporary Theories of Knowledge*, 70.
19. Foley, *Theory of Epistemic Rationlity*, 50.

20. Coherence considerations thus seem one ground for warranted belief. See Dauer, "Warrant, Coherence and Evaluative Certainties," 503.
21. Foley, *Theory of Epistemic Rationality*, 55. Notation altered.
22. But see Foley's discussion of self-evident propositions. Ibid., p. 54.
23. See Triplett, "Recent Work on Foundationalism," 93.
24. By "strength" of justification here I mean that the component beliefs are more strongly justified in the senses canvassed in sec. 3.4. The "$\rightleftarrows$" stands for "inferentially justify each other."
25. The "$\rightarrow$" stands for "inferentially justifies."
26. Ampliative justification serves to blunt the problem of chains of inferences that lose justification (see the last paragraph of sec. 3.4). Because several inferences may support the same belief, this would appear typically crucial in offsetting the loss of justification through singular linear chains.
27. See Dawes, "The Robust Beauty of Improper Linear Models in Decision Making," 405.
28. Ewing, *Ethics*, 120. Ewing's argument for this conclusion differs from that presented here.
29. See Sidgwick, *Methods of Ethics*, 374–75. For a survey of intuitionist theories, see Hudson, *Ethical Intuitionism*. See also Mabbott, *Introduction to Ethics*, chap. 4.
30. Prichard, *Moral Obligation*, 16.
31. See D. Ross, *Foundations of Ethics*, chap. 8.
32. See Sidgwick, *Methods of Ethics*, 374–80; D. Ross, *Foundations of Ethics*, 168 ff. On degrees of justification and knowledge claims, see Dauer, "Warrant, Coherence," 499 ff.
33. Platts, "Moral Reality," 285; Ewing, *Ethics*, 122.
34. See Feinberg, "Rawls and Intuitionism."
35. D. Ross, *Foundations of Ethics*, 187.
36. Sidgwick, *Methods of Ethics*, chap. 8. See Brink, "Common Sense and First Principles in Sidgwick's *Methods*," 188. "Nonetheless," Brink observes, "Sidgwick believes that justification in ethics has a certain structure that supports philosophical intuitionism [which concerns intuitions about first principles]. . . ." Ibid. Cf. D. Ross, *Foundations of Ethics*, 168 ff.
37. Platts, "Moral Reality," 282.
38. See Mabbott, *Introduction to Ethics*, 33 ff.
39. See Snare, *The Nature of Moral Thinking*, 165–66.
40. To be sure, one could attribute an emotional basis to recognition of moral facts, and yet hold them to be objective. See Gaus, *Value and Justification*, 81–84; Hudson, *Ethical Intuitionism*; Gibbard, *Wise Choices, Apt Feelings*, chaps. 8, 9.
41. Ewing, *Ethics*, 117.
42. Sidgwick, *Methods of Ethics*, 382. Emphasis added.
43. Brink, "Common Sense and First Principles," 191. In addition to *Methods of Ethics*, Brink also draws on Sidgwick's "The Establishment of Ethical First Principles."
44. Brink considers and rejects this as an interpretation of Sidgwick. One reason for rejecting it is that "Sidgwick motivates intuitionism at least in part by the regress argument. . . . But that argument has as one of its premises the claim that circular reasoning confers no justification." In sec. 6.1 I rejected this interpretation of the regress argument. In a note, Brink recognizes that the regress argument can be understood as maintaining simply that initial credibility is necessary for circles to justify; but he holds that this was not Sidgwick's understanding of it. Brink, "Common Sense and First Principles," 192.
45. Sidgwick, *Methods of Ethics*, 379. See Brink, "Common Sense and First Principles," 187–91.
46. Norman Daniels defends Rawls against this "charge" in "Wide Reflective Equilibrium and Theory Acceptance in Ethics." R.B. Brandt stresses the intuitionist "charge" in *A Theory of the Good and the Right*, chap. 1.

47. This charge is discussed and dismissed by Michael R. DePaul in "Reflective Equilibrium and Foundationalism." For an example of the charge, see Hare, "Rawls' Theory of Justice."

48. This is not unique to my proposal. As Ernest Sosa points out, "foundationalism . . . does not reject coherence as *one* factor relevant to epistemic justification"; "Nature Unmirrored, Epistemology Naturalized," 97. Emphasis in original.

49. Rawls, *A Theory of Justice*, 21.

50. Goodman, *Fact, Fiction and Forecast*, 63–64. Emphasis in original.

51. Rawls actually supposes that the beliefs do indeed possess an initial credibility; *Political Liberalism*, 8n. See also the quote from Goodman in sec. 7.1.2 above.

52. Brandt makes a criticism of Rawls's method of reflective equilibrium that is similar to (but not the same as) that advanced here. He writes: "There is a problem here quite similar to that which faces the traditional coherence theory of justification of belief: that the theory claims that a more coherent system of beliefs is better justified than a less coherent one, but there is no reason to think this claim true unless some of the beliefs are initially credible—and not merely initially believed—for some other reasons than their coherence, say, because they state facts of observation. In the case of normative beliefs, no reason has been offered why we should think that initial credence levels, for a person, correspond to credibilities"; *A Theory of the Good and the Right*, 20. In responding to this, Daniels focuses on the lack of analogy between observation reports and moral judgments: "The 'no credibility' argument gains its plausibility from the assumption that the analogy of observation reports *should* hold and then denigrates moral judgments when it is pointed out that they differ from observation reports. . . . If the *should* and *do* function differently—because they are different kinds of judgments—that is not something we should hold against the moral judgments"; "Wide Reflective Equilibrium," 271. Though this is relevant to one part of Brandt's argument, it is not to the point here. What is crucial is that coherence presupposes that the beliefs to be made coherent possess some credibility not derivative of coherence, and thus no justification can derive purely from coherence.

53. I am supposing here that reflective equilibrium is a *method* to be employed in organizing and justifying our belief system rather than a theory about how belief structures develop or about the very meaning of justification. It is no doubt all these things, but exposition is easier if we focus on it as a method. In assuming a temporal sequence I am loosely following DePaul, "Reflective Equilibrium and Foundationalism."

54. Bonjour, *Structure of Empirical Knowledge*, 98–99; Cornman, "Foundational versus Nonfoundational Theories of Empirical Justification," 241–47; Lycan, *Judgment and Justification*, 169 ff; Lehrer, *Theory of Knowledge*, chap. 5.

55. Sosa, "Epistemology Today," 81.

56. Note that the belief to be explained must itself be justified. Explanatory coherence is ampliative, and therefore cannot be used as the sole justificatory principle, as coherence theorists are sometimes wont to do.

57. See Rawls, *Theory of Justice*, 48.

58. See Lycan, *Judgment and Justification*, 129 ff.

59. DePaul, "Reflective Equilibrium and Foundationalism," 65.

60. DePaul recognizes this. See his discussion of the view that "a person's considered judgments . . . have some epistemic privilege on their own, and that the moral theory he accepts in narrow reflective equilibrium must have its status because it systematizes these judgments, if the person knows or is justified in accepting that moral theory"; ibid., 66.

61. For charges that it is an overly conservative method, see Brandt, *Theory of the Good and the Right*, 21–22. See the discussion in DePaul, "Reflective Equilibrium and Foundationalism" of R.M. Hare's and Peter Singer's charge of conservativism.

62. Rawls, *Political Liberalism*, 8.

63. Daniels, "Wide Reflective Equilibrium," 258. Notice in this quote that Daniels conceives of reflective equilibrium as applying to an individual's set of beliefs. Sosa distinguishes this individual version from a social version, in which coherence of judgments across people is the aim. As Sosa argues, the epistemologist's concern is individual reflective equilibrium; "Equilibrium in Coherence?", 263–64. However, it remains unclear to what extent Rawls was interested in the individual rather than the social version. Fred D'Agostino presents a strong case for the primacy of the social in "Relativism and Reflective Equilibrium."

64. Cf. Daniels, "Wide Reflective Equilibrium," 266 ff; DePaul, "Reflective Equilibrium and Foundationalism"; Sosa, "Equilibrium in Coherence?," 262.

65. Sandel, *Liberalism and the Limits of Justice*, chap. 1.

66. Daniels, "Wide Reflective Equilibrium," 266. Emphasis in original.

67. See Parfit, *Reasons and Persons*, pt. 3.

68. Rawls, *Political Liberalism*, 110.

69. Cherniak, *Minimal Rationality*, 67–68. The quote from Simon is from *Administrative Behavior*, 80–81.

70. Lycan notes similar problems in *Judgment and Justification*, 179 ff.

71. For an overview of the evidence, see Nisbett and Ross, *Human Inference*, chap. 8.

72. See Stich and Nisbett, "Justification and the Psychology of Human Reasoning."

CHAPTER 8

1. Hurley, *Natural Reasons*, 91. The quotation from Wittgenstein is from *Remarks on the Foundations of Mathematics*.

2. See Hurley, *Natural Reasons*, 93–94.

3. This is not to say that Alf's rules interpret themselves. Cf. ibid., 33–35, 318.

4. Ibid., 93–94.

5. It is worth noting in this regard that one of Wittgenstein's most powerful statements of the argument against private rules asked us to imagine a case where only *one* person followed a rule on only *one* occasion. See *Philosophical Investigations*, sec. 199.

6. Dworkin, *Law's Empire*, 52, 88.

7. Some may argue that, since Dworkin is concerned with the interpretation of practices (*Law's Empire*, 66), this does not in any way provide grist to the anti-Wittgensteinian mill. But, as we shall see, I do not deny that participation in practices is an important background in deliberation; I am merely stressing here that, in any specific case, private reasoning about the application of rules achieves determinacy through systemic considerations.

8. Dworkin, *Taking Rights Seriously*, 107.

9. Ibid. The case being discussed in *Chatwin v. United States*, 326 U.S. 455 (1946).

10. My point is not to defend the thesis that there is always a correct answer as to how to go on with such rules, only that systematic considerations greatly reduce the eligible interpretations. For a formal analysis of Dworkin's argument that there is always a right answer as to how to apply a rule, see Skubik, *At the Intersection of Legality and Morality*, 209–21. See further sec. 16.1 below.

11. Cf. Habermas, *Theory of Communicative Action*, 1:100.

12. The possibility of error is, of course, even clearer under open justification, which, as it were, treats the belief system of another as only the alpha. See sec. 3.1 above.

13. Because we have rejected the radical principle of charity, according to which rendering others' beliefs intelligible can only be achieved by endorsing them.

14. This is Habermas's gloss on Rorty's "particular version of discourse theory"; *Moral Consciousness and Communicative Action*, 14. Rorty sometimes suggests such a view, though,

as he is apt to do, he also sometimes draws back from more radical statements of it. Cf., for instance, *Philosophy and the Mirror of Nature*, 156–57, 176, 183, 190.

15. Is this inconsistent with Peirce's account of truth as "the opinion fated to be ultimately agreed by all"? Much depends here on just how we cash out "ultimately," but I see no reason to preclude the idea that some truths may be permanently unrecognizable by some. Truth, I suspect, cannot be explicated in terms of justified belief, or even the future convergence of justified belief. Cf. Rorty, *Philosophy and the Mirror of Nature*, 297 ff.

16. Ibid., 9, 186.

17. Habermas, *Communication and the Evolution of Society*, 3.

18. Habermas, *Moral Consciousness and Communicative Action*, 30–31. See also his *Theory of Communicative Action*, 1:10 ff.

19. That is, a rational agreement that would be achieved if "argumentation were conducted openly and continued long enough." Habermas, *Moral Consciousness and Communicative Action*, 105.

20. Rorty, "Science as Solidarity," esp. 38–41. See also his Introduction to *Objectivity, Relativism and Truth*, 13.

21. Rorty, *Philosophy and the Mirror of Nature*, 178. Rorty mistakenly believes that this supports coherence theories of justified belief. See above, chap. 6, n. 13. See also D'Agostino, "Transcendence and Conversation."

22. I am indebted to Fred D'Agostino for his assistance with the remainder of sec. 8.2.

23. Habermas, *Moral Consciousness and Communicative Action*, 8, 132, 139, 159.

24. Margaret Urban Walker rightly questions the intelligibility of this view: "God sees everything, but how should we imagine the salience and priority for God of what God sees from God's point of view, and what has this to do with (our) morality?"; "Partial Considerations," 764.

25. T. Nagel, *View from Nowhere*, 63.

26. As Rorty recognizes, rather than climbing up out of our minds, as we achieve objectivity our perspectives grow larger and stronger; Introduction to *Objectivity, Relativism and Truth*, 14.

27. Rorty, "Solidarity or Objectivity?," 23.

28. Nagel, *View from Nowhere*, 63.

29. Evolutionary epistemologists put considerable store in it, but it is controversial nonetheless. See Stich, *Fragmentation of Reason*, chap. 3.

30. Kant, *Critique of Judgment*, sec. 40 (p. 160). See also Beiner, *Political Judgment*, 51 ff.

31. O'Neill, "The Public Use of Reason," esp. 46. See also Kant, "What Is Enlightenment?" For a survey of use of the idea of public reason by Hobbes, Rousseau, Jefferson, Kant, and Rawls, see Solum, "Constructing Public Reason," 745–762.

32. In this paragraph I claim that "we" possess the capacity to engage in public reasoning. This is a little too broad; evidence indicates that psychopaths have difficulty decentering, and so find it exceedingly difficult to think from the standpoint of others. I consider this evidence in Gaus, *Value and Justification*, 292–300. However, as broad generalizations go, this one is fairly sound; evidence indicates that normal adults possess the capacity to think from the standpoint of others.

33. MacIntyre, *Whose Justice? Which Rationality?*, 6. Cf. Rorty, "The Priority of Democracy to Philosophy," 175–76.

34. It is perhaps worth noting that some philosophers have responded to the debunking of the Enlightenment's claims of universal public reason as the ultimate standard of justification in all matters by retreating to local intersubjective agreement as the standard. But this seems still under the spell of the Enlightenment insofar as all justification must be public, though of course now the boundaries of the relevant public have shrunk considerably.

35. The relevant public, however, can be circumscribed; there is no need for us to think from the standpoint of absolutely everyone else. On the different levels of publicness, see Benn and Gaus, "The Liberal Conception of the Public and Private." See also Gaus, *Value and Justification*, 322 ff.

36. Kant, "What Is Enlightenment?," 57.

37. Habermas, *Moral Consciousness and Communicative Action*, 178. Emphasis in original. But cf. ibid., 203. Habermas follows Kant in linking morality, universality, and public reasoning. Cf. ibid., 178, and Kant, *Critique of Judgment*, sec. 40 (pp. 160–61).

38. See McCarthy, Introduction to *Moral Consciousness and Communicative Action*, xi. See also S. K. White, *Recent Work of Jürgen Habermas*, chap. 3.

39. Kupperman, *The Foundations of Morality*, chap. 1.

40. On the relation of these moral emotions to judgments of right and wrong, see Richards, *A Theory of Reasons for Action*, 250 ff; Fried, *An Anatomy of Values*, 56–57; T. Nagel, *The Possibility of Altruism*, 84–85; Benn, *Theory of Freedom*, 97–121; Strawson, *Freedom and Resentment*, chap. 1; Gaus, *Value and Justification*, 281–86.

41. Kupperman, *Foundations of Morality*, 3. I defend this interpretation of Nietzsche at some length in Gaus, *Value and Justification*.

42. See Feinberg, "Duties, Rights and Claims," 136. The idea of a "responsibility" also is relevant. Ibid., 137. Cf. Mill's claim that "It is part of the notion of Duty in every one of its forms, that a person may rightfully be compelled to fulfill it"; *Utilitarianism*, 184.

43. Mill, *Utilitarianism*, 185.

44. Ibid., 184. David Lyons has developed this conception of morality more fully in "Mill's Theory of Morality." I discuss Lyons's interpretation in Gaus, "Mill's Theory of Moral Rules."

45. See T. Nagel, "Moral Conflict and Political Legitimacy;" Rawls, *Political Liberalism*, 216 ff.

46. I have argued this point in more detail in Gaus, *Value and Justification*, 278 ff.

47. Gibbard, *Wise Choices, Apt Feelings*, 171. Emphasis added.

48. Ibid., 173.

49. In Gaus, *Value and Justification* (278 ff), I argue that such browbeating does not ground the moral emotions of resentment, indignation, and guilt. Consequently, our moral practice and discourse cannot be reduced to browbeating.

50. For the idea of "an authority" see R. B. Friedman, "On the Concept of Authority in Political Philosophy." See secs. 11.2.2–3 below.

51. Gibbard, *Wise Choices, Apt Feelings*, 174.

52. Ibid., 174–75.

53. Ibid., 176.

54. Ibid., 175.

55. Ibid., 180.

56. Ibid., 180–81.

57. Ibid., 176. Gibbard holds out the possibility that it may be "fully" credible in this way.

58. Ibid., 179.

59. For Gibbard such a person abjures any claim to epistemic objectivity, according to which "none may give special weight to his own judgment simply as his own" (ibid., 182). Here, as is so often the case in philosophy, appeals to "objectivity" seem to befuddle more than enlighten. Deliberators are certainly not objective qua impartial between their own judgments about what they should believe and the judgments of others as to what they should believe. Such partiality toward one's own deliberations is intrinsic to selfhood; if objectivity requires one to abjure that, objectivity is unattainable. A person, then, claims a privileged status as a privileged determiner of what she has reason to believe. But this does not, as I have stressed, collapse into subjectivism: A person can still be wrong in what she believes (see sec. 4.5 below). So, insofar as there is an objective

answer to the question, "What is Betty justified in believing?" my account maintains epistemic objectivity. On the other hand, we have seen that Betty might possess a norm that warrants her in believing β, while Alf does not, and so is not warranted in believing it. So, in this sense of epistemic objectivity (qua universal warrant for belief), the account I have defended is not "epistemically objective." Cf. Gibbard, *Wise Choices, Apt Feelings*, 180, 213–14.

60. This is not precisely the view of browbeating that Gibbard considers and rejects on p.191 of *Wise Choices, Apt Feelings*, in that anything is browbeating that demands more than follows from premises you already accept plus my own observations. I may argue that, given your current system of beliefs, you are committed to major revisions and new norms. The starting point of the argument is your current beliefs, but the conclusion may require new premises not a part of the current system.

61. See Gaus, *Value and Justification*, chaps. 6, 7.

CHAPTER 9

1. Rawls, *Political Liberalism*, 19.
2. See Ewin, *Virtues and Rights*, 35.
3. On impositions and their relation to freedom and coercion, see Kleinig, *Paternalism*, 6 ff.
4. This can be expressed as a second-order thesis. It might be claimed that, while one or the other may in fact have the sounder belief about *N*, neither can be *confident* that he or she has the sounder case (say, due to general conditions of fallibility). Consequently, for one to impose his view on the other is for him to assert his second-order belief that he is correct, but this second-order belief in the correctness of his own opinions is no better grounded than the other's second-order belief in the soundness of her own opinions. Again, the conclusion is that, in the crucial respect, their epistemological positions are on par.
5. This is different from the claim that objectivity simply is defined by intersubjective agreement. See sec. 8.3 above.
6. Whether it is sufficient is a rather more interesting question. See secs. 8.4, 9.3.3.
7. See Larmore, "Pluralism and Reasonable Disagreement."
8. Rawls, *Political Liberalism*, 119.
9. Ibid., 49–52.
10. Ibid., 54–58.
11. Rawls is referring here to what he calls "comprehensive" doctrines. Ibid., 60.
12. Ibid., 119.
13. Ibid., 76, 162–63, 229.
14. Ibid., 62, 144.
15. Of course it is not the same. I shall argue in chap. 11 that a justified authority can legitimately prohibit people from acting on their justifiable views.
16. Michael J. Perry retracts his endorsement of the accessibility condition in his "Religious Morality and Political Choice: Further Thoughts—and Second Thoughts—on *Love and Power*."
17. Macedo, *Liberal Virtues*, 50.
18. Rawls, *Political Liberalism*, 60n, 225; Macedo, *Liberal Virtues*, 48–49.
19. See Stich and Nisbett, "Justification and the Psychology of Human Reasoning." See sec. 4.5 above.
20. See esp. Wason and Johnson-Laird, *Psychology of Reasoning*, esp. chaps. 6 ff.
21. D. Kuhn, *The Skills of Argument*, 174–75.
22. Their fundamental nature is important here; it implies that even if others accept inferential norms that I do not, they will not override the inferences sanctioned by the fundamental bridgehead norms.

23. Cf. Rawls, *Political Liberalism*, 67.
24. This, of course, was the point of the belief perseverance experiment analyzed in pt. I. See also Kuhn, *Skills of Argument*.
25. See Rawls, *Political Liberalism*, 78.
26. Macedo, *Liberal Virtues*, 51.
27. Rawls, *Political Liberalism*, 136. Emphasis added.
28. For this fundamental point I am indebted to Julian Lamont, who pressed it upon me so often that I finally understood it.
29. This is related to what Gibbard called "Socratic influence." See sec. 8.4 above.
30. Cf. Habermas's claim that in discourse one advances claims that one believes to be true; *Theory of Communicative Action*, 1:99. Habermas would, I think, classify the parent's insincere reply as a case of strategic, not communicative, interaction; *Moral Consciousness and Communicative Action*, 133–34. See also Gibbard's analysis of expressing a belief in *Wise Choices, Apt Feelings*, 84–86, and D'Agostino's analysis of scientific discourse, and in particular the principle of rationalism, in "Adjudication as an Epistemological Concept."
31. Galston, *Liberal Purposes*, 109. Emphasis in last sentence added.
32. Lomasky, *Persons, Rights and the Moral Community*, 28. Emphasis in original. I have defended a similar view of the reasons associated with valuings in Gaus, *Value and Justification*, pt. 1.
33. Harman, "Human Flourishing, Ethics and Liberty," 321.
34. T. Nagel, *Equality and Partiality*, 156. Cf. Larmore, *Patterns of Moral Complexity*, 73; Galston, *Liberal Purposes*, 102.
35. In the passage leading up to the above quote, for example, Nagel is clear that by "the values a person can appeal to in conducting his own life" he has in mind religious convictions. I made a similar comment in Gaus, "Public Reason and the Rule of Law."
36. Some may be justifiable. See Greenawalt, "Grounds for Political Judgment," 648–54.
37. Greenawalt, *Religious Convictions and Political Choice*, 155.
38. Ibid., 176. Eric Mack essentially agrees with Greenawalt here, but charitably concedes that the position I endorse in the text is "not at all loony"; "Liberalism, Neutralism and Rights," 57.
39. This is a weaker form of secularism than that defended by Audi, "The Place of Religious Argument in a Free Society."
40. See Waldron, "Enough and as Good Left for Others."
41. See Wellman, *Challenge and Response: Justification in Ethics*, chap. 3.
42. For a different analysis of this distinction, see Bittner, *What Reason Demands*, 11 ff.
43. As Jan Narveson remarks, "It is widely, if not quite universally, accepted by moral philosophers that morality involves—somehow, some way—some such requirement as universalizability." This is not to say, of course, that it is easy to explicate just what this involves. See Narveson's essay, "The How and Why of Universalizability," 3. It must be acknowledged that some recent writers have questioned this understanding of the moral point of view, sometimes as part of a general project questioning the possibility or desirability of impartiality. See, e.g., M. Friedman, "The Impracticality of Impartiality." It should be remembered, however, that I have already articulated a view of morality as demands based on public reason; given that understanding of morality, that public morality involves universalizability seems uncontroversial.
44. See Kant, *Critique of Judgment*, 160 (sec. 40); Beiner, *Political Judgment*, 52; O'Neil, "Public Use of Reason," 46 ff.
45. See Habermas, *Moral Consciousness and Communicative Action*, 64 ff; Sullivan, *Immanuel Kant's Moral Theory*, 249 ff.
46. Cf. Wellman's claim that "one 'has justified' something to someone when one has met every challenge . . . that actually has been made to it on that occasion, by that challenger"; *Challenge and Response*, 130.

47. D. Kuhn, *Skills of Argument*, 139.
48. See McCarthy, Introduction, viii, and Habermas, *Moral Consciousness and Communicative Action*, 57 ff, 203 ff.
49. As Wellman remarks, "one may actually meet a challenge even though the challenger does not admit that one has done so"; *Challenge and Response*, 130. But we must be careful not to present too simple a picture of Habermas, for he, too, insists on distinguishing "between the social fact that a norm is intersubjectively recognized and its worthiness to be recognized"; *Moral Consciousness and Communicative Action*, 61.
50. D. Kuhn, *Skills of Argument*, 146 ff.
51. William Galston traces this view back to Plato, according to whom "justified belief . . . is opinion that has survived the most rigorous testing in contestation with the available contrasting views"; *Liberal Purposes*, 33.
52. Cf. Rawls, *Political Liberalism*, 66 ff; Sullivan, *Kant's Moral Theory*, 249–50.
53. Such a dissociation is even more radical than the split between true self and self as doer that seems characteristic of schizoid personalities. I consider such personalities in Gaus, *Value and Justification*, 386–90, 402–4.
54. John Wilson, "Indoctrination and Rationality," 18.
55. Reiman, *Justice and Modern Moral Philosophy*, 1–2.
56. Ibid., 1.
57. Ibid., 5.
58. Wellman, *Challenge and Response*, 98.
59. Ibid., 130–31. For rather different reasons, Lehrer also indicates that there are but two possibilities. *Theory of Knowledge*, 151 ff.
60. I think it is manifest that these conditions are not independent; given the limits on our cognitive resources, the high standard of proof cannot be attained unless the publicity condition is met—reasonable doubts will remain.
61. Williams, *Ethics and the Limits of Philosophy*, 85.
62. Gray, "Contractarian Method, Private Property and the Market Economy," 169 ff, 186 ff.
63. Or, rather, "sentences" or "propositions." See chap. 2, n. 7.
64. This, of course, is not to say that the belief systems are logically incompletable—they do not violate Ellis' completability (i.e., rationality) requirement. See Ellis, *Rational Belief Systems*, 9, and also his "Epistemic Foundations of Logic," 190–92. See also Gärdenfors, *Knowledge in Flux*, 21–28.
65. Seung and Bonevac, "Plural Values and Indeterminate Rankings," 802.
66. Ibid.
67. Ibid., 803. Their "epistemological indeterminacy" sounds more like the roots of inclusiveness.
68. Of course this inconsistency can be avoided by analyzing the situation in terms of having a reason to choose A over B, and a reason to choose B over A. As we have seen, reasons can come into conflict (sec. 5.3).
69. Greenawalt, *Religious Convictions and Political Choice*, 39 ff, chaps. 6–8.
70. See Rawls, "Domain of the Political and Overlapping Consensus," 237; Perry, *Morality, Politics and the Law*, 148 ff.
71. Greenawalt, *Religious Convictions and Political Choice*, chap. 6.
72. See T. Regan, *The Case for Animal Rights*; Singer, *Practical Ethics*, chap. 5.
73. Elster, *Solomonic Judgments*, 134.
74. Ibid., 137.
75. Rawls, *A Theory of Justice*, 5. Cf. Hart, *The Concept of Law*, 155 ff.
76. Dworkin, *Law's Empire*, 71. Cf. D'Agostino, *Free Public Reason*, sec. 4.

CHAPTER 10

1. The problem of drawing the boundaries of the public is considered in Gaus, *Value and Justification*, 367–76.
2. T. Nagel, *Equality and Partiality*, 57. Cf. Hobhouse's list of the "Elements of Liberalism" in his *Liberalism*, chap. 2.
3. The rights associated with the rule of law and democracy are defended in chaps. 12 and 13 below.
4. See further Gaus, "Subjective Value and Justificatory Political Theory," 256–57.
5. Moreover, in Gaus, *Value and Justification*, I presented a defense of liberal liberty. See secs. 24, 28.4.
6. I make this point about rights theory in somewhat more detail in Gaus, "Property, Rights and Freedom."
7. On the new liberalism, see Michael Freeden's excellent study, *The New Liberalism: An Ideology of Social Reform*, and Gaus, *Modern Liberal Theory of Man*. See also Hobhouse's *Liberalism*. On the varieties of classical liberalism see N. Barry, *On Classical Liberalism and Libertarianism*. For comparison of classical and new liberalism, see Gaus, "Public and Private Interests in Liberal Political Economy, Old and New."
8. Rawls describes his theory as "an egalitarian form of liberalism"; *Political Liberalism*, 6. Rawls tells us explicitly that "the question of private ownership in the means of production or their social ownership and similar questions are not settled at the level of the first principles of justice." Ibid., 338.
9. Ibid., 338–39. Emphasis added.
10. Though probably not universal assent. See Rorty, "Priority of Democracy to Philosophy," 190 ff.
11. It is worth pointing out that one can uphold a regime based on private property and the market even if one believes that reasoning on these issues is inconclusive. But then the protection of private property rights and market freedoms could not be an issue removed from the political agenda.
12. Again, though, I think that this supposition can be defended. I argue elsewhere that nonpsychopathic valuers are committed to the notion of public justification. See Gaus *Value and Justification*, chap. 6. See also Benn, *Theory of Freedom*, chaps. 5–6.
13. Arkes, *First Things: An Inquiry into the First Principles of Morals and Justice*, 70. Emphasis omitted.
14. Benn and Peters, *Social Principles and the Democratic State*, 110. Emphasis in original.
15. Ibid., 111.
16. See Flathman, "Equality and Generalization: A Formal Analysis," 38–60; Berlin, "Equality as an Ideal," 128–50; Frankena, "The Concept of Social Justice," 1–29. For a dissenting view see Norman, *Free and Equal*, 57–58.
17. Benn, "Human Rights—For Whom and for What?," p. 67. Emphasis in original. See also Flathman, "Equality and Generalization," p.39; Berlin, "Equality as an Ideal," 131, 133.
18. For such a criticism of Benn's egalitarianism, see Holborow, "Benn, Mackie, and Basic Rights." In his final work Benn weakens his egalitarian principle so as not to undermine the liberal principle. See *Theory of Freedom*, 117–21.
19. Stanley Benn and I discuss such a norm—*The Race Relations Act* of 1968—in our essay, "Liberal Conception of the Public and Private," 36–38.
20. See King, *Toleration*, 21. Needless to say, toleration is entirely distinct from the celebration of cultural diversity.
21. Ackerman, *Social Justice and the Liberal State*, 305.
22. In this regard classical liberals are correct: noninterference is the basic liberal commitment. See Lomasky, *Persons, Rights and the Moral Community*, 94 ff.
23. Feinberg, *Harm to Others*, 9. See also his *Social Philosophy*, 21.

24. I employ the interference formulation in Gaus, "Does Compensation Restore Equality?" See also sec.11.2.2 below. For a comparison of coercion, interference, and imposition, see Kleinig, *Paternalism*, 5–7.
25. Bickel, *The Least Dangerous Branch*, 36–37. As Macedo observes, "The contours of every one of our most basic liberties remains a matter of lively disagreement"; *Liberal Virtues*, 57.
26. Rawls, *Political Liberalism*, 45–46, citation omitted.
27. Stephen Holmes (properly, I think) interprets Rawls's method of avoidance in this more pragmatic way: "To establish a public conception of justice acceptable to all members of a diverse society, we must abstract from questions which elicit radical disagreement. In a liberal social order, the basic normative framework must be able to command the loyalty of individuals and groups with widely differing self-understandings and conceptions of personal fulfillment"; "Gag Rules or the Politics of Omission," 20–21.
28. Richards, *Toleration and the Constitution*. Cf. Tribe and Dorf, *On Reading the Constitution*, 28–29.
29. Mill, *On Liberty*, 24 (chap. 2, para. 6).
30. As Stephen Holmes shows, however, in some circumstances debate may be furthered by keeping some issues off the agenda through, for instance, gag rules. See Holmes, "Gag Rules or the Politics of Omission."
31. Kant, "What Is Enlightenment?," 55.
32. See R. M. Smith, *Liberalism and American Constitutional Law*, 26.
33. Mill, *On Liberty*, 62 (chap. 3, para. 1).
34. See Holmes, "Gag Rules or the Politics of Omission."
35. See Wellington, *Interpreting the Constitution: The Supreme Court and the Process of Adjudication*, 58 ff; Bork, "Neutral Principles and Some First Amendment Problems," 21. For a Rawlsian-inspired theory resolving conflicts of speech and other interests, see Tucker, *Law, Liberalism and Free Speech*, esp. pt. 2.
36. Though it does announce the right of the people to assemble peacefully, and to petition the government for a redress of grievance.
37. For Hohfeld's classic analysis, see his "Some Fundamental Legal Conceptions as Applied in Judicial Reasoning." For an excellent explication and development of Hohfeld's analysis, see Robinson, Coval and Smith, "The Logic of Rights," 267–78.
38. Locke, *A Letter Concerning Toleration*, 25. Emphasis added.
39. "Locke's principle was naturally opposed as undermining public morality and political stability, especially when it was later elaborated to include disestablishment in Virginia and under the First Amendment of the United States Constitution. Political experience thereto had associated religion with state coercive and other support, so that many wondered how a state could be stable when all religions were independent of it. Bayle and Locke responded that a peaceful civility can be restored only when religious persecution is abandoned; persecution itself creates the instabilities of intractable, sectarian conflict." Richards, "Religion, Public Morality and Constitutional Law," 155. See, however, John Plamenatz's discussion of the Rousseauean character of Locke's intolerance toward atheism in *Man and Society*, 1: 86.
40. Holmes, "Gag Rules or the Politics of Omission" 31.
41. See, e.g., Galston, *Justice and the Human Good*; Perry, *Morality, Politics and the Law*.
42. Larmore, "Pluralism and Reasonable Disagreement," 74. But Cf. Moon, *Constructing Community*, chaps. 1, 2.
43. Benn, *Theory of Freedom*, 268.
44. Mill, *On Liberty*, 14 (chap. 1, para. 9).
45. Anshutz, *The Philosophy of John Stuart Mill*, 48. See also Wolff, *The Poverty of Liberalism*, 22 ff.
46. Ten, *Mill on Liberty*, 40–41.

47. According to Mill, harm to others is a necessary, not a sufficient, condition for intervention. Ten suggests that it may not even be a necessary condition. Ten, *Mill On Liberty*, 66–67.
48. Mill, *The Subjection of Women*, 472.
49. Locke, *Letter Concerning Toleration*, 17.
50. On Locke and consent theory, see Simmons, *On the Edge of Anarchy*. For a general defense of consent theory, see Beran, *The Consent Theory of Political Obligation*.
51. Baier, *The Moral Point of View*, 154. See also Kavka, *Hobbesian Moral and Political Theory*, chap. 9; Gert, *Morality*, chap. 6.
52. Gauthier, *Morals by Agreement*, 11.
53. See Rex Martin's analysis of civil rights in *A System of Rights*, 102 ff. I have stressed the importance of the idea of the common good to liberalism in Gaus, *Value and Justification*, 334 ff.
54. On the interest in such privacy, see Benn, *Theory of Freedom*, chap. 15; Fried, "Privacy."
55. The definitive work here is Joel Feinberg's *Harm to Others*.
56. See, for example: D'Agostino, "The Idea and the Ideal of Public Justification;" D'Agostino, *Free Public Reason*, Part Two; Lawrence B. Solum, "Constructing an Ideal of Public Reason," p.735; Larry Alexander, "Liberalism, Religion and the Unity of Epistemology."
57. See Alexander,"Liberalism, Religion and the Unity of Epistemology."

CHAPTER 11

1. I leave aside nested indeterminacy until sec. 11.2.3.
2. Rawls has argued that the difference principle is not a constitutional essential; *Political Liberalism*, 229.
3. Ibid., 14n.
4. See Shearmur, "Epistemological Limits of the State: Reflections on Popper's *Open Society*," 124.
5. This distinction, of course, can occur at many levels; there could, for instance, be a victoriously justified principle that does have a victoriously justified interpretation I_1, but the interpretation of I_1 itself is open to dispute in some cases. Although for ease of exposition I only deal with two levels—the abstract and the specific—it should be clear that many interpretive levels can arise. The regulative idea is that, to be a case of nested inconclusiveness, the inconclusive proposal must be an interpretation of, and so consistent with, all "higher level" victoriously justified articulations of the idea.
6. Rawls, *Political Liberalism*, 137. Emphasis added.
7. Kant, *The Metaphysical Elements of Justice*, 76 (sec.44). Emphasis in original.
8. Ibid.
9. For Hobbes, see Ewin, *Virtues and Rights*, 27, 43–44, 67, 125–26, 196–205; for Locke, see his *The Second Treatise of Government*, secs. 13, 87–89, 123–131.
10. See Gaus, "Does Compensation Restore Equality?," 67 ff; Macedo, *Liberal Virtues*, 67.
11. Ewin, *Virtues and Rights*, 32. The main theme of Ewin's work is the necessity of abandoning reliance on "private" judgment to achieve cooperation. See also his *Liberty, Community and Justice*.
12. Macedo, *Liberal Virutes* 72.
13. Kant, *Metaphysical Elements of Justice*, 76 (sec. 44).
14. Hobbes, *Leviathan*, 102 (chap. 15.) Emphasis in original. See Ewin, *Virtues and Rights*, 34.

15. Hobbes, *Leviathan*, 291 (chap. 37). See also Solum, "Constructing Public Reason," 754. This is the central theme of Ewin, *Virtues and Rights.*
16. E.D. Watt strongly defends the notion of moral authority in his *Authority*, chap. 6.
17. I borrow this characterization from Hardin, *Morality Within the Limits of Reason*, 179.
18. Narveson, *The Libertarian Idea*, 125.
19. R. B. Friedman, "On the Concept of Authority in Political Philosophy," 142–43. See also Peters, "Authority."
20. Friedman, "On the Concept of Authority," 129. Cf. Raz, *The Morality of Freedom*, 39 ff.
21. As Russell Hardin notes, "coordination problems are at best on the fringes of ethics"; *Morality Within the Limits of Reason*, 48. See sec. 9.4.3. below.
22. It is thus not surprising that Hobbesian theory, which is often interpreted as focusing on a conflict of wills rather than a disagreement about the content of the law of nature, seems at least partially captured by an analysis of coordination games. See Hampton, *Hobbes and the Social Contract Tradition.* However, Ewin's excellent study of Hobbes points to an analysis much closer to that presented here; see *Virtue and Rights.*
23. L. Green, *Authority of the State*, 56.
24. For a helpful discussions, see Watt, *Authority*, chap. 4; D'Agostino, "The Ethos of Games."
25. See Raz, *Practical Reason and Norms*, 35 ff.
26. Ibid., 42. Cf. Friedman's reference to "surrendering judgment" at n.20 above.
27. Raz, *Practical Reason and Norms*, 46.
28. L. Green, *Authority of the State*, 41–42.
29. Often this can be discerned because justifications are provided; when no justification is provided the subject of authority can still infer if it is "a reasonable call." Think of the umpire who consistently calls out the base runner well before the ball is caught by the first baseman. He doesn't offer a justification, but such calls are nevertheless illegitimate. See secs.16.3–16.4 below on the evaluation of illegitimate directives.
30. I believe that Raz and Green would interpret this as a limitation of scope. But the crucial issue here is *not* Betty's reasons (are they within the set of reasons that the umpire can exclude her from acting on?), but *the content* of the umpire's directive.

CHAPTER 12

1. Locke, *Second Treatise*, sec. 87.
2. Hobbes, *Leviathan*, p. 173 (ch. 26). Emphasis in original. See Ewin, *Virtues and Rights*, pp. 32, 67.
3. Nozick, *Anarchy, State and Utopia*, 98.
4. Dicey, *Introduction to the Study of the Law of the Constitution*, 188. See Marshall's discussion of the elements of the rule of law in "Due Process in England," 69–88.
5. But cf. here E.C.S. Wade's Introduction to Dicey's *Law of the Constitution*, xciii–xcix.
6. See Fuller, *The Morality of Law*, chap. 2. See also Rawls, *Theory of Justice*, 235–43.
7. Dicey, *Law of the Constitution*, 195 ff, chaps. 5–7. Dicey made a great deal of the distinction between Britain, where the constitution was founded *on* personal freedom (enforced through the common law) and those countries that protected freedom *through* a constitution.
8. Dworkin, "Political Judges and the Rule of Law," 11–12, emphasis in original.
9. See Lucas, *Principles of Politics*, sec. 25. This also relates to Madison's argument in *Federalist 47*; see Madison, Hamilton and Jay, *The Federalist Papers.*
10. Madison, Hamilton and Jay, *The Federalist Papers* (Hamilton, *Federalist 78*).
11. To be sure, it may be that they *are* simply a hodgepodge, which would be to say that

the rule of law is not a coherent concept. I believe that we have reason to prefer accounts of basic practical concepts that show them to be coherent. I consider this issue in Gaus, *Value and Justification*, 4–10.

12. See Rawls, "The Idea of an Overlapping Consensus," 18n.

13. It may be objected that this is a meaningless idea—how can we determine whether a theory approaches a goal that cannot be stated in advance? I consider this issue in sec. 13.4. See T.H. Green, *Prolegomena to Ethics*, sec. 353.

14. This, perhaps, is not strictly true: What if lm_2 tracks LM better than does lm_1, but lm_2 is a sort of evolutionary dead end; i.e., it is impossible to develop it in a way that gets any closer to LM, whereas lm_1 is rich in possibilities for such development? I set this problem aside, as it doesn't affect the point I wish to stress in the text.

15. Fuller, *Morality of Law*, 37.

16. Again, if the prohibition of retroactive laws is a part of LM, then epistemologically motivated agents would, of course, reject them.

17. This relates to the distinction between being "an authority" (i.e., an expert) and being "in authority." See sec. 11.2.3.

18. See Fuller, *Morality of Law*, chaps. 3, 4.

19. Hobbes, *Leviathan*, 102 (chap. 15).

20. Stanley Benn and I explore this matter more thoroughly in Benn and Gaus, "Public and Private: Concepts and Action."

21. I have considered this principle in more depth in Gaus, "Does Compensation Restore Equality?", 48–54.

22. Locke explicitly denies that the "magistrate" has any right to impose laws that reflect merely his private views; *A Letter Concerning Toleration*, 49.

23. See Ewin, *Virtues and Rights*, chap. 2.

24. I am supposing that it is clear that this idea of disputed jurisdiction applies to all areas of social life, and not simply property. Alf might claim jurisdiction over what Betty believes, what she wears, how she educates her children, the language she speaks, the way she weighs her meat for sale (pounds or kilos), what she ingests, the side of the road she drives on, her political views, what she does with her time, and on and on.

25. Ewin, *Liberty, Community and Justice*, 41. Citation omitted. In secs. 12.3.2 and 16.3– 16.4 I criticize Ewin's claim that politically recognized rights can *never* be overridden on substantive grounds.

26. I do not mean to imply here that Betty's having a right to Φ is sufficient to justify her Φ-ing; rights can be overridden. What is important is that Alf *can* reason in this way, though step (2) supposes that no overriding conditions are present. On overriding reasons, see sec. 5.3.2.

27. See Waldron, "A Right to Do Wrong."

28. Ewin, *Liberty, Community and Justice*, 41–43.

29. T.H. Green, *Lectures on the Principles of Political Obligation*, 107. See Martin, *A System of Rights*, chaps. 5–7. See also Cacoullos, *Thomas Hill Green: Philosopher of Rights*.

30. See also Martin, *System of Rights*, chaps. 2–3.

31. Nozick, *Anarchy, State and Utopia*, 11–12.

32. Martin, *System of Rights*, 125.

33. This argument is made with great care, and in considerable detail, by Martin. See ibid., chaps. 2–7.

34. I shall sidestep here the controversial issue as to whether rights should be understood in terms of justified claims, or whether a more complex analysis is required. For the most part, I follow Wesley Hohfeld's division of rights into liberties, claims, powers and immunities. See Hohfeld, "Some Fundamental Legal Conceptions as Applied in Judicial Reasoning." For a recent development of Hohfeld's analysis, see Robinson, Coval, and Smith, "The Logic of Rights."

35. Ewin, *Virtue and Rights,* 19. Emphasis added.
36. Hobbes's theory gets into trouble on precisely this point. Although he wants to uphold C1 and C2, he also argues that individuals cannot renounce their right to self-preservation, thus contradicting C2. See Ewin, *Virtues and Rights,* esp. chap. 3.
37. This points to a contrast between Locke's genuinely liberal view and Hobbes's. In contrast to Locke, Hobbes wants to leave behind questions about "What is right?" and focus purely on the practical matter of "What are we to do?" Given that Hobbes wishes to focus exclusively on the practical problems engendered by reliance on individual judgment, he does his best to avoid any substantive limits on what the umpire can legally accomplish. The sovereign's task is simply to resolve any and all disputes between individuals, and thus in a sense he cannot go beyond his charge. Even if all the citizens disagree with the umpire, there is still the clash between his judgment and theirs, which he resolves in his own favor. See Ewin, *Virtues and Rights,* 38. See secs. 16.3–16.4 below.
38. This, of course, is a weaker view of natural rights than is to be found in Locke—as I have depicted them, natural rights are prepolitical, but need not be universal. See Gaus, *Value and Justification,* 23.
39. Dworkin, "Political Judges and the Rule of Law," 12.
40. Locke, *Second Treatise,* 199–202.
41. R. M. Smith, *Liberalism and American Constitutional Law,* 32–33.
42. Snowiss, *Judicial Review and the Law of the Constitution,* 29.
43. Madison, Hamilton and Jay, *Federalist Papers* (Hamilton, *Federalist 78*), 467.
44. Macedo, *Liberal Virtues,* 171.
45. Although it is often disputed. For different attacks on this idea, see Reynolds, "The Ethical Foundations of Constitutional Order"; Ely, *Democracy and Distrust.*
46. On Madisonian constitutionalism and substantive limits, see, e.g., Richards, *Toleration and the Constitution,* 40–41; M. White, *Philosophy, The Federalist and the Constitution,* 220–21. Although constitutional political economy stresses the importance of procedural constraints in Madison's thought, substantive constraints play a role as well. For public choice perspectives on Madison, see Dorn, "Public Choice and The Constitution: A Madisonian Perspective"; Dorn, "Madison's Constitutional Political Economy: Principles for a Liberal Order"; Wagner and Gwartney, "Public Choice and Constitutional Order." On Madison and bills of rights, see Rumble, "James Madison on the Value of Bills of Rights."
47. This distinction is recognized by Holcombe, "Constitutions as Constraints," 303.
48. Rumble, "James Madison on the Value of Bills of Rights," 124.
49. This is not quite right; the legislation must be authorized by the relevant secondary rules. As Locke stressed, a government can go astray in two ways: by legislating in a way that violates natural rights (tyranny) or by doing what may be just, but what it is not authorized to do (usurpation.). See Locke, *The Second Treatise of Government,* sec. 199. See below, 12.4.3. As Jonathan Riley points out, Madison uses "tyranny" in a different way, which is "unrelated to any particular conception of injustice and, indeed, carries no necessary ethical connotation whatsoever"; "American Democracy and Majority Rule," 284.
50. Bork, *The Tempting of America,* 139. Compare Justice Holmes's assertion of "the right of the majority to embody their opinions in law" in *Lochner v. New York,* 189 US 45 (1905). Robert Dahl advances a similar interpretation of Madisonian democracy in *A Preface to Democratic Theory,* 31.
51. "Conservative strict constructionists, like Bork, argue in effect that judges should enforce only explicit rights, rights plainly stated in the Constitution's text or very clearly implied in it. Legislators, on the other hand, may do anything that is not plainly forbidden by the Constitution's text and its clear implications"; Macedo, *The New Right v. The Constitution,* 27.

52. See Mill's distinction between authoritative and nonauthoritative government interventions. My focus here is on authoritative interventions—those that aim at "controlling the free agency of individuals." Mill, *Principles of Political Economy*, bk. 5, chap. 11, sec. 1.
53. Dahl, *Democracy and Its Critics*, 113. Dahl accepts that the majority has no authority to rescind rights essential to the democratic process, such as free speech and freedom of assembly. Ibid., 169 ff.
54. Of course, Dahl never purports to present a Madisonian theory. Dahl's *Preface to Democratic Theory* is, indeed, a classic critique of "Madisonian theory." For a much more sympathetic interpretation of Madison, and a rebuttal of Dahl's criticism of the American constitution, see Riley, "American Democracy and Majority Rule."
55. Madison, Hamilton and Jay, *Federalist Papers* (Madison, *Federalist 51*), 324.
56. Quoted in Slagstad, "Liberal Constitutionalism and Its Critics," 107.
57. Macedo, *Liberal Virtues*, 277.
58. Ibid., 120. Citation omitted. Emphasis added. I will not enter into the debate here as to whether Oakeshott is best understood as a critic or as a member of the liberal tradition. Kirk Koerner depicts Oakeshott as a critic of liberalism in his *Liberalism and Its Critics*, while Paul Franco interprets Oakeshott as offering a restatement of liberalism in *The Political Philosophy of Michael Oakeshott*. John Chapman also understands Oakeshott as essentially a liberal in his "Justice, Freedom and Property."
59. Dworkin, *Taking Rights Seriously*, 82.
60. Ibid., xi, 90–100. See D. Regan, "Glosses on Dworkin: Rights, Principles, and Policies."
61. Dworkin, "Neutrality, Equality and Liberalism," 6.
62. Cf. Rawls, *Theory of Justice*, 331–32.
63. R. M. Smith, *Liberalism and American Constitutional Law*, 31.
64. Locke, *Second Treatise*, sec. 131. Emphasis in original.
65. See M. White, *Philosophy, The Federalist and the Constitution*, 194.
66. Stanley Benn and I have argued this more fully in Benn and Gaus, "Liberal Conception of the Public and the Private."
67. See Ibid. Collectivist common good arguments are characteristic of Roman Catholic thought. See Rommen, *The State in Catholic Thought*, chap. 13; Maritain, *The Person and the Common Good*. On types of common good arguments, see Gaus, *Value and Justification*, 336–58.
68. As in the following argument from *The Economist:* "Taxes are imposed for what government believes to be the common good. Some people will condemn the ends the government decides on: pacifists may object to defence spending, or greens to spending on new roads. Most pay anyway. They have other ways of making their case: through the press, through the legislature and even, as a last resort, by sitting down in the streets. But at the end of the day government must govern, and tax, in the interests of the majority." August 6, 1994, p. 20, col. 2.
69. On the idea of sections of the public, see Benn and Gaus, "The Liberal Conception of the Public and the Private," 36–38.
70. This point is emphasized by Wagner and Gwartney, "Public Choice and Constitutional Order."
71. Hart, *Concept of Law*, 75. Emphasis in original.
72. Madison, Hamilton and Jay, *Federalist Papers* (Madison, *Federalist 51*), 324–25.
73. Ibid., (Madison, *Federalist 49*), 315.
74. Ibid. (Madison, *Federalist 50*), 319.
75. Cf. Shapiro, "Three Ways to Be a Democrat," 127 ff.
76. At this point I have not distinguished the legislative and judicial aspects of liberal authority. That will be the task of chaps. 13–16.
77. In this regard it seems to me that liberalism is indeed rationalistic. See Oakeshott, "Rationalism in Politics."

78. See Ackerman, *We the People*, chap. 10. This is not to say that I accept Ackerman's way of distinguishing constitutional and normal politics; I criticize it below in secs. 13.2, 15.3, and 16.2. See also Rawls, *Political Liberalism*, 334 ff; D'Agostino, *Free Public Reason*, pt. three.

79. Henry Knox, quoted in Crosskey and Jeffrey, *Politics and the Constitution in the History of the United States*, vol. 3, *The Political Background of the Federal Constitution*, 368–69. Even John Jay, who stressed that constitutional politics must be in the voice of "the people," recognized this pragmatic aspect of widespread assent. Ibid., 373.

CHAPTER 13

1. Rex Martin provides a thorough account of the state's authority to punish in *A System of Rights*, chaps. 9–11.

2. I thus put aside here the important area of administrative law, which is adjudication by the executive. See Ehr-Soon Tay and Kamenka, "Public Law—Private Law." See also Hayek's concerns about administrative law in *The Constitution of Liberty*, chap. 14.

3. I have considered some of the problems with specifying the boundaries of the public in Gaus, *Value and Justification*, 367–76. See Appendix below.

4. See Sen, *Collective Choice and Social Welfare*, 22 ff. On the idea of a social welfare function, see ibid., 35 ff.

5. Riker, *Liberalism Against Populism*, 45.

6. Ibid., 47–51; Foron and Kronick, "Single Transferrable Vote: An Example of a Perverse Social Choice Function."

7. Austen-Smith and Banks, "Monotonicity in Electoral Systems."

8. Ibid., 531.

9. See Hardin, "Public Choice Versus Democracy." Arrow's controversial condition I—the independence of irrelevant alternatives—can also be interpreted in a way that tends to eliminate procedures in which voters vote "strategically," that is, cast their votes in ways that misstate their true preferences in relation to some alternatives. Since logrolling can be understood as a form of strategic voting, condition I is also relevant to this problem. On the interpretation of condition I and how it helps make voting procedures immune to strategic voting, see Mueller, *Public Choice II*, 393–95; Karni and Schmeidler, "Independence of Nonfeasible Alternatives, and Independence of Nonoptimal Alternatives"; Bordes and Tideman, "Independence of Irrelevant Alternatives in the Theory of Voting"; Osborne, "Irrelevant Alternatives and Social Welfare." For discussions of logrolling, strategic voting, and democracy, see Riker, *Liberalism Against Populism*, chap. 6; Christiano, "Social Choice and Democracy." See sec. 15.4 below.

10. On the justificatory force of hypothetical contractual arguments, see Gaus, *Value and Justification*, 328 ff.

11. Of course, a chief virtue is that it is fair, but fairness is part of the internal morality of the law, and so is presupposed by the idea of a *law*-making procedure (sec. 12.2 above).

12. See Gaus, *Value and Justification*, chaps. 7–9.

13. Rawls, "Kantian Constructivism in Moral Theory," 533–35, 567 ff.

14. Hume, "Of the Independency of Parliament," 42–43.

15. Madison, Hamilton and Jay, *Federalist Papers* (Madison, *Federalist 51*), 322. See M. White, *Philosophy*, The Federalist *and the Constitution*, 95–99.

16. See M. White, *Philosophy*, the Federalist *and the Constitution*, 200 ff.

17. For a brief history, which points to its recent decline, see Jane J. Mansbridge, "The Rise and Fall of Self-Interest in the Explanation of Political Life."

18. Machiavelli, *Discourses on Livy*, bk. 1, chap. 18.

19. R. D. Putnam, *Making Democracy Work*, 88.

20. Madison, Hamilton and Jay, *Federalist Papers* (Madison, *Federalist 55*), 346.
21. See Sears, Lau, Tyler, and Allen, "Self-Interest vs. Symbolic Politics in Policy Attitudes and Presidential Voting"; Sears and Funk, "Self-Interest in Americans' Political Opinions." But Cf. Weatherford, "Economic Voting and the 'Symbolic Politics' Argument: A Reinterpretation and Synthesis."
22. If we add to the assumption that people are generally self-interested the claim that when they are not self-interested they tend to be malicious, then what Madison called republican government seems quite impossible. See Geoffrey Brennan and Loren Lomasky, "Large Numbers, Small Costs: The Uneasy Foundation of Democratic Rule," 53–54. See sec. 15.3.
23. Bentham, *Manual of Political Economy*, 1:226.
24. See Elster, "The Market and the Forum: Three Varieties of Political Theory"; D. Miller, "The Competitive Model of Democracy."
25. See Pettit, "Consequentialism and Respect for Persons," 124 ff. I criticize Pettit's proposal in Gaus, "Practical Reason and Moral Persons," 144 ff.
26. For a wide-ranging analysis demonstrating the limits of self-interest as a motivation, see James Q. Wilson, *The Moral Sense.*
27. See Tyler, "Justice, Self-Interest, and the Legitimacy of Legal and Political Authority."
28. See, e.g., D'Agostino, "Ethical Pluralism and the Role of Opposition in Democratic Politics." Writing in favor of choosing representatives (not policies) by lot, Barbara Goodwin notes "that going over to the lot-representative system would signify the abandonment of the view that the purpose of democratic procedures is to light upon the "right" answers to political questions, or to achieve the 'common good' "; *Justice by Lottery*, 162.
29. Ackerman, *Social Justice in the Liberal State*, 289. Ackerman is writing here of what he calls "responsive lotteries," which are much the same as the system described by Wolff at notes 33 and 34 below.
30. Elster, *Solomonic Judgments*, 107.
31. For Elster, a problem is typically indeterminate unless: (1) all the options are known; (2) all the possible outcomes of each option are known; (3) the probabilities of each outcome are known; (4) the value attached to each outcome is known. These conditions seem more relevant to inconclusiveness. Ibid., 134. However, that the idea that indeterminacy is closely linked with incommensurability (p. 38) seems quite right. Cf. Goodwin, who follows Elster: "The arguments for a Total Social Lottery assume that there are far more indeterminacies and incommensurabilities in human life and society than would generally be acknowledged, and that conventional distributive criteria are therefore rarely conclusive or just"; *Justice by Lottery*, 151.
32. Elster, *Solomonic Judgments*, 38. In reference to the "random dictator" proposal, Elster writes: "This proposal would appear strange, to say the least, yet surprisingly there are a large number of arguments to be made for it. Not surprisingly, however, the counterarguments are stronger." Ibid., 87.
33. Wolff, *In Defense of Anarchism*, 44–45. Emphasis in original.
34. Ibid. 45.
35. Walzer, *Spheres of Justice*, 305. Even Barbara Goodwin, who seems inclined toward a thoroughgoing use of lotteries to shape almost all areas of social life, shies away from complete legislation by lottery. See her *Justice by Lottery*, 161.
36. It is important to stress that my concern here is with law-making institutions, not with, say, allocative decisions within a system of laws. There may well be good reasons to allocate some burdens or resources by lot. If conscription can be publicly justified, a lottery to select conscripts may be justified.
37. See Luce and Raiffa, *Games and Decisions*, 9 ff; Hampton, *Hobbes and the Social Contract Tradition*, 154 ff.

38. As Hampton notes, game theorists have proposed a variety of "fair" solutions to the Battle of the Sexes problem. *Hobbes and the Social Contract Tradition*, 153.
39. This is even true of that paradigm of a "pure" coordination game, which side of the road to drive on (sec. 9.4.3). Left-handed drivers may plausibly be attributed a slight preference for driving on the left side of the road, as they can shift gears with their left hand.
40. For critical analyses of "best answer" or "consequentialist" justifications of democracy, see Elster, "Arguments for Constitutional Choice"; Beitz, *Political Equality*, chap. 3.
41. Quoted in Snowiss, *Judicial Review and the Law of the Constitution*, 14–15.
42. Mill, *Considerations on Representative Government*, 245 (chap. 3).
43. On responsiveness, see Pennock, *Democratic Political Theory*, chap. 7.
44. See, e.g., Arneson, "Democratic Rights at National and Workplace Levels"; Nelson, *On Justifying Democracy*, chap. 6; Lively, *Democracy*, 126–31; Hayek, *The Political Order of a Free People*, 5.
45. See Brennan and Lomasky, "Large Numbers, Small Costs," in which they argue at length for this claim.
46. Shklar, *The Faces of Injustice*, chap. 3.
47. This feature of democracy is stressed by Von Mises in *Liberalism in the Classical Tradition*, 39 ff; Riker, *Liberalism Against Populism*.
48. Much depends here on whether the corporatist arrangement is one in which the government controls the groups. See Gaus, "Public and Private Interests in Liberal Political Economy, Old and New," 207–11.
49. See Mill, *Considerations on Representative Government*, 334 ff. At one point Mill provides the following scale of voting power: Unskilled laborers—1 vote; Skilled laborers—2 votes; Foremen—3 votes; Farmers, manufacturers, and traders—3 or 4 Votes; Professionals—5 or 6 votes; University graduates—at least 5 or 6 votes. Mill, "Thoughts on Parliamentary Reform," 324–25. See also Thompson, *John Stuart Mill and Representative Government*, chap. 2; Arneson, "Democratic Rights at National and Workplace Levels,"133 ff.
50. For evidence that public opinion does indeed affect policy, see Page and Shapiro, "Effects of Public Opinion on Policy."
51. See, for example, Ackerman, "Why Dialogue?"; Benhabib, "Liberal Dialogue Versus a Critical Theory of Discursive Legitimation"; Benjamin Barber, *Strong Democracy*, 178 ff.
52. Rawls, *Political Liberalism*, 227–30.
53. Geoffrey Brennan and Loren Lomasky show that a unanimity rule can lead to results that no one thinks are desirable in *Democracy and Decision*, chap. 8.
54. See Giovanni Sartori, *The Theory of Democracy Revisited*, pt. 1, 227–32. My notion of a side payment is not quite the same as Sartori's.
55. To be sure, it might simply be rejected as hopelessly corrupt, to be replaced by a communitarian political life characterized by deep consensus. Again we are back to the charge of utopianism; such consensus does not characterize our judgments, and given our epistemic situation, it seems unlikely to arise. "The communitarian alternative is not one we can simply adopt. . . . [W]e are not a community." Hardin, "Public Choice Versus Democracy," 167–68. See sec. 15.4 below.
56. See Ackerman, *We The People*; Bickel, *Least Dangerous Branch*, 24–26, 30–31, 88 ff.
57. Rawls, *Political Liberalism*, 231; Bickel, *Least Dangerous Branch*, 199. Rawls cites Ackerman's work on this page.
58. Rawls, *Political Liberalism*, 214.
59. Ibid., 215.
60. Gutmann and Thompson, "Moral Conflict and Political Consensus," 79.
61. Ibid., 88.
62. Ibid., 77.
63. Ibid., 85.

64. Nelson, *On Justifying Democracy*, 115.
65. Mill, *Considerations on Representative Government*, 283 (chap. 5). As Mill himself clearly recognized, this justification of representative institutions as widely deliberative provides a powerful argument for some form of proportional representation—the deliberation should encompass "every interest and shade of opinion." In his study of the political consequences of electoral laws from 1945–85, Arend Lijphart found that proportional representation rules are effective in generating legislatures in which the electoral popularity of parties is reflected in the legislature; plurality and majority systems tend to yield results that are twice as disproportional as the least proportional PR method. Lijphart, "The Political Consequences of Electoral Laws, 1945–85," 485. This is one of the few conclusions of Douglas Rea's classic study, *The Political Consequences of Electoral Laws*, with which Lijphart agrees. Lijphart also finds that the number of representatives returned from each district is an independent predictor of proportionality. For a critical appraisal of proportional representation systems, with special reference to Nelson's defense of open government, see Beitz, *Political Equality*, chap. 6.
66. Nelson, *On Justifying Democracy*, 117. See also his "Evaluating the Institutions of Liberal Democracy."
67. Nelson, *On Justifying Democracy*, 119.
68. Ibid., 118. Emphasis added.
69. Nelson, "Evaluating the Institutions of Liberal Democracy," 72. In sec. 13.4 I endorsed the other type of tracking argument; I believe the two are indeed "complementary."
70. This point is stressed by Beitz, *Political Equality*, 41–46.
71. See Goodin, "Laundering Preferences," pp. 86 ff.
72. Madison, Hamilton and Jay, *Federalist Papers* (Madison, *Federalist 50*), 317.
73. Ibid. (Madison, *Federalist 10*), 82. For a discussion, see Fishkin, *Democracy and Deliberation*, 35–41.
74. Morton White uses this phrase to describe the *Federalist Papers;* e.g., M. White, *Philosophy, The Federalist and the Constitution*, 216. Mill, of course, has also been described as an "elitist." For an excellent discussion see Garforth, *Educative Democracy*, chap. 4. I am neither affirming nor denying that epistemological elitism is well-grounded; see sec. 14.1 below.
75. Burnheim, *Is Democracy Possible?*, 106 ff.; Fishkin, *Democracy and Deliberation*.
76. But see sec. 15.2 below.
77. Systems employing essentially random devices to select a deliberative assembly could also be justified on this ground, and thus are not subject to the objections raised in sec. 13.3 to policy lotteries. See Goodwin, *Justice by Lottery*, 156 ff; Norman, *Free and Equal*, 168–69.
78. See Ackerman, *We the People*, 278–80; Nozick, *Anarchy, State and Utopia*, 96–7.
79. Nozick, *Anarchy, State and Utopia*, 98.
80. Indeed, requiring unanimity or even near unanimity may undermine public justification. See 15.5 below.
81. See Benn and Peters, *Social Principles and the Democratic State*, 347 ff; Fishkin, *Tyranny and Legitimacy*, chap. 8.
82. Neutrality is presented as an important part of the case for democracy by Ackerman (he calls it "outcome indifference") in *Social Justice in the Liberal State*, 278 ff. See also Christiano, "Political Equality," 154–57. For another democratic theorist who ascribes too much importance to neutrality, see Gaus, "Public Justification and Democratic Adjudication," 277–78.
83. See Mueller, *Public Choice II*, 96–100.
84. B. Barry, *Political Argument*, 312. Emphasis in original. Today, of course, even if there were four smokers to only one nonsmoker, the nonsmoker would carry the day, and

would probably sue the smokers if they indulged. Indeed, even if there were five smokers, they might all sue the railway for letting them smoke.

85. Elaine Spitz understands majority rule as a way to resolve disputes among equals; see her *Majority Rule.*
86. Martin, *System of Rights,* 142. See also Spitz, *Majority Rule,* 206; B. Barry, "The Public Interest"; Grofman and Feld, "Rousseau's General Will: A Condorcetian Perspective." For discussions of Grofman and Feld, see the responses by David Estlund and Jeremy Waldron, as well as Grofman's and Feld's rejoinder, in vol. 83 of the *American Political Science Review,* 1315–35.
87. Kuflik, "Majority Rule Procedure," 306.
88. Ibid.
89. See Estlund, "Making Truth Safe for Democracy," 93.
90. I owe this point to Loren Lomasky.
91. This point is stressed by Riker, *Liberalism Against Populism,* chap. 7. For some additional fascinating examples, see Riker's *The Art of Political Manipulation,* esp. chap. 3.
92. It is tempting to think that this problem can be dispelled simply by applying the majoritarian procedure to the agenda-setting problem, but the possibilities of manipulation merely reproduce themselves at new levels.
93. Dewey, *Intelligence in the Modern World,* 402
94. For a useful overview of this distinction see Bernholz and Faber, "Reflections on a Normative Economic Theory."
95. Buchanan, *Limits of Liberty,* 94–96.
96. Cf. Mill, *Principles of Political Economy,* bk. 5, chap. 11, sec. 5; Mill, *On Liberty,* chap. 3.
97. Brennan and Buchanan, *The Reason of Rules,* 137. Wicksell proposed a joint requirement: (1) "no public expenditures ever be voted on without simultaneous determination of the means of covering their costs" and (2) "approximate unanimity of decisions— absolute unanimity may have to be ruled out for practical reasons." Wicksell, "A New Principle of Just Taxation," 121–22. See sec. 15.5 below.

CHAPTER 14

1. Hurley, *Natural Reasons,* 341.
2. For strong arguments in favor of consequential justifications of democracy, see Arneson, "Democratic Rights at National and Workplace Levels"; Nelson, *On Justifying Democracy.*
3. Mill, *Considerations on Representative Government,* 335 (chap. 8). See also Arneson, "Democratic Rights at National and Workplace Levels," 133 ff.
4. Beitz, *Political Equality,* 38.
5. Ibid., 103.
6. Gutmann, "How Liberal Is Democracy?" 38.
7. Christiano, "Social Choice and Democracy," 182.
8. Ibid., 189.
9. Ibid. See also Nielsen, *Equality and Liberty,* 48; Norman, *Free and Equal.*
10. Cf. Waldron, "Religious Contributions to Public Deliberation," 827 ff.
11. Estlund, "Making Truth Safe for Democracy," 84.
12. Arneson, "Democratic Rights at National and Workplace Levels," 137–38.
13. Cf. Singer, *Democracy and Disobedience.*
14. See Weaver and Rockman, "Institutional Reform and Constitutional Design," 470–71. See also their "Assessing the Effects of Institutions," 8 ff.
15. For advocates of a link, see, e.g., Gutmann, *Liberal Equality,* chap. 7; Dahl, *Dilemmas*

of Pluralist Democracy, 170 ff; Cohen and Rogers, *On Democracy,* 149 ff; Nedelsky, "American Constitutionalism and the Paradox of Private Property."

16. Christiano, "Social Choice and Democracy," 190.
17. Dahl, *Preface to Economic Democracy,* 60.
18. But cf. Weaver and Rockman, "Institutional Reform and Constitution Design," 470–71, who place this in the "third tier" of institutional structures.

CHAPTER 15

1. This point is made by David M. Estlund in his contribution to the debate concerning Grofman and Feld's essay, "Rousseau's General Will: A Condorcetian Perspective." The comments of Estlund and Jeremy Waldron and Grofman and Feld's replies are published under the title "Democratic Theory and The Public Interest: Condorcet and Rousseau Revisited." *American Political Science Review* 83 (December 1989): 1317–40; for Estlund's point, see 1321.
2. See Gibbard, "Manipulation of Voting Schemes: A General Result"; Riker, *Liberalism Against Populism,* chap. 6; Christiano, "Social Choice and Democracy," 175 ff.
3. Riker, *Liberalism Against Populism,* 239.
4. Arrow, *Social Choice and Individual Values.* The literature on Arrow's theorem is enormous. For useful explications, see MacKay, *Arrow's Theorem: The Paradox;* Craven, *Social Choice,* chap. 3; Sen, *Collective Choice and Social Welfare,* chap. 3; Riley, *Liberal Utilitarianism,* 21–24.
5. See Sen, *Collective Choice and Social Welfare,* chap. 4. For a helpful discussion of Arrow's social welfare functions, see Riley, *Liberal Utilitarianism,* chap. 2.
6. Monotonicity enters Arrow's theorem via the Pareto condition. See Riker, *Liberalism Against Populism,* 117.
7. This, I think, is the truth behind Elaine Spitz's rather quick dismissal of Arrow's theorem because "its relevance to the real world is doubtful"; *Majority Rule,* 24. In *Liberalism Against Populism,* Riker, I believe, shows that Arrow's work has relevance for understanding politics, but it remains true that the justification for, and results of, the application of the formal conditions to entire electoral systems remain obscure.
8. This point can be generalized to D'Agostino's "impossibility theorem," which seeks to construct a list of desiderata for public justifications that is intuitively obvious and more or less freestanding. Each political theory offers an account of why public justification is important, what we aim for it to do, etc., and these accounts will determine the set of desiderata, and their relative importance, relevant to that theory. See D'Agostino, *Free Public Reason* and "The Idea and the Ideal of Public Justification."
9. See Coleman and Ferejohn, "Democracy and Social Choice"; Cohen, "An Epistemic Conception of Democracy." For a different way of understanding the relation between epistemic democracy and social choice theory, see Hurley, *Natural Reasons,* 322 ff. On epistemic democracy, see also Martin, *System of Rights,* chap. 6; Grofman and Feld, "Rousseau's General Will."
10. Riker, *Liberalism Against Populism,* 11 ff.
11. Rousseau, *The Social Contract,* 184–86 (bk. 2, chap. 2).
12. Fishkin, *Democracy and Deliberation,* 21.
13. Converse and Markus, "Plus ça change . . . : The New CPS Election Study Panel."
14. Converse, "The Nature of Belief Systems in Mass Publics."
15. Brennan and Lomasky, *Democracy and Decision,* 211.
16. Converse and Markus, "Plus ça change."
17. Page and Shapiro, *The Rational Public,* 16–17. For an overview of their analysis, see their "The Rational Public and Democracy."

18. Page and Shapiro, *Rational Public,* 45.
19. Ibid., 50.
20. Ibid, 54.
21. Ibid., 108, 385.
22. Ibid., 26, 388.
23. Ibid., 389.
24. The first question is the precise wording of the Gallup poll; the second is an approximation of a Harris poll item. Page and Shapiro, *Rational Public,* 110.
25. Ibid., 111.
26. Madison, Hamilton and Jay, *Federalist Papers* (Madison, *Federalist 10*), 79.
27. Locke, *The Second Treatise of Government,* 13.
28. Rousseau, *Social Contract,* 185 (bk. 2, chap. 2). See Grofman and Feld, "Rousseau's General Will," 57–72.
29. Rousseau, *Social Contract,* 185 (bk. 2 chap. 2).
30. Madison, Hamilton and Jay, *Federalist Papers* (Madison, *Federalist 10*), 78.
31. Ibid.
32. Brennan and Lomasky, *Democracy and Decision,* 124.
33. See Hirschman, *The Passions and the Interests.*
34. See Olson, *The Logic of Collective Action.*
35. The alternative approach of many rational choice theorists is to find some way that this behavior is self-interested, since the model backs them into assuming that if it is rational, it must, somehow, aim at self-interest. I plan to examine these responses in detail sometime in the future, but note for now *how* long economic theorists of democracy have been trying to show that voting is self-interested.
36. For an overview, see Kingdon, "Politicians, Self-Interest and Ideas," 75–77.
37. Ibid., 85.
38. Bickel, *The Least Dangerous Branch,* 25.
39. See Macedo, *Liberal Virtues,* 149n.
40. Ibid., 113.
41. Ibid., 117.
42. Riker, *Liberalism Against Populism,* 159.
43. On the relation of independence and the problem of "strategic voting," see chap. 13, n. 9.
44. Riker, *Liberalism Against Populism,* chaps. 8–10.
45. This idea was suggested to me by Geoff Sayre-McCord's work on moral kinds, though, of course, he does not bear responsibility for this corruption of his work.
46. See, e.g., Pennock, *Democratic Political Theory,* 389 ff.
47. See Martin, *System of Rights,* 178; Christiano, "Social Choice and Democracy," 184–85: D'Agostino, "Ethical Pluralism." It is somewhat puzzling that Martin appears to approve of vote trading but not strategic voting; *System of Rights,* 180–81.
48. See Gibbard, "Manipulation of Voting Schemes."
49. Brams and Fishburn, "Approval Voting."
50. See B. Barry, *Political Argument,* 318; Pennock, *Democratic Political Theory,* 389. On Wicksellian rules, see chap. 13, note 97.
51. See Mansbridge, *Beyond Adversary Democracy.* For an analysis of a cooperative conception of democratic life, see Berry, *The Idea of a Democratic Community.*
52. In particular, see Lijphart's analysis of the consensus mode of democracy in *Democracies,* chap. 2.
53. D'Agostino, *Free Public Reason,* sec. 9. See also T. Nagel, "Moral Conflict and Political Legitimacy," 218.
54. This is R.M. MacIver's characterization of the interest group school of politics of political scientists, characterized by Arthur F. Bentley. In opposition to this view, MacIver insists

that "Democracy is itself the organization of the common interest"; *The Web of Govern-ment*, 220. Cf. Bentley, *The Institution of Government*. Many pluralists simply, and no doubt rightly, make no claim that the outcome of group competition is the public inter-est. Indeed, they are apt to dismiss the very idea of the public interest. For a general discussion, see Dunleavy and O'Leary, *Theories of the State*, chap. 2.

55. Mill, *Considerations on Representative Government*, 255 (chap. 3).

CHAPTER 16

1. Hart, *Concept of Law*, 138.
2. Ibid., 139.
3. Madison, Hamilton and Jay, *Federalist Papers* (Hamilton, *Federalist 78*), 471.
4. For the same reason it is improper for jurors to disregard laws with which they disagree. Cf. here the views of the "Fully Informed Jury Association." *Wall Street Journal*, Janu-ary 4, 1991, p. 1.
5. Hart, *Concept of Law*, 123.
6. "The interpretation of a statute, therefore," wrote Hans Kelsen, "need not necessarily lead to a single decision as the only correct one, but possibly to several, which are all of equal value, though only one of them in the action of the law-applying organ (especially the court) becomes positive law." Kelsen, *The Pure Theory of Law*, 351.
7. See Wasserstrom, *The Judicial Decision*, 28; MacCormick, *Legal Reasoning and Legal Theory*, 72 ff; Skubik, *At the Intersection of Legality and Morality*, 42 ff.
8. Dworkin, *Taking Rights Seriously*, 107.
9. "According to law as integrity, propositions of law are true if they figure in or follow from the principles of justice, fairness, and procedural due process that provide the best constructive interpretation of the community's legal practice." Dworkin, *Law's Empire*, 225.
10. Bickel, *Least Dangerous Branch*, 188, 199; Wellington, *Interpreting the Constitution*, 83 ff.
11. Rawls, *Political Liberalism*, 235.
12. For a criticism of this view, see R. F. Nagel, *Constitutional Cultures*, 22 f.
13. Macedo, *Liberal Virtues*, 144–45.
14. Ibid., 181.
15. This point is stressed by Ely, *Democracy and Distrust*; see, e.g., chap. 3, 102.
16. Dahl, *Democracy and Its Critics*, 155.
17. Lijphart, *Democracies*, 191–96.
18. Dahl, *Democracy and Its Critics*, 187–91.
19. Snowiss, *Judicial Review*, 2.
20. Ibid., 50 ff.
21. A famous latter-day proponent of the second position is James B. Thayer, "The Origins and Scope of the American Doctrine of Constitutional Law."
22. R. Nagel, *Constitutional Cultures*, 3.
23. Ely, *Democracy and Distrust*, 92.
24. Ibid., 844 ff. For a criticism that Ely "reads things out" of the Constitution to fit his interpretative theory, see Tribe and Dorf, *On Reading the Constitution*, 26–27.
25. But cf. Smith, *Liberalism and American Constitutional Law*, 90–91, 172 ff.
26. Ely, *Democracy and Distrust*, chap. 4.
27. Ibid., 102–3. Two citations omitted.
28. Ibid., 102.
29. See Wellington, *Interpreting the Constitution*, 66–69.

30. Graham W. Walker notes the similarity of Ely to Robert Bork in this regard in *Moral Foundations of Constitutional Thought*, 15. See also Macedo, *Liberal Virtues*, 103. On Bork's majoritarianism, see sec. 12.4.1.

31. Complications arise here. In sec. 14.3 I distinguished features "internal" to the political institution and "background" conditions. The courts clearly should be the guardian of the integrity of the institution, ensuring that representation is fair, districting arrangements do not conspire to deprive some of their political voice, and so on. And indeed these are the sorts of issues on which the courts have spoken. Wider issues—for example, whether political inequalities arising from property rights or free speech rights can be justified—concern the relative weights of liberal principles, and are properly part of the political institution. Rather than characterizing the court's role in terms of "gate keeping"—which seems to involve abstract "background" questions about the justification of private property—the court's job is better described as "guardian of the procedures." Ultimately, I think, Ely endorses a more activist agenda for the court than that justified here.

32. Who wrote the majority decision in *Roe v. Wade*.

33. For the charge of "fetishism" see Perry, *Morality, Politics and the Law*, 110.

34. Ewin, *Liberty, Community and Justice*, 42–43. This also suggests that the place of the ideal of autonomy in liberal theory is rather more complex than is usually thought.

35. Thus the umpire account of political obligation can meet what A. John Simmons calls the "particularity" requirement: Citizens are bound to the laws of *their own* state. A citizen is bound to a law because it is the decision given by an umpiring procedure to which he is justifiably subject; the calls of other umpires do not bind him. See Simmons, *Moral Principles and Political Obligations*, 31; L. Green, *Authority of the State*, 227–28. See Appendix A below.

36. See Perry, *Morality, Politics and Law*, 110; L. Green, *Authority of the State*, 228 ff.

37. Ewin, *Liberty, Community and Justice*, 113–14. See also his *Virtues and Rights*, 32, 49–50, chap. 8.

38. Cf. Ewin, *Virtues and Rights*, 166. Of course, citizen Alf may well conclude that for reasons such as civility, keeping the peace, or upholding a nearly just institution, he will comply even though he is not morally obligated. See sec. 16.4.

39. See Holmes, "Gag Rules or the Politics of Omission." See sec. 10.2.2 above.

40. Just how fanciful it is depends on one's theory of how to attribute responsibility for many acts, each of which produces a very small effect, but the totality of which produces great evil. See, e.g., Parfit's proposal in *Reasons and Persons*, 75–78.

41. *Declaration of Independence*, emphasis added. Although a similar passage occurs in Locke's *Second Treatise* (sec. 225), Locke appears more concerned with explaining when revolutions occur than when revolution is a right and duty.

42. May, "A Set of Independent Necessary and Sufficient Conditions for Simple Majority Decisions."

CHAPTER 17

1. Macedo, *Liberal Virtues*, 78.
2. Locke, *Second Treatise*, 241.

APPENDIX

1. Hobhouse, *Liberalism*, 57.
2. Benn, "Private and Public Morality," 164–65.

3. Hobhouse, *Liberalism*, 57.
4. von Mises, *Liberalism in the Classical Tradition*, 109.
5. See Wight, "Western Values in International Society." See also Feuchtwanger, *Gladstone*, 161; Doyle, "Kant, Liberal Legacies and Foreign Affairs," 332.
6. Beitz, *Political Theory and International Relations*, 71, 1833.
7. Beitz, "Bounded Morality," 408.
8. See Hehir, "The Ethics of Intervention," 127 ff. Emphasis added.
9. Grotius, *De Juri Belli ac Pacis*, Bk. II, chap. xxv, 8.
10. A. C. Campbell's translation of Grotius, *The Law of War and Peace*, Book II, chap. xxv, 8.
11. Kant, *Metaphysical Elements of Justice*, 67 (sec. 44).
12. See Kant, "On the Common Saying: 'This May Be True in Theory, but It Does Not Apply in Practice'," 90. See also P. Riley, *Kant's Political Philosophy*, 115.
13. See Hayek, *The Mirage of Social Justice*, 144 ff.

BIBLIOGRAPHY

Ackerman, Bruce A. *Social Justice in the Liberal State.* New Haven, CT: Yale University Press, 1980.
———. *We The People.* Vol. 2, *Foundations.* Cambridge, MA: Belknap Press of Harvard University Press, 1991.
———. "What Is Neutral About Neutrality?" *Ethics* 93 (January 1983): 372–90.
———. "Why Dialogue?" *Journal of Philosophy* 86 (January 1989): 5–22.
Alexander, Larry. "Liberalism, Religion, and the Unity of Epistemology." *San Diego Law Review* 30 (Fall 1993): 763–97.
Alston, William P. "Self-Warrant: A Neglected Form of Privileged Access." *American Philosophical Quarterly* 13 (October 1976): 257–72.
———. "Two Types of Foundationalism." *Journal of Philosophy* 73 (April 1976): 165–86.
Anshutz, R. P. *The Philosophy of John Stuart Mill.* Oxford: Clarendon Press, 1953.
Aristotle. *Nicomachean Ethics.* Trans. Sir David Ross. London: Oxford University Press, 1925.
Arkes, Hadley. *First Things: An Inquiry into the First Principles of Morals and Justice.* Princeton, NJ: Princeton University Press, 1986.
Armstrong, David. *Belief, Truth and Knowledge.* Cambridge: Cambridge University Press, 1973.
Arneson, Richard J. "Democratic Rights at National and Workplace Levels." In David Copp, Jean Hampton, and John E. Roemer, eds., *The Idea of Democracy,* 118–48. Cambridge: Cambridge University Press, 1993.
———. "Neutrality and Utility." *Canadian Journal of Philosophy* 20 (June 1990): 215–40.
Arrow, Kenneth. *Social Choice and Individual Values.* 2d ed. New Haven, CT: Yale University Press, 1963.
Audi, Robert. "The Place of Religious Argument in a Free Society." *San Diego Law Review* 30 (Fall 1993): 677–702.
———. *The Structure of Justification.* Cambridge: Cambridge University Press, 1993.
Austen-Smith, David, and Jeffrey Banks, "Monotonicity in Electoral Systems." *American Political Science Review* 85 (June 1991): 531–37.
Baier, Kurt. *The Moral Point of View: A Rational Basis of Ethics.* Abr. ed. New York: Random House, 1965.
Barber, Benjamin. *Strong Democracy: Participatory Politics for a New Age.* Berkeley: University of California Press, 1984.
Barry, Brian. "Is Democracy Special?" In Peter Laslett and James Fishkin, eds., *Philosophy, Politics and Society,* 5th ser., 155–96. Oxford: Basil Blackwell, 1979.
———. *Political Argument.* London: Routledge and Kegan Paul, 1965.
———. "The Public Interest." In Anthony Quinton, ed., *Political Philosophy,* 112–26. New York: Oxford University Press, 1967.

Barry, Norman. *On Classical Liberalism and Libertarianism.* New York: St. Martin's Press, 1987.

Beiner, Ronald. *Political Judgment.* London: Methuen, 1983.

Beitz, Charles. "Bounded Morality: Justice and the State in World Politics." *International Organization* 33 (1979): 405–27.

———. *Political Equality.* Princeton, NJ: Princeton University Press, 1989.

———. *Political Theory and International RElations.* Princeton, NJ: Princeton University Press, 1979.

Benhabib, Seyla. "Liberal Dialogue Versus a Critical Theory of Discursive Legitimation." In Nancy Rosenblum, ed., *Liberalism and the Moral Life,* 143–56. Cambridge, MA: Harvard University Press, 1989.

Benn, Stanley I. "Human Rights—For Whom and for What?" In Eugene Kamenka and Alice Erh-Soon Tay, eds., *Human Rights,* 57–73. New York: St. Martin's Press, 1978.

———. "Individuality, Autonomy and Community." In Eugene Kamenka, ed., *Community as a Social Ideal,* 42–62. London: Edward Arnold, 1982.

———. *A Theory of Freedom.* Cambridge: Cambridge University Press, 1988.

Benn, S. I., and G. F. Gaus. "The Liberal Conception of the Public and the Private." In S. I. Benn and G. F. Gaus, eds., *Public and Private in Social Life,* 31–65. New York: St. Martin's Press, 1983.

———. "Practical Rationality and Commitment." *American Philosophical Quarterly* 23 (July 1986): 255–66.

———. "Public and Private: Concepts and Action." In S.I. Benn and G.F. Gaus, eds., *Public and Private in Social Life,* 3–27. New York: St. Martin's Press, 1983.

Benn, S. I., and R. S. Peters. *Social Principles and the Democratic State.* London: George Allen & Unwin, 1959.

Bentham, Jeremy. *Manual of Political Economy.* In W. Stark, ed., *Jeremy Bentham's Economic Writings,* vol. 1. London: Allen and Unwin, 1952.

Bentley, Arthur F. *The Process of Government.* Bloomington, IN: Principia Press, 1949.

Beran, Harry. *The Consent Theory of Political Obligation.* London: Croom Helm, 1987.

Berlin, Isaiah. "Equality as an Ideal." In Frederick A. Olafson, ed., *Justice and Social Policy,* 128–50. Englewood Cliffs, NJ: Prentice-Hall, 1961.

———. "Two Concepts of Liberty." In Isaiah Berlin, *Four Essays on Liberty,* 118–72. Oxford: Oxford University Press, 1969.

Bernholz, Peter, and Malte Faber. "Refections on a Normative Economic Theory of Law." In James D. Gwartney and Richard E. Wagner, eds., 229–49. *Public Choice and Constitutional Economics.* Greenwich, CT: JAI Press, 1988.

Berry, Christopher J. *The Idea of a Democratic Community.* New York: St. Martin's Press, 1989.

Bickel, Alexander M. *The Least Dangerous Branch: The Supreme Court at the Bar of Politics,* 2d ed. New Haven, CT: Yale University Press, 1986.

Bittner, Rüdiger. *What Reason Demands.* Trans. Theodore Talbot. Cambridge: Cambridge University Press, 1989.

Blanshard, Brand. *The Nature of Thought.* London: George Allen and Unwin, 1939.

342 *Bibliography*

Bonjour, Laurence. *The Structure of Empirical Knowledge.* Cambridge, MA: Harvard University Press, 1985.

Bordes, Georges, and Nicolaus Tideman. "Independence of Irrelevant Alternatives in the Theory of Voting." *Theory and Decision* 30 (1991): 163–83.

Bork, Robert H. "Neutral Principles and Some First Amendment Problems." *Indiana Law Journal* 47 (Fall 1971): 1–35.

———. *The Tempting of America: The Political Seduction of the Law.* New York: Simon & Schuster, 1990.

Bosanquet, Bernard. *The Value and Destiny of the Individual.* London: Macmillan, 1913.

Braine, Martin D.S. "On the Relation Between the Natural Logic of Reasoning and Standard Logic." *Psychological Review* 85 (January 1978): 1–21.

Braine, Martin, and B. Rumain. "Development of Comprehension of 'or': Evidence for a Sequence of Competencies." *Journal of Experimental Child Psychology* 31 (1981): 46–70.

Brams, Steven J., and Peter C. Fishburn. "Approval Voting." *American Political Science Review* 72 (September 1978): 831–47.

Brandt, Richard B. "An Emotional Theory of the Judgment of Moral Worth." *Ethics* 52 (October 1941): 41–79.

———. "The Emotive Theory of Ethics." *Philosophical Review* 59 (July 1950): 305–18.

———. "Stevenson's Defense of the Emotive Theory." *Philosophical Review* 59 (October 1950): 535–40.

———. *A Theory of the Good and the Right.* Oxford: Clarendon Press, 1979.

Brennan, Geoffrey, and James M. Buchanan. *The Reason of Rules.* Cambridge: Cambridge University Press, 1985.

Brennan, Geoffrey, and Loren E. Lomasky. *Democracy and Decision: The Pure Theory of Electoral Preference.* Cambridge: Cambridge University Press, 1993.

———. "Large Numbers, Small Costs: The Uneasy Foundation of Democratic Rule." In Geoffrey Brennan and Loren E. Lomasky, eds., *Politics and Process: New Essays in Democratic Thought,* 42–59. Cambridge: Cambridge University Press, 1989.

Brink, David O. "Common Sense and First Principles in Sidgwick's *Methods.*" *Social Philosophy & Policy* 11 (Winter 1994): 179–201

———. *Moral Realism and the Foundations of Ethics.* Cambridge: Cambridge University Press, 1989.

Buchanan, James. *The Limits of Liberty: Between Anarchy and Leviathan.* Chicago: University of Chicago Press, 1975.

Buckle, Stephen. *Natural Law and the Theory of Property: Grotius to Hume.* Oxford: Clarendon Press, 1991.

Burnheim, John. *Is Democracy Possible?: An Alternative to Electoral Politics.* Cambridge: Polity Press, 1985.

Cacoullos, Ann R. *Thomas Hill Green: Philosopher of Rights.* New York: Twayne, 1974.

Chapman, John. "Justice, Freedom and Property." In J. Roland Pennock and John W. Chapman, eds., NOMOS XXII: *Property,* 289–324. New York: New York University Press, 1980.

————. "Political Theory: Logical Structures and Enduring Types." In *L'idée de philosophie politique*, 57–96. Paris: Presses Universitaires de France, 1965.

Cherniak, Christopher. *Minimal Rationality*. Cambridge, MA: MIT Press, 1986.

Chisholm, Roderick M. "The Foundation of Empirical Statements." In Michael D. Roth and Leon Galis, eds., *Knowing: Essays in the Analysis of Knowledge*, 39–53. Lanham, MD: University Press of America, 1984.

————. *The Foundations of Knowing*. Minneapolis: University of Minnesota Press, 1982.

Christiano, Thomas. "Political Equality." In John W. Chapman and Alan Wertheimer, eds., *NOMOS XXXIII Majorities and Minorities*, 151–83. New York: New York University Press, 1990.

————. "Social Choice and Democracy." In David Copp, Jean Hampton, and John E. Roemer, eds., *The Idea of Democracy*, 173–95. Cambridge: Cambridge University Press, 1993.

Cohen, Joshua. "An Epistemic Conception of Democracy." *Ethics* 97 (October 1986): 26–38.

————. "Moral Pluralism and Political Consensus." In David Copp, Jean Hampton, and John E. Roemer, eds., *The Idea of Democracy*, 270–91. Cambridge: Cambridge University Press, 1993.

Cohen, Joshua, and Joel Rogers. *On Democracy: Toward a Transformation of American Society*. Harmondsworth: Penguin, 1983.

Coleman, Jules. "Democracy and Social Choice." In Jules Coleman, *Markets, Morals and the Law*, 290–310. Cambridge: Cambridge University Press, 1988.

Coleman, Jules, and John Ferejohn. "Democracy and Social Choice." *Ethics* 97 (October 1986): 6–25.

Constant, Benjamin. "The Liberty of the Ancients Compared with That of the Moderns." In *Benjamin Constant: Political Writings*. Ed. and trans. Biancamaria Fontana, 308–28. Cambridge: Cambridge University Press, 1988.

Converse, Philip E. "The Nature of Belief Systems in Mass Publics." In David E. Apter, ed., *Ideology and Discontent*, 206–61. Glencoe: The Free Press, 1964.

Converse, Philip E., and Gregory B. Markus, "Plus ça change . . . : The New CPS Election Study Panel." *American Political Science Review* 73 (March 1979): 32–49.

Cooper, David E. "Moral Relativism." In Peter A. French, Theodore E. Uehling, Jr., and Howard K. Wettstein, eds., *Midwest Studies in Philosophy*. Vol. 3, *Studies in Ethical Theory*, 97–108. Morris, MN: University of Minnesota, Morris, 1978.

Cornman, James W. "Foundational Versus Nonfoundational Theories of Empirical Justification," In George S. Pappas and Marshall Swain, eds., *Essays on Knowledge and Justification*, 229–52. Ithaca, NY: Cornell University Press, 1978.

Craven, John. *Social Choice: A Framework for Collective Decisions and Individual Judgments*. Cambridge: Cambridge University Press, 1992.

Crosskey, William Winslow, and William Jeffrey, Jr. *Politics and the Constitution in the History of the United States*. Chicago: University of Chicago Press, 1980.

Crossley, David. "Self-Conscious Agency and the Eternal Consciousness: Ultimate

Reality in Thomas Hill Green." *Ultimate Meaning and Reality* 13 (1990): 3–20.

D'Agostino, F. B. "Adjudication as an Epistemological Concept." *Synthese* 79 (1989): 21–39.

———. "Ethical Pluralism and the Role of Opposition in Democratic Politics." *Monist* 73 (1990): 437–63.

———. The Ethos of Games." *Journal of the Philosophy of Sport* 8 (1981): 7–18.

———. *Free Public Reason*. New York: Oxford University Press, forthcoming.

———. "The Idea and the Ideal of Public Justification." *Social Theory and Practice* 18 (Summer 1992): 143–64.

———. "Relativism and Reflective Equilibrium." *Monist* 71 (1988): 420–36.

———. "Some Modes of Public Justification." *Australasian Journal of Philosophy* 69 (December 1991): 390–414.

———. "Transcendence and Conversation: Two Conceptions of Objectivity." *American Philosophical Quarterly* 30 (1993): 87–108.

Dahl, Robert. *Democracy and Its Critics*. New Haven, CT: Yale University Press, 1989.

———. *Dilemmas of Pluralist Democracy: Autonomy vs. Control*. New Haven, CT: Yale University Press, 1982.

———. *A Preface to Democratic Theory*. Chicago: University of Chicago Press, 1956.

———. *A Preface to Economic Democracy*. Berkeley: University of California Press, 1985.

Daniels, Norman. "Wide Reflective Equilibrium and Theory Acceptance in Ethics." *Journal of Philosophy* 76 (1979): 256–82.

Darwall, Stephen L. *Impartial Reason*. Ithaca, NY: Cornell University Press, 1983.

Dauer, Francis W. "Warrant, Coherence and Evaluative Certainties." *Noûs* 14 (November 1980): 499–515.

Davidson, Donald. "A Coherence Theory of Truth and Knowledge." In Alan Malachowski, ed., *Reading Rorty*, 120–38. Oxford: Basil Blackwell, 1990.

———. "On the Very Idea of a Conceptual Scheme." In Donald Davidson, *Inquiries into Truth and Interpretation*, 183–98. Oxford: Oxford University Press, 1984.

———. "Paradoxes of Irrationality." In Paul K. Moser, ed., *Rationality in Action: Contemporary Approaches*, 449–64. Cambridge: Cambridge University Press, 1990.

———. "Radical Interpretation." In Donald Davidson, *Inquiries into Truth and Interpretation*, 125–39. Oxford: Clarendon Press, 1984.

Dawes, Robyn. "The Robust Beauty of Improper Linear Models in Decision Making." In Daniel Kahneman, Paul Slovic, and Amos Tversky, eds., *Judgments Under Uncertainty: Heuristics and Biases*, 391–407. Cambridge: Cambridge University Press, 1982.

de Jasay, Anthony. *Social Contract, Free Ride: A Study of the Public Goods Problem*. Oxford: Clarendon Press, 1989.

Deigh, John. "Cognitivism in the Theory of Emotions." *Ethics* 104 (July 1994): 824–54.

"Democratic Theory and the Public Interest: Condorcet and Rousseau Revisited." Symposium with contributions by Jeremy Waldron, David Estlund, Bernard Grofman and Scot L. Feld. *American Political Science Review* 83 (December 1989): 1317–40.

Dennett, Daniel C. *The Intentional Stance.* Cambridge, MA: MIT Press, 1987.

DePaul, Michael R. "Reflective Equilibrium and Foundationalism." *American Philosophical Quarterly* 23 (January 1986): 59–69.

Dewey, John. *Intelligence in the Modern World: John Dewey's Philosophy.* Ed. Joseph Ranter. New York: Modern Library, 1939.

Dicey, A. V. *Introduction to the Study of the Law of the Constitution* 9th ed. London: Macmillan, 1948.

Dorn, James A. "Madison's Constitutional Political Economy: Principles for a Liberal Order." *Constitutional Political Economy* 2 (Spring/Summer 1991): 163–86.

———. "Public Choice and the Constitution: A Madisonian Perspective." In James D. Gwartney and Richard E. Wagner, eds., *Public Choice and Constitutional Economics,* 57–102. Greenwich, CT: JAI Press, 1988.

Downs, Anthony. *An Economic Theory of Democracy.* New York: Harper & Row, 1957.

Doyle, Arthur Conan. *A Study in Scarlet.* In Arthur Conan Doyle, *The Complete Sherlock Holmes,* 15–86. New York: Doubleday, 1930.

Doyle, Michael. "Kant, Liberal Legacies, and Foreign Affairs (Parts 1 and 2)." *Philosophy & Public Affairs,* 12 (1983): 205–35, 325–353.

Dunleavy, Patrick, and Brenden O'Leary. *Theories of the State: The Politics of Liberal Democracy.* London: Macmillan Educational, 1987.

Dworkin, Ronald. *Law's Empire.* Cambridge, MA: Belknap Press of Harvard University Press, 1986.

———. "Neutrality, Equality and Liberalism." In Douglas MacLean and Claudia Mills, eds., *Liberalism Reconsidered,* 1–11. Totowa, NJ: Rowman & Allenheld, 1983.

———. "Political Judges and the Rule of Law." In Ronald Dworkin, *A Matter of Principle,* 9–32. Cambridge, MA: Harvard University Press, 1985.

———. *Taking Rights Seriously.* Cambridge, MA: Harvard University Press, 1978.

Ellis, Brian. "Epistemic Foundations of Logic." *Journal of Philosophic Logic* 5 (1975): 187–204.

———. *Rational Belief Systems.* Totowa, NJ: Rowman and Littlefield, 1979.

Elster, Jon, "Arguments for Constitutional Choice." In Jon Elster and Rune Slagstad, eds., *Constitutionalism and Democracy,* 303–23. Cambridge: Cambridge University Press, 1988.

———. "Belief, Bias and Ideology." In Martin Hollis and Steven Lukes, eds., *Rationality and Relativism,* 123–48. Cambridge, MA: MIT Press, 1982.

———. "The Market and the Forum: Three Varieties of Political Theory." In Jon Elster and Aanund Hylland, eds., *Foundations of Social Choice Theory,* 103–32. Cambridge: Cambridge University Press, 1986.

———. *Solomonic Judgments: Studies in the Limits of Rationality.* Cambridge: Cambridge University Press, 1989.

Ely, John Hart. *Democracy and Distrust: A Theory of Judicial Review.* Cambridge, MA.: Harvard University Press, 1980.

Estlund, David. "Making Truth Safe for Democracy." In David Copp, Jean

Hampton, and John E. Roemer, eds., *The Idea of Democracy*, 71–100. Cambridge: Cambridge University Press, 1993.

Ewin, R. E. *Liberty, Community and Justice*. Totowa, NJ: Rowman and Littlefield, 1987.

———. *Virtues and Rights: The Moral Philosophy of Thomas Hobbes*. Boulder, CO: Westview Press, 1991.

Ewing, A. C. *Ethics*. New York: Free Press, 1953.

Feinberg, Joel. "Duties, Rights and Claims." In Joel Feinberg, *Rights, Justice and the Bounds of Liberty*, 131–42. Princeton, NJ: Princeton University Press, 1980.

———. *Harm to Others*. New York: Oxford University Press, 1984.

———. "Rawls and Intuitionism." In Norman Daniels, ed., *Reading Rawls: Critical Studies of* A Theory of Justice, 108–124. Oxford: Basil Blackwell, 1975.

———. *Social Philosophy*. Englewood Cliffs, NJ: Prentice-Hall, 1973.

Fetzer, James H. "The Argument for Mental Models is Unsound." *Behavioral and Brain Sciences* 16 (1993): 347–48.

———. *Scientific Knowledge*. Dordrecht: Reidel, 1981.

Feuchtwanger, E. J. *Gladstone*. New York: St. Martin's Press, 1975.

Field, Hartry. "Mental Representations." *Erkenntnis* 13 (1978): 9–61.

Findley, J. N. *Meinong's Theory of Objects and Values*. 2d ed. Oxford: Clarendon Press, 1963.

Fischhoff, Baruch. "For Those Condemned to Study the Past: Heuristics and the Bias of Hindsight." In Daniel Kahneman, Paul Slovic, and Amos Tversky, eds., *Judgments Under Uncertainty: Heuristics and Biases*, 335–51. Cambridge: Cambridge University Press, 1982.

Fishkin, James. *Democracy and Deliberation*. New Haven, CT: Yale University Press, 1991.

———. *Tyranny and Legitimacy,: A Critique of Political Theories*. Baltimore, MD: Johns Hopkins University Press, 1979.

Flathman, Richard E. "Equality and Generalization: A Formal Analysis." In J. Roland Pennock and John W. Chapman, eds., *NOMOS IX: Equality*, 38–60. New York: Atherton Press, 1967.

———. *The Practice of Rights*. Cambridge: Cambridge University Press, 1976.

Foley, Richard. *The Theory of Epistemic Rationality*. Cambridge, MA: Harvard University Press, 1987.

Foron, Gideon, and Richard Kronick. "Single Transferrable Vote: An Example of a Perverse Social Choice Function." *American Political Science Review* 21 (May 1977): 303–11.

Forrest, Peter. *The Dynamics of Belief: A Normative Logic*. Oxford: Basil Blackwell, 1986.

Franco, Paul. *The Political Philosophy of Michael Oakeshott*. New Haven, CT: Yale University Press, 1990.

Frankena, William K. "The Concept of Social Justice." In R.B. Brandt, ed., *Social Justice*, 1–29. Englewood Cliffs, NJ: Prentice-Hall, 1962.

Freeden, Michael. *The New Liberalism: An Ideology of Social Reform*. Oxford: Clarendon Press, 1978.

Freud, Sigmund. *The Ego and the Id*. Trans. Joan Riviere, ed. James Strachey. New York: W.W. Norton, 1962.

———. "Inhibitions, Symptoms and Anxiety." In *On Psychopathology*. Ed. Angela Richards, 227–315. Harmondsworth: Penguin, 1979.

Fried, Charles. *An Anatomy of Values*. Cambridge, MA: Harvard University Press, 1970.

———. "Privacy." In Ferdinand D. Schoeman, ed., *Philosophical Dimensions of Privacy*, 203–222. Cambridge: Cambridge University Press, 1984.

Friedman, Marilyn. "The Impracticality of Impartiality." *Journal of Philosophy* 96 (1989): 645–56.

Friedman, Richard B. "On the Concept of Authority in Political Philosophy." In Richard E. Flathman, ed., *Concepts in Social and Political Philosophy*, 121–46 New York: Macmillan, 1973.

Fuller, Lon. *The Morality of Law*. Rev. ed. New Haven, CT: Yale University Press, 1964.

Galston, William A. *Justice and the Human Good*. Chicago: University of Chicago Press, 1980.

———. *Liberal Purposes: Goods, Virtues and Diversity in the Liberal State*. Cambridge: Cambridge University Press, 1991.

Gärdenfors, Peter. *Knowledge in Flux: Modeling the Dynamics of Epistemic States*. Cambridge, MA: MIT Press, 1988.

———. "Positionalist Voting Functions." *Theory and Decision* 4 (1973): 1–24.

Garforth, F. W. *Educative Democracy: John Stuart Mill on Education and Society*. Oxford: Oxford University Press, 1980.

Gaus, Gerald F. "A Contractual Justification of Redistributive Capitalism." In John W. Chapman and J. Roland Pennock, eds., *NOMOS XXXI: Markets and Justice*, 89–121. New York: New York University Press, 1989.

———. "Does Compensation Restore Equality?" In John W. Chapman, ed., *NOMOS XXXIII: Compensatory Justice*, 45–81. New York: New York University Press, 1991.

———. "Mill's Theory of Moral Rules." *Australasian Journal of Philosophy* 57 (September 1980): 265–79.

———. *The Modern Liberal Theory of Man*. New York: St. Martin's Press, 1983.

———. "Practical Reason and Moral Persons." *Ethics* 100 (October 1988): 127–48.

———. "Property, Rights and Freedom." *Social Philosophy & Policy* 11 (Summer 1994): 209–40.

———"Public Justification and Democratic Adjudication." *Constitutional Political Economy*, vol. 2 (1991): 251–81.

———. "Public and Private Interests in Liberal Political Economy, Old and New." In S. I. Benn and G. F. Gaus, eds., *Public and Private in Social Life*, 183–222. New York: St. Martin's Press, 1983.

———. "Public Reason and the Rule of Law." In Ian Shapiro, ed., *NOMOS XXXVI: The Rule of Law*, 328–63. New York: New York University Press, 1994.

———. "The Rational, the Reasonable and Justification." *Journal of Political Philosophy*, 3(September 1995): 232–56.

———. "Subjective Value and Justificatory Political Theory." In J. Roland Pennock and John W. Chapman, eds., *NOMOS XXVIII: Justification*, 241–69. New York: New York University Press, 1986.

———. "Green, Bosanquet and the Philosophy of Coherence." In C. L. Ten, ed.,

The Routledge History of Philosophy. Vol. 7, The Nineteenth Century, 408–36. London: Routledge, 1994.

———. Value and Justification: The Foundations of Liberal Theory. Cambridge: Cambridge University Press, 1990.

Gaus, Gerald F., and Loren E. Lomasky. "Are Property Rights Problematic?" Monist 73 (October 1991): 483–503.

Gauthier, David. Morals by Agreement. Oxford: Clarendon Press, 1986.

Gert, Bernard. Morality: A New Justification of the Moral Rules. New York: Oxford University Press, 1988.

Gibbard, Alan. "Manipulation of Voting Schemes: A General Result." Econometrica 41 (July 1973): 587–601.

———. Wise Choices, Apt Feelings: A Theory of Normative Judgment. Cambridge, MA: Harvard University Press, 1990.

Golding, Martin. "Towards a Theory of Human Rights." Monist 52 (1968): 540–48.

Goldman, Alan H. Empirical Knowledge. Berkeley: University of California Press, 1988.

Goldman, Alvin I. "What Is Justified Belief?" In Paul K. Moser, ed., Empirical Knowledge: Readings in Contemporary Epistemology, 171–92. Totowa, NJ: Rowman & Littlefield, 1986.

Goodin, Robert E. "Laundering Preferences." In Jon Elster and Aanund Hylland, eds., Foundations of Social Choice Theory, 74–101. Cambridge: Cambridge University Press, 1986.

Goodman, Nelson. Fact, Fiction and Forecast 4th ed. Cambridge, MA: Harvard University Press, 1983.

———. "Sense and Certainty." Philosophical Review 61 (April 1952): 160–68.

Goodwin, Barbara. Justice by Lottery. Chicago: University of Chicago Press, 1992.

Grandy, R. "Reference, Meaning and Belief." Journal of Philosophy 70 (1973): 439–52.

Gray, John. "Contractarian Method, Private Property and the Market Economy." In John Gray, Liberalisms, 161–98. London: Routledge, 1989.

———. Liberalism. Milton Keynes: Open University Press, 1986.

Green, Leslie. The Authority of the State. Oxford: Clarendon Press, 1990.

Green, T. H. Lectures on the Principles of Political Obligation and Other Writings. Ed. Paul Harris and John Morrow. Cambridge: Cambridge University Press, 1986.

———. Prolegomena to Ethics. Ed. A. C. Bradley. Oxford: Clarendon Press, 1890.

Greenawalt, Kent. "Grounds for Political Judgment: The Status of Personal Experience and the Autonomy and Generality of Principles of Restraint." San Diego Law Review 30 (Fall 1993): 647–75.

———. Religious Convictions and Political Choice. New York: Oxford University Press, 1988.

Grofman, Bernard, and Scott L. Feld. "Rousseau's General Will: A Condorcetian Perspective." American Political Science Review 82 (June 1988): 567–76.

Grotius, Hugo. De Juri Belli ac Pacis. Trans. Francis W. Kelsey. London: Wiley and Sons, 1964.

———. *The Law of War and Peace*. Trans. A. C. Campbell. Westport: Hyperion Press, 1979.

Gutmann, Amy. "How Liberal Is Democracy?" In Douglas MacLean and Claudia Mills, eds., *Liberalism Reconsidered*, 25–50. Totowa, NJ: Rowman and Allenheld, 1983.

———. *Liberal Equality*. Cambridge: Cambridge University Press, 1980.

Gutmann, Amy, and Dennis Thompson. "Moral Conflict and Political Consensus." *Ethics* 101 (October 1990): 64–88.

Haack, Susan. "Theories of Knowledge: An Analytic Framework." *Proceedings of the Aristotelian Society* 83 (1982–1983): 143–47.

Habermas, Jürgen. *Communication and the Evolution of Society*. Trans. Thomas McCarthy. London: Heinemann, 1976.

———. *Knowledge and Human Interests*. Trans. Jeremy J. Shapiro. Boston: Beacon Press, 1971.

———. *Moral Consciousness and Communicative Action*. Trans. Christian Lenhardt and Shierry Weber Nicolsen. Cambridge, MA: MIT Press, 1991.

———. *The Philosophical Discourse of Modernity*. Trans. Frederick Lawrence. Cambridge, MA: MIT Press, 1987.

———. *The Theory of Communicative Action*. Trans. Thomas McCarthy. Boston: Beacon Press, 1984.

Hampton, Jean. *Hobbes and the Social Contract Tradition*. Cambridge: Cambridge University Press, 1986.

Hansson, Bengt. "The Independence Condition in the Theory of Social Choice." *Theory and Decision* 4 (1973): 25–49.

Hardin, Russell. *Morality Within The Limits of Reason*. Chicago: University of Chicago Press, 1988.

———. "Public Choice Versus Democracy." In David Copp, Jean Hampton, and John E. Roemer, eds., *The Idea of Democracy*, 157–72. Cambridge: Cambridge University Press, 1993.

Hare, R. M. "Rawls' Theory of Justice." In Norman Daniels, ed., *Reading Rawls: Critical Studies of* A Theory of Justice, 81–107. Oxford: Basil Blackwell, 1975.

Harman, Gilbert. *Change in View: Principles of Reasoning*. Cambridge, MA: MIT Press, 1986.

———. "Human Flourishing, Ethics and Liberty." *Philosophy & Public Affairs* 12 (Fall 1983): 307–22.

Hart, H. L. A. *The Concept of Law*. Oxford: Clarendon Press, 1961.

Hayek, F. A. *The Constitution of Liberty*. London: Routledge & Kegan Paul, 1960.

———. *The Mirage of Social Justice*. Chicago: University of Chicago Press, 1976.

———. *The Political Order of a Free People*. Chicago: University of Chicago Press, 1979.

———. "Liberalism." In F. A. Hayek, *New Studies in Philosophy, Politics, Economics and the History of Ideas*, 119–61. London: Routledge & Kegan Paul, 1978.

Heir, J. Bryan. "The Ethics of Intervention: Two Normative Traditions." In Peter G. Brown and Douglas MacLean, eds., *Human Rights and U.S. Foreign Policy*, 121–39. Lexington, MA: Lexington Books, 1979.

Herzog, Don. *Without Foundations: Justification in Political Theory.* Ithaca, NY: Cornell University Press, 1985.

Hirschman, Albert O. *The Passions and the Interests.* Princeton, NJ: Princeton University Press, 1977.

Hobbes, Thomas. *Leviathan.* Ed. Michael Oakeshott. Oxford: Basil Blackwell, 1948.

Hobhouse, L. T. *Liberalism.* New York: Oxford University Press, 1964.

Hogarth, Robin M. *Judgment and Choice: The Psychology of Decision.* New York: John Wiley & Sons, 1980.

Hohfeld, Wesley. "Some Fundamental Legal Conceptions As Applied in Judicial Reasoning." *Yale Law Review* 23 (1913): 16–59.

Holborow, Les. "Benn, Mackie, and Basic Rights." *Australasian Journal of Philosophy* 63 (March 1985): 11–25.

Holcombe, Randall G. "Constitutions as Constraints: A Case Study of Three American Constitutions." *Constitutional Political Economy* 2 (Fall 1991): 303–28.

Hollis, Martin. "The Limits of Irrationality." In Bryan Wilson, ed., *Rationality,* 214–20. Oxford: Basil Blackwell, 1970.

———. "Reason and Ritual." In Bryan Wilson, ed., *Rationality,* 221–39. Oxford: Basil Blackwell, 1970.

———. "The Social Destruction of Reality." In Martin Hollis and Steven Lukes, eds., *Rationality and Relativism,* 67–86. Cambridge, MA: MIT Press, 1982.

Holmes, Stephen. "Gag Rules or the Politics of Omission." In Jon Elster and Rune Slagstad, eds., *Constitutionalism and Democracy,* 19–58. Cambridge: Cambridge University Press, 1988.

———. "Precommitment and the Paradox of Democracy." In John Elster and Rune Slagstad, eds., *Constitutionalism and Democracy,* 195–240. Cambridge: Cambridge University Press, 1988.

Hookway, Christopher. "Indeterminacy and Interpretation." In Christopher Hookway and Philip Pettit, eds., *Action and Interpretation,* 17–41. Cambridge: Cambridge University Press, 1978.

Hudson, W. D. *Ethical Intuitionism.* London: Macmillan, 1967.

Hume, David. "Of the Independency of Parliament." In David Hume, *Essays Moral, Political and Literary,* 40–47. Oxford: Oxford University Press, 1963.

Hurley, Susan. *Natural Reasons: Personality and Polity.* New York: Oxford University Press, 1989.

Jarvie, I. C., and Joseph Agassi. "The Problem of the Rationality of Magic." In Bryan Wilson, ed., *Rationality,* 172–93. Oxford: Basil Blackwell, 1970.

Johnson-Laird, P. N. "Reasoning Without Logic." In Terry Myers, Keith Brown, and Brenden McGonigle, eds., *Reasoning and Discourse Processes,* 13–49. New York: Academic Press, 1986.

Jones, Peter. "The Ideal of the Neutral State." In Robert E. Goodin and Andrew Reeve, eds., *Liberal Neutrality,* 9–38. London: Routledge & Kegan Paul, 1989.

Kagan, Jerome. *The Nature of the Child.* New York: Basic Books, 1984.

Kahneman, Daniel, and Amos Tversky. "On the Psychology of Prediction." In Daniel Kahneman, Paul Slovic, and Amos Tversky, eds., *Judgments Under*

Uncertainty: Heuristics and Biases, 48–68. Cambridge: Cambridge University Press, 1982.

Kant, Immanuel. *Critique of Judgment*. Trans. Werner S. Pluhar. Indianapolis: Hackett, 1987.

———. *The Metaphysical Elements of Justice*. Trans. John Ladd. Indianapolis: Bobbs-Merrill, 1965.

———. "On the Common Saying: 'This May be True in Theory, But it Does Not Apply in Practice.' " In Hans Reiss, ed., *Kant's Political Writings*, Trans. H. B. Nisbett. 61–92. Cambridge: Cambridge University Press, 1977.

———. "What Is Enlightenment?" In Hans Reiss, ed., *Kant's Political Writings*. Trans. H.B. Nisbett, 54–60. Cambridge: Cambridge University Press, 1970.

Karni, Edi, and David Schmeidler. "Independence of Nonfeasible Alternatives, and Independence of Nonoptimal Alternatives." *Journal of Economic Theory* 12 (1976): 488–93.

Kavka, Gregory S. *Hobbesian Moral and Political Theory*. Princeton, NJ: Princeton University Press, 1986.

Kelsen, Hans. *The Pure Theory of Law*. Trans. Max Knight. Berkeley: University of California Press, 1967.

King, Preston. *Toleration*. London: Allen and Unwin, 1976.

Kingdon, John W. "Politicians, Self-Interest and Ideas." In George E. Marcus and Russell L. Hanson, eds., *Reconsidering the Democratic Public*, 73–89. University Park, PA: Pennsylvania State University Press, 1993.

Kleinig, John. *Paternalism*. Totowa, NJ: Rowman & Allenheld, 1983.

Koerner, Kirk. *Liberalism and Its Critics*. London: Croom-Helm, 1985.

Kohlberg, Lawrence. *The Philosophy of Moral Development: Moral Stages and the Idea of Justice*. New York: Harper & Row, 1981.

Kuflik, Arthur. "Majority Rule Procedure." In J. Roland Pennock and John W. Chapman, eds., *NOMOS XVIII: Due Process*, 296–332. New York: New York University Press, 1977.

Kuhn, Deanna. *The Skills of Argument*. Cambridge: Cambridge University Press, 1991.

Kuhn, Thomas S. *The Structure of Scientific Revolutions* 2d ed. Chicago: University of Chicago Press, 1970.

Kunda, Ziva, and Richard Nisbett. "Prediction and the Partial Understanding of the Law of Large Numbers." *Journal of Experimental Social Psychology* 22 (1986): 339–54.

Kupperman, Joel J. *The Foundations of Morality*. London: Allen and Unwin, 1983.

Lane, P. H. *An Introduction to the Australian Constitution* 5th ed. Sydney: The Law Book Company, 1990.

Larmore, Charles. "Beyond Religion and Enlightenment." *San Diego Law Review* 30 (Fall 1993): 799–815.

———. *Patterns of Moral Complexity*. Cambridge: Cambridge University Press, 1987.

———. "Pluralism and Reasonable Disagreement." *Social Philosophy & Policy* 11 (Winter 1994): 61–79.

———. "Political Liberalism." *Political Theory* 18 (August 1990): 339–60.

Lawson, Gary. "Proving the Law." *Northwestern Law Review* 4 (Summer 1992): 859–903.

Lehman, Darrin R., and Richard E. Nisbett. "A Longitudinal Study of Undergraduate Training on Reasoning." *Developmental Psychology* 26 (1990): 952–60.

Lehrer, Keith. *Theory of Knowledge*. Boulder, CO: Westview, 1990.

Levi, Isaac. *The Enterprise of Knowledge*. Cambridge, MA: MIT Press, 1980.

Lewis, C. I. *An Analysis of Knowledge and Valuation*. LaSalle, IL: Open Court, 1946.

Lijphart, Arend. *Democracies: Patterns of Majoritarian and Consensus Government in Twenty-one Countries*. New Haven, CT: Yale University Press, 1984.

———. "The Political Consequences of Electoral Laws, 1945–85." *American Political Science Review* 84 (June 1990): 481–96.

Lively, Jack. *Democracy*. Oxford: Basil Blackwell, 1975.

Locke, John. *A Letter Concerning Toleration*. Indianapolis: Bobbs-Merrill, 1955.

———. *The Second Treatise of Government* in *Two Treatises of Government*. Ed. Peter Laslett. Cambridge: Cambridge University Press, 1960.

Lomasky, Loren E. *Persons, Rights and the Moral Community*. New York: Oxford University Press, 1987.

Lucas, J. R. *The Principles of Politics*. Oxford: Clarendon Press, 1966.

Luce, R. Duncan, and Howard Raiffa, *Games and Decisions: Introduction and Critical Survey*. New York: John Wiley & Sons, 1957.

Lukes, Steven. "Relativism in Its Place." In Martin Hollis and Steven Lukes, eds., *Rationality and Relativism*, 261–305. Cambridge, MA: MIT Press, 1982.

———. "Some Problems About Rationality." In Bryan Wilson, ed., *Rationality*, 195–213. Oxford: Basil Blackwell, 1970.

Lycan, William. *Judgment and Justification*. Cambridge: Cambridge University Press, 1988.

Lyons, David. *Ethics and the Rule of Law*. Cambridge: Cambridge University Press, 1984.

———. "Mill's Theory of Morality." *Noûs* 10 (1976): 101–20.

———. "Rights, Claims and Beneficiaries." *American Philosophical Quarterly* 6 (July 1969): 173–85.

Mabbott, J. D. *An Introduction to Ethics*. London: Hutchinson, 1966.

MacCormick, Neil. *Legal Reasoning and Legal Theory*. Oxford: Clarendon Press, 1978.

Macedo, Stephen. *Liberal Virtues: Citizenship, Virtue and Community in Liberal Constitutionalism*. Oxford: Clarendon Press, 1991.

———. *The New Right v. the Constitution*. Washington, DC: The Cato Institute, 1987.

Machan, Tibor. *Individuals and Their Rights*. La Salle, IL: Open Court, 1989.

Machiavelli, Niccoló. *Discourses on Livy*. Trans. Harvey Mansfield and Nathan Tarcov. Chicago: University of Chicago Press, forthcoming.

MacIntyre, Alasdair. *Whose Justice? Which Rationality?* Notre Dame, IN: University of Notre Dame Press, 1987.

MacIver, R. M. *The Web of Government*. New York: Macmillan, 1947.

Mack, Eric. "Liberalism, Neutralism and Rights." In J. Roland Pennock and John

W. Chapman, eds., *NOMOS* XXX: *Religion, Morality and the Law*, 46–70. New York: New York University Press, 1988.

MacKay, Alfred. *Arrow's Theorem: The Paradox*. New Haven, CT: Yale University Press, 1980.

Mackie, J. L. *Ethics: Inventing Right and Wrong*. Harmondsworth: Penguin, 1977.

Madison, James, Alexander Hamilton, and John Jay. *The Federalist Papers*. Ed. Clinton Rossiter. New York: New American Library, 1961.

Mansbridge, Jane J. *Beyond Adversary Democracy*. New York: Basic Books, 1980.

———. "The Rise and Fall of Self-Interest in the Explanation of Political Life." In Jane J. Mansbridge, ed., *Beyond Self-Interest*, 3–22. Chicago: University of Chicago Press, 1990.

Maritain, Jacques. *The Person and the Common Good*. London: Geoffrey Bles, 1948.

Marshall, Geoffrey. "Due Process in England." In J. Roland Pennock and John W. Chapman, eds., *NOMOS* XVIII: *Due Process*, 69–88. New York: New York University Press, 1977.

———. "The Role of Rules." In David Miller and Larry Siedentop, eds., *The Nature of Political Theory*, 183–96. Oxford: Clarendon Press, 1983.

Martin, Rex. *A System of Rights*. Oxford: Clarendon Press, 1993.

May, Kenneth O. "A Set of Independent Necessary and Sufficient Conditions for Simple Majority Decisions." *Econometrica* 20 (October 1952): 680–84.

McCarthy, Thomas. Introduction to Jürgen Habermas, *Moral Consciousness and Communicative Action*. Trans. Christian Lenhardt and Shierry Weber Nicolsen, vi–xiii. Cambridge, MA: MIT Press, 1991.

Meinong, Alexis. *On Emotional Presentation*. Trans. Marie-Luise Schubert Kalsi. Evanston, IL: Northwestern University Press, 1972.

Mill, John Stuart. *Considerations on Representative Government*. In John Stuart Mill, *On Liberty and Other Essays*, 203–467. Ed. John Gray. New York: Oxford University Press, 1991.

———. *An Examination of Sir William Hamilton's Philosophy*. In *The Collected Works of John Stuart Mill*, Vol. 9. Ed. J.M. Robson. Toronto: University of Toronto Press, 1979.

———. *On Liberty*. In John Stuart Mill, *On Liberty and Other Essays*, 1–128. Ed. John Gray. New York: Oxford University Press, 1991.

———. *Principles of Political Economy*. In *The Collected Works of John Stuart Mill*. Vols. 2 & 3, Ed. J. M. Robson. Toronto: University of Toronto Press, 1965.

———. *The Subjection of Women*. In John Stuart Mill, *On Liberty and Other Essays*, 469–582. Ed. John Gray. New York: Oxford University Press, 1991.

———. *A System of Logic*. In *The Collected Works of John Stuart Mill*, Vols. 7 & 8. Ed. J. M. Robson. Toronto: University of Toronto Press, 1974.

———. "Thoughts on Parliamentary Reform." In *The Collected Works of John Stuart Mill*, Vol. 19. Ed. J. M. Robson. Toronto: University of Toronto Press, 1977.

———. *Utilitarianism*. In *On Liberty and Other Essays*. Ed. John Gray. New York: Oxford University Press, 1991.

Miller, David. "The Competitive Model of Democracy." In Graeme Duncan, ed., *Democratic Theory and Practice*, 132–155. Cambridge: Cambridge University Press, 1983.

Miller, Richard W. "Marx and Morality." In J. Roland Pennock and John W. Chapman, eds., *NOMOS XXVI: Marxism*, 3–32. New York: New York University Press, 1986.

Moon, J. Donald. *Constructing Community: Moral Pluralism and Tragic Conflicts*. Princeton, NJ: Princeton University Press, 1993.

Mueller, Dennis C. *Public Choice II*. Cambridge: Cambridge University Press, 1989.

Munzer, Stephen R. *A Theory of Property*. Cambridge: Cambridge University Press, 1990.

Nagel, Robert F. *Constitutional Cultures: The Mentality and Consequences of Judicial Review*. Berkeley: University of California Press, 1989.

Nagel, Thomas. *Equality and Partiality*. New York: Oxford University Press, 1991.

———. "Moral Conflict and Political Legitimacy." *Philosophy & Public Affairs* 16 (Summer 1987): 215–40.

———. *The Possibility of Altruism*. Princeton, NJ: Princeton University Press, 1979.

———. *The View from Nowhere*. New York: Oxford University Press, 1986.

Narveson, Jan. "The How and Why of Universalizability." In Nelson T. Potter and Mark Timmons, eds., *Morality and Universalizability*, 3–44. Boston: D. Reidel, 1985.

———. *The Libertarian Idea*. Philadelphia: Temple University Press, 1988.

Nedelsky, Jennifer. "American Constitutionalism and the Paradox of Private Property." In Jon Elster and Rune Slagstad, eds., *Constitutionalism and Democracy*, 241–73. Cambridge: Cambridge University Press, 1988.

Nelson, William. "Evaluating the Institutions of Liberal Democracy." In Geoffrey Brennan and Loren E. Lomasky, eds., *Politics and Process: New Essays in Democratic Thought*, 60–77. Cambridge: Cambridge University Press, 1989.

———. *On Justifying Democracy*. London: Routledge & Kegan Paul, 1980.

Newton-Smith, W. "Relativism and the Possibility of Interpretation." In Martin Hollis and Steven Lukes, eds., *Rationality and Relativism*, 106–22. Cambridge, MA: MIT Press, 1982.

Nielsen, Kai. *Equality and Liberty: A Defense of Radical Egalitarianism*. Totowa, NJ: Rowman & Allenhead, 1985.

Nietzsche, Frederick. *On the Genealogy of Morals*. Trans. Walter Kaufmann and R. J. Hollingwood. New York: Vintage Books, 1967.

Nisbett, Richard E., Geoffrey T. Fong, Darrin R. Lehman, and Patricia W. Cheng. "Teaching Reasoning." *Science* 238 (October 1987): 625–31.

Nisbett, Richard E., David H. Krantz, Christopher Jepson, and Ziva Kunda. "The Use of Statistical Heuristics in Everyday Reasoning." *Psychological Review* 90 (1983): 339–63.

Nisbett, Richard, and Lee Ross. *Human Inference: Strategies and Shortcomings of Social Judgment*. Englewood Cliffs, NJ: Prentice-Hall, 1980.

Norman, Richard. *Free and Equal: A Philosophical Examination of Political Values*. Oxford: Oxford University Press, 1987.

Nozick, Robert. *Anarchy, State and Utopia.* New York: Basic Books, 1974.

———. *The Nature of Rationality.* Princeton, NJ: Princeton University Press, 1993.

———. *Philosophical Explanations.* Oxford: Clarendon Press, 1981.

Oakeshott, Michael. *On Human Conduct.* Oxford: Clarendon Press, 1975.

———. "Rationalism in Politics." In Michael Oakeshott, *Rationalism in Politics,* 5–42. Indianapolis, IN: Liberty Press, 1962.

Olson, Mancur, Jr. *The Logic of Collective Action: Public Goods and the Theory of Groups.* New York: Schocken Books, 1968.

O'Neill, Onora. "The Public Use of Reason." In Onora O'Neill, *Constructions of Reason: Explorations of Kant's Practical Philosophy,* 28–50. Cambridge: Cambridge University Press, 1989.

Osborne, D. K. "Irrelevant Alternatives and Social Welfare." *Econometrica* 44 (September 1976): 1001–15.

Page, Benjamin I., and Robert Y. Shapiro. "Effects of Public Opinion on Policy." *American Political Science Review* 77 (March 1983): 175–90.

———. *The Rational Public: Fifty Years of Trends in Americans' Policy Preferences.* Chicago: University of Chicago Press, 1992.

———. "The Rational Public and Democracy." In George E. Marcus and Russell L. Hanson, eds., *Reconsidering the Democratic Public,* 35–64. University Park, PA: Pennsylvania State University Press, 1993.

Pappas, George S. "Basing Relations." In George S. Pappas, ed., *Justification and Knowledge: New Studies in Epistemology,* 51–63. Boston: D. Reidel, 1979.

Pappas, George S. and Marshall Swain. "Introduction." In George S. Pappas and Marshall Swain, eds., *Essays on Knowledge and Justification,* 11–40. Ithaca, NY: Cornell University Press, 1978.

Parfit, Derek. *Reasons and Persons.* Oxford: Clarendon Press, 1984.

Pastin, Mark. "Modest Foundationalism and Self-Warrant." In George S. Pappas and Marshall Swain, eds., *Essays on Knowledge and Justification,* 279–88. Ithaca, NY: Cornell University Press, 1978.

Pennock, J. Roland. *Democratic Political Theory.* Princeton, NJ: Princeton University Press, 1979.

Perry, Michael J. *Morality, Politics and the Law.* New York: Oxford University Press, 1988.

———. "Religious Morality and Political Choice: Further Thoughts—and Second Thoughts—on *Love and Power.*" *San Diego Law Review* 30 (Fall 1993): 703–27.

Peters, Richard. "Authority." In Anthony Quinton, ed., *Political Philosophy,* 82–96. Oxford: Oxford University Press, 1967.

Pettit, Philip. *The Common Mind.* New York: Oxford University Press, 1993.

———. "Consequentialism and Respect for Persons." *Ethics* 100 (October 1988): 117–26.

Piaget, Jean. "The Growth of Logical Thinking from Childhood to Adolescence." In Howard Gruber and J. Jacques Voneché, eds. Anne Parson and Stanley Milgram, trans., *The Essential Piaget,* 404–44. London: Routledge & Kegan Paul, 1977.

———. "Logic and Psychology." In Howard Gruber and J. Jacques Voneché, eds., *The Essential Piaget,* 445–77. London: Routledge & Kegan Paul, 1977.

————. *The Moral Development of the Child,* Marjorie Gabain, trans. New York: Free Press, 1965.

Pinkard, Terry. *Democratic Liberalism and Social Union.* Philadelphia: Temple University Press, 1987.

Plamenatz, John. *Man and Society: A Critical Examination of Some Important Social and Political Theories from Machiavelli to Marx.* London: Longman, 1963.

Plantinga, Alvin. "Reason and Belief in God." In Alvin Plantinga and Nicholas Wolterstorff, eds., *Faith and Rationality,* 16–93. Notre Dame, IN: University of Notre Dame Press, 1983.

Platts, Mark. "Moral Reality." In Geoffrey Sayre-McCord, ed., *Essays on Moral Realism,* 282–300. Ithaca, NY: Cornell University Press, 1988.

Pollock, John L. *Contemporary Theories of Knowledge.* Totowa, NJ: Roman & Littlefield, 1986.

————. "A Plethora of Epistemological Theories." In George S. Pappas, ed., *Justification and Knowledge: New Studies in Epistemology,* 93–113. Boston: D. Reidel, 1979.

Prichard, H. A. *Moral Obligation: Essays and Lectures.* Oxford: Clarendon Press, 1949.

Putnam, Hilary. *Reason, Truth and History.* Cambridge: Cambridge University Press, 1981.

Putnam, Robert D. *Making Democracy Work: Civic Traditions in Modern Italy.* Princeton, NJ: Princeton University Press, 1993.

Quine, W. V. *Pursuit of Truth.* Rev. ed. Cambridge, MA: Harvard University Press, 1992.

Quine, W. V., and J. S. Ullian. *The Web of Belief.* New York: Random House, 1970.

Quinton, Anthony. *The Nature of Things.* London: Routledge & Kegan Paul, 1973.

Rae, Douglas. *The Political Consequences of Electoral Laws.* New Haven, CT: Yale University Press, 1971.

Raphael, D. D. *Moral Judgement.* London: Allen and Unwin, 1955.

Rasmussen, Douglas B., and Douglas J. Den Uyl. *Liberty and Nature: An Aristotelian Defense of Liberal Order.* La Salle, IL: Open Court, 1991.

Rawls, John. "The Domain of the Political and Overlapping Consensus." *New York University Law Review* 64 (May 1989): 233–55.

————. "The Idea of an Overlapping Consensus" *Oxford Journal of Legal Studies* 7 (1987): 1–25.

————. "Justice as Fairness: Political Not Metaphysical." *Philosophy & Public Affairs* 14 (Summer 1985): 223–51.

————. "Kantian Constructivism in Moral Theory." *Journal of Philosophy* 77 (September 1980): 515–72.

————. *Political Liberalism.* New York: Columbia University Press, 1993.

————. "The Priority of Right and Ideas of the Good." *Philosophy & Public Affairs* 17 (1988): 251–76.

————. *A Theory of Justice.* Cambridge, MA: Belknap Press of Harvard University Press, 1971.

Raz, Joseph. "Facing Diversity: The Case of Epistemic Abstinence." *Philosophy & Public Affairs* 19 (1990): 3–46.

———. *The Morality of Freedom.* Oxford: Clarendon Pres, 1986.

———. *Practical Reason and Norms.* London: Hutchinson, 1975.

Regan, Donald H. "Glosses on Dworkin: Rights, Principles, and Policies." In Marshall Cohen, ed., *Ronald Dworkin and Contemporary Jurisprudence,* 119–60. Totowa, NJ: Rowman & Allanheld, 1984.

Regan, Tom. *The Case for Animal Rights.* Berkeley: University of California Press, 1983.

Reiman, Jeffrey. *Justice and Modern Moral Philosophy.* New Haven, CT: Yale University Press, 1990.

Reynolds, Noel B. "The Ethical Foundations of Constitutional Order: A Conventionalist Perspective." *Constitutional Political Economy* 4 (Winter 1993): 79–95.

Richards, David A. J. "Religion, Public Morality and Constitutional Law." In J. Roland Pennock and John W. Chapman, eds., *NOMOS XXX: Religion, Morality and the Law,* 152–78. New York: New York University Press, 1988.

———. *A Theory of Reasons for Action.* Oxford: Clarendon Press, 1971.

———. *Toleration and the Constitution.* New York: Oxford University Press, 1986.

Riker, William H. *The Art of Political Manipulation.* New Haven, CT: Yale University Press, 1986.

———. *Liberalism Against Populism: A Confrontation Between the Theory of Democracy and the Theory of Social Choice.* San Francisco: W.H. Freeman, 1982.

Riley, Jonathan. "American Democracy and Majority Rule." In John W. Chapman and Alan Wertheimer, eds., *NOMOS XXXII: Majorities and Minorities,* 267–307. New York: New York University Press, 1990.

———. *Liberal Utilitarianism: Social Choice Theory and J.S. Mill's Philosophy.* Cambridge: Cambridge University Press, 1988.

Riley, Patrick. *Kant's Political Philosophy.* Totowa, NJ: Rowman and Littlefield, 1983.

Rips, Lance J. "Cognitive Processes and Propositional Reasoning." *Psychological Review* 90 (1983): 38–71.

Robinson, R. E., S. C. Coval, and J. C. Smith. "The Logic of Rights." *University of Toronto Law Review* 33 (1983): 267–78.

Rommen, Heinrich A. *The State in Catholic Thought.* London: B. Herder, 1950.

Rorty, Richard. "Introduction". In Richard Rorty, *Objectivity, Relativism and Truth,* 1–17. Cambridge: Cambridge University Press, 1991.

———. *Philosophy and the Mirror of Nature.* Princeton, NJ: Princeton University Press, 1979.

———. "The Priority of Democracy to Philosophy." In Richard Rorty, *Objectivity, Relativism and Truth,* 175–96. Cambridge: Cambridge University Press, 1991.

———. "Science as Solidarity." In Richard Rorty, *Objectivism, Relativism and Truth,* 35–45. Cambridge: Cambridge University Press, 1991.

———. "Solidarity or Objectivity?" In Richard Rorty, *Objectivity, Relativism and Truth,* 21–34. Cambridge: Cambridge University Press, 1991.

Ross, David. *The Foundations of Ethics.* Oxford: Clarendon Press, 1939.

Ross, Lee, and Craig A. Anderson. "Shortcomings in the Attribution Process: On the Origins and Maintenance of Erroneous Social Assessments." In Daniel Kahneman, Paul Slovic, and Amos Tversky, eds., *Judgments Under Uncertainty: Heuristics and Biases*, 129–52. Cambridge: Cambridge University Press, 1982.

Ross, Lee, and Richard E. Nisbett. *The Person and the Situation: Perspectives of Social Psychology*. Philadelphia: Temple University Press, 1991.

Ross, Michael, and Fiore Sicoly. "Egocentric Biases in Availability and Attribution." In Daniel Kahneman, Paul Slovic, and Amos Tversky, eds., *Judgments Under Uncertainty: Heuristics and Biases*, 179–89. Cambridge: Cambridge University Press, 1982.

Rousseau, Jean-Jacques. *The Social Contract*. In Jean-Jacques Rousseau, *The Social Contract and Discourses*. Trans. G.D.H. Cole. London: Dent, 1973.

Rumble, Wilfred E. "James Madison on the Value of Bills of Rights." In J. Roland Pennock and John W. Chapman, eds., *NOMOS XX: Constitutionalism*, 122–62. New York: New York University Press, 1979.

Ryan, Alan. "Public and Private Property." In S. I. Benn and G. F. Gaus, eds., *Public and Private in Social Life*, 223–45. New York: St. Martin's Press, 1983.

Sandel, Michael. *Liberalism and the Limits of Justice*. Cambridge: Cambridge University Press, 1982.

Sartori, Giovanni. *The Theory of Democracy Revisited*. Chatham, NJ: Chatham House, 1987.

Schauer, Frederick. *Free Speech: A Philosophical Enquiry*. Cambridge: Cambridge University Press, 1982.

Scheffler, Samuel. *Human Morality*. New York: Oxford University Press, 1992.

Schick, Frederic. *Understanding Action: An Essay on Reasons*. Cambridge: Cambridge University Press., 1991.

Schmidtz, David. *The Limits of Government: An Essay on the Public Goods Argument*. Boulder, CO: Westview, 1990.

Schumpeter, Joseph. *Capitalism, Socialism and Democracy*. London: Allen and Unwin, 1943.

Sears, David O., and Carolyn L. Funk. "Self-Interest in Americans' Political Opinions." In Jane J. Mansbridge, ed., *Beyond Self-Interest*, 147–70. Chicago: University of Chicago Press, 1990.

Sears, David O., Richard R. Lau, Tom R. Tyler, and Harris M. Allen, Jr. "Self-Interest vs. Symbolic Politics in Policy Attitudes and Presidential Voting." *American Political Science Review* 74 (March 1980): 670–84.

Sen, A. K. *Collective Choice and Social Welfare*. San Francisco: Holden-Day 1970.

———. "The Impossibility of a Paretian Liberal." *Journal of Political Economy* 78 (January/February 1970): 152–57.

Seung, T. K., and Daniel Bonevac. "Plural Values and Indeterminate Rankings." *Ethics* 102 (July 1992): 799–813.

Shapiro, Ian. "Three Ways to Be a Democrat." *Political Theory* 22 (February 1994): 124–51.

Shearmur, Jeremy. "Epistemological Limits of the State: Reflections on Popper's *Open Society*." *Political Studies* 38 (1990): 116–25.

Shklar, Judith. *The Faces of Injustice*. New Haven, CT: Yale University Press, 1990.

Shope, Robert K. *The Analysis of Knowing: A Decade of Research*. Princeton, NJ: Princeton University Press, 1983.

Sidgwick, Henry. "The Establishment of Ethical First Principles." *Mind* 4 (1879).

———. *The Methods of Ethics*, 7th ed. Chicago: University of Chicago Press, 1907.

Simmons, A. John. *On the Edge of Anarchy: Locke, Consent and the Limits of Society*. Princeton, NJ: Princeton University Press, 1993.

———. *The Lockean Theory of Rights*. Princeton, NJ: Princeton University Press, 1992.

———. *Moral Principles and Political Obligations*. Princeton, NJ: Princeton University Press, 1979.

Simon, Herbert. *Administrative Behavior*. New York: Macmillan, 1947.

Singer, Peter. *Practical Ethics*. Cambridge: Cambridge University Press, 1979.

———. *Democracy and Disobedience*. Oxford: Clarendon Press, 1973.

Skubik, Daniel W. *At the Intersection of Legality and Morality: Hartian Law as Natural Law*. New York: Peter Lang, 1990.

Slagstad, Rune. "Liberal Constitutionalism and Its Critics." In Jon Elster and Rune Slagstad, eds., *Constitutionalism and Democracy*, 103–29. Cambridge: Cambridge University Press, 1988.

Smith, Adam. *An Enquiry into the Nature and Causes of the Wealth of Nations*. Ed. W. B. Todd. Oxford: Clarendon Press, 1976.

Smith, Rogers M. *Liberalism and American Constitutional Law*. Cambridge, MA: Harvard University Press, 1990.

Snare, Francis. *The Nature of Moral Thinking*. London: Routledge & Kegan Paul, 1992.

Snowiss, Sylvia. *Judicial Review and the Law of the Constitution*. New Haven, CT: Yale University Press, 1990.

Solum, Lawrence B. "Constructing an Ideal of Public Reason." *San Diego Law Review*, 30 (Fall 1993): 729–62.

Sosa, Ernest. "Epistemology Today." In Ernest Sosa, *Knowledge in Perspective: Selected Essays in Epistemology*, 65–85. Cambridge: Cambridge University Press, 1991.

———. "Equilibrium in Coherence?" In his *Knowledge in Perspective*, 257–69. Cambridge: Cambridge University Press, 1991.

———. "The Foundations of Foundationalism." In his *Knowledge in Perspective*, 149–64. Cambridge: Cambridge University Press, 1991.

———. "Nature Unmirrored, Epistemology Naturalized." In his *Knowledge in Perspective*, 86–107. Cambridge: Cambridge University Press, 1991.

Spector, Horacio. *Autonomy and Rights: The Moral Foundations of Liberalism*. Oxford: Clarendon Press, 1992.

Spitz, Elaine. *Majority Rule*. Chatham, NJ: Chatham House, 1984.

Stich, Stephen. *The Fragmentation of Reason*. Cambridge, MA: MIT Press, 1990.

Stich, Stephen P. and Richard E. Nisbett. "Justification and the Psychology of Human Reasoning." *Philosophy of Science* 47 (June 1980): 188–202.

Strawson, P. *Freedom and Resentment and Other Essays.* London: Methuen, 1974.

Sullivan, Roger J. *Immanuel Kant's Moral Theory.* Cambridge: Cambridge University Press, 1989.

Sumner, L.W. *The Moral Foundations of Rights.* Oxford: Clarendon Press, 1987.

Swain, Marshall. "Justification and the Basis of Belief." In George S. Pappas, ed., *Justification and Knowledge: New Essays in Epistemology,* 25–49. Boston: D. Reidel, 1979.

Tay, Alice Ehr-Soon, and Eugene Kamenka. "Public Law—Private Law." In S.I. Benn and G.F. Gaus, eds., *Public and Private in Social Life,* 67–92. New York: St. Martin's Press, 1983.

Ten, C.L. *Mill on Liberty.* Oxford: Clarendon Press, 1980.

Thayer, James B. "The Origins and Scope of the American Doctrine of Constitutional Law." *Harvard Law Review* 7 (October 1893): 129–56.

Thompson, Dennis F. *John Stuart Mill and Representative Government.* Princeton: Princeton University Press, 1976.

Thomson, Judith Jarvis. *The Realm of Rights.* Cambridge, MA: Harvard University Press, 1990.

Toulmin, Stephen. *An Examination of the Place of Reason in Ethics.* Cambridge: Cambridge University Press, 1953.

Tribe Laurence H., and Michael C. Dorf. *On Reading the Constitution.* Cambridge, MA: Harvard University Press, 1991.

Triplett, Timm. "Recent Work on Foundationalism." *American Philosophical Quarterly* 27 (April 1990): 93–116.

Tucker, D. F. B. *Law, Liberalism and Free Speech.* Totowa, NJ: Rowman & Allanheld, 1985.

Tversky, Amos, and Daniel Kahneman. "Availability: A Heuristic for Judging Frequency and Probability." In Daniel Kahneman, Paul Slovic, and Amos Tversky, eds., *Judgments Under Uncertainty: Heuristics and Biases,* 163–78. Cambridge: Cambridge University Press, 1982.

———. "Belief in the Law of Small Numbers." In Daniel Kahneman, Paul Slovic, and Amos Tversky, eds., *Judgments Under Uncertainty: Heuristics and Biases,* 23–31. Cambridge: Cambridge University Press, 1982.

———. "Judgment Under Uncertainty: Heuristics and Biases." In Daniel Kahneman, Paul Slovic, and Amos Tversky, eds., *Judgments Under Uncertainty: Heuristics and Biases,* 3–20. Cambridge: Cambridge University Press, 1982.

———. "Judgments of and by Representativeness." In Daniel Kahneman, Paul Slovic, and Amos Tversky, eds., *Judgments Under Uncertainty: Heuristics and Biases,* 84–98. Cambridge: Cambridge University Press, 1982.

Tyler, Tom R. "Justice, Self-Interest, and the Legitimacy of Legal and Political Authority." In Jane J. Mansbridge, ed., *Beyond Self-Interest,* 171–79. Chicago: University of Chicago Press, 1990.

Urmson, J. O. *The Emotive Theory of Ethics.* New York: Oxford University Press, 1968.

Van Cleve, James. "Foundationalism, Epistemic Principles and the Cartesian Circle." *Philosophical Review* 88 (January 1979): 55–91.

Von Mises, Ludwig. *Liberalism in the Classical Tradition.* Trans. Ralph Raico. San Francisco: Cobden Press, 1985.

Wade, E. C. S. "Introduction." In A.V. Dicey, *Introduction to the Study of the Law of the Constitution*, ninth edn, xxvii–clvi. London: Macmillan, 1948.

Wagner, Richard E. and Gwartney, James D. "Public Choice and Constitutional Order." In James D. Gwartney and Richard E. Wagner, eds., *Public Choice and Constitutional Economics*, 3–28. Greenwich, CT: JAI Press, 1988.

Waldron, Jeremy. "Enough and as Good Left for Others." *Philosophical Quarterly* 29 (1979): 319–28.

———. "Legislation and Moral Neutrality." In Robert E. Goodin and Andrew Reeve, eds., *Liberal Neutrality*, 61–83. London: Routledge & Kegan Paul, 1989.

———. "Religious Contributions to Public Deliberation." *San Diego Law Review* 30 (Fall 1993): 817–48.

———. "A Right to Do Wrong." *Ethics* 92 (1981): 21–39.

———. *The Right to Private Property*. Oxford: Clarendon Press, 1988.

———. "Theoretical Foundations of Liberalism." In Jeremy Waldron, *Liberal Rights: Collected Papers, 1981–91*, 35–62. Cambridge: Cambridge University Press, 1993.

Walker, Graham. *Moral Foundations of Constitutional Thought: Current Problems, Augustinian Prospects*. Princeton, NJ: Princeton University Press, 1990.

Walker, Margaret Urban. "Partial Considerations." *Ethics* 101 (1991): 758–74.

Walzer, Michael. *Spheres of Justice: A Defense of Pluralism and Equality*. Oxford: Basil Blackwell, 1983.

Wason, P. C., and P. N. Johnson-Laird. *The Psychology of Reasoning: Structure and Content*. London: B.T. Batsford, 1972.

Wasstersrom, Richard. *The Judicial Decision: Toward a Theory of Legal Justification*. Stanford: Stanford University Press, 1961.

Watt, E. D. *Authority*. London: Croom Helm, 1982.

Weatherford, M. Stephen. "Economic Voting and the 'Symbolic Politics' Argument: A Reinterpretation and Synthesis." *American Political Science Review* 77 (March 1983): 158–74.

Weaver, R. Kent, and Bert A. Rockman. "Assessing the Effects of Institutions." In R. Kent Weaver and Bert A. Rockman, eds., *Do Institutions Matter?*, 1–41. Washington, DC: The Brookings Institution, 1993.

———. "Institutional Reform and Constitutional Design." In R. Kent Weaver and Bert A. Rockman, eds., *Do Institutions Matter?*, 462–81. Washington, DC: The Brookings Institution, 1993.

Wellington, Harry H. *Interpreting the Constitution: The Supreme Court and the Process of Adjudication*. New Haven, CT: Yale University Press, 1990.

Wellman, Carl. *Challenge and Response: Justification in Ethics*. Carbondale and Edwardsville: Southern Illinois University Press, 1971.

———. *Welfare Rights*. Totowa, NJ: Rowman & Littlefield, 1982.

White, Alan R. *Rights*. Oxford: Clarendon Press, 1984.

White, Morton. *Philosophy, The Federalist and the Constitution*. New York: Oxford University Press, 1987.

White, Stephen K. *The Recent Work of Jürgen Habermas: Reason, Justice and Modernity*. Cambridge: Cambridge University Press, 1988.

Wicksell, Knut. "A New Principle of Just Taxation." Trans. James Buchanan. In

James D. Gwartney and Richard E. Wagner, eds. *Public Choice and Constitutional Economics*, 117–130. Greenwich, CT: JAI Press, 1988.

Wight, Martin. "Western Values in International Society." In Herbert Butterfield and Martin Wight, eds., *Diplomatic Investigations*, 89–131. Cambridge, MA: Harvard University Press, 1966.

Williams, Bernard. "A Critique of Utilitarianism." In J. J. C. Smart and Bernard Williams, *Utilitarianism: For and Against*, 77–150. Cambridge: Cambridge University Press, 1973.

———. "Deciding to Believe." In Bernard Williams, *Problems of the Self*, 136–51. Cambridge: Cambridge University Press, 1973.

———. "Ethical Consistency." In Bernard Williams, *Problems of the Self*, 166–86. Cambridge: Cambridge University Press, 1973.

———. *Ethics and the Limits of Philosophy*. London: Fontana/Collins, 1985.

———. "Internal and External Reasons." In Bernard Williams, *Moral Luck*, 101–113. Cambridge: Cambridge University Press, 1981.

———. "*Ought* and Moral Obligation." In Bernard Williams, *Moral Luck*, 114–23. Cambridge: Cambridge University Press, 1981.

———. "The Truth in Relativism." In Bernard Williams, *Moral Luck*, 132–43. Cambridge: Cambridge University Press, 1981.

Wilson, James Q. *The Moral Sense*. New York: The Free Press, 1993.

Wilson, John. "Indoctrination and Rationality." In I. A. Snook, ed., *Concepts of Indoctrination: Philosophical Essays*, 17–24. London: Routledge & Kegan Paul, 1972.

Winch, Peter. *The Idea of a Social Science*. London: Routledge & Kegan Paul, 1958.

Wittgenstein, Ludwig. *Philosophical Investigations*, 3d ed., Trans. G. E. M. Anscombe. London: Macmillan, 1958.

———. *Remarks on the Foundations of Mathematics* Trans. G. H. von Wright, R. Rhees, and G. E. M. Anscombe. Oxford: Basil Blackwell, 1978.

Wolff, Robert Paul. *In Defense of Anarchism*. New York: Harper & Row, 1970.

———. *The Poverty of Liberalism*. Boston: Beacon Press, 1968.

INDEX

Abduction, 102–4
Accessibility condition, 132, 135, 136
Ackerman, Bruce A., 164, 223, 232, 303, 304, 323, 330–33
Actual assent thesis, 3, 130, 166, 173
Adjudication. *See also* Authority; Democracy; Tracking; Umpire
and liberal *Rechtstaat*, 207ff
and self-interest, 263ff
as response to inconclusiveness, 188ff
contrasted to mediation, 271–74
democratic, 223ff
two phases of, 271ff
Affective judgments, 8, 9, 28
Agassi, Joseph, 310
Agenda manipulation, 243, 267ff
Agglomeration principle, 43
Akrasia
epistemic, 48, 59, 70–73, 133
of action, 70, 71
Alexander, Larry, 325
Allen, Harris M., Jr., 331
Alston, William P., 313, 314
Ampliative justification, 76, 96, 103, 315, 316
Anderson, C.A., 305
Anshutz, R.P., 324
Arkes, Hadley, 163, 323
Armstrong, David, 20, 305, 306, 313
Arneson, Richard J., 252, 303, 332, 334
Arrow, Kenneth, 217, 235, 258, 259, 335
Audi, Robert, 305, 308, 313, 314, 321
Austen-Smith, David, 216, 217, 330
Authority. *See also* Umpire
and office of voter, 249ff
and rights, 199–202
and Socratic influence, 125
contextual, 124, 125, 138, 150, 185, 186, 276
coordinating, 186, 187
epistemic, 128, 129, 149–51, 173, 180, 181
fundamental, 125–29, 149, 159
legal not simply derived from content, 212
liberal, 184–91, 195

moral, 123, 124, 127, 185, 230, 276, 279–81
of law, 211
of judges, 276ff
umpire model of, 184–91

Baier, Kurt, 173, 325
Balinese, 301
Banks, Jeffrey, 216, 217, 330
Barber, Benjamin, 332
Barry, Brian, 240, 333, 334, 336
Barry, Norman, 323
Beiner, Ronald, 318
Beitz, Charles R., 248, 250, 251, 297, 332–34, 339
Belief commitments, 35, 37, 38, 64
Belief perseverance, 20, 21, 31
Beliefs. *See also* Justified beliefs
causal theory of, 51
conscious, 37
explicit, 37, 53
how many we can have, 36
obviously derivable, 37
spontaneous, 89, 90, 92–95
tacit, 35–38
unjustified, 64, 65, 75, 86, 87
Benhabib, Seyla, 332
Benn, Stanley, xxxv, 11, 12, 19, 28, 35, 163, 171, 304–7, 312, 313, 319, 323, 325, 327, 329, 333, 338
Bentham, Jeremy, 331
Bentley, Arthur F., 336, 337
Beran, Harry, 325
Berlin, Isaiah, 73, 163, 313, 323
Bernholz, Peter, 334
Berry, Christopher J., 336
Bickel, Alexander M., 165, 232, 266, 279, 324, 332, 336, 337
Bill of Rights, 205, 284
Bittner, Rüdiger, 321
Black, Hugo L., 168
Blackmun, Harry, 286
Blackstone, William, 226
Blanshard, Brand, 82, 314
Bonevac, Daniel, 153, 322

Bonjour, Laurence, 7, 75, 82, 96, 102, 304, 313, 314, 316
Bordes, Georges, 330
Bork, Robert H., 206, 209, 324, 328, 338
Bosanquet, Bernard, 7, 313
Brain attic theory, 36, 37, 53
Braine, Martin D.S., 47, 308, 309
Brams, Stephen J., 336
Brandt, Richard B., 8, 304, 307, 315, 316
Brennan, Geoffrey, 228, 244, 261, 264, 265, 331, 332, 334–36
Bridgehead, 48–53, 135, 136, 310, 320
Brink, David O., 78, 303, 304, 313–15
  characterization of coherence theory, 76, 77
  characterization of moral realism, 6, 7
  claim that no beliefs are non-inferentially justified in coherence theory, 85
  criticism of self-justification, 89–91
  on Sidgwick, 99, 100
Browbeating, 123, 124, 176, 319
Brown v. Board of Education, 266, 281
Brute strength thesis, 41
Buchanan, James, 243, 244, 334
Buckle, Stephen, xxxv
Burdens of judgment, 131, 134, 135
Burnett, Sterling, xxxvi
Burnheim, John, 236, 333

Cacoullos, Ann R., 327
Campbell, A.C., 339
Chapman, John W., xxxv, 329
Charity, Principle of, 49–51, 114, 118, 317
Cheng, Patricia W., 311
Cherniak, Christopher, 52–54, 107, 143, 307, 310, 311, 317
Chisholm, Roderick M., 306, 313
Christiano, Thomas, 249, 254, 330, 333–36
Civil interests, 172–74, 267
Civil Rights Act of 1964, 266
Clinton, Bill and Hillary, 238
Closed justification, 30–32, 138–40. *See also* Inferential justification; Justified beliefs; Systems of reasons and beliefs
Cobden, Richard, 296
Cognitive efficiency
  and compartmentalizing belief system, 107
  and democracy, 229ff
  and heuristics, 58, 60
  and wide reflective equilibrium, 107

justification of embracing spontaneous beliefs, 90
Cognitivism, 7, 8, 99
Cohen, Joshua, 335
Coherence justification
  absolutist coherence, 78, 79
  and comprehensiveness, 82, 87
  and Dworkin's legal theory, 279
  and justificatory discourse, 80
  and moral intuitions, 99, 100
  and moral realism, 304
  and principle of conservation, 85–87
  and self-justified beliefs, 85, 91
  and Socratic influence, 125
  and the basing relation, 80, 81
  and truth, 7
  assumes self-justified beliefs, 88, 89
  claim that there is only one coherent system, 308
  claimed to be purely inferential, 76
  coherence defined, 82
  global, 76–81, 84, 159
  local, 81–84
  multi-dimensional nature of, 82, 83
  not purely inferential, 88, 89
  principle of, 76, 77
  situated, 79, 85, 87, 88
  supposes initially credible beliefs, 316
  web coherentism, 82, 83
Coleman, Jules, 335
Common good, 209–11
  and convergence verdicts, 273–74
  and logrolling, 270–71
  and morality, 173–74
  as an end of politics, 222
  procedures appropriate for determining, 243–45
Common sense reasoning, 4, 132–36, 292ff
Compromise, 183–84
Condorcet, M.-J.A.C, 335
Condorcet jury theorem, 241–43, 262
Consensus, 116–19, 183, 184, 230ff, 271, 272, 293
Conservation of beliefs, principle of, 85, 86, 87, 94–96, 102
Constitutional politics, 213, 214, 232
Constitutionalism. *See also* Madisonian constitutionalism
  and defending justified principles, 239
  and procedural provisions, 211–13
  as limiting government, 205ff
  political liberals' view of, 231

specifying fundamental law, 204–7
specifying purposes of government, 206ff
requirement of efficacy, 214
Converse, Philip E., 260, 261, 335
Cooper, David E., 310
Coordination problems, 116, 156–58, 187, 188, 225–26
Cornman, James W., 316
Counter-examples in philosophy, 19, 305
Coval, S.C., 324, 327
Craven, John, 335
Credulity, principle of, 86, 102
Crosskey, William Winslow, 330
Crossley, David, 313

D'Agostino, Fred, xxxv, 4, 5, 175, 271, 303, 309, 317, 318, 321, 322, 325, 326, 330, 331, 335, 336
Dahl, Robert, 206, 256, 281, 328, 329, 334, 335, 337
Daniels, Norman, 105, 315–17
Darwall, Stephen L., 307
Dauer, Francis W., 315
Davidson, Donald, 49, 53, 54, 310, 311
Dawes, Robyn, 315
Decentering, 46, 118
Defeated justifications, 12, 13, 147
and immunities, 168–71
public, 144–46
Defeating reasons
and epistemic akrasia, 71, 72
defined, 66, 67
rebutting, 66, 67
undermining, 67–69
Degree of implicatedness thesis, 41
Deigh, John, 304
Democracy. *See also* Political equality
adjudicative contrasted to mediation-based views, 271–74
and charge of public incompetence, 260–63
and deliberative bodies, 235
and economy of virtue, 267
and epistemic scarcity, 229–30
and non-neutral procedures, 237–45
and problem of self-interested voting, 227–29, 263–67
and responsive procedures, 226–30
and self-protection, 227–29
and vote trading, 267–71
challenge from social choice theory, 258–60

challenges to adjudicative theory of, chp. 15
epistemic conception of, 247, 259–60
fairness of, 253
limits to consequentialist justification of, 246–48
not well grounded on indeterminancy, 223–26
pluralist conception of, 232, 292
random, 223–26
voting in as expressing judgment of justice, 228
Dennett, Daniel C., 307
DePaul, Michael R., 104, 316
Dewey, John, 243, 334
Dicey, A.V., 196, 326
Disobedience to the law, 288–91
"Doctrine of Signatures," 50
Dorf, Michael C., 324, 337
Dorn, James A., 328
Doxastic presupposition, 28
Doyle, Arthur Conan, 307
Doyle, Michael, 339
Dred Scott decision, 281
Dunleavy, Patrick, 337
Dworkin, Ronald, 114, 115, 158, 196, 204, 208, 278, 279, 317, 322, 326, 328, 329, 337

Einstein, Albert, 72
Ellis, Brian, 40, 41, 43, 47, 153, 307–9, 322
Elster, Jon, 19, 157, 223, 224, 305, 306, 322, 331, 332
Ely, John Hart, 284–86, 328, 337, 338
Emotivism, 6, 8, 9, 28, 29
Enlightenment, 65, 318
Epistemic clutter, 312
Epistemic irrationality, 60, 61, 64, 65, 70, 72, 74
Epistemic relativism
and moral logic, 43, 44
and public justification, 159
belief relativism, 43
defended, 38–40
distinguished from normative cognitive pluralism, 45
distinguished from relativism of truth, 39
logical relativism, 43
tamed by mental logic, 47, 48
tamed by mutual intelligibility, 48–52, 114
two routes to, 43

Epistemology
  and liberalism, chps. 1, 17
  and moral theory, 6ff
  as a comprehensive doctrine, 303
  as theory of justified belief, 7, 303
  practicality of, 26, 27
Equality, principle of, 163, 169, 215
  and due process, 213
  and rule of law, 206
  as basis of political equality, 248–55
  basic to rule of law, 199
  defined, 164
  not fundamental principle of liberal
    morality, 164ff
Estlund, David M., 251, 334 335
Ewin, R.E., xxxv, 183 201, 202, 287, 304,
    320, 325–28, 338
Ewing, A.C., 97–99, 315
Exclusionary reasons, 190–91, 201
Externalism, 33–35

Faber, Malte, 334
Factions, 264ff, 293
Feinberg, Joel, 165, 315, 319, 323, 325
Feld, Scott L., 334–36
Ferejohn, John, 335
Fetzer, James H., xxxv, 305, 309
Feuchtwanger, E.J., 339
Field, Hartry, 37, 307
First Amendment, 168–70, 324. *See also*
    Freedom of speech
Fishburn, Peter C., 336
Fishkin, James, 236, 260, 261, 333
Flathman, Richard E., 163, 323
Foley, Richard, 78, 92, 93, 306–8, 312, 314,
    315
Following a rule, 113–17, 129, 317
Fong, Geoffrey T., 311
Foron, Gideon, 330
Forrest, Peter, 41, 308
Foundationalism. *See also* Weak
    foundationalism, chp. 7
  and certainty, 90, 92
  and coherence, 316
  and incorrigibility, 90, 92
  and indubitability, 92
  and infallibility, 90
  and spontaneous beliefs, 90
  and the regress argument, 74
  foundationalism defined, 92
Frankena, William K., 163, 323
Frazer, James George, 310

Freeden, Michael, 323
Freedom of speech, 68, 160, 161, 166–68,
    213
Freud, Sigmund, 24, 305–7
Fried, Charles, 319, 325
Friedman, Marilyn, 321
Friedman, Richard, 186, 319, 326
Fuller, Lon, 196, 198, 326, 327
Fundamental law. *See also*
    Constitutionalism; Law, 196, 201–7,
    226, 227, 237ff, 282, 283
Fundamental Liberal Principle, 162–66 171,
    180, 199, 206, 238
  See also Liberal principles.

Gag rules, 167–70
Galston, William A., 140, 141, 310, 321,
    322, 324
Gambler's fallacy, 61, 133, 311, 312
Gärdenfors, Peter, 41, 308, 322
Garforth, F.W., 333
Gaus, Gerald F., 303, 304, 306–10, 312,
    313, 315, 318, 319, 321–25, 327–33
Gauthier, David, 174, 325
General Will, 260, 264, 272, 273
Gert, Bernard, 325
Gettier problem, 305
Gibbard, Alan, 123–29, 137, 150, 303, 304,
    307, 315, 319, 320, 321, 335, 336
Gladstone, William, 296, 297, 339
Goldman, Alan H., 308
Goldman, Alvin I., 306
Goodin, Robert, 333
Goodman, Nelson, 88, 101, 103, 314, 316
Goodwin, Barbara, 331, 333
Gow, David, xxxv
Grandy, Richard E., 51, 310
Gray, John, 152, 165, 179, 322
Green, Leslie, 188, 191, 326, 338
Green, T.H., 202, 327
Greenawalt, Kent, 142, 143, 154–56, 225,
    277, 321, 322
Grofman, Bernard, 334–36
Grotius, Hugo, 298, 339
Gutmann, Amy, 233, 249, 332, 334
Gwartney, James D., 328, 329

Haack, Susan, 314
Habermas, Jürgen, 10–12, 118, 121, 148,
    305, 304, 309, 313, 317–19, 321, 322
Hamilton, Alexander, 205, 326, 328, 329,
    331, 333, 336, 337

Hampton, Jean, 331, 332
Hard cases, 115, 277–79
Hardin, Russell, 314, 326, 330, 332
Hare, R.M., 316
Harm, 172ff
Harman, Gilbert, 142, 305, 312, 314, 321
Hart, H.L.A., 158, 196, 211, 212, 275–77, 322, 329, 337
Hayek, F.A., 301, 330, 332, 339
Hehir, J. Brian, 339
Herzog, Don, 303, 314
Heuristics, 56, 60–62, 133, 136
   availability heuristic, 56, 58, 108
   and gambler's fallacy, 61
   and inferential errors, 62
   representativeness heuristic, 55–58
   vividness heuristic, 58, 59, 108
Hirschman, Albert O., 336
Hobbes, Thomas, 173, 182–84, 190, 195, 198, 200, 203, 275, 287, 290, 318, 325–28, 331, 332
Hobhouse, L.T., 296, 323, 338, 339
Hohfeld, Wesley, 168, 324, 327
Holborow, Les, 323
Hollis, Martin, 48–51, 135, 310
Holmes, Oliver Wendell, 328
Holmes, Sherlock, 36, 37, 53
Holmes, Stephen, 167–69, 324, 338
Homo politicus, 221–23
Hookway, Christopher, 310
Hudson, W.D., 315
Hume, David, 220, 303, 330
Hurley, Susan, 44, 70–73, 113, 114, 247, 309, 310, 313, 317, 334, 335

Idealism, 78, 82, 308, 313
Inconclusive reasoning, 12, 13, 151–56, chp. 11
   and democracy, 223–26
   and hard cases in law, 277–79
   and internal morality of law, 197
   merely, 180–82, 207
   nested, 157–58, 166, 180–82, 207
Independence condition, 259, 269
Indeterminate reasoning, 114–16, 151–54, 156–58
   and democracy, 223–26
   and hard cases in law, 277–79
   nested, 156, 157, 187
Inferences
   can be taught, 61, 62
   feasibility ordering of, 52–55

not always epistemic assets, 97
ultimately undefeated, 69
Inferential errors, 48, 50, 51, 58, 59
   and closed justification, 140
   and commonsense reasoning, 133
   and feasibility orderings, 54, 55
   and heuristics, 55–61
   and reasonable people, 136
   can be source of intelligibility, 50–52
   can be taught, 61, 62
   casual mistakes, 54
   in probability judgments, 56–59
   of reasonable people, 134, 135
Inferential justification, 17, 81, 82, chp. 5.
   See also Justified beliefs; Reasons for beliefs
   and affective reasons, 29
   and ampliative justification, 96
   and causal theory of belief, 19
   and circles, 74, 75, 89, 96, 103
   and coherence, 76–84, 93
   and likelihood of error, 42
   and principle of conservation of belief, 95
   and reflective equilibrium, 102
   and the regress argument, 75
   axioms of, 64–69, 75, 76, 86, 95
   defeated, 144–47
   distinguished from self-justification, 91
   errors in, 48, 50, 51 58, 59
   linear nature of, 81
   not necessarily conscious, 305
   telos of, 66, 75, 86
   undefeated, 151–58
   victorious, 147–51
   why all justification cannot be purely inferential, 74, chp. 6.
Interpretation, 48ff, 113ff, 279. *See also* Mutual intelligibility
Intuitions, 97–99, 100, 101, 104, 126, 161
Invisible hand theory of politics, 220
Issue individuation, 217, 231, 269ff
Italy, 221

Jarvie, I.C., 310
Jay, John, 326, 328–31, 333, 336, 337
Jefferson, Thomas, 318
Jeffrey, William, 330
Jepson, Christopher, 311
Johnson-Laird, P.N., 48, 60, 309–11, 320
Jones, Peter, 303
Judicial review, 279–86

Judiciary, chp. 16. *See also* Supreme Court
and the rule of law, 196
judges as umpires, 275–79
not to simply express their own moral
views, 276ff
Juridical state, 207–11, 215, 263–67
Justice
and consensus verdicts, 273–74
and coordination problems, 225
and logrolling, 270–71
as end of government, 212, 222, 267
coinciding with interest, 227
procedures appropriate for determining,
243–45
Justifiable beliefs, 17–19, 35ff, 69, 81, 138,
160
Justification. *See also* Justified beliefs;
Public justification
contrasted with persuasion, 139
monological, 113
to what extent a social phenomenon, 117,
118
Justification tracking procedures. *See* Law-
making institutions; Tracking
Justificatory liberalism
and cognitivism, 8
and its rivals, 3ff, 161, chp. 17
and substantive liberalism, 160
as explaining reasonable pluralism, 11
as a moralistic theory of politics, 266–67
based on moral epistemology, 4, 292ff
robust in relation to truth, 43
Justified beliefs. *See also* Inferential
justification; Reasons for beliefs
and circles, 76
and efficient causation, 25
and Socratic influence, 125, 137
and sustaining causation, 23
as based on good reasons, 19
as epistemic assets, 86, 87
as ultimately undefeated, 69
can be false, 39
contrasted with justifiable beliefs, 17, 18
internal and external perspectives on, 30
logically prior to truth, 26, 27, 40, 42, 63
not distinguished from justifiable beliefs
in coherence theory, 81
self-justification, 64, 75, 76, 85, 88–92,
95, 126, 161
telos of inferential justification, 66

Kagan, Jerome, 305
Kahneman, Daniel, 56, 57, 60, 311

Kamenka, Eugene, 330
Kant, Immanuel, 98, 120, 121, 146, 182–84,
190, 195, 265, 275, 290, 299, 303, 318,
319, 321, 324, 325, 339
Karni, Edi, 330
Kavka, Gregory S., 325
Kelsen, Hans, 337
King, Preston, 323
Kingdon, John W., 266, 336
Kleinig, John, xxxv, 320, 324
Knox, Henry, 214, 330
Koerner, Kirk, 329
Kohlberg, Lawrence, 23, 305
Krantz, David H., 311
Kronick, Richard, 330
Kuflik, Arthur, 241, 242, 334
Kuhn, Deanna, 134, 148, 320–22
Kuhn, Thomas, 72, 313
Kunda, Ziva, 311
Kupperman, Joel J., 121, 319

Lamont, Julian, xxxv, 321
Larmore, Charles, 3, 4, 65, 141, 170, 303,
304, 312, 320, 321, 324
Lau, Richard R., 331
Law. *See also* Fundamental law; Law-
making institutions; Rule of law
and rights, 196
and secondary rules, 211–12
as coordination device, 224–25
content independence of, 212
internal morality of, 196–99
justified disobedience to, 288–91
moral obligation to obey, 286–88, 295
telos of, 198, 204
Law of small numbers, 57
Law-making institutions, chp. 13
and deliberative procedures, 230–37
and judicial review, 279–86
and judicial role, 276ff
and non-neutral procedures, 237–45
and principle of political equality, 253
and responsiveness, 226ff
assumes constraints of rule of law,
219
boundaries of, 253ff
cannot be justified in detail, 290
distinguished from collective choice rules,
215–17
four steps in, 216
malfunctions in, 285
Laws of thought, 47, 48, 54, 55
Lawson, Gary, 308

Legislators, 233, 266, 267, 272
Lehman, Darrin R., 61, 311
Lehrer, Keith, 23–25, 305, 306, 313, 314, 316, 322
Lewis, C.I., 313
Liberal politics
and international politics, 296–301
and moral community, 288
and revolution, 288ff
epistemological basis of, 292ff
Lockean v. Hobbesian conceptions of, 286ff
moral basis of, 292ff
requirements for, 294–95
Liberal principles, 3, 152, 174, 175. *See also* Fundamental liberal principle
abstractness of, 165, 174
and constitutionalism, 213
and Great Society, 301
and inconclusiveness, 152, 166
whether they are universal, 296–301
Liberal *Rechtstaat*, 207–11, 215, 263–67
Liberalism. *See also* Justificatory liberalism; Political liberalism
and antiestablishmentarianism, 168–71
and civil interests, 172–74
and defeater doctrines, 171
and immunities, 168–71
and rights, 168, 201
and robustness, 6
and rule of law, 205
and the private sphere, 171–72
based on public justification, 3
basic elements of, 160, 161
classical, 161, 162
libertarian, 239
new, 161, 162
victorious justification of, 161–78
Lijphart, Arend, 281, 333, 336, 337
Likelihood of error thesis, 41
Lively, Jack, 332
Lochner v. New York, 328
Locke, John, 167–69, 172, 173, 182–84, 190, 195, 198, 202, 204, 205, 209, 275, 287, 290, 295, 324–28, 329, 338
Logrolling. *See* Vote trading
Lomasky, Loren, xxxv, 142, 228, 261, 264, 265, 321, 323, 331, 332, 334–36
Luce, R. Duncan, 331
Lukes, Stephen, 48, 49, 51, 135, 309, 310
Lycan, William, 28–29, 37, 89, 306, 307, 314, 316, 317
Lyons, David, 319

Mabbott, J.D., 315, 304
MacCormick, Neil, 337
Macedo, Stephen, xxxv, 3, 132, 135, 136, 183, 205, 208, 266, 267, 280, 293, 303, 320, 321, 324, 325, 328, 329, 336–38
Machiavelli, Niccoló, 221, 330
MacIntyre, Alasdair, 120, 309, 318
MacIver, R.M., 336
Mack, Eric, xxxv, 321
MacKay, Alfred, 335
Mackie, J.L., 303
Madison, James, 206, 212, 235, 263–65, 273, 293, 326, 328, 329, 331, 333, 336, 337
Madisonian constitutionalism, 220, 221, 238. *See also* Constitutionalism
Madisonian democracy
and procedural constraints, 328
and procedural provisions, 211
Bork's view of as majoritarian, 209
justice, the end of, 206
not majoritarian, 206
Majoritarianism, 206, 224, 240–243, 285, 292
Mansbridge, Jane J., 330, 336
Marbury v. Madison, 282
Maritain, Jacques, 329
Markus, Gregory B., 260, 335
Marshall, John, 282, 283
Marshall, Geoffrey, 326
Martin, Rex, 202, 241, 325, 327, 330, 334–36
May, Kenneth O., 290, 338
McCarthy, Thomas, 319, 322
Meinong, Alexis, 26, 306
Mill, John Stuart, 47, 50, 51, 54, 55, 104, 122, 160, 166, 167, 171, 172, 200, 224, 227, 233, 234, 236, 244, 246–48, 251, 252, 273, 309–11, 319, 324, 325, 329, 332–34, 337
Mill's plural voting scheme, 228–29, 234, 247ff
Miller, David, 331
Miller, Fred, xxxvi
Monotonicity, 216, 217
Moon, J. Donald, 324
Moral anarchism, 180–82
Moral dogmatism, 182–89
Moral emotions, 122, 123
Moral experts, 185, 186, 230, 276, 279–81
Moral intuitionism, 97–98
Moral obligation to obey the law, 286–88, 295

Moral realism, 7, 304
Moral sages. *See* Moral experts
Morality as a system of demands, 122–24, 129, 174
Moralized social relations, 214, 288–91
Morillo, Carolyn, xxxv
Morris, Christopher, xxxv
Mueller, Dennis C., 330, 333
Mutual intelligibility, 114, 117, 160. *See also* Interpretation

Nagel, Robert F., 337
Nagel, Thomas, 118, 119, 142, 160, 307, 318, 319, 323, 336
Narveson, Jan, 186, 321, 326
National Australian Convention of 1897–1898, 290
Natural mental logic, 47, 48, 50
Nedelsky, Jennifer, 335
Nelson, William, xxxv, 233, 234, 236, 332–34
Neutrality, 237–45, 303
Newton-Smith, W., 38, 39, 307
Nielson, Kai, 334
Nietzsche, Frederick, 319
Nisbett, Richard E., 51, 57, 59, 61, 62, 320, 305, 310, 311, 312, 317
Non-intervention, principle of, 296ff
Non-neutral procedures, 237ff, 280
Norman, Richard, 323, 333, 334
Normative cognitive pluralism, 45–47, 51, 53
Nozick, Robert, 26, 195, 202, 237, 306, 326, 327, 333

O'Leary, Brenden, 337
O'Neil, Onora, 318, 321
Oakeshott, Michael, 208, 329
Objectivity, 319
  and convergence, 119, 120
  and decentering, 46, 118, 119
  and intersubjective agreement, 118
  and public justification, 144
  and public reasoning, 143
  as expanding of system of belief, 46
  as God's eye view, 46, 118
  as thinning of self, 46, 118
  contrasted to impartiality, 46, 118
  epistemic, 119, 120, 320
  metaphysical, 119
  Rawls on, 131
Olson, Mancur, Jr., 336

Open justification. *See also* Inferential justification; Justifiable beliefs; Justified beliefs; Reasons for beliefs
  and contextual authority, 124
  and mutual intelligibility, 117
  and public justification, 137–40
  as weakly externalist, 32, 34, 63
  characterized, 30ff
Open-texture of legal rules, 276ff
Opinion polls, 235–36, 361–63

Page, Benjamin I., 261–64, 332, 335, 336
Pappas, George S., 305, 313
Parfit, Derek, 106, 317, 338
Paris, Dr., 50
Pennock, J. Roland, 332, 336
Perry, Michael J., 320, 322, 324, 338
Personal justification. *See also* Justified beliefs; Justifiable beliefs; Private reasoners
  and public justification, 10, 11, 120ff, 129
  and social reasoning, 12, 113ff
  relying solely on, 182–84
Peters, R.S., 163, 323, 326, 333
Pettit, Philip, xxxv, 331
Piaget, Jean, 23, 46, 118, 305, 309
Pierce, C.S., 75
Plamenatz, John, 324
Plantinga, Alvin, 310
Plato, 322
Platts, Mark, 98, 99, 315
Plessy v. Ferguson, 281
Pluralism, 73, 155, 170, 171
Policy, 207–11
Political contract, 217ff
Political equality, chp. 14. *See also* Democracy; Equality—principle of
  and economic equality, 254–57
  argument for in terms of distribution of a personal good, 248–50
  Mill's case against, 247ff
  principle of, 252
Political liberalism. *See also* Rawls, John
  and consensus, 214, 231
  and justificatory populism, 130–36, 293
  and reasonable pluralism, 11, 131ff
  as avoiding moral epistemology, 4ff, 132ff, 293ff
  as relying on normative theory of justification, 5, 12, 134
  as seeking robustness, 6
  as self-destructive, 293

on private property, 161–62
unclarity about view of politics, 231–33
Pollock, John L., 30, 66, 67, 91, 144, 305, 306, 307, 312–14
Prichard, H.A., 98, 315
Prisoner's Dilemma, 222
Privacy, 171, 172, 283, 286
Private property, 161, 162, 172, 239, 256, 257, 323
Private reasoners,113–16, 195, 200–202. *See also* Personal justification
Productive state, 243–45, 273, 274. *See also* Common good; Coordination problems
Property. *See* Private property
Protective state, 243–45, 270–74. *See also* Juridical state; Justice
Psychoanalysis, 18, 30
Public good. *See* Common good
Public justification. *See also* Justificatory liberalism; Political liberalism; Public reasoning
  and actual discourse, 148
  and agreeing to differ, 180–82
  and closed justification, 138–40
  and consensus, 230ff
  and cosmopolitan state, 299–301
  and defeater doctrines, 171
  and democracy, 234
  and diversity of individual values, 141
  and diversity of religious views, 142–44, 167, 168
  and epistemic scarcity, 229, 230
  and fundamental liberal principle, 162–66
  and judicial decisions, 277
  and legitimacy, 10
  and need for a moral epistemology, 3
  and normal politics, 231–33
  and personal, 10, 11, 120ff, 129
  and religious beliefs, 154, 155, 163
  and respect for others, 141
  as an essentially contested concept, 4, 175ff
  as basis of liberalism, 3, 293ff
  as open justification, 137–40, 147
  as social, 12, 116ff
  defeated, 144–47
  inconclusive, 151–56, 179ff
  indeterminate, 151–54, 156–58
  intimate relation to free speech, 166
  of liberal principles, 161–78
  our commitment to and social contract, 218, 219

populist theories of, 130–36, 160
reflexivity of, 175ff
undefeated, 151–58
victorious, 147–51, 159, 160
Public opinion, 235ff, 260–63
Public reasoning. *See also* Public justification
  and Enlightenment, 120
  and free speech, 167
  and Madisonian constitutionalism, 212
  and morality, 121–23, 129
  and mutual intelligibility, 121
  and objectivity, 120
  and open government, 233–35
  and open justification, 121
  and religious views, 143
  and rule of law, 195
  and social reasoning, 120
  and Supreme Court, 232
  and umpires, 184ff
  and universalizability, 146
  as basis for democratic verdicts, 273
  inconclusive, 154
  ought to control government, 235
  two aspects of, 181–82
  why engage in it?, 120, 121
Publicity condition, 147, 148, 166, 230
Pure inferential closed justification, 90. *See also* Closed justification; Inferential justification
Putnam, H., 310
Putnam, Robert D., 221, 330

Quine, W.V., 86, 309, 314
Quinton, Anthony, 313, 314

Raiffa, Howard, 331
Random procedures, 223–26
Rawls, John, 4, 5, 58, 103–5, 107, 158, 219, 231, 264, 279, 293, 303, 304, 306, 316, 318–27, 329, 330, 332, 337
  and commonsense reasoning, 134, 135
  and reasonable pluralism, 11
  as a populist, 136
  as focusing on justification not truth, 7
  his conception of the reasonable, 131, 132
  method of avoidance, 166
  on actual assent thesis, 130
  on concept/conception distinction, 179
  on private property, 161–62
  on relective equilibrium, 101
  on two aspects of public reason, 181–82

Rawls, John (*Continued*)
  pragmatic notion of justification, 4
  seeking robustness for liberalism, 6
Raz, Joseph, 33, 190, 303, 306, 307, 312,
  326
Rea, Douglas, 333
Realism in politics, 220
Reasonable people thesis, 131, 133–36, 170
Reasons for beliefs. *See also* Beliefs;
    Inferential justification; Justified
    beliefs; Systems of reasons and beliefs
  and efficient causation of beliefs, 20, 127
  and overdetermination, 20ff
  as causes of beliefs, 19 ff
  as commitments, 36ff
  as efficient causes, 23–25
  as justificatory, 30
  as sustaining causes, 20ff, 127, 306
  giving and having, 17
  internal to cognitive systems, 34
  not always beliefs, 28–30, 91
  prima facie and pro tanto, 70–72
  strong externalist account of rejected, 33–
    35, 39, 41, 159
Reflective equilibrium, 115, 316, 317
  and coherence, 101, 102
  and heuristics, 108
  and intuitionism, 101
  and principle of abduction, 102–4
  based on self-justified beliefs, 104
  explanatory coherence interpretation of,
    103–5
  justification of, 101
  narrow, 103, 108
  wide, 105–8
Reflexivity requirement, 175–78
Regan, Donald H., 329
Regan, Tom, 155, 322
Regress argument, 74–76, 95
Reiman, Jeffrey, 150, 151, 182, 322
Reliabilism, 26, 27
Rent seeking, 292
Representative assemblies, 233–37
Republican virtue, 221, 227, 267
Revolution, 289–91, 295
Reynolds, Noel B., 328
Richards, David A.J., 166, 319, 324, 328
Rights
  and liberalism, 160
  and recognition, 202–4
  and rule of law, 196
  as demands, 122

as spheres of authority, 199–202, 327
as valid claims, 202
disputes about, 182
inconclusively justified, 203
natural, 203–4
to do wrong, 201
Riker, William H., 216, 259, 260, 268, 269,
  330, 332, 335, 336
Riley, Jonathan, xxxv, 328, 329, 335
Riley, Patrick, 339
Rips, Lance J., 47, 54, 55, 309, 311
Robinson, R.E., 324, 327
Robustness
  and political liberalism, 6
  as feature of justificatory liberalism, 5ff
  contrasted to content independence, 191
  distinguished from uncontroversiality, 9
  of account of inferential justification, 29,
    42
Rockman, Bert A., 254, 255, 334, 335
Roe v. Wade, 283, 338
Rogers, Joel, 335
Rommen, Heinrich A., 329
Rorty, Richard, 27, 117–20, 306, 309, 314,
  317, 318, 323
Ross, David, 310, 311, 315, 317
Ross, Lee, 20–22, 31, 32, 51, 98 57, 60, 305
Rousseau, Jean-Jacques, 260, 264, 272, 273,
  318, 334–36
Rule of law. *See also* Law
  and fundamental law, 204–7
  and internal morality of law, 197–99
  and liberalism, 205
  and limits of policy, 207–11
  and moral obligation to obey the law,
    286ff
  and pursuit of the common good, 209
  and rights, 199–204
  role of judges in, 275ff
  and social contract theory, 195
  three aspects of, 196–97
Rumain, B., 309
Rumble, Wilfred E., 328
Ryan, Alan, xxxvi

Sandel, Michael, 317
Sartori, Giovanni, 332
Sayre-McCord, Geoffrey, 336
Schauer, Frederick, 312
Scheffler, Samuel, 306
Schick, Frederic, 310
Schmeidler, David, 330

Schmitt, Carl, 208
Sears, David, 331
Self-determination, principle of, 296
Self-interest theory of politics, 220–23, 232, 263–67, 292ff
Sen, A.K., 216, 235, 330, 335
Seung, T.K., 153, 322
Shapiro, Daniel, xxxv
Shapiro, Ian, xxxv, xxxvi, 329
Shapiro, Robert Y., 261–64, 332, 335, 336
Shearmur, Jeremy, xxxv, 325
Shklar, Judith, 228, 332
Shope, Robert, 305
Sidgwick, Henry, 99, 100, 315
Simmons, A. John, 325, 338
Simon, Herbert, 317
Sincerity, Principle of, 139, 140, 145
Singer, Peter, 155, 316, 322, 334
Single transferable vote, 216
Skubik, Daniel, 317, 337
Slagstad, Rune, 329
Smith, Adam, 220, 222, 223
Smith, J.C., 324, 327
Smith, Rogers M., 205, 209, 324, 328, 329, 337
Snare, Francis, 304, 315
Snowiss, Sylvia, 281, 282, 328, 332, 337
Social contract
    and justice, 206
    and rule of law, 195, 199–200
    and Socratic influence, 137
    as articulating fundamental law, 204–7
    hypothetical, 173
    moral distinguished from political, 218
    three perspectives in contractual arguments, 219–20
Social reasoners, 12, 116–20. *See also* Public reasoning
Socrates, 125
Solum, Lawrence B., 318, 325, 326
Sosa, Ernest, 102, 313, 316, 317
Spitz, Elaine, 334, 335
Standards of proof, 42, 149, 150
State sovereignty, 296–301
State, extent of, 299–301
Stevenson, C.L., 8
Stich, Stephen, 45, 47, 52, 53, 59, 61, 62, 305, 309–12, 317, 318, 320
Strawson, P., 319
Subjective theory of justification, 60–63
Subjugation, 150, 183
Sullivan, Roger J., 321, 322

Supreme Court, 266, 279, 285, 338. *See also* Judiciary; Judicial review
    and legal expertise, 281–84
    anti-democratic view of, 281
    as guardians of procedure, 284–86, 338
    as referee, 285
    not moral experts, 279–81
    view of as exemplar, 232, 266, 279–81
Swain, Marshall, 305, 313
Swanson, Kory, xxxvi
Systems of reasons and beliefs. *See also* Justified beliefs; Open justification; Reasons for beliefs; Weak foundationalism
    and ampliative justification, 96
    and constructive interpretation, 115
    and open and closed justification, 30ff
    and reflective equilibrium, 101ff
    and relativism, 42
    coherentist accounts of, 76ff
    compartmentalization of, 107, 142, 143
    foundationalist accounts of, 85ff
    limits on divergence of, 48ff
    rational, 40–42

Tay, Ehr-Soon, 330
Ten, C.L., 172, 181, 324
Thayer, James B., 337
Thompson, Dennis F., 233, 332
Toleration, 160, 161ff, 171, 213
Toulmin, S., 304
Tracking, chp. 13, 327. *See also* Lawmaking institutions; Umpire
    and adjudication, 271–74
    and deliberative procedures, 230–37
    and law, 197, 198, 275ff, 286ff
    and non-neutral procedures, 237–45
    and public opinion, 260–63
    and responsive procedures, 226–30
    and self-interested voting, 263–67
    and social choice theory, 258–60
    and the problem of vote trading, 267–71
    as main aim of the political contract, 218
    not the sole aim of democracy, 235
    summary of requirements for, 246–47
Tribe, Laurence H., 324, 337
Triplett, Timm, 314, 315
Tucker, D.F.B., 324
Tversky, Amos, 56, 57, 60, 311
Tyler, Tom R., 331
Tyranny, 204, 212, 213, 237ff, 299, 328

Ullian, J.S., 85, 86, 314
Umpire. *See also* Authority; Juridical state;
   Law-making institutions; Protective
   state; Tracking
and exclusionary reasons, 190, 191
and fairness, 198
as central to social contract theory, 183,
   195, 275
can be final, yet fallible, 275–79, 282
distinguished from coordinator, 225
elements of, 215
judges as, 275–79
model of authority, 184–91
unreasonable, 226
when competent to rule, 207ff
Unanimity, 244–45, 270, 271
Urmson, J.O., 304
Utilitarianism, 38, 84

Van Cleve, James, 314
Veil of insignificance, 264
Victorious reasons, 12, 13 147–51, 159, 160,
   177. *See also* Justified beliefs; Public
   justification
Von Mises, Ludwig, 296, 332, 339
Vote trading, 217, 231, 267–71

Wade, E.C.S., 326
Wagner, Richard E., 328, 329
Waldron, Jeremy, 3, 303, 321, 327, 334,
   335
Walker, Graham W., 338
Walker, Margaret Urban, 318
Walzer, Michael, 224, 331
Warner, Stuart, xxxv

Wason, P.C., 36, 50, 309, 311, 320
Wasserstrom, Richard, 337
Watt, E.D., 326
Weak foundationalism. *See also*
   Foundationalism
and ampliative justification, 96
and coherence, 93
and fundamental authority, 127
and local justification, 160
and moral intuitionism, 97
and principle of conservation of beliefs,
   94–96
and reflective equilibrium, 101
and relativism of reasons, 146
and victorious justifications, 159
based on spontaneous beliefs, 92–94
contrasted to coherence theory, 94
defined, 92
not publicly justified, 176
objection to spontaneous moral beliefs, 94
Weatherford, M. Stephen, 331
Weaver, R. Kent, 254, 255, 334, 335
Wellington, Harry H., 324, 337
Wellman, Carl, 151, 321, 322
White, Morton, 328, 329, 330, 333
White, S.K., 310, 319
Wicksell, Knut, 244, 334, 336
Wight, Martin, 339
Williams, Bernard, 19, 38, 43, 44, 152, 305,
   307, 309, 310, 322
Wilson, James Q., 331
Wilson, John, 149, 322
Winch, Peter, 310
Wittgenstein, Ludwig, 113–16, 317
Wolff, Robert Paul, 224, 324, 331

9 780195 094406

Printed in Great Britain
by Amazon.co.uk, Ltd.,
Marston Gate.